Mastering Adobe Photoshop Elements 2020

Second Edition

Supercharge your image editing using the latest features and techniques in Photoshop Elements

Robin Nichols

Packt>

BIRMINGHAM—MUMBAI

Mastering Adobe Photoshop Elements 2020
Second Edition

Commissioning Editor: Pavan Ramchandani
Acquisition Editor: Ashitosh Gupta
Senior Editor: Hayden Edwards
Content Development Editor: Aamir Ahmed
Technical Editor: Sachin Sunilkumar
Copy Editor: Safis Editing
Project Coordinator: Manthan Patel
Proofreader: Safis Editing
Indexer: Rekha Nair
Production Designer: Aparna Bhagat

First published: August 2019

Second edition: April 2020

Production reference: 1240420

Published by Packt Publishing Ltd.
Livery Place
35 Livery Street
Birmingham
B3 2PB, UK.

ISBN 978-1-80020-420-1

www.packt.com

To my wonderful wife, Natalie, whose love of life, great humor,
and joyful attitude

helped sustain me through the long hours spent putting this book together...

- Robin Nichols, Sydney, 2020

Packt>

Packt.com

Subscribe to our online digital library for full access to over 7,000 books and videos, as well as industry leading tools to help you plan your personal development and advance your career. For more information, please visit our website.

Why subscribe?

- Spend less time learning and more time coding with practical eBooks and Videos from over 4,000 industry professionals

- Improve your learning with Skill Plans built especially for you

- Get a free eBook or video every month

- Fully searchable for easy access to vital information

- Copy and paste, print, and bookmark content

Did you know that Packt offers eBook versions of every book published, with PDF and ePub files available? You can upgrade to the eBook version at packt.com and as a print book customer, you are entitled to a discount on the eBook copy. Get in touch with us at customercare@packtpub.com for more details.

At www.packt.com, you can also read a collection of free technical articles, sign up for a range of free newsletters, and receive exclusive discounts and offers on Packt books and eBooks.

Contributors

About the author

Born in the UK, **Robin Nichols** has always had a great love for recording the world with a camera. After finishing school, he studied Fine Art, before moving to Nottingham Trent University where he attained a degree in creative photography.

He subsequently worked in the advertising industry for several years, before emigrating to Australia in 1985. Robin has always worked in photography: as a black-and-white printer, a cameraman, a stock photographer, and as a freelance photographer.

In the 1990s, Robin contributed to several publications in Australia, New Zealand, Singapore, and the UK. This led to a full-time position as the editor of the Sydney-based Commercial Photography magazine, and later, Australian Photography magazine, a post that he held for five years.

In 1997, he founded the critically acclaimed Digital Photography and Design magazine. During this period, he also wrote books for Focal Press and Octopus Press, lectured at seminars in Sydney, Melbourne, and Brisbane, as well as in Seattle and Chicago, and ran highly successful photographic workshops in Dubai for seven years.

In 2000, he started his own publishing business, launching Australia's best-selling specialist photo publication: Better Digital Magazine. With this, he pursued his goal of producing clear, well-illustrated information written in jargon-free English. As a publisher during this period, Robin has been lucky enough to interview some of the biggest names in photography: Elliott Erwitt, David Doubilet, Joe McNally, Gregory Heisler, David Hobby, and even jazz legend Don Burrows on one occasion.

Both magazines ran for more than 10 years but, as distribution and paper costs spiralled, and access to free information on the internet exploded, he made the move into teaching. Robin now concentrates on teaching everything photographic, locally through Sydney University's Centre for Continuing Education, and through several online institutions including Udemy, Skillshare, and Eduonix. When not writing or teaching locally, Robin plans, organizes, and conducts specialist small group photographic tours to photo-centric locations such as South Africa, Botswana, Namibia, Zimbabwe, Tanzania, Oman, Ethiopia, Japan, Iceland, Bali, Sri Lanka, Madagascar, and Cuba.

About the reviewer

Liz Staley is a visual artist and blogger who loves horses, animation, comics, and true crime. She began her digital art journey using Adobe Photoshop, but in recent years has started using Clip Studio Paint. She is the author of Mastering Manga Studio 5, Manga Studio EX5 Cookbook, and Learn Clip Studio Paint. When she isn't creating art, she can be found at the barn with her horse. She currently lives in Pennsylvania, USA, with her husband.

Packt is searching for authors like you

If you're interested in becoming an author for Packt, please visit `authors.packtpub.com` and apply today. We have worked with thousands of developers and tech professionals, just like you, to help them share their insight with the global tech community. You can make a general application, apply for a specific hot topic that we are recruiting an author for, or submit your own idea.

Table of Contents

Preface

1

Photoshop Elements Features Overview

What's new in Elements 2020?	2	The Create and Share menus	16
The Home screen	4	Working with video and Premiere Elements	17
The Organizer	6		
The catalog	7	Working with panels and the Panel Bin	19
The edit modes	9	What do these panels do?	21
Quick edit mode	9		
		Summary	25
The Guided edit mode	11		
The Expert edit mode	13		

2

Setting Up Photoshop Elements from Scratch

Color spaces	28	Organizing your work	45
File formats – JPEG and RAW	29	Star-rating your photos	46
File format characteristics	30	Using metadata	47
		Organizing your work – keyword tags	49
Setting up a photo-editing computer	33	Organizing your work – places	53
		Organizing your work – events	54
Media backup	38	Organizing your work – people	56
Importing photos and other media into Elements Organizer	39		
		Backing up your media and the Catalog	58
Reviewing the media	43	Managing Catalogs	61
Suggested editing workflow	45		

Working with plugins 63

Additional resources – keyboard shortcuts and working tips 65

Color management options 65

Screen calibration 66

Organizer keyboard shortcuts 67

Summary 68

3

The Basics of Image Editing

The editing workflow and best practices 71

Ten ways to open a photo for editing 72

Editing RAW files 73

RAW files – a brief overview 74

The Basic tab – RAW processing tools 77

Camera RAW – profile browser 80

The Detail tab – sharpening and noise reduction tools 81

Understanding picture resolution 89

Cropping for better composition 92

How does the Crop tool work? 93

Straightening horizons 95

Resampling 97

Instant photo-fixing in Organizer 100

Saving files and Version Sets 101

Using autocorrection tools 104

Mastering contrast, color, sharpness, and clarity 107

Adjusting the contrast using Levels 107

Adjusting color using Hue/Saturation 113

Creating high-impact black and white images 118

Perfecting skin tone color 120

Skin smoothing 122

Simple retouching – spot removal 123

Modifying facial expressions 126

Eyes wide shut 128

Additional resources 130

Summary 131

4

Image Makeover

Basic edit workflow 134

Creative edit workflow 134

Makeover example one 135

Makeover example two 137

Makeover example three 145

Makeover example four 151

Makeover example five 155

Makeover example six 161

Summary 175

5

Easy Creative Projects

Finding inspiration on the
Home Page   178
Adding artistic effects   181
Exploit the easy stuff   184
Colorize – AI-driven creativity   187
Creating widescreen
panoramas   193
Panoramas the easy way   195
Working tips   198

Advanced panorama
techniques   199

Making a jigsaw panorama   200
Using Photomerge Scene
Cleaner   201
Making a simple slideshow   205
Creating custom Photo
Calendars   209
Creating custom greeting cards 213
Making a custom Facebook
page   216
Keyboard shortcuts   218
Summary   219

6

Advanced Techniques – Layers and Masking

Introduction to layers   223
Other features on the Layer panel   232
Blending modes   234
Layer opacity   240
Merging layers   240

Adjustment Layers   241
Adjustment Layer masking   243
Pseudo layer masks   245
Combining pictures – posters
and flyers   252

Correcting perspective with
Transformations   259
Other Transformation modes   263

Correcting skewed perspectives 264
Working tips   271
Layer Masking   272
Erasing Tools   277
The Gradient tool   280

Keyboard shortcuts   284
Summary   285

7

Advanced Techniques: Retouching, Selections, and Text

Beauty retouching   288
The Clone Stamp tool explained   288
Retouching in practice   290

Combining the Spot Healing Brush and
the Clone Stamp tools   295

The Burn, Dodge, and Sponge
tools   299
The selection tools   306
Easy object removal   306
Selecting your subject   308
The Lasso tool   310
The Magic Wand tool   314
Saving a selection   322
Feathering selections   323
The Selection Brush tool   325
The Quick Selection tool   326
The Refine Selection Brush tool   327
The Auto Selection tool   328
The Refine Edge function   329

Removing large objects   330

Finishing tips   334
Brush and Pencil tools   335

Working with graphic elements 338
Text graphics   340
Regular Shape tool   341

Custom Shape tool   341
Cookie Cutter tool   342
Paint Bucket tool   344

Adding text to images   346
Using the Type options panel   352
Text styles and special effects   353
Custom fonts   355

Keyboard shortcuts   357
Summary   358

8

Advanced Drawing and Painting Techniques

Illustration – drawing and
painting techniques   360
The View menu   361
Using a graphics tablet   363
Using brushes   366
Brush behavior   366

Drawing a sphere from scratch 370
Impressionist Brush   375
Color Replacement tool   377

Working with Brushes   378
Importing and using custom Brushes   378
Custom lightning brushes   386

Adobe vectors   390
Creating custom vector illustrations   393

Effects filters   399
Keyboard shortcuts   400
Summary   401

9

Exporting the Finished Work

Resolution revisited   404
Online – web and blogging   404
Facebook   405

Instagram   406
Flickr   407

Print resolution	409	The High Pass sharpening technique	432
Local printing	410	General sharpen filters	434
Page Setup	417	The Haze Removal tool	435
Save for Web	418	Export as New Files	439
Sharpening	423	Process Multiple Files	441
Unsharp Mask	424	Keyboard shortcuts	447
The Adjust Sharpness tool	429	Summary	448
The Shake Reduction tool	431		

10
Best Practices

Finding lost or disconnected files	450	underexposure	460
Using the Find menu	452	Underexposure	460
Adjusting dates for different time zones	454	Overexposure	464
Reinstating your catalog	455	Fixing blurred images	466
		People and face-swapping	468
Resolution problems – resampling or adding more pixels	456	Content-Aware Move tool	473
		Recompose tool	475
Dealing with gross overexposure or		Using the Help menu	478
		Summary	481

11
Feature Appendix

Home Screen	484	Fun Edits	496
Organizer – Import (button)	484	Special Edits	497
Organizer – the five view spaces	485	Photomerge	497
Expert Edit mode – the Tool bar	486	Panels overview	505
Quick Edit: Tool bar	494	More tabs	506
Adjustments	494		
Guided edit space	494	Create Menu (Organizer and Editor)	508
Basics	494		
Color	495	Share Menu (Organizer and Editor)	510
Black and White	495		

Other Books You May Enjoy

Leave a review - let other
readers know what you think   513

Index

Preface

Welcome to *Mastering Adobe Photoshop Elements 2020*. This book is designed to highlight, explain, and teach the most important aspects of this long-lasting, comprehensive, powerful, and ever-popular photo editing application.

Who this book is for

Mastering Adobe Photoshop Elements 2020 is written by a photographer for photographers of all skill levels. Its target audience is anyone with a thirst for knowledge, a desire to get on top of their file organization, and a wish to improve their visual creativity through the incredible power of photo editing.

Although novices might be advised to start right at the beginning, the book's structure is one that can be sampled almost at random, depending on your skill level and the direction in which you might want to take your work.

It's certainly not an attempt to be the only book you'll ever need on the subject, but I hope it will entertain and inform those who want to escalate their level of expertise, from basic through intermediate levels, and eventually toward a degree of professionalism.

What this book covers

Chapter 1, *Photoshop Elements Features Overview*, firstly introduces the reader to what's new in this application – and there are several really useful automated AI features that everyone is sure to be impressed with.

This chapter also features detailed explanations on how the different parts of Photoshop Elements operate. This includes a clear examination of its **Home Screen**, the **Organizer**, the all-important Edit workspaces (**Quick**, **Guided**, and **Expert**), plus an overview of how Elements works with its video-editing sister application, **Premiere Elements**, finishing with a detailed look at how all the different **Panels** function.

Chapter 2, *Setting Up Photoshop Elements from Scratch*, helps you overcome the first hurdle of buying and installing the software. The next step is to learn how to set up the application to produce the quickest and most efficient results.

This chapter deals with how to prepare your camera (by setting the correct **color space** in its menu), the **best practices** for imaging computers (Windows and Mac), and understanding the differences between **file formats**. Once the computer is set up, we look at the importance of **backing up** your work effectively.

This chapter then describes the best ways to begin: by importing picture files into the Organizer, plus all the techniques Elements provides for **organizing your media**, such as **keywords**, **albums**, tags, and **metadata**.

Also, it describes how to use and manage its all-important **catalogs**, plus some ideas on the benefits of working with third-party plugins.

Chapter 3, The Basics of Editing, discusses the editing workflow and suggests a number of best practices. It illustrates how to get started with photo editing by covering a range of topics, including an in-depth look at the business of **RAW file editing**, understanding **picture resolution** (including the process of resampling files to make them larger or smaller), **cropping** images, **straightening** horizons, and using the **Instant Fix** feature in **Organizer**.

Besides getting up to speed with the basics, this chapter covers how to work with **Version Sets** and auto correction tools, as well as showing you how to master contrast, color, sharpness, clarity, skin tones, and black-and-white conversions using **Levels, Hue/Saturation** and the **black-and-white** conversion tool. Once you understand this, you are set up to create basic, but effective, retouching techniques, including using the fun **Adjust Facial Features** function and the surprisingly effective **Open Closed Eyes** feature.

Chapter 4, Image Makeover, helps you to learn photo editing by seeing it work in real-life examples.

In this chapter, we study several different image makeover examples that include fixing poor exposure (that is, poor contrast and brightness), how to get the most out of a RAW file, perfecting color inconsistencies, mastering the retouching (**Healing**) brushes, and how to combine multiple images to create one **complete collage**.

Chapter 5, Easy Creative Projects, looks at some truly impressive and highly useful features of Photoshop Elements. This application started life as a simple project-based program, but it has continued to expand its repertoire, both creatively and practically.

In this chapter, these features include finding additional inspiration through the **Home Page**, (including several new project display features) adding **artistic effects**, creating wide-screen **panoramas**, shooting and making random jigsaw panoramas, delving into Elements' amazing many-faceted **Photomerge** feature (particularly with its **Scene Cleaner**), putting together **slideshows**, and creating custom **calendars** and **greeting cards**. The chapter finishes off with how to create your own customized **Facebook** or **blog** page.

Chapter 6, Advanced Editing Techniques: Layers and Masking, focuses on the basics described in chapter 3 and the and the techniques practiced in *Chapter 4* and *Chapter 5*, you'll be ready to turbo-charge your creativity using the power of **layers** and **masking**.

Despite being classed as advanced, layers and masking can be picked up quite quickly and used for a huge range of different photographic projects. Once mastered, these techniques will change the way you edit for good.

This chapter introduces you to the nuts and bolts of image **layers**, including layer **Blend Modes**, **Adjustment Layers** (for lossless editing), and quick and easy pseudo image masks. If that isn't enough, we also demonstrate how to combine pictures to make posters and flyers, how to correct **perspective distortion**, how to master full **layer masking** – the ultimate in controlled layer editing – plus the **Eraser** and the little-used **Gradient** tools.

Chapter 7, Advanced Techniques: Retouching, Selections, and Text, follows a step-by-step approach from the power of layers to fine-tune the use of retouching tools in examples of **beauty retouching**, using of the incredible **Clone Stamp** tool, the magical **Healing Brush** tools, and the highly underrated **Burn**, **Dodge**, and **Sponge** brushes.

We also tackle the complex world of **selections**, which, like layers and masking, once mastered, will change the way you view image editing forever.

And while learning all about selections, we also cover how to **refine selections**, **save selections**, and **remove large objects** from any scene. What most people never appreciate is that Elements also features some great graphics tools – this section highlights its drawing capabilities (brush, eraser and pencil tools), **vector custom shapes**, the **Cookie Cutter**, the **Paint Bucket** tool and everything to do with adding **text** and **text effect**s to an image.

Chapter 8, Advanced Drawing and Painting Techniques, begins by highlighting the best ways to master the handy **design** and **layout helpers** located in the **View Menu**, the benefits of using a **graphics tablet** (over a mouse), how to use Elements' many **brushes**, and engaging you in some simple drawing exercises.

Amazingly, Elements ships with a wide range of very credible **graphics** and **illustration tools**, making it more of an all-round creative powerhouse than many give it credit for.

The chapter then shifts gear to highlight a range of features that include the **Impressionist Brush**, the **Color Replace Tool**, the **Preset Manager**, importing and using **Custom Brushes**, illustrative **vectors**, custom **text effects**, and finally, getting the most out of the program's many and varied **effects filters**.

Chapter 9, Exporting the Finished Work, encourages you to consider export options once your masterpiece has been fully edited.

In this chapter, we look at the various resolution requirements for different social media platforms, as well as how to prepare files for print. Because so many photographers are now so reliant on the internet, it's important to get a handle on how to prepare pictures for best display (using the **Save for the Web** feature), as well as how best to **sharpen** files for different print and online applications using the industry standard **Unsharp Mask** tool, the generic Sharpen filters, **High Pass** sharpening, and more, including how to use the amazing **Haze Reduction** tool.

Finally, this chapter takes a good look at how to export multiple instances of your work (with the **Export as New Files** feature), as well as how to bulk-process files using the effective **Process Multiple Files** utility.

Chapter 10, Best Practices, looks at how to fix all those things that can go horribly wrong when trying to manage a database of thousands, or tens of thousands, of images, when processing damaged or poor-quality files, or when dealing with images that are just not 100% sharp.

One of the best places to start is the powerful **Find** menu, which allows you to locate missing files based on a wide range of criteria, to how to adjust dates for different **time zones**, how to re-instate a lost or damaged **Catalog**, how to resize files (via the **Image Size** resampling feature), and to deal with gross over- and under exposure.

In this section, you'll also find information for fixing, or at least improving, less-than-perfectly-sharp files (using **Levels**, **Contrast**, **Clarity**, **Unsharp Mask**, **Shake Reduction**, and **Haze Removal**), how to extend your editing prowess using the amazing **Photomerge Face** and **People Swap** features, how to rearrange large objects around your image with the **Content Aware Move Tool**, or indeed change the composition using the impressive **Recompose** feature.

Appendix, Common Features, features a breakdown of all the features found in Photoshop Elements.

To get the most out of this book

The point of this publication is that you really don't need to have much experience before starting out in the world of photo editing. That was the premise of the original Adobe application a dozen or so versions ago, and today, that idea still stands.

That said, it would be immensely useful to have a fundamental knowledge of how computers operate, including Macs and Windows, and perhaps an inkling of basic image editing, just to get started. Also, be prepared to experiment with your images as much as possible.

Develop a network of friends or mentors who might be able to help you if you get stuck. To do this, you may find that it's a good idea to join a camera club in order to get help with both your photography and post-processing.

Above all, have fun, and experiment as much as you have the time for…

Conventions used

There are a number of text conventions used throughout this book.

`Code in text`: Indicates code words in text, database table names, folder names, filenames, file extensions, pathnames, dummy URLs, user input, and Twitter handles. Here is an example: "Mount the downloaded `WebStorm-10*.dmg` disk image file as another disk in your system."

Bold: Indicates a new term, an important word, or words that you see onscreen. For example, words in menus or dialog boxes appear in the text like this. Here is an example: "Select **System info** from the **Administration** panel."

Tips or important notes
Appear like this.

Get in touch

Feedback from our readers is always welcome.

General feedback: If you have questions about any aspect of this book, mention the book title in the subject of your message and email us at `customercare@packtpub.com`.

Errata: Although we have taken every care to ensure the accuracy of our content, mistakes do happen. If you have found a mistake in this book, we would be grateful if you would report this to us. Please visit `www.packtpub.com/support/errata`, selecting your book, clicking on the Errata Submission Form link, and entering the details.

Piracy: If you come across any illegal copies of our works in any form on the Internet, we would be grateful if you would provide us with the location address or website name. Please contact us at `copyright@packt.com` with a link to the material.

If you are interested in becoming an author: If there is a topic that you have expertise in and you are interested in either writing or contributing to a book, please visit `authors.packtpub.com`.

Reviews

Please leave a review. Once you have read and used this book, why not leave a review on the site that you purchased it from? Potential readers can then see and use your unbiased opinion to make purchase decisions, we at Packt can understand what you think about our products, and our authors can see your feedback on their book. Thank you!

For more information about Packt, please visit `packt.com`.

1
Photoshop Elements Features Overview

Adobe Photoshop Elements is a pixel-based graphics photo-editing application that was first released in 2001. Its appearance followed on from an entry-level program called **Photoshop LE**, a light edition of Photoshop, which was a product made available mostly for students and teachers, and sometimes bundled with other hardware products at the point of sale. If you count its LE predecessor, Photoshop Elements 2020 is now in its twentieth version.

Initially, Photoshop Elements was released as a basic, entry-level tool for the consumer; mums and dads trying to get their collective heads around digital technology. But over the years, it has dramatically expanded its feature set, inheriting many significant professional-level tools from its more complex sibling, Adobe Photoshop.

So, how different is Elements from Photoshop? Interestingly, Adobe maintains that the principal difference between the two is that Elements is still essentially a screen-based, **RGB** (Red, Green and Blue) program, whereas Photoshop CC is designed to convert RGB files for work in the commercial **CMYK print space**—making it the go-to graphics application for all professionals working in print.

However, the market has changed significantly in the past 15 years, with so many more businesses trading online; therefore, the demand for print-ready conversions has reduced significantly. In my own experience, I have found that any good commercial print shop will gladly convert Elements' RGB files to its preferred CMYK color space, usually with only a nominal prepress charge, thus enabling everything produced out of Elements to be commercially printed to the highest degree of quality.

In this version, you'll find an astonishing range of sophisticated tools, features, and capabilities packed into a very affordable editing package, making it not only a serious professional tool but also one that is simpler to use than Photoshop CC.

As you will quickly come to appreciate, this software is, in fact, made up of two separate applications and a number of different modes designed to address different user experience levels, all rolled into one bundle called Elements. Although it has technically evolved from other products, such as Adobe Photoshop LE and Photoshop Album, it's now an incredibly powerful and cohesive standalone tool designed for transforming photographic images, while remaining both affordable and fairly easy to use.

What's important to understand is that it's not necessary to know everything about this application to succeed at producing beautiful results—you can use just one, or a combination, of its components to produce impressive edits, depending on your experience, creativity, and, indeed, your drive for editing perfection.

Because Adobe Photoshop Elements 2020 is made up of several quite different parts, treat this first chapter very much as a general overview. Once you better understand what each section offers, you'll find it significantly easier to navigate the various features, which, in turn, will enable you to produce great results more efficiently.

What you will see in this first section:

- New features in Adobe Photoshop Elements 2020
- Importing files and the Organizer
- Storing your edit information in the Catalog
- Editing modes, including the Quick Edit, Guided Edit, and Expert Edit modes
- The Create and Share menus explained
- Working with video and Premiere Elements
- Working with Panels, the Panel Bin, and Panel functionality

What's new in Elements 2020?

Although recent updates in the last couple of versions have appeared to be little more than stability and reliance fixes, Adobe has pushed ahead by interlacing its **artificial intelligence technology** (AI) with a range of automated features—making complex and time-consuming processes easier, quicker, and more reliable.

I'd be the first to suggest that such technology would, at best, be fraught with errors, but this new version proves me wrong. Its new AI-driven automated features—notably, tools for **Colorizing** black and white images, **Skin Smoothing** and **Object Removal**, and **Subject Selection**—are remarkably effective and pretty much do what Adobe claims them to be capable of, that is, to colorize black and white images with a single click, select and remove objects automatically, smooth skin tones flatteringly, and instantly isolate your subjects from busy backgrounds without the usual time-consuming selection tool process:

And while the success of these new AI-driven features does rely, to an extent, on the content of the images in question, I find that even if the result is not entirely as expected, the effect created is invariably something very desirable.

As with most new features introduced in the 2020 version, if the AI-generated version does not turn out as you'd hoped, you can apply the effect manually with greater control—but that takes more experience. That said, in the example of this classic Hollywood image, I think the automated results (the three color versions to the left of the main image) are as good as the manually created, and more time-consuming, version seen on the right-hand side.

Users might also note that the application is now compatible with HEIF and HEVC (photo and video) files, further streamlining performance, especially when using files sourced from Apple iPhones.

The Home screen

What was referred to in **Adobe Photoshop Elements 2018** as the **eLive** screen is now the **Home screen**. It's the first thing you see when Elements starts and, like its predecessor, is there to provide users with creative inspiration on how to edit images, embark on creative projects, and how to best use its many **Auto Creations** (circled in red). You can use it for learning how to accomplish basic editing tasks and for fun activities such as creating YouTube memes, automated slideshows, movies, and more, simply by clicking any of the pictorial links on the Home screen—which then take you to an online tutorial hosted by Adobe.

The screen displays a short (text) list of previously opened files, which is a nice feature, plus shortcuts to open the photo editor, the media browser (called the **Organizer**), and the video editor, plus links to Adobe, Facebook, and Twitter:

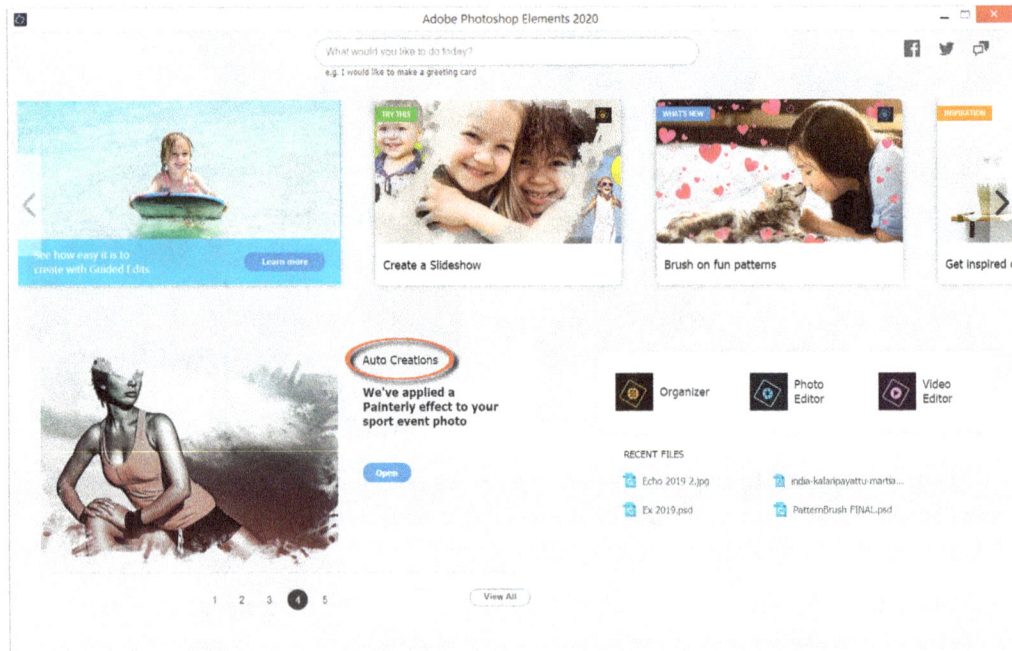

As you can see, this is the new Elements 2020 Home screen. You can use it as a source of creative inspiration, but also as the go-to screen to open previously edited files or to start one of the application links: **Organizer**, **Photo Editor**, or **Video Editor**.

It's important to note that if you've not bought Elements and Premiere Elements together as a bundle, clicking the third icon, **Video Editor**, will prompt you to download and 'try' Premiere Elements. Buying the bundle saves a fair chunk of money and makes sense because so many of us shoot video and stills.

If you are already using Premiere Elements 2020, you will notice several new features, including **Smart Tags** to help organization, simplified noise reduction, a sky replacement tool, and more. But those are topics for another book...

Photoshop Elements users will note that there are now more **Auto Creations** that appear on the lower left-hand side of the screen. These include the **Pattern Brush**, **Black and White Selection**, **Depth of Field**, and **Painterly** effects, as seen in the following screenshot. Not a massive enhancement on its own, but, as a source of inspiration, it's always interesting to see how your own images look incorporated into different creative styles that you might never have considered previously:

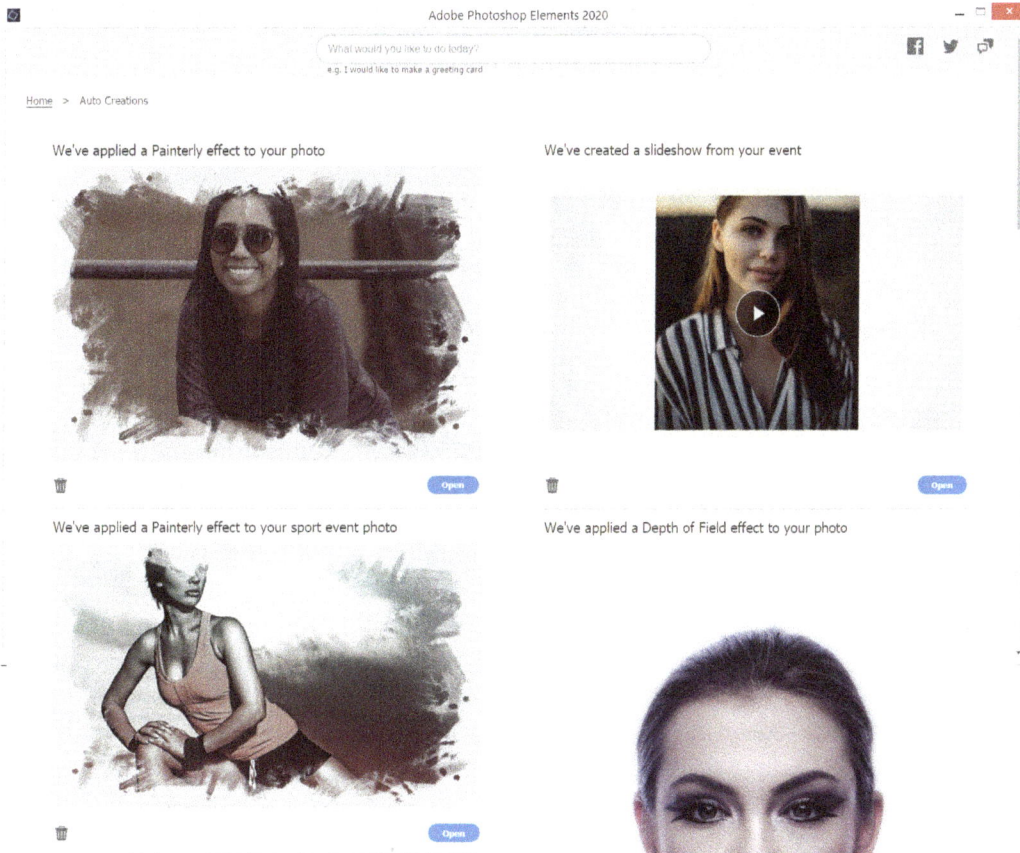

Because the Home page is linked to Adobe's servers, it also provides access to the **Help** menu, plus thousands of pages of inspiration covering a massive range of topics, from basic tone enhancement and scrapbooking to professional standard retouching techniques and more.

The Organizer

One drawback of digital photography is that we accumulate masses of digital images and other assets, such as audio tracks and video clips. Keeping track of everything on a monthly basis, let alone annually, becomes something of a nightmare, especially if you plan on upgrading your skillset from amateur status to professional.

Sorting everything into meaningful collections, therefore, is the main function of the **Organizer**. Once installed, you'll note that it runs as a separate application, albeit one with almost inseparable ties to the photo editing part of Elements, and indeed to its video-editing partner, Adobe Premiere Elements, which is often sold with Elements as a bundle:

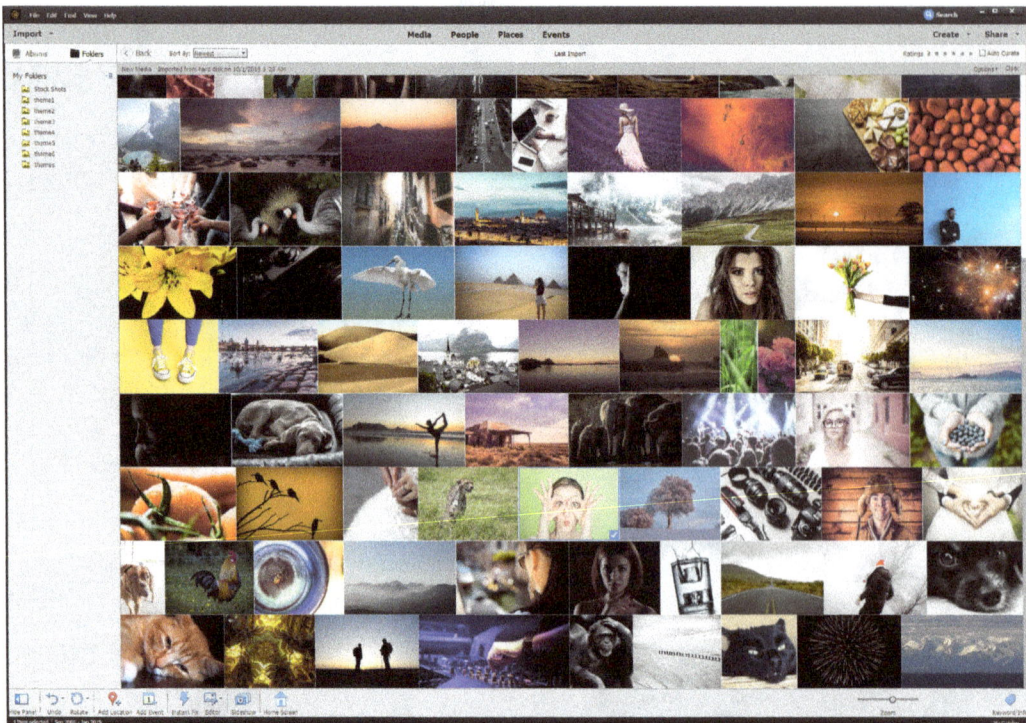

Images and other digital assets are imported into the **Organizer** and sorted into a meaningful order using a range of clever tools such as albums, keywords, labels, place and people tags, star ratings, and metadata. Because all of these attributes can be applied to your images, its organizational and file search capabilities are extensive, making it one of the best asset management systems in the business.

> **Tip**
>
> Before you start, it's important to note that when Adobe states that you **Import** assets into the **Organizer**, what it actually does is create links to your files wherever they might be stored. Nothing is physically moved or copied into the **Organizer**; instead, it's just linked to wherever the files have been stored. This is a good thing in case you ever have to reinstall the program because of a computer malfunction or hardware issue, but it can be a bad thing if you habitually move or rename files using only the computer's finder system, and not through Elements itself. We will cover this in more detail later.

The **Organizer** is also the place we go to for quick fixes—Adobe calls these **Instant Fixes**—as well as a number of other creative activities, such as making collages, calendars, greeting cards, and slideshows. We also use the **Organizer** as a platform for uploading our creations to social media such as Facebook, Vimeo, Twitter, and YouTube.

The catalog

Occasionally, users will be reminded to back up the catalog. If you have simply downloaded and installed Elements and proceeded to get on with your image organization and editing, you might not even know what this **catalog** is. It's important! Let's take a look at the following screenshot:

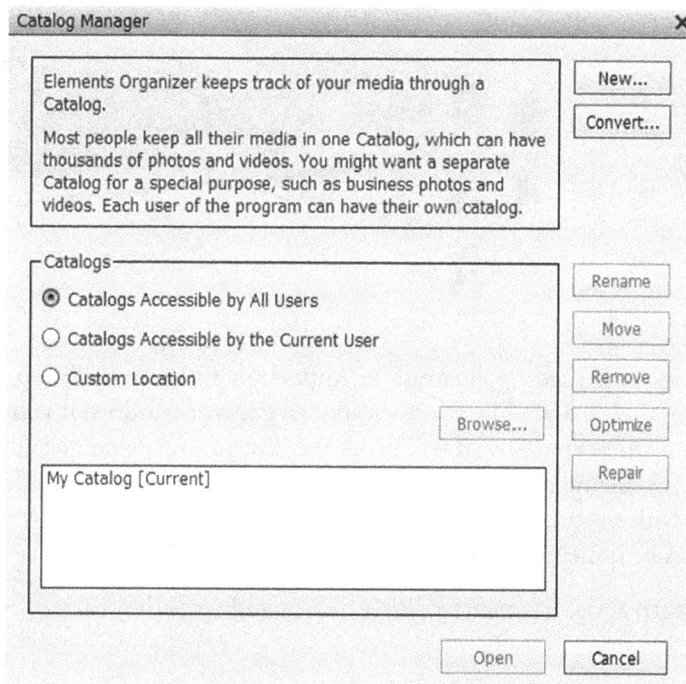

The **Catalog Manager** provides the ability to monitor multiple catalogs. To start, I'd recommend just having one catalog. Having multiple catalogs is a good idea if you share Elements with your partner, your children, or perhaps your work colleagues.

Elements refers to your images using **links**—nothing is ever physically moved into the application. When files are imported, Elements makes links to where the images are usually kept (normally in the Pictures folder). This linking information, along with all the metadata, thumbnails, tags, attributes, and keywords—in fact, everything you do with the program, is saved to the catalog. While you can have multiple catalogs, you can only open one at a time. Your original **high-resolution** files are stored elsewhere (see *Chapter 2, Setting Up Photoshop Elements from Scratch*). Catalogs should be backed up periodically onto a disk or a hard drive that does not contain your images—it's usually considerably smaller than the hi-res images it lists, so it can be backed up to the cloud or even a small-capacity hard drive. We will cover this in more detail in *Chapter 2, Setting Up Photoshop Elements from Scratch*:

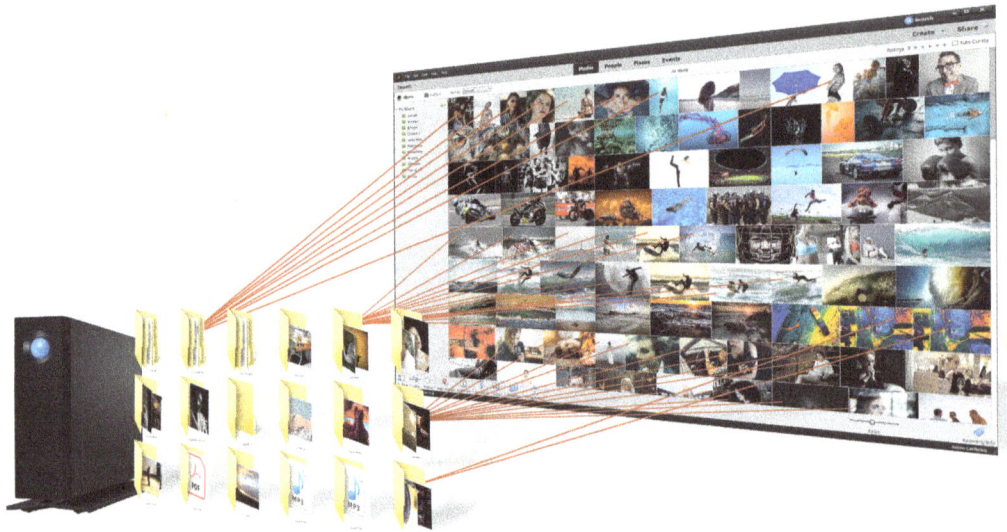

As you can see from the preceding illustration, 'importing' files is actually a process of 'linking' files—from their original location—to the **Organizer** window. If you delete, move, or rename any imported files, it will break the link and you won't be able to edit them. If this happens, Elements will immediately search for the missing file based on the name it imported with the metadata. If it locates the lost file, it automatically re-links it. If not, then this can be done manually.

Let's move on to learn about Elements' editing modes and what they offer.

The edit modes

Unlike many image-editing applications, Adobe presents its editing features in three different windows or edit modes that are separate from the Organizer window. If you are a complete novice, start with the Quick edit mode. If you know what you want but are not sure how to do it, try the comprehensive step-by-step Guided edit mode. And if you have some experience editing your work, you can also go fully manual using the Expert edit mode. Here's a brief overview of what you can expect from each mode:

Quick edit mode

As you can see, in the **Quick** edit mode, the image currently being edited can be displayed in a *before*, *after*, or, as seen in the preceding screenshot, *before and after* display mode. The right-hand side of the following screenshot displays some of the excellent effects available in this mode.

In fact, there are 55 to choose from (5 variants of 11 originals). I think this is a fantastic feature because it gives you instant results, most of which, I think, serve as great inspiration for the creative mind. You might not like all of them, but they at least are a terrific starting point...

The following screenshot is an enlarged view of the **Quick** mode toolbar on the left-hand side of the main edit screen:

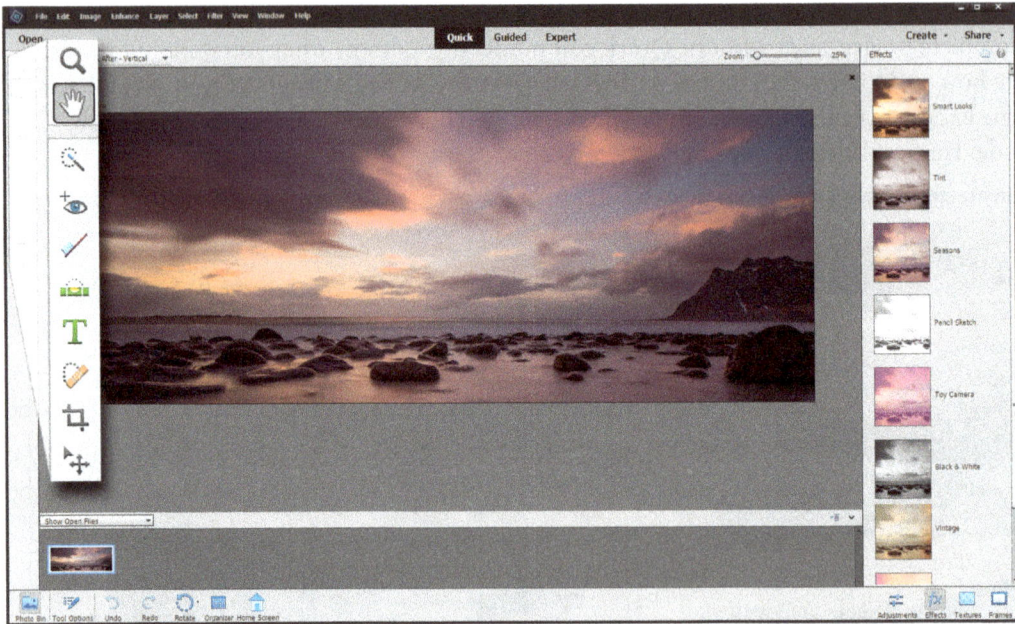

During the edit process, you'll use the **Organizer** to search for and find images that are then opened in one or, depending on your creative requirements, several of the three edit modes. After editing, they are saved and appear updated back in the **Organizer**. The process of getting images from the **Organizer** to the editor is dealt with in detail in *Chapter 3, The Basics of Image Editing*.

As the name suggests, the **Quick** edit mode enables users to make simple but significant improvements to any picture file using adjustments specifically ordered, so as to produce the best editing workflow. These adjustments can include **Smart Fix**, **Exposure**, **Lighting** (contrast), **Color**, and finally, **Sharpness**.

To make the editing process more visual, both this and the **Guided** edit mode offer the user a handy *before* and *after* viewing window, making it easy to see what the original looked like alongside the new, edited version. All three edit modes are interchangeable. This means that you can easily transfer an image from Quick, to Guided, to Expert, and back again, should you need to.

This mode also features a range of tools that cover the most commonly used editing tasks. These tools include the following:

- The **Zoom** tool—used for enlarging/reducing the size of images
- The **Hand** tool—used for moving a greatly enlarged image around the screen
- The **Quick Selection** tool—ideal for isolating parts of the image
- The **Eye** tool—specializes in fixing red-eye and (green) pet-eye
- The **Whiten Teeth** tool—click on teeth and this tool automatically selects and brightens teeth in one easy action
- The **Straighten** tool—an easy way to level wonky horizons
- The **Type** tool—specifically for adding text to an image
- The **Spot Healing** and **Healing Brush** tools—both powerful and very effective tools used for retouching photos

And, curiously, at the bottom of the list (I think these two features really should be at the top of the toolbar) you'll find the following tools:

- **Crop**—a ubiquitous tool for cutting bits off your image to recompose the frame
- The **Move** tool—the ideal tool for moving extra elements such as text about the screen

The performance of each tool, throughout all of Elements' edit modes, can be modified using the **Tool Options** panel, which pops up from the bottom of the screen when clicked on. Additionally, note that each tool has different options. For many time-poor photographers, these features provide a good level of editing capability.

The Guided edit mode

As the name suggests, the **Guided** edit workspace is packed with step-by-step advice to guide you through a range of editing tasks; there are 47 to be exact. These are presented in a beautifully designed and easy-to-use format. All that's needed is for you to choose one of the effects and follow the steps—easy!

Topics include **Basics, Color, Black & White, Fun Edits** (highlighted overleaf), **Special Edits,** and **Photomerge**, which is a mini-application designed for stitching images together into widescreen panoramas, among other things:

The screenshot shows what the **Guided** edit screen looks like (with the **Fun Edits** tab selected). Note that while this screen is visually quite busy, its interactive design makes it quite clear what each of these effects looks like when applied to the samples pictured:

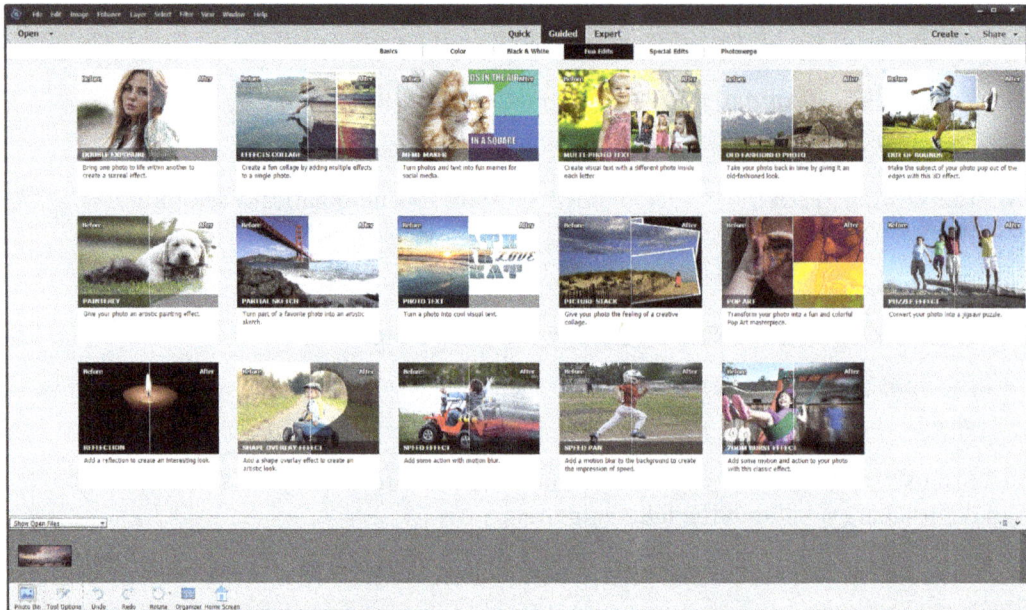

All that's needed is for you to swipe the cursor left or right to reveal the effect in a before/after style. This is a good, practical software design that, in my opinion at least, should be incorporated into many other software applications.

The **Guided** edit mode is a great source of creativity, more so perhaps than the current Home screen. For example, if you are a bit stuck with what direction to take your photo editing in, just open a picture in this mode and try some of the effects offered; most of them are bound to get your creative juices flowing nicely.

It's hard to illustrate the **Guided** edit mode because it's packed with so many great features, so where do you start? The screenshot of the suit-wearing man perfectly illustrates a feature new to Elements 2020 called the **Pattern Brush**.

There's been a Pattern Stamp tool in Photoshop CC for years and I always found it hard to use—and rarely will you ever see anyone else demonstrating its application, I suspect, because it's not very good. This new feature is completely different as it combines an automated subject selection algorithm to mask the important parts of the shot, in this case, the seated male model, while adding a range of patterns in the background. All you do is click and drag the mouse across the image to make it happen. It's fun, easy, and effective:

Another Guided Edit that's new to Elements 2020 is called **Object Removal** (under the Basic tab). Again, this renders a complex editing action involving selections and object cloning to a swish of the cursor. Brilliant! More on this feature in *Chapter 6, Advanced Techniques – Layers and Masking*.

The Expert edit mode

Having played with the **Quick** and **Guided** edit modes, you'll find this advanced editing workspace a little challenging, especially if you are a newcomer to photo editing.

The **Expert** edit mode essentially relies on the user having an **editing plan**. It's good to have a basic idea of what you'd like to achieve with the image open on the desktop, as well as having some degree of experience with the tools needed to complete the job. In many ways, this part of Elements resembles Adobe Photoshop quite closely—although I would add that it also contains a good range of very cool processes that you will not find in Photoshop. We will cover this in more detail in *Chapter 5, Easy Creative Projects*:

Don't let the name **Expert** put you off; its basic tools (which are dealt with in more depth in *Chapter 3, The Basics of Image Editing*) are easily mastered and provide any photographer or designer with a raft of powerful creative options.

Essentially, the tools and features offered in this part of Elements' workspace are far more customizable than those in the **Quick** and **Guided** edit modes.

For example, if you are trying to change the color in part of an image, but find the semi-automatic **Quick Selection** tool in **Quick** edit to be clunky and hard to control, the **Expert** edit mode offers not 1, but 11 different selection tools (including the new **Select>Subject** feature), all of which are interchangeable with one another, and all of which can be fine-tuned using a range of sophisticated modification features.

This all takes time and experience but, once you have played with some of the tools in the first two modes, moving into the Expert domain will be significantly easier:

As with all the edit modes, the main window displays a **Photo Bin** (highlighted in pink), where currently, open image files are stashed before being moved into the main edit space. There are also **Rotate** buttons, **Undo** and **Redo** buttons, and a **Tool Options** panel, which allows you to fine-tune the performance of every tool in the program—a very handy panel to familiarize yourself with because it allows you to finely control the efficacy of each tool.

Once your images have been edited to perfection, you'll need to either incorporate them into a project, such as a slide show or photo book, export them to a printer, or upload them to your favorite social media site. This is where the **Create** and **Share** menus come in very handy. Let's take a look at what these menus offer.

Tip

Don't worry about the Mac or Windows dilemma either. After many years of producing two quite different versions of this excellent software, Adobe has finally settled its differences with Apple (over iPhoto). Now, the only difference between Elements running on the two operating systems comes down to the *Command* and *Control* keys, making life for those of us switching between Mac and Windows a breeze.

The Create and Share menus

When digital photography became mainstream 20 years ago, there were precious few things you could do with your images other than look at them on low-resolution screens—digital printing was in its infancy, as were reliable computers, the internet, and editing software.

It took programs such as Photoshop Elements to introduce us to the concept of doing something more than just looking at images on screen. It began with a few creative projects and is now driving a wide range of activities, ranging from book printing to slideshows, scrapbooking, and stationery:

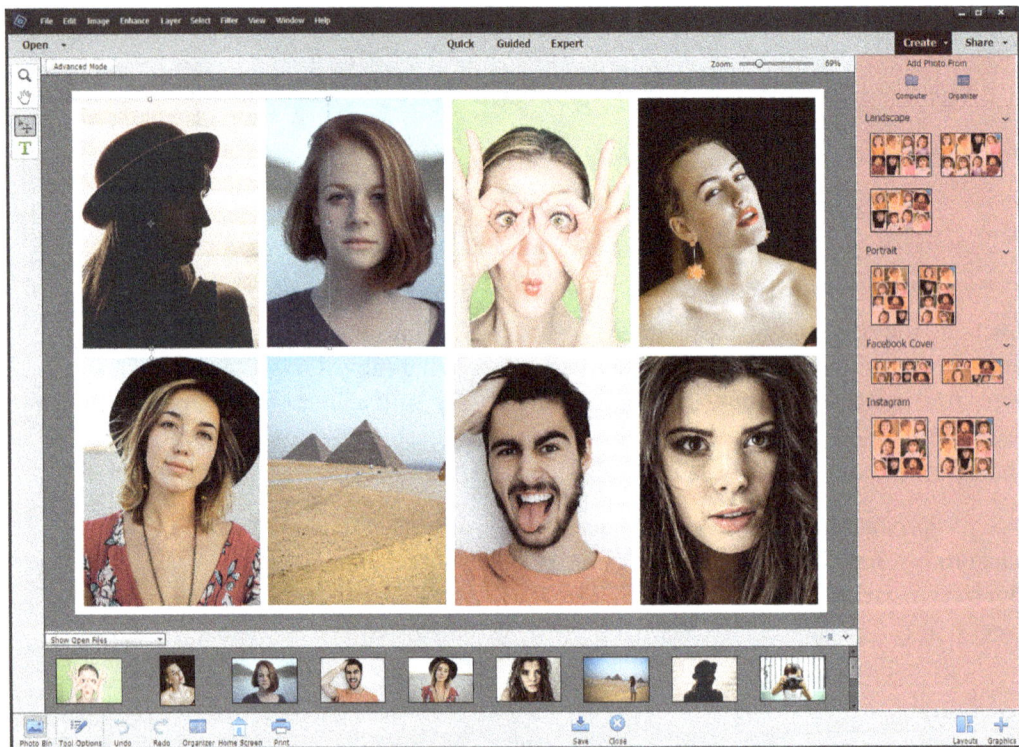

Creative projects are an excellent way to perform relatively complex actions with ease. In the preceding screenshot, all I had to do was find eight images, open them, and choose **Create | Photo Collage**. The application automatically arranges the files according to the layout chosen in the right-hand panel and it's done. A time-consuming process performed automatically in less than a minute—genius!

Running through both the Organizer and all three edit modes, you'll spot the highly useful **Create** and **Share** menus. The **Organizer** is used as a **media browser** for still images, music files, and video clips, so it's designed to work with both Elements and its consumer video editing sibling, **Premiere Elements**. In it, you'll find a few additional features offered, in both the **Create** and **Share** menus, notably for producing video projects and uploading them to video-centric sites such as YouTube and Vimeo.

Otherwise, these two drop-down menus are identical, enabling users, after the editing is done, to incorporate them into one of the many creative projects offered, and then to share them immediately, directly out of Elements, with a range of social media platforms or local destinations such as the desktop.

Some of its original projects provide the user with great creative options; for example, anything from making a slideshow, photo collage, photo book, greeting card, or calendar, to producing your own instant movie, DVD labels, and photo prints. As indicated, its **Share** menu just provides you with the easy option of uploading your newly crafted work directly to Facebook, Twitter, email, Vimeo, YouTube, or the desktop.

It's possible to buy Photoshop Elements as a standalone photo editor but, as is often the case, it's also sold bundled with its moving-picture sibling, **Adobe Premiere Elements**, simply because the line between still images and video has become increasingly blurred (no pun intended). Let's take a brief look at what this video-editing powerhouse has to offer the budding filmmaker.

Working with video and Premiere Elements

Adobe Premiere Elements targets the consumer video-editing market and, increasingly so, these two applications are often sold as a bundle, which incidentally should save you 25% or more compared to buying the two applications separately.

We can use the **Organizer** to catalog still images, as well as HD video clips, GIFs (Graphics Interchange Format files used to record short animations), audio tracks, and music, together or separately, depending on the work planned. Once organized, files can then be opened in either application—Elements or Premiere Elements—depending on how they are to be used. I edit quite a lot of video, so I find this close relationship incredibly convenient, especially where I might need to use still images in a video project, or video clips in a still image story that's, for example, to be exported to Facebook or Vimeo.

To the novice, **Premiere Elements** might seem unduly complex. Being a video editing application, it does deal with images and time in a single process, but this application is very much like the photo editor: you can skim through it using the automated video tools, or explore its many professional standard editing features to produce a movie of outstanding quality.

The relationship between Premiere Elements and **Adobe Premiere Pro**, Adobe's industry-standard editing suite, is similar to that of Elements and Photoshop CC. It began as a dumbed-down version of the high-end commercial product, but it is now one of the best video editors on the market. Additionally, like Elements, Premiere employs some incredibly powerful features that include **image stabilization**; an amazing **instant movie** feature; a wide range of professional effect *looks* (a *look* is a prerecorded editing recipe designed to add a specific color, tone, or emotion to a video clip—they are great time-savers); sophisticated **brightness**, **contrast**, **color**, and **sharpness** tools; and an export function that allows you to easily upload any completed video project to social media effortlessly.

If you are considering moving into video production, this is a very capable and professional tool with a great range of guided and automated functions that makes the often tedious job of editing video clips a breeze. Note that Premiere Elements 2020 now handles HEIF and HEVC files (PC and Mac), while updating its noise reduction capabilities and speeding up file organization using Adobe Sensei technology and a feature called **Smart Tags**.

Over the years and versions, Photoshop Elements has grown to contain a staggering number of effects, automated processes, editing tools, and presets. So many, in fact, that storing them in a tidy manner, while presenting them for easy access, has become something of a challenge. To this end, Adobe employs a feature called panels to catalog these features while keeping them relatively accessible in a tabbed format. The following is an overview of how this works.

Working with panels and the Panel Bin

You'll find the most important panels in the **Panel Bin**, located on the right-hand side of the main screen in the **Quick** and **Expert** edit modes. While they might not be the most glamorous part of this editing application, panels still play an important part in your day-to-day workflow:

In the preceding screenshot, I have highlighted the **Styles** panel where, with an image open in the main window, a specific pre-recorded *recipe* can be applied—this could be anything from a color tweak to contrast, brightness, and sharpness adjustments. Even special effects can be applied to a file with a click of the mouse.

Principal panels in the **Quick** edit mode are the **Adjustments** panel (*Chapter 3*, *The Basics of Image Editing*), **Effects**, **Textures**, and **Frames** (*Chapter 5*, *Easy Creative Projects*). Naturally, the **Expert** mode has a wider selection of panels that include **Layers**, **Effects**, **Filters**, **Styles**, and **Graphics** (*Chapter 6*, *Advanced Techniques – Layers and Masking*).

There are eight more panels to be found, either by clicking on the **More** button or by using the **Window** drop-down menu at the top of the page. Most panels also have their own drop-down menus to help organize the staggering array of features each one holds and, most importantly, to help you find the stuff you really need:

In the preceding screenshot, most of the panels have been dragged out from the right-hand **Bin** and attached side by side to demonstrate how customizable panels can be. Because there are so many panels in this arrangement, this format wouldn't be practical unless you either had a large computer monitor or were using two monitors. Panels can also be made smaller and made to float freely over the workspace.

> **Tip**
> Although the panels live in the **Panel Bin**, you can drag them out of the bin and over the work area by clicking, holding, and dragging the appropriate name tab.

What do these panels do?

There are many panels in Photoshop Elements, with each providing essential help with the editing process. Some just refer to the **Quick** edit mode (such as **Adjustments**), while some only appear in the **Expert** mode (such as the **Info** panel). Here's an overview of what each panel offers:

- **Adjustments**: This provides sliders to adjust the **Exposure**, **Lighting** (contrast), **Color**, **Balance**, and **Sharpness**.

- **Effects**: This provides the user with a great range of *looks*, automated colors, and special effects; in essence, these are *recipes* that can be applied to an image with a single click.

- **Textures**: Elements comes with a wide range of creative assets—such as surface textures that, once clicked, apply to the opened image as a textured overlay. These are good for backgrounds, web pages, and more.

- **Frames**: This is used for graphic artwork. You can click on a frame thumbnail in the panel and, if never used before, it downloads it from www.adobe.com, and then automatically resizes and applies itself to the image. Clever stuff!

- **Layers**: This is probably the most important panel for advanced projects where text, multiple images, or other assets are added to different layers in the document, thus maintaining editability throughout the production process.

- **Filter**: The small filter thumbnails try to illustrate the effect of each FX filter. You can click on the thumbnail to apply the effect. You can also use the associated slider to vary the intensity of each effect. There are 98 different filters and billions of possible combinations.

- **Styles**: Like filters, Styles are one-click presets that are used to change the image—mostly by adding an effect to the entire layer. Where **Filters** and **Effects** presets are applied to the surface of the image to give it a different *look*, Styles are used to add more esoteric features such as drop shadows, bevels, glows, patterns, and glass button effects. Though there's a small photographic subset in Styles, most are used for the purposes of design rather than to improve the image. This panel holds some 176 different styles.

- **Graphics**: This panel contains a lot of (downloadable) clip art, text effects, scalable vector shapes, and a bucketload of picture frame styles—all of which can be applied to an image by simply clicking on the thumbnail. Because there are so many items in this panel, you can filter or sort them, according to **Type**, **Activity**, **Mood**, **Event**, **Object**, **Season**, and more. As there are well over 1,000 assets listed that can be used, most will have to be downloaded from Adobe first before they are ready to use:

I consider the **Layer** panel to be one of the most useful simply because the Layers feature enables you to combine text, selections, and multiple images and mask them all in the same (multi-layered) file. Aside from being able to combine multiple assets in a single file, each individual layer remains independently editable. In the preceding screenshot, you can see that the image has its original photo layer (the cat), plus two non-destructive Adjustment Layers, which are used to change the tone in the image without compromising the quality.

Other panels

Once you get started with the editing process, you'll notice even more panels lurking in the back of the **Panel Bin**. While still very useful, these particular panels provide slightly more esoteric assistance to the editing process and should probably be left until you have developed a reasonable skill level. These panels include the following:

- **Actions**: Essentially, this is a watered-down preset feature that's been copied over from Photoshop. The supplied Actions can be replayed on images to achieve goals such as adding a photo border, resizing, and cropping. An Action is just a small file of instructions—you can find more Actions online, download them, and import them into Elements to boost the paltry range supplied by default.

- **Color Swatches**: These are used to choose colors for a range of features, from type to pencil, to paintbrush to background colors. The panel allows you to make your own custom Swatch for specific projects.

- **Histogram**: This displays the range of tones present in any image and, more accurately, where in the brightness range those tones sit (such as mid-tone, highlights, whites, blacks, underexposed, and overexposed).

- **History**: This is a useful panel that displays your editing steps—from opening the image to saving the new work. By clicking on one of the steps displayed in the panel, you can go back in time to a previous state, mouse click by mouse click. This is handy if you decide that you have edited the image a bit too much; just click back a few steps to a previous version.

- **Favorites**: This is a big time-saver; you can keep your frequently used **Styles** and **Graphics** in one place by dragging the relevant thumbnail into the **Favorites** panel.

Here's what a floating panel might look like:

This is convenient because it provides a wider view of the main image while the panel can be manually shifted to "float" over the least important part of the image being edited:

- **Navigator**: This is another unsung hero of this program. The Navigator panel displays the image you have open in the main window. This is especially useful when the main window display is enlarged so that it is bigger than the screen, because it's then hard to know which part of the image you are seeing.

- **Info**: This is a useful panel that displays the RGB brightness values in any part of the image that you mouse over. The readout works regardless of the tool currently being used. It can be set to display RGB values (0-255); web color; grayscale; **Hue**, **Saturation**, **Brightness** (**HSB**); and measurement dimensions. It is a handy helper if your computer monitor is not calibrated correctly.

Tip

If you accidentally close a panel by clicking on the **x** icon at the top-right of the panel on Windows, or the top-left of the panel on a Mac, it's simple enough to reinstate that same panel from the **Window** drop-down menu.

Important note

Custom workspace? One of the big differences between Adobe Photoshop and Photoshop Elements is in the former's ability to save various processes that you might be working on as a **custom preset** so that they can be reused at another time. This is especially useful in the matter of a **workspace configuration** (essentially, a workspace is a record of where all the panels and tools are placed while working in the main window). In Photoshop, you can open the panels you prefer to use and close the ones you don't, and then save that configuration as a personal "workspace." If the desktop gets messy and you accidentally close a few of your favorite panels, that original workspace can be reloaded from the **Window** menu, and everything returns to the way it was before you messed it up. However, it's a curious thing—though you can create a custom workspace in Elements, there's no function to save it for use at a later time. In the Expert edit mode, point your cursor to the **More** tab at the bottom right-hand side of the main window (to the right of the **Graphics** panel) and click on the tiny arrowed symbol to the right of the rectangular **More** tab. This produces a drop-down menu displaying the panels that are not currently docked in the Panel Bin. Choose the **Custom Workspace** option, and then go ahead and close the panels you don't use and open and reposition the panels you need to see all the time. They can either float over the main window (which can be annoying unless you have a big screen), or drag the new panel to the top of the Panel Bin and you'll see it highlighted in blue as it *docks*, or plugs, into the existing set of tabs. You can arrange them to be stacked, tabbed, or to sit side by side. However, if you close and restart the program, all your panels will default back to their original layout.

Using the new **Subject Selection** feature, you can now make accurate and quite complex selections, like the one above, with nothing more than the click of a mouse, thanks mostly to Adobe's artificial intelligence. This analyzes the image and automatically finds the subject and selects it. This technology is all way above my pay grade but, after some testing on images that have fairly strong, bold subjects, I can say that it really works! For more information on this impressive new feature, refer to *Chapter 6, Advanced Techniques – Layers and Masking*.

Summary

In this chapter, we have learned about the different parts that make up the Photoshop Elements image-editing application. We now understand that this package not only offers a comprehensive suite of powerful editing tools, but its **Organizer**, running as a separate application to the editing program, can be used to catalog all our assets in one place: as stills, music, clips, and HD videos.

Then, depending on the level of editing required and your user experience, it's relatively simple to achieve quite complex edits using any of the semi-automated processes seen in the **Quick** mode. That said, we now know that it's also possible to take far greater control by exploring the **Expert** edit mode in greater depth.

The next chapter highlights the best way to set up a powerful editing computer, how to import images into the **Organizer**, how to work with **catalog** backups, and how to get your media into a cohesive order using albums, tags, metadata, keywords, and the powerful search facility.

2
Setting Up Photoshop Elements from Scratch

If you are new to Photoshop Elements, then setting up your camera, computer, monitor, data storage, and media backup are very important steps in the editing process. The correct setup at the outset will enable you to plunge straight into the learning process without having to waste time renaming files or folders, going looking for lost images, or worse, losing materials because it never occurred to you to back up your original files in a timely fashion.

And even if you are not new to Elements, take some time here to check that your camera settings, screen calibration, photo import, and backup workflow are correct. This might save you a lot of grief later on.

The following topics are covered in this chapter:

- Preparing your camera, selecting a color space, and learning about different file formats
- Setting up a photo-editing computer
- Backing up files
- Importing media into Elements Organizer
- Reviewing the media

- Backing up your media and the Catalog
- Managing Catalogs
- Organizing your work – ratings, keywords, and more
- Working with plugins
- Additional resources – keyboard shortcuts and working tips

Color spaces

Cameras, all monitors, and most printers can display only a limited range of colors – this is called the **color space**. The industry-standard space is called **sRGB color** (standard, red, green, and blue), but there are many other *spaces* such as **Adobe RGB (1998)** and **ProPhoto RGB**, to name just two.

Most color spaces correctly claim to encompass a broader range of color than sRGB. While this is certainly true, actually being able to see an increase in the range of colors on both a computer screen and in print is a characteristic that's hard to evaluate because most screens and printers cannot recreate the number of colors captured by the camera.

Most consumer cameras can be set to capture only one of two different spaces: **sRGB** or **Adobe RGB (1998)**. The best practice for amateur photographers is to choose sRGB. This matches the range of colors that most monitors can display, plus it matches the gamut, or range, of most consumer photo inkjet printers. That said, some commercial lithographic print businesses now require files to be Adobe RGB (1998) in order to match the high-end print machines they use. If you are considering a move to commercial photography, then Adobe RGB (1998) is the best color space setting. That said, a good color pre-press business should also be able to make these space conversions for you, for a fee. Camera menus tend to be very different – refer to the manual to find the all-important option of color space. The following image shows the Canon screen with my preference for the **sRGB color space**:

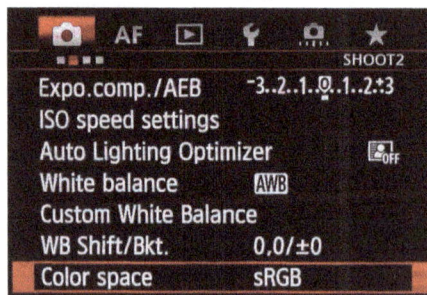

While Photoshop Elements was initially designed as a pixel-based editor for the JPEG file format some 15 years ago, it's now fully compatible with most RAW file formats.

Let's take a closer look at how different file formats work in the editing process.

File formats – JPEG and RAW

Nearly all digital cameras these days can shoot and record two formats of image files: JPEG and RAW files. Some newer models can also record digital negative RAW files. We'll look at these later in this chapter.

The difference between JPEGs and RAW files is simple: JPEG files are 8-bit picture files. These are processed in-camera and then compressed (squashed) to maximize storage space, before being saved to the memory card.

RAW files are usually 10-bit files that have little or no processing applied in-camera, and they are not compressed before being saved to the memory card. The result is a file that is several times larger than a JPEG, but one that can be edited to a far higher degree of accuracy than the humble JPEG.

Tip

Bit depth relates to the amount of color information held in an image file. The higher the bit depth in that file, the more color information it contains; more information produces smoother tonal gradation. Single-bit color is made up of two colors only: black and white. 8-bit color produces 256 tones, while 24-bit color can have millions of tones.

Although shooting with RAW files is highly recommended, you will find that your camera's files are quite different to another model's (RAW) files. For example, Sony RAW files use the suffix .ARN; Olympus uses .ORW; Nikon uses .NEF; and Pentax uses .PEF. The following is a view of an original (Canon) RAW file displayed in a browser window. It has the .CR2 suffix common to all Canon cameras:

Although each camera manufacturer shares the same three-letter suffix across all of its camera range, RAW files produced by different models are quite different to each other (that is, RAW files from the Nikon D7000 are different to the Nikon D7200, D800, and D850 RAW files. This is why it takes companies such as Adobe several months to provide an update for the different RAW file types designed for each new camera make and model. If you are an early adopter, waiting for Adobe to "catch up" and release a compatibility update can be a source of frustration.

RAW files have to be edited in a specific RAW editing window, called **Camera RAW**, which is separate from the regular **Quick**, **Guided**, or **Expert** mode windows. Once edited in this space, a RAW file must be either closed (there's no *saving* with RAW files – it automatically records all the edits applied to it), or it can be saved in a more universally acceptable file format for storage, backup, or later distribution.

Such formats include JPEGs, TIFF files, digital negative files, and even Photoshop files. But what's the difference between these formats and when would be the best situation for us to use each of them?

File format characteristics

Choosing the right format to save your edited work can be an important decision because it can have direct ramifications on both the final image quality and your backup and archiving practices:

- **JPEG (.jpg)**: This is a compressed *lossy* format (*lossy* means it loses quality when saved and compressed) that's ideal for emailing, photo books, web, social media, and photo lab printing (note: most photo book companies only accept JPEG and PNG files).
- **RAW**: RAW files are essentially untouched data straight from the camera. They typically contain four times more picture information than a JPEG and are therefore a good choice for shooting in tricky lighting. RAW files are big, can take any amount of editing, do not deteriorate (as JPEGs do with too much editing), and have to be saved in a more universal format such as JPEG in order to be printed or included in a digital photo book.
- **DNG (.dng)**: A digital negative file is like a universal RAW file, retaining all of the benefits of regular RAW files while retaining a higher degree of application than a regular RAW file. Adobe Lightroom, for example, is a program optimized to work best with .dng files.
- **PSD (.psd)**: Photoshop files have no compression and can store extra Photoshop data within the file itself, such as layers, paths, selections, and more advanced features. Because everything can be saved in layers, you retain a high degree of editability. This is good for preserving the best quality for complex editing and commercial print projects.

- **TIFF**: Similar to `.psd` files, TIFF files can be compressed by up to 25% with no loss of quality (this is called LZW or *lossless* compression). It also preserves many features including selections and layers. It's good for preserving the best quality for editing and commercial printing. TIFF files can end up being larger than the same file saved in `.psd` format.

- **Photoshop PDF**: These files are very similar to regular Acrobat PDF files. These are good for general distribution.

- **PNG**: **Portable Network Graphics (PNG)** files are used primarily for website design and in photo books, where background transparency is a requirement.

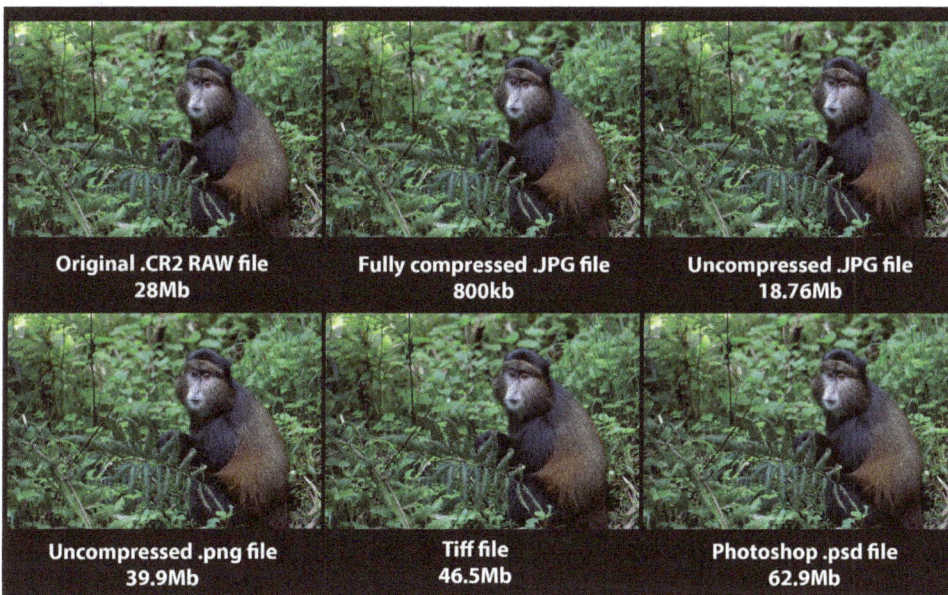

To illustrate the different properties of image files, I saved the same image (a golden monkey) in six different file formats. Because the JPEG format is compressible, its saved state is considerably smaller than everything else, hence its popularity in social media, on the web, and for emailing, among other uses. Compressing it to the maximum (that is, the smallest possible file size) brings it out at only 800 KB—less than 1 MB—but the extreme compression would damage the quality irreparably.

Despite my original `.CR2` RAW file being 28.99 MB, the `.png` file is larger (39.9 MB), followed by the slightly compressed (though lossless) TIFF file (46.5 MB), the Photoshop file (62.9 MB), and the uncompressed TIFF file (63.3 MB).

Of all the file formats available in Elements, the one that's perhaps the most useful is JPEG. The following close-ups of this bespectacled gentleman nicely display the problems that over-compressing JPEG files might create:

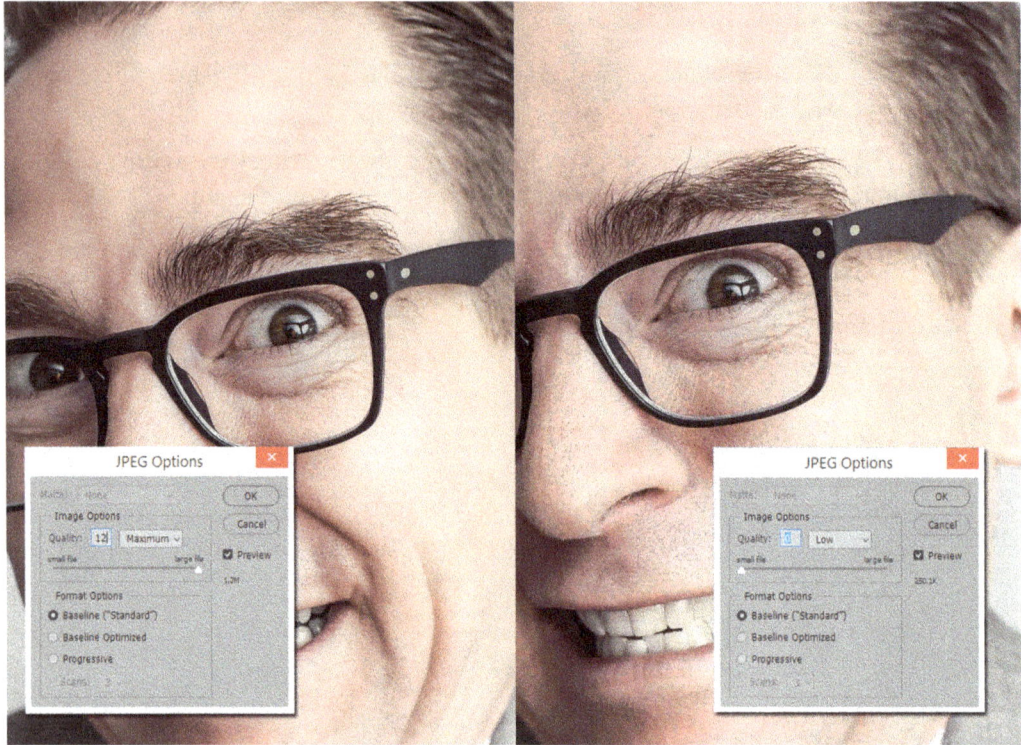

Don't get me wrong here – JPEG files are great because they can be compressed. However, if they are compressed too much (that is, set to level 7 or lower in the **JPEG Options** box), you'll see a significant deterioration in image clarity and color (the right half of the previous composite image was set to **Quality**: 0, producing a tiny file).

However, too much compression at this stage or repeated saving (and therefore repeated compression) will generate image artifacts, for example, in the form of posterization (banding) seen mostly in the smoother tones. Overcompression will also create inaccurate color, and might even introduce blocky-looking pixels when compared to the minimal compression setting of level 12, as seen on the left of the preceding screenshot, producing a far larger saved file with smoother, more accurate tones.

Let's now go ahead and look at how we can create the ideal imaging computer.

Setting up a photo-editing computer

Although we take computers much for granted these days, using such a machine to store, process, and edit high-resolution stills and video data requires a totally different set of features compared to a machine that's only used for web browsing, social media, emailing, or downloading music.

Although the interoperability of Windows and Mac computers used to be very minimal, their **operating systems** (**OSes**) are now far more user-friendly, both in the way third-party hardware interacts (such as external drives) and in the fact that most software is now available for both systems:

Is there a difference between running Elements on Windows or a Mac? The answer to this often-asked question can get you into a lot of hot water, depending on the technical leaning of the person being asked. To be honest, I have used Windows and Macs and both desktops and laptops for a long time and find that, when editing images, there's really no big difference in performance between the two OSes.

In the early years, Elements was a different application on a Mac because Adobe was in contention with Apple over iPhoto (being the default image browser), but that's all sorted now. Macs are certainly beautifully designed, but providing you have the same processing power, RAM chips, graphics cards, and screen resolution settings, you'd be hard pushed to pick out any real performance difference.

However, you will experience a significant cost difference between the two platforms. Macs have always sold at a premium compared to Windows gear.

An imaging computer needs to have a very fast processor (the **Central Processing Unit (CPU)**). This is the bit that does all the calculations. A computer with one of the latest CPU chips installed will certainly future-proof your investment for several years to come. That said, I don't advise you to purchase the very latest technology, simply because you'll pay an absolute premium for it without necessarily gaining a commensurate speed advantage. Such is the downside of being an early adopter.

It's far better to buy something that is just about to be replaced—which means it might only be 5 months old—and spend the cash saved on installing additional memory (also called **Random Access Memory** or **RAM**). The more memory installed, the more images, video clips, and applications you can have running at the same time without the computer visibly struggling. I'd recommend at least 16 GB of RAM to start with, and more if you can afford it.

> **Tip**
>
> Because most computers are sold off the shelf with the minimum workable amount of RAM installed to keep the cost down, it always pays to top up the RAM, either at the point of purchase, or later, where you might save money buying it from the local computer shop or online. Increasing the amount of RAM in an older computer can also be hugely beneficial – almost giving it a new lease of life. This is worth considering if a new machine is out of your price range.

Currently, screen resolutions are impressively high, with 4K (3,840 x 2,160 pixels) and now 5K (5,120 x 2,880 pixels) curved and flat screens becoming *the norm*. A flat screen is best for your imaging needs. Curved screens certainly appear tempting but, because of their shape, will never give accurate feedback when trying to adjust characteristics like proportion and perspective. The size of the screen you have is also partially dictated by the capability of the computer's graphics card. That said, most preinstalled graphics cards are very powerful and are easily capable of running a very high-resolution 4 or 5K screen, and in many models, even two screens at the same time. If it's an entry-level video card not suited to a high-resolution output, you might encounter a lot of onscreen flickering, which can be quite disturbing. Check carefully before you buy.

The best image editing computer monitors are made by Eizo—these have superb edge-to-edge brightness, are easily (color-)calibrated, come with a hood (pictured), and produce extremely reliable, accurate color. However, they are expensive, so they are really only practical if you plan on running a commercial business. If you want to save some money, look at buying a monitor from Dell, BenQ, or even LG—three companies that produce pretty good display products that are considerably less expensive than the Eizo example pictured here:

Then there is the very real problem of storage. Most photographers are prolific shooters and, with consumer camera resolutions generally passing the 25-megapixel mark at present, it won't take long to fill the computer's hard drive with media.

My best advice is always to use a desktop computer, Windows or Mac, because, though large and bulky, they are significantly cheaper than laptops.

Apart from that, their size, notably Windows PCs, permit the addition of further internal hard drives when more storage space is needed and even the upgrading of internal components such as video cards and motherboards for improved performance. Mac desktop computers are a little harder to upgrade partly because of their design and partly because, if you do, you might well void your original warranty.

If you absolutely have to use a laptop (and a lot of photographers are entirely mobile these days), this is also a good option, although its storage space, CPU, and screen size will all be compromised unless you spend a lot of money. One answer is to buy several external storage drives and a large desktop screen that can be hooked up to the laptop when you are working locally in the home office:

Laptops are designed to be lightweight and compact, so there's never much storage space in them for all your files. Typically, we would buy a portable USB-powered hard drive for backups while traveling. Once home, it might make better sense to transfer all your work from the USB-powered hard drive to a physically larger desktop drive—these are usually cheaper, have far greater data capacity, and are (mostly) more reliable.

Desktop hard drives are the perfect way to keep up to date with your backups – they are relatively inexpensive for the capacity offered, and if one fills up, it's simple enough to buy another drive. There are a number of excellent devices currently available from Seagate, LaCie, and Western Digital, to name a few. In the following image, the device on the left is a single drive unit from LaCie (the company has a unique Porsche-style design for its products). A single drive, such as this 6 TB model, would suit most beginners. The Western Digital *My Book Duo*, shown in the middle, is a RAID drive containing two hard drive units in one box. This offers a mirroring feature, where it backs up two copies of everything, or it can be programmed for extreme speed if this is needed.

Most drives are set to RAID level 1, which mirrors the copy to give a second identical backup automatically. On the right of the following image, we have another RAID drive. This unit is designed more for busy commercial studios where speed and high capacity are crucial. This unit from Drobo can take up to five hard drives:

For absolute speed freaks, **solid state drives** (**SSDs**) are the best option – both as an internal drive in your Windows or Mac, and also as an external option. Expensive and not as high a capacity as their older SATA drive companions, SSDs are small, light, require no additional power, and are incredibly fast:

The best practice is to install just your OS and software applications onto the computer's hard drive. Everything else – photos, music, and video – is saved to an external hard drive (or drives). That way, your computer can run at its optimum, while accessing your photo library on an external drive. Once that external drive is full, it's simple enough to carry on with a second, or even a third, external hard drive.

Media backup

As we expand our image and media collection, we'll not only need large-capacity hard drives, but also backups. It's important to perform backups in case the original drive corrupts, or suffers a mechanical failure. Nothing is forever and even though the drive might be a premium brand, things can still go wrong, usually when you least expect it.

There's no point in backing up images, or your Elements Catalog, to the same place where everything else is stored—typically your computer's hard drive. If it becomes corrupted, everything will be lost. For this reason, it's important to consider buying a large-capacity hard drive, preferably one with a higher capacity than the computer's drive, which is then used only for backing up your data: images, music, Elements' Catalog, and so on. Most PCs have room for additional internal drives. If you use a Mac, you'd do best to buy an external hard drive.

If you are using a Mac, backing up your data is very easy using a pre-installed Apple application called Time Machine. Windows users also have it easy because most good quality external drives (such as Seagate and Western Digital) come with automated backup software included.

This software takes only a few moments to set up. Once done, you can forget it, because it automatically backs all your new material up every hour, day, or week (depending on how you initially set up its preferences).

The two screenshots here show Western Digital's free backup software (available for Mac and Windows) on the left, and Apple's excellent Time Machine software utility that comes pre-loaded on every Mac, on the right:

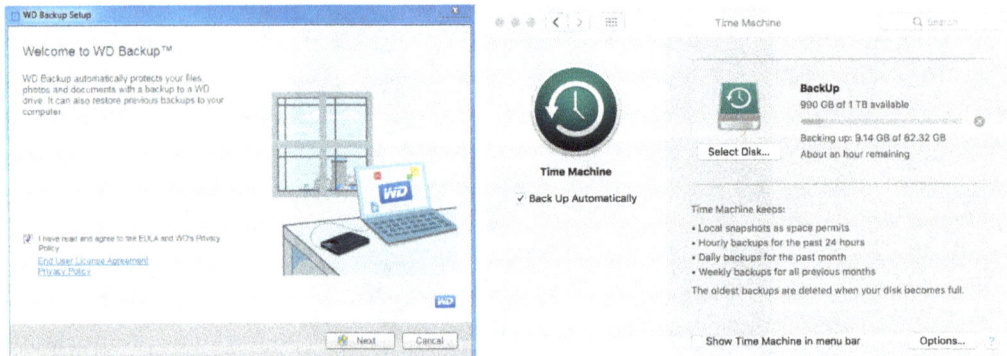

Let's move on and learn how to get our pictures into the Organizer so that we can begin the exacting process of image organization and then dive into some editing.

Importing photos and other media into Elements Organizer

As already mentioned, when images are *imported* into Elements **Organizer**, they are not really copied into the application at all; they are just linked from the place where they physically reside (typically, this is the **Pictures** folder) to the **Organizer**. This is so that if Elements develops some kind of technical issue and you have to delete and reinstall the application, you simply reinstate the **catalog** from the backup version, and it automatically relinks all missing files. Sometimes, it's necessary to actually point the program to the hard drive where the images are stored, but more often than not, Elements will search and find every image that was previously linked in the catalog. It's a very clever program.

Using the **Import** button (on the top left-hand side in the **Organizer**), you can bring images, audio, or video clips into Elements Organizer directly using the **From Files and Folders** option. These files can physically reside anywhere – locally, on the computer, or externally on a drive. There are also options to import files directly from a camera or a card reader, or in bulk from pre-organized folders. The panel on the right-hand side of the main window holds both **Keyword** and **Metadata** information about each file. Click the small **Keyword/Info** button on the lower right-hand side of the main screen to open/close this panel (highlighted in red):

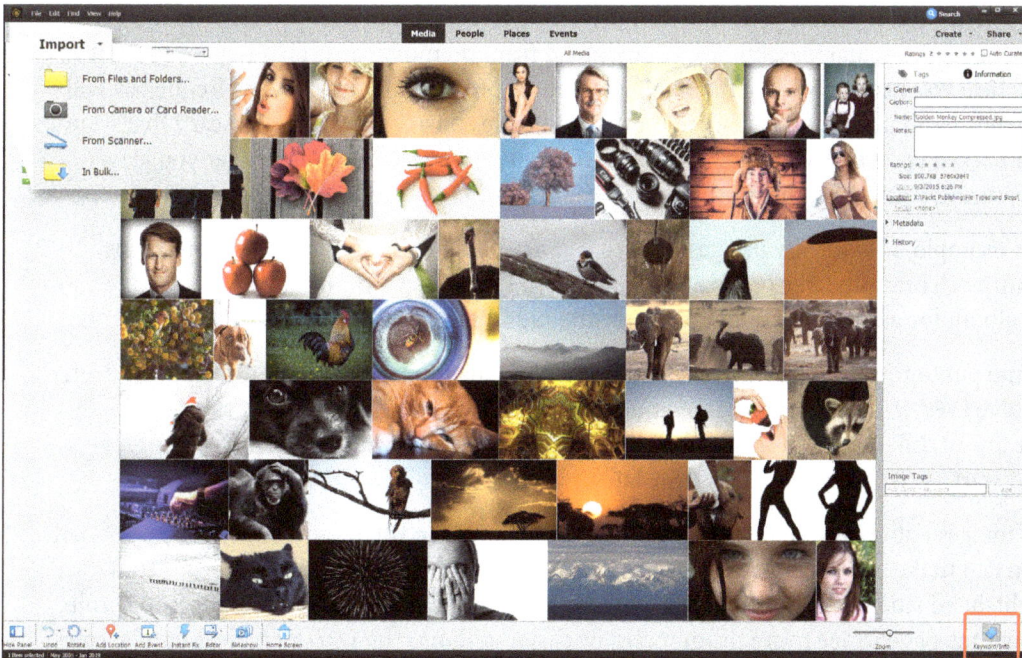

Because of this linking process, it's not advisable to rename or move files that have already been imported into Elements. If files are moved or renamed using the Windows **Explorer** or Mac's **Finder**, the next time Elements is used, it will prompt you that the file is missing and immediately start a search for the file. This is fine if the name remains the same, but if it has a new name, it will have to be re-imported. You can leave Elements to complete the search, or do it yourself if you know where the file was moved to. How long Elements takes to locate a moved file depends on how big your photo collection is.

The import process is fast because, remember, Elements does not copy the full pixel data – it only takes small thumbnails and the metadata (essentially text) when it forms a link to the location of your original files. So, to avoid wasting time searching for files that have been renamed or moved after they were imported into the Organizer, it makes sense to sort out the storage hierarchy on the computer or external drives before importing into the application.

We all have different ways with which to organize our busy photographic lives. Some prefer to store files by date, while others prefer to name everything according to events in their lives. There is no *right* or *wrong* way to do this. The best method is the one that you are going to remember in months or years to come.

That said, there are basic rules I can suggest that will make the editing process flow better. Download and organize your files into pre-made folders as often as you can. There's no need to rename the actual files, but if you download from memory cards on a regular basis, it will help you keep abreast of the Elements import processes. Downloading frequently will also ensure that you don't accidentally overwrite files on a camera memory card that were not backed up. Always add keyword tags to freshly imported files. The longer you leave organizing your work, the more confusing it gets.

For example, I divide my images up into events. These might typically be work, trips, family, celebrations, weekends away, and so on. I create an album for each big trip, an album for a conference, an album for the kids' birthdays, and so on.

Some photographers prefer to file and search for images based solely on the date. I prefer to give everything a proper name and only search by date when nothing else works. We are all different, so it is important to consider your naming conventions before you start—it'll save you a lot of time later on.

As images come into Elements Organizer, they appear in the main window as thumbnails. You can make the thumbnails bigger or smaller using the zoom slider at the bottom right-hand side of the main screen. You can also use the edge-of-screen sliders to scroll down the page to see more thumbnails, or easier still, use the *Up/Down* keyboard arrows.

As a suggestion, before you import a second batch of images, it makes a lot of sense to sort out the first batch, because if you continue to import folder after folder of images, before long, you'll have thousands displayed in the main screen, and that can get very confusing. Once imported into the **Organizer**, you can see exactly where on your hard drives those imported files reside through the **Folders** menu in the left-hand bin.

Another best practice is to sort any new files into what Adobe calls **Albums**, which you make in the **Organizer**. These are essentially virtual folders that are used for compartmentalizing image files inside Photoshop Elements. Dragging image thumbnails to populate these albums doesn't alter the location of the originals. You can then apply keywords, tags, and star ratings, and even rank them according to the places and people that Elements identifies for you during the import process. I particularly like ranking images according to keywords and the star attribute hierarchy because they are easy to use. Use one or a combination of these filing systems to bring greater order to your image library. Everything can, of course, be renamed, copied, and moved while it's inside Elements.

In the following screenshot, I have created an album called **Animals**. Selecting the album on the left-hand side of the window will display the contents of that album in the main window. As with most features in Elements, an album can be renamed:

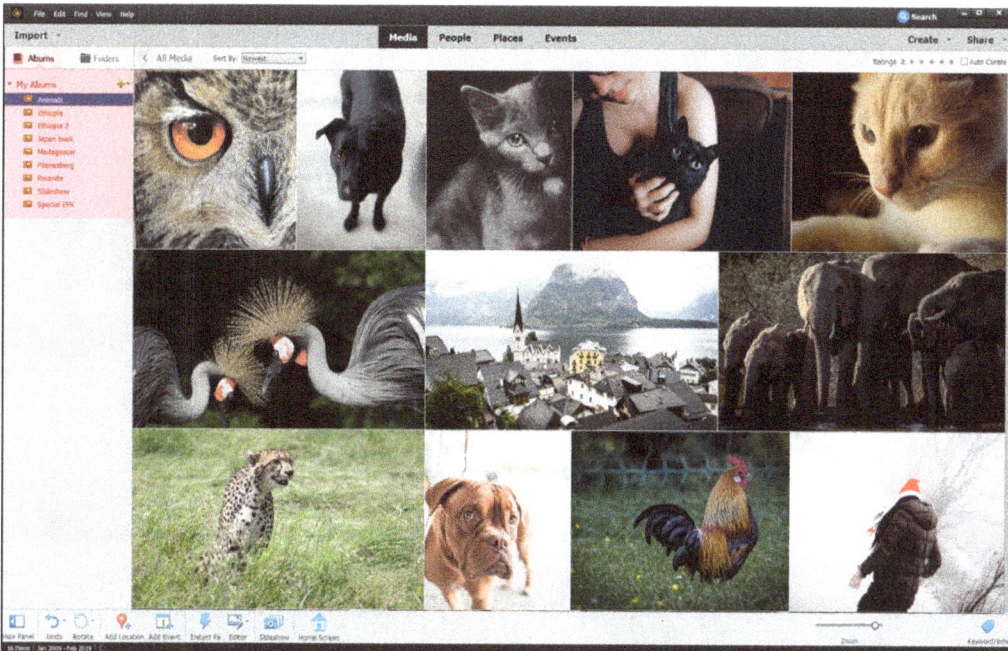

The huge advantage of creating albums, apart from enabling you to easily compartmentalize your work into smaller, more practical collections, is that you can have the same image or images in multiple albums without increasing the space taken up on the storage drive.

All the details of this filing system (albums, tags, keywords, thumbnails, original files, and so on) are part of the Elements catalog, which in itself is something that also needs to be backed up to a location that's different to where the original RAW files are backed up. Some photographers prefer to divide image collections up into multiple different catalogs. For example, wedding photographers might have a separate catalog for each client.

The main disadvantage of organizing your work this way is that you can only ever open one catalog at a time, which is why it works for wedding and portrait professionals – each client is entirely separate from the other. You might like to have two catalogs – one for work and one for the family – but most photographers use just the one.

Photoshop Elements has a number of quite powerful but often overlooked features – including this one, called **Auto Curate**, highlighted here in red, which picks the top 500 images from the **Organizer**. The results might surprise you:

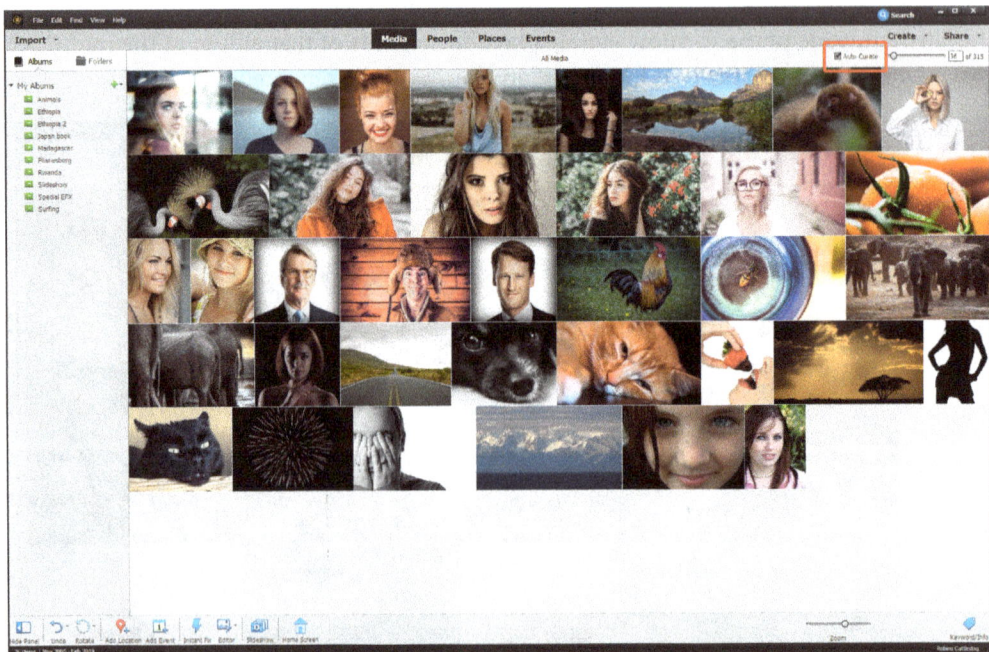

With your media displayed in the main window, check the **Auto Curate** box and watch as Elements finds 50 of the best images from anything up to 20,000 images (according to Adobe). As I think most of the images in my test media are good anyway, it's a mystery how it finds 50 (or any number you choose) of the best. Nonetheless, this is worth a look for a quick, frustration-free selection.

Reviewing the media

Looking at your media in the Organizer couldn't be easier. The main window displays all media files in a mode called **Grid View**—these are adjustable-size thumbnails, as displayed in the background of this image here. But if you create and populate albums, the main window will only display what's in each album.

Compartmentalizing an image collection into multiple albums, therefore, is an effective way to break up what would otherwise be a confusing mass of images on the main screen, into smaller, more visually digestible quantities:

One quick tip for anyone wanting to sort through a lot of images is to maximize the *thumbnail* size so the screen effectively only displays one image at a time, as seen in the preceding coastal seascape image, then use the up/down arrows on the keyboard to scroll through the latest import while examining each file's full size. Every time you find an image that you love, want to keep, or think needs editing, you can classify it using the number keys to add one, two, three, four, or five stars (see the *Organizing your work – ratings* section later in this chapter). Use these to sort and search for images later. (Pressing the number zero on the keypad removes all star attributes.) You can also see that, once expanded to fullscreen, you can also type in a caption for the displayed image and play any associated sound (that is, if it's a movie clip).

Even better, there are no restrictions as to how many albums you can create and, since they are essentially *virtual* folders, they don't take up much storage space.

While sorting through recently imported images, get into the habit of right-clicking an image thumbnail – this reveals a contextual menu that offers many options, but in particular reference to sorting images, you can choose from any of the following:

- **Delete from Catalog**
- **Edit with Photoshop Elements Editor**
- **Edit with Premiere Elements Editor**
- **Adjust Date and Time** (this is good for when you cross different time zones)
- **Add Caption**
- **Add a Rating** (that is, 1-5 stars)
- **Add a Person** (identified in the image for later searches)
- **Create a Slideshow** (when more than one image thumbnail is selected)
- **Show File Info** (that is, view the file's metadata)

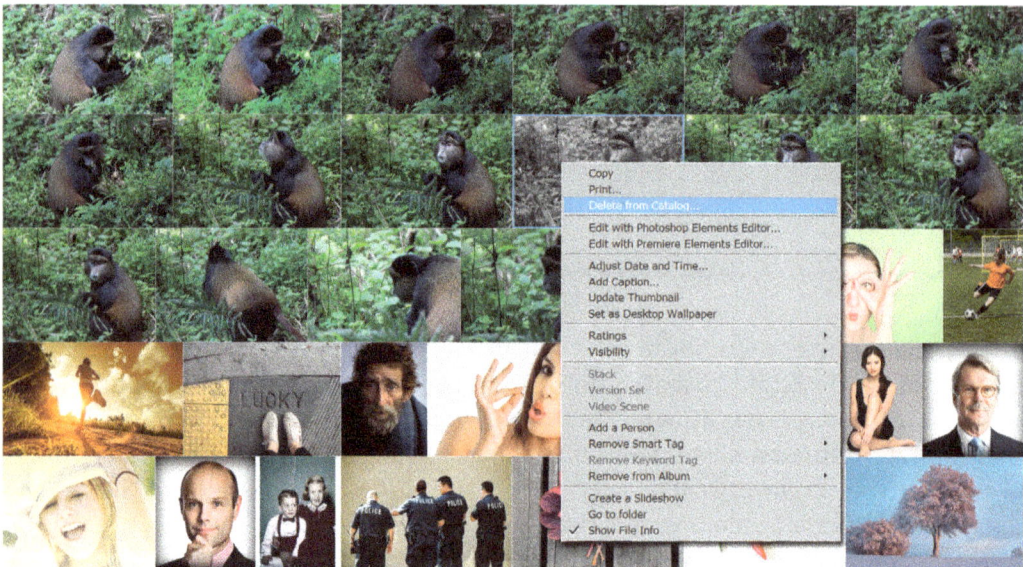

One question often asked is "*In what order do I make my edits?*" Follow some of the guidelines in the next section to learn the most efficient way to process and organize your photographic output.

Suggested editing workflow

Finding the best processes to sort out all your work is important. You really don't want to keep going back and forth importing, re-importing, then losing image files because they were not keyworded, labeled, or stored correctly.

The following is a list of my workflow actions:

1. I always run through my latest import quickly, checking for quality.

2. Files that are **blurry**, **unsharp**, or just **not interesting** get deleted. (Right-click to choose **Delete from Catalog**.)

> **Tip**
> You can also delete the original file entirely if required. This saves time and hard drive space if the image really is that poor and not worth keeping.

3. Everything in that import then gets added to **custom-named albums**.

4. Another important habit to get into is **keywording**. Select one or multiple images and add keywords. This is an invaluable search tool. You can add multiple keywords to one or hundreds of images at the same time.

5. Import another batch of images and repeat the same steps.

Do not try to rename your files or folders in the Mac Finder app or Windows Explorer because this is liable to confuse Elements. Do all your renaming from within Elements and you should experience few problems.

Organizing your work

Some of you might be familiar with the Windows OS's star ratings. This is a feature that allows you to award a file anything from one to five stars, depending on its merit. You can then search for files (in this context, images) that are displaying X number of stars. You might give your best images five stars, and those that need editing three stars – that kind of thing. Ratings appear in a wide range of photo-editing applications, including Adobe Bridge, Lightroom, and Camera Bits' Photo Mechanic, for good reason—it's a system that's easy to implement and effective in its organizational potential.

Star-rating your photos

If photo organization and image management are new concepts for you, I recommend you start out using Elements' **Ratings** feature because it's simple and works well. Here's how to get this happening:

1. Right-click an image in the **Organizer**.

2. From **Ratings** in the contextual menu, slide over the number of stars you'd like to award the selected image (that is, from 1-5). Or, faster still, select one or more images in the main window, and hit any number key between *1* and *5* (use the top of the keyboard, not the number keypad) to add a rating.

3. To search for an already-rated image, click the appropriate star symbol in the **Ratings** search field (at the top of the screen, just under the **Create** tab), and everything in the main screen with that star rating will remain. Everything else is hidden until you click the same star rating again to zero the search.

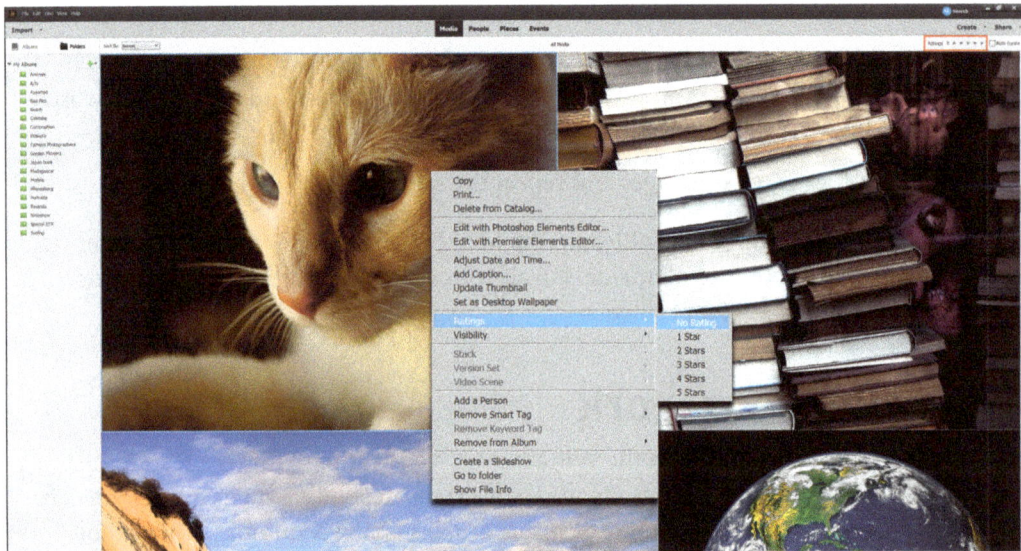

Note that this search can be refined by clicking the tiny symbol to the right of the word **Ratings** to set **Greater than, or equal to**; **Less than, or equal to**; or **Rating is equal to**. It can make a big difference to your search results.

This is an exceptionally intuitive system that's easy to set up, easy to modify, and very efficient in its search results – just use that pop-out menu to lower, raise, or delete the rating if required.

Using metadata

Metadata is little more than a small text file that records all your camera details at the time the photo is taken. We rarely see what's in the metadata unless we specifically need to look it up or, in this context, use it to search for images. Metadata records camera and lens details, the date and time, and, if your camera has it, a set of GPS coordinates.

So, without having to enter any data first (like we have to when using keywords and tags), we can use **Organizer** to search our image database using any of those pre-recorded metadata details:

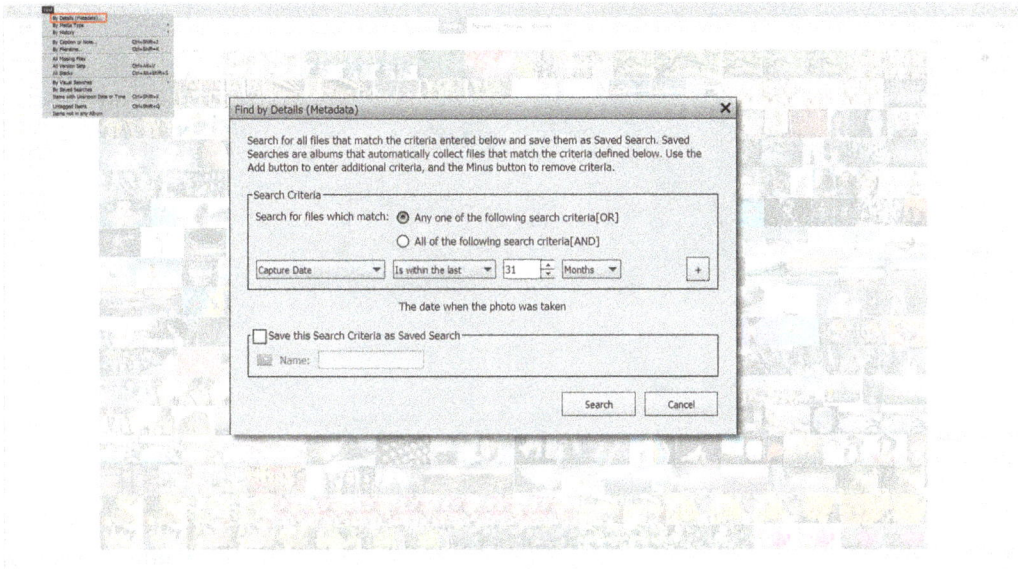

You might find the **Find by Details (Metadata)** search field a bit confusing because it offers so many ways to look for your images. You can also use this dialog box to save frequently used searches—a real time-saver. It can also be used to search for images by the date and time captured. This is useful if you holiday in different time zones.

The easiest way to do this is to use the aptly named **Find** menu. By selecting **Find | By Details**, we can choose from a staggering range of parameters with which to search.

The obvious choices would be to search for camera type, or the date taken—but you can also look for files based on the lens' focal length, the f-stop value, ISO, shutter speed, exposure settings, and many more characteristics. In the **Find by Details** window (shown in the preceding screenshot), enter your search criteria using the drop-down menu. If what you see in the menu is not specific enough, simply add a second or a third "rule" to the search by clicking the + button to the right of the **Search Criteria** window.

The **Information** panel shown here shares space in the right-hand panel with tags, and is quite comprehensive—there's a compact version and an extended version (seen here currently occupying the entire right-hand panel):

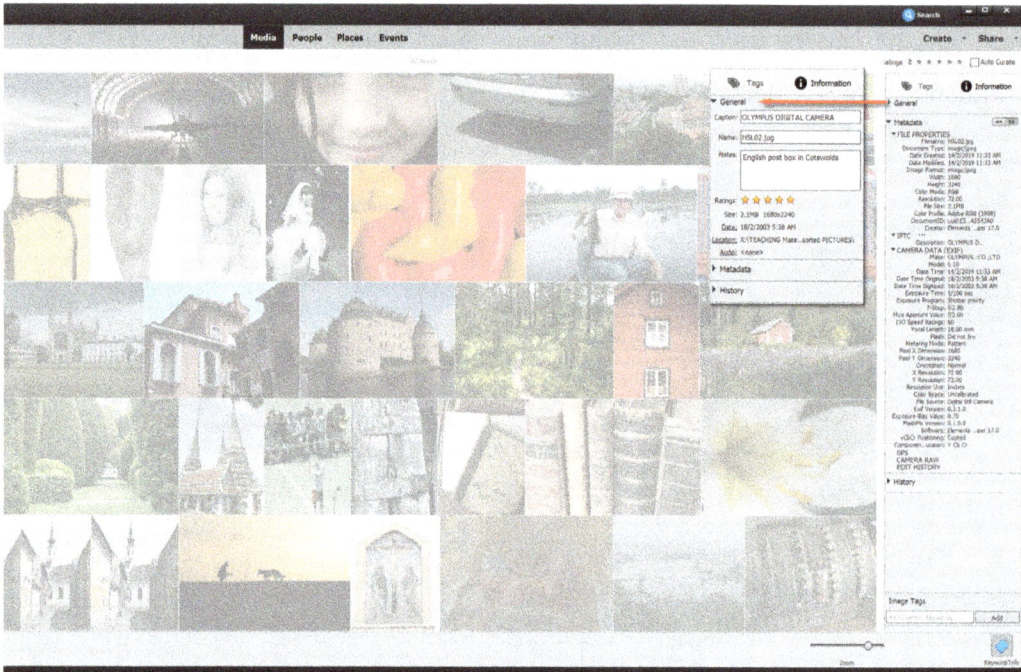

Above that is the **General** menu (for the purposes of this illustration, it's floating over the thumbnail picture grid, to the left of the extended **Information** panel). This displays a few snippets of that file's metadata, as well as the star rating and where it physically resides on your hard drives.

Note that searches can be set to use **Any one of the following search criteria** or **All of the following search criteria**. Choosing one of these over the other might have a significant effect on the search result. If it is not finding the media you are searching for, flick over to the other search rule and see if that works.

Now let's move on and have a look at what many professionals consider to be the best way to organize your photos, video clips, music files, and more: keyword tags.

Organizing your work – keyword tags

One of the best features in Elements is its ability to sort out hundreds, thousands, or even tens of thousands of images using the tested method of **keyword tags**.

While viewing a newly imported batch of pictures, select a file by clicking it once and, on the bottom right-hand side of the screen, type in a keyword.

I think keywording is one of the most important setup features in this program. Get in the habit of adding a keyword (or keywords) to everything you import into the Organizer and you will be able to search and find almost any image weeks, months, and even years later. It's an incredibly efficient and effective system of image retrieval.

You can see that, in the pink highlighted area in the following screenshot, I have entered the words surfing and Australia. If I import and add keywords to hundreds of surfing images in the Organizer, all I need do is click in the **Surfing** and/or the **Australia** tag (both highlighted in blue in the screenshot) to find all those images, which can then be placed in a specific album called **Surfing**:

Let's say you have got back home from a vacation. Select all the images from the vacation and type the name of the place you visited. If you went to Australia, for example, all images could be keyworded as Australia. But if half that time was spent in the mountains around the town of Katoomba, re-select those images of Katoomba alone and add Katoomba as the keyword. If three days in Australia were spent surfing, select those images only, and add the keyword surfing. This takes only a few minutes and, with a little forethought, you'll quickly be able to keyword all the important events in this album (named Holiday in Australia) so that, months or years later, you can search for Australia, surfing, or cocktails, for example, and Elements will locate those images almost instantly.

> **Tip**
>
> You can take your keywording as far as you have the time and patience for by being increasingly specific. For example, I could also keyword my holiday pictures with the words beaches, restaurants, funny signs, people, markets, nightlife, sunsets, palm trees, cocktails, and so on.
>
> If you add multiple keywords, separate them with a comma (,) to avoid confusing the search engine. Also, limit your keywords to five or six per image. Too many keywords can be counter-productive.

It's an easy process, but the real magic only really begins when you try to search for specific images shot on that trip:

In the **Search** field (the blue magnifying glass icon at the top right-hand side of the **Organizer** screen), type in a location and maybe an event using whatever keywords are appropriate (such as Surfing or Australia), and the **Organizer** will find those images within seconds. It's fast because it only has to sort through its database (which is essentially a text record), not through gigabytes of high-resolution RAW files.

In the following screenshot, I right-clicked my **Surfing** keyword tag in the right-hand bin and chose **Edit** from the contextual menu. This brings up the **Edit Keyword Tag** window (on the left). You can edit the name of the **Tag** and add comments. Clicking the **Edit Icon** tab brings up another, larger window, into which you can load a surfing picture. It's a cute feature, but it won't really improve your workflow:

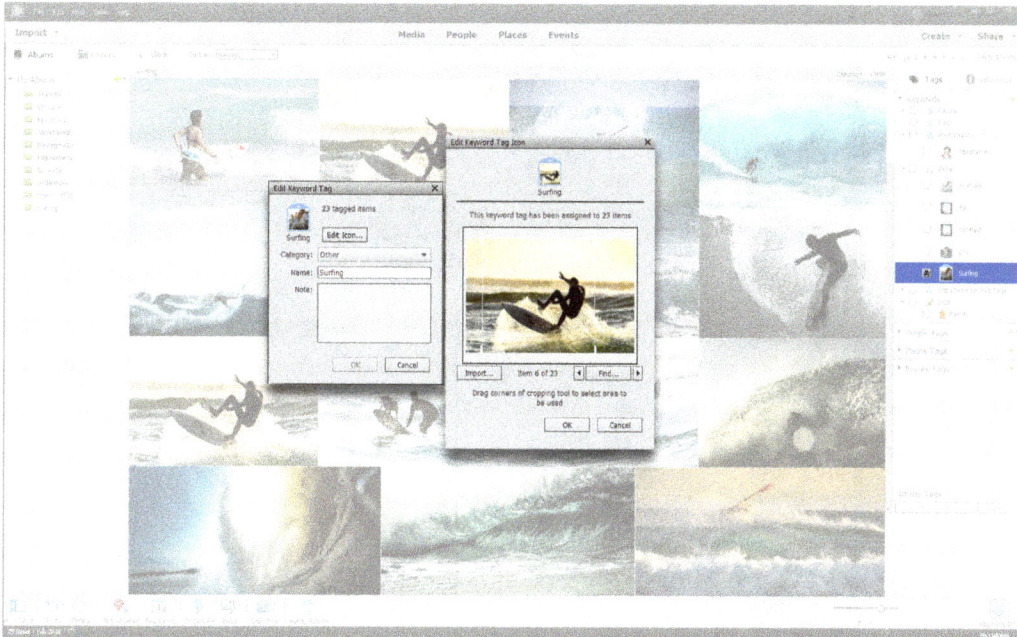

Keyword tags are written into the file so that if I sent a bunch of my (tagged) images to a third party, they would be able to sort them using my attached tags. Elements' tags can be read by a range of other image-editing software programs. An album, on the other hand, is a purely Elements-only feature.

If you create a new tag in the right-hand tag bin, you can apply it to any image simply by dragging that tag onto the photo thumbnail—easy! If you have 100 images that need the same tag, select all of them first, drag the newly made tag onto any one of the selected thumbnails, and it will automatically apply that tag to all selected images. Very smart!

In the following screenshot, I have enlarged the pop-out **Tags** menu to show its various options. There's everything here that you need to fully label anything you bring into Elements. Pay attention to the tagging process and you'll never lose an image again:

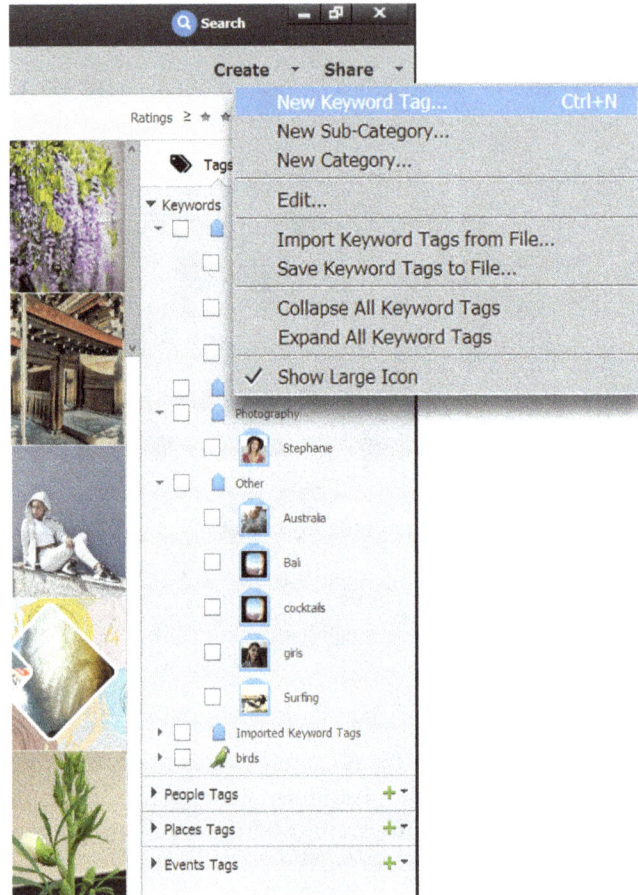

A green + symbol in the **Tags** bin, or elsewhere in this application, always points to the ability to create a new feature. In the example here, use it to create a new keyword tag, new category, new sub-category, or to import tags from a file, to save tags to a file, or to expand and collapse the tag hierarchy.

> **Tip**
>
> Don't forget that you can also create your own keyword categories and sub-categories to further refine your search criteria.
>
> Elements provides a default subset of People, Places, and Events tags that can easily be expanded as and when needed.

Organizing your work – places

The Organizer has a huge range of features designed to help photographers keep track of, and search for, their images. I think there are too many—but that's just a personal opinion.

The **Places** feature has been in Elements for many years. Its principal use is to automatically place any image that contains GPS data onto an internet-driven world map so that users can identify pictures simply by seeing the locations where they were actually shot, as shown in the following screenshot:

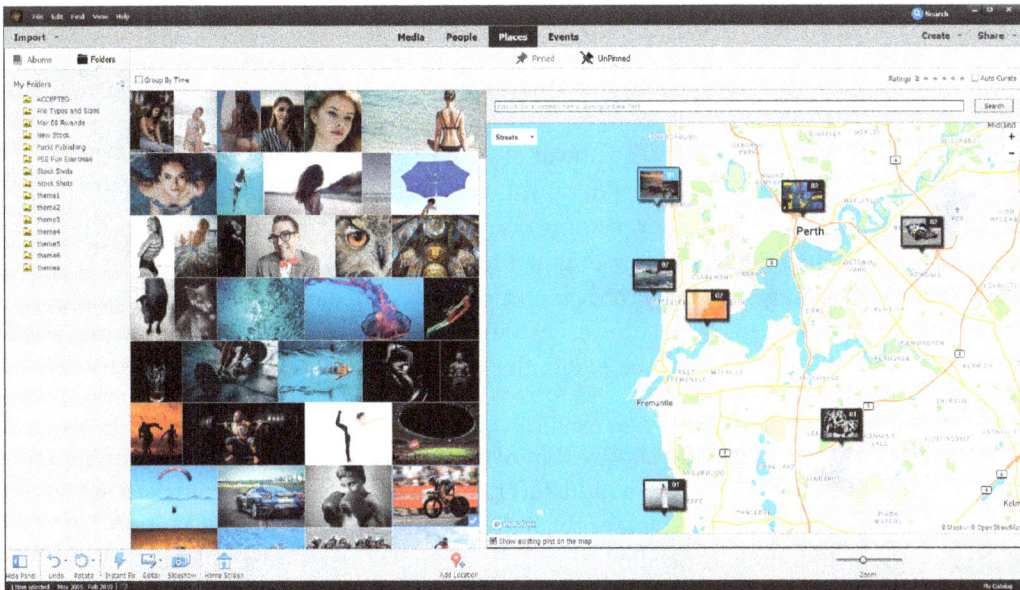

In earlier versions of this program (several years ago), few cameras had GPS capabilities, so you had to drag images from the grid on the left-hand side of the screen onto the map to pin them in place instead. You can still do this.

The feature has two view modes: **Pinned** and **UnPinned**. In the latter mode, you can select single or multiple images and drag them to the location where they were shot—they are then pinned to the map. Once pinned, they automatically appear under the **Pinned** tab. If you get the location wrong, simply click and drag the pinned image(s) to a new location. Double-clicking the pinned image thumbnails opens them in **Grid** view. Double-click once more and they open in fullscreen.

On paper, Places appears to be a nice feature, but after years of teaching Elements, I have yet to meet anyone that uses this feature exclusively. That might well change once all cameras record GPS data. Since 2018, Places no longer works in any of the previous versions of Elements. At the time of going to press, Adobe was not forthcoming about why this is so. It's fully functional in Elements 2020.

Organizing your work – events

The **Events** category is, I think, more useful to everyday photographers. Why? Because Events starts off by using dates as a way to categorize images. We might take a bunch of shots over a family weekend or on our 12-day trip to Bali. Using the **Events** feature, these images can be grouped into either events dictated solely by the date, read from the metadata, or they can be grouped and renamed into something more memorable, such as `Family Weekend, 2019`, or simply `Bali Vacation`.

Events has two view modes: **Named** and **Suggested**. I normally dislike anything that *suggests* things to me (that is, predictive text), but in this case, it presents all your images grouped by date. This is quite useful because it instantly orders everything in the main window, whether from an album, folder, or all media. That's a good start.

The following screenshot illustrates the power of sorting by date. The base window shows **Events**, with the **Number of Groups** slider positioned to the left-hand side (highlighted in red). Everything is pushed against everything else because the search engine is effectively compressing time. The middle window (highlighted in blue) shows how, if the slider is pushed to the right, images are displayed on an almost day-by-day basis, making it easier to find photos from a day shoot or some other short-running function. The front window illustrates what the named Events look like in the **Named** tab (highlighted in orange). Events can be modified.

To delete an Event, right-click and choose **Remove this Event**. This pop-out menu also allows you to **Edit** the Event (that is, to add/subtract images to/from the Event); to **Set as Cover**, which makes the displayed image the default front page; to **Create a Slideshow**, which takes all the files in that specific Event stack and puts them into a slideshow that can be saved for further editing in the **Organizer**; or it can be directly uploaded to social media via the **Share** menu (at the top right-hand side of the **Organizer**).

Tip

When drawing a marquee, simply click and drag the cursor so it draws a rectangle over all the images you need. Blue checkmarks appear in all those that are selected. If you accidentally miss one image, add it by holding the *Ctrl* or the *Cmd* key down while you click the mouse once (Windows or Mac, respectively). By the same process, if you select too many by accident, you can hold *Ctrl* or *Cmd* and click the file to deselect it.

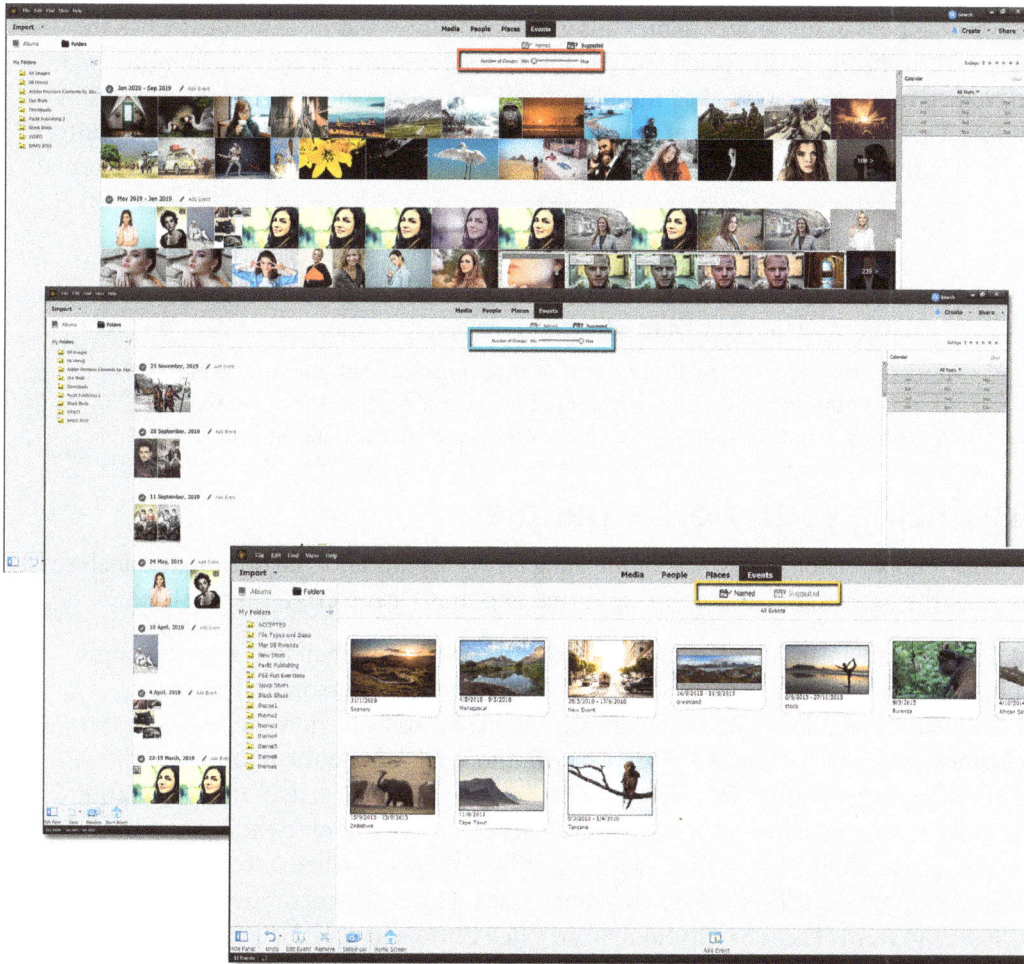

I give my albums and folders real names, rather than going on just the dates—the same can be done using **Places**. Shift the **Number of Groups** slider so the setting that displays your **Event** does so in one group of images (that is, selecting just the weekend, or just that week). Physically select all those images (do this by holding the *Shift* key down, and clicking the first and then the last image in the group). They are now all selected. If the images you need are in more than one group, it's easy enough to select multiple groups by drawing a marquee around those groups.

Once selected, click the **Add Event** button at the base of the page and, in the dialog box that opens, give the event a proper name, check the dates to ensure you have grabbed the right sequence, select a **Group** if that's needed, add a description if required, and click **OK**.

But what happens to the proper names this group of pictures was just awarded? Click the **Named** tab at the top of the screen and you'll see all the images that were custom-grouped and **Named** now appear as stacked thumbnails. Sliding the cursor over a group displays its contents. Double-clicking an **Event** stack reveals the individual images it contains. Clicking the **Back** button on the same screen moves those spread-out images back into a stack format.

> **Tip**
>
> As your image collection grows, you can further refine a search, or just what's displayed in this main window, by selecting different dates from the calendar that's posted on the right-hand side of the screen.
>
> You can also create a **New Event** in the **Media** window. Click the **Add Event** tab at the bottom of the page, drag those images you'd like in the new Event to the right-hand side bin, give it a proper name, check the date, and click **OK**.

Organizing your work – people

Elements' **People** mode is really all about using face recognition, an algorithm that analyzes images in the background as they are imported into the **Organizer** for the first time.

If it detects a face in an image, it presents it as a circular thumbnail in the main **People** window. If it *thinks* that there are several images of the same person in the import, these will be automatically stacked like a deck of cards. You can view the results in the **UnNamed** panel. Every image will appear with the label **Add Name** underneath the thumbnail to begin with. If you recognize the person depicted, click in the **Add Name** field and type in the name. As soon as you click the check symbol to the right of the field to lock it in, the thumbnail stack disappears. Where's it gone? Click into the **Named** window and there you'll see the newly named stack. Hover the cursor over the stack and you'll see the words **Faces** or **Photos** appear. Click **Photos** to reveal the full image in which the face was detected, or click **Faces** to reveal just the face or faces in that group:

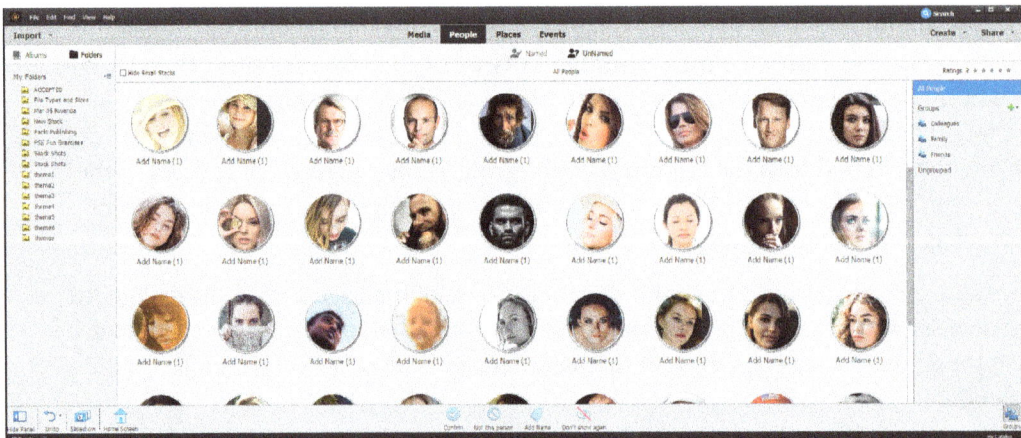

Elements' **People** window will find images of your friends—but it also finds every image that looks like a face, including in posters and abstract backgrounds, for example. These can easily be discounted by right-clicking the icon and choosing **Don't Show Again**. As you can clearly see here, I have some naming to do—as soon as an image gets a proper name, it is moved into the **Named** tab, and stacks with similarly named images.

Tip

You can merge one stack into another simply by click-dragging one file over another. You can further refine the sort process by adding stacks to **Groups**, such as `Family`. Click the **Groups** tab on the bottom-right side of the main window, and either use one of the default groups, or make a new one by clicking the green + symbol. As with most Elements' features, there is no limit to the number of groups you can have.

If you discover an inappropriate face in a stack, open the stack and right-click the **Faces** icon and choose **Not…**, or just rename it, which places it out of that stack into its own new stack. You can also use this pop-out menu to **Assign** that image as a profile photo (that is, this is the default top of the stack). Finally, there's the **Don't Show Again** command, which hides that image from ever appearing in the **People** view again.

For those of us that prefer to identify our images based on the content, and specifically on the people depicted in the files, you'll find the **People** feature very handy:

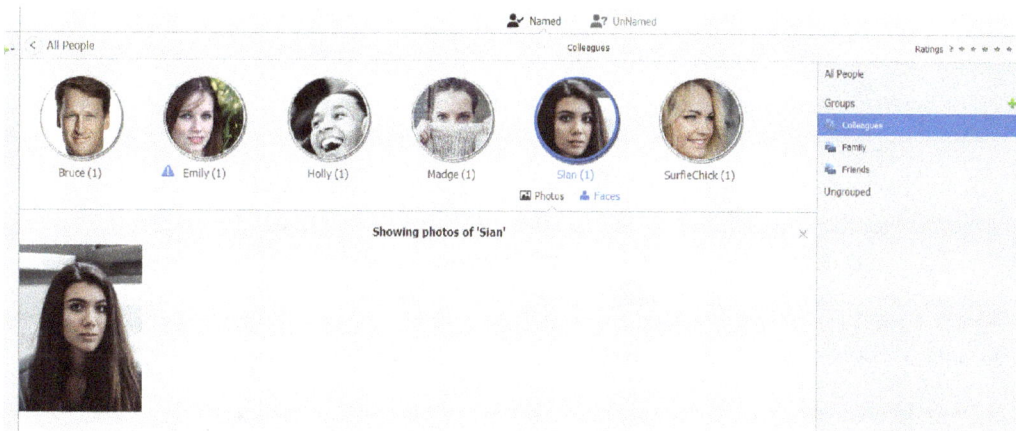

Like the **Keywords** feature, the **People** feature, shown in the preceding screenshot, allows you to subdivide your found faces into smaller categories, or **Groups**, as seen on the right-hand side of the screen. Elements starts you off with **Colleagues**, **Family**, and **Friends** but, of course, clicking the green plus (+) symbol allows you to add new group categories when needed.

Like most organizational tools in Elements, you can choose to work simply by adopting just keywords, or maybe ratings, or you can use a combination of everything covered in this section to create a sophisticated and deep searchable database. The best advice is to make up your mind regarding which way is best for you before you start; that way, you can streamline your workload from day one rather than having to go back over everything that's been imported into the **Organizer** because you changed your mind about how to organize your images.

Pre-planning will save you a lot of time and effort.

Backing up your media and the Catalog

As I mentioned in the introduction to this section, keeping media backups is very important. Once lost, there's little chance you'll ever get your images back if there's a major technical problem, so be warned!

If you have a Mac, follow these steps:

1. Buy an external hard drive that's at least twice the capacity of your Mac's internal drive (that is, if your Mac's drive is 1 TB capacity, buy a 2 TB drive, or better still, a 4 TB drive).

2. Plug the drive into the Mac.

3. Format the drive for FAT32 (which means it'll work on a Mac or Windows) or Mac OS Extended (a Mac-only format) using the Mac's included Disk Utility.

4. Find and start the Time Machine app.

5. Follow the onscreen prompts. It takes 2 minutes to set up. You can set it to back up only your photos, only specific folders, or everything!

6. A full backup might take several hours, depending on the amount of stuff that's already on the computer. It backs up **all** your documents, emails, messages, music, images, and documents. Once done, it just backs up new files only, every day or every hour. It's a fast and totally seamless operation.

If you have Windows, follow these steps:

1. Plug the external hard drive into the PC.

2. Locate the backup software—this should be on the hard drive when you buy it. Most good-quality drives from companies such as Seagate or Western Digital come pre-loaded with their own proprietary software backup programs. If not, you might have to either download it from that company's website, or buy a backup application to do it for you (this is unlikely).

3. Run the application and follow the onscreen prompts to set up the data you need copied, plus the frequency.

4. Some proprietary software apps allow you to set up a terrestrial backup or a cloud backup (that is, backing up to a service such as Dropbox). Western Digital drives offer a third-party application (from Acronis) that, like Apple's Time Machine, can be set up to copy everything on the PC to the external drive, not just pictures. Also, note that the Windows operating system also has restore functionality, should you need to recover lost, corrupted, or deleted files.

If you are a little more familiar with computers, it's easy enough to perform **manual backups** when needed. The process is the same for Mac or Windows:

1. Start the computer.

2. Locate the file or folders that you need to back up.

3. Locate the drive icon for the backup drive unit.

4. Drag the files or folders across from your local drive onto the external drive icon. You'll see a progress bar appear to indicate that it is under way.

This is an easy method of backup, but essentially relies on the operator remembering when to do the backups!

If you have never tried manually backing data up to an external drive, it can be a little daunting because, if you release the mouse at the wrong moment, the images might scatter all over the computer, making them hard to locate. To make this easy, I usually open two windows (in the regular **Mac Finder**, or **Windows Explorer**) and arrange them approximately side by side. The left-hand window displays all my images on the computer (that is, in the `Pictures` folder). The right-hand window displays the content of my external hard drive. Locate the file or folder that you want to back up, then click and drag it from the left window to the right-hand window and release. It copies over to the external drive. If you subsequently add more images to the computer's hard drive, when you manually back that up, it will ask if you want to *overwrite the existing files* on the external drive. You can do this, but it just takes a bit longer because everything is copied again (including those files that have already been copied). If you say **No**, it only copies new files, which is a much faster option.

The following screenshot demonstrates how this drag and drop process can work:

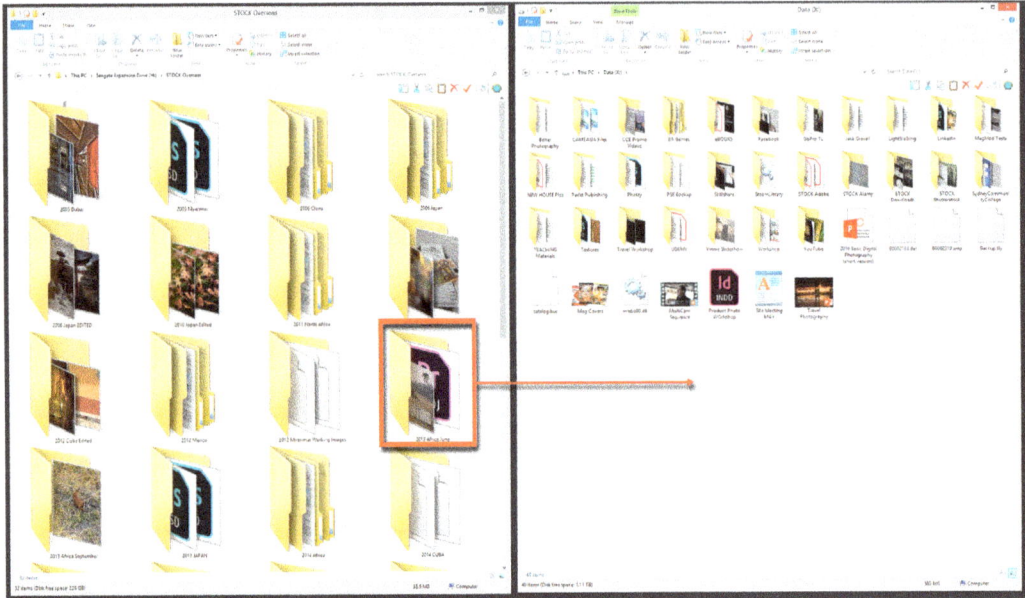

Note that although the select, drag, and drop method of backing up files is specific and fast, you can also use the time-honored method of select, copy, and paste.

Do this by selecting the appropriate files first (**Select | All** or *Ctrl/cmd + A*), then copying the selected images onto the computer's clipboard (**Edit | Copy** or *Ctrl/cmd + C*). Before you paste anything, select the destination (that is, the backup drive) and paste the contents of the selection to the new location (**Edit | Paste** or *Ctrl/cmd + V*).

> **Tip**
>
> If you purchase a RAID drive (essentially two or more hard drives in one box), you can program it to back up once to each drive, essentially giving you two complete backups in one operation so if one drive fails, you still have a second copy to use. Another use of the RAID drive is to split backups 50/50. This greatly enhances the read/write speeds of the device but, in this mode, if one drive goes down, you lose everything because the process actually splits files rather than putting one file on disk A then the next file on disk B, and so on. Nothing in digital imaging can be 100% safe but if you use a reliable RAID system it should give you years of good service.

Note that the **Select All** command selects everything in the open window. If you specifically want to select one image file, one folder, or a few selected folders on their own, you must either draw a marquee around those folders or files that you need, or hold the *Ctrl/cmd* key while clicking the files to be included. If you accidentally select one file/folder that you do not need, simply *Ctrl/cmd* click it a second time to deselect it.

Managing Catalogs

The Catalog Manager dialog box (**Organizer | File | Manage Catalogs**) is used for several tasks. These include the following:

- Creating new catalogs

- Renaming existing catalogs

- Converting a previous, older version of Elements catalogs to the new version of the software

- Optimizing a catalog—this helps reduce its size, making it more efficient

It's quite important to ensure that your backed-up catalog is saved to a location that is different to where the default catalog is stored. For most, this means saving it to an entirely different drive – in the following illustration, there are five different drives available for backup:

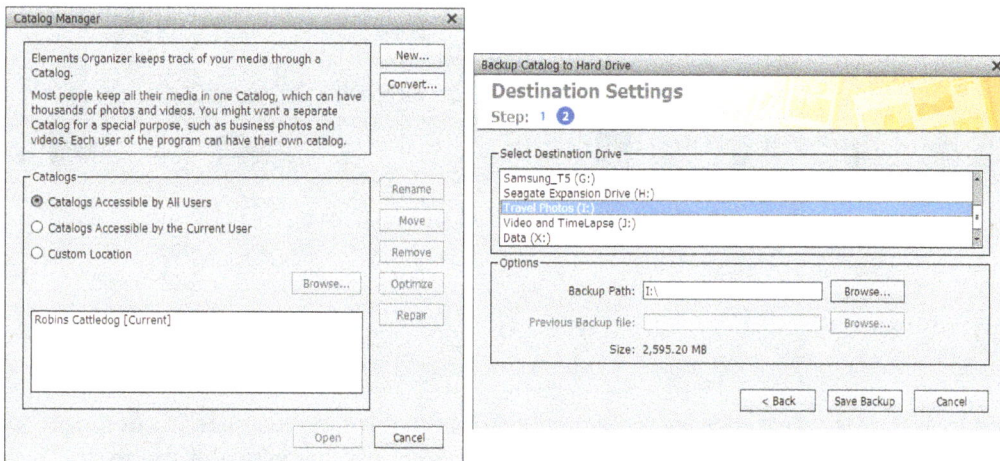

While a software-driven data backup is a good procedure to set up for all users, it might not back up your Photoshop Elements catalog. And even if it did, it wouldn't be in a format that Elements can recognize, should you need to restore it after a software mishap.

The catalog is where all your hard work is stored: tags, keywords, albums, captions, places, maps, and events; as well as your images, as RAW, JPEG, TIFF, PNG or PSD files; plus a lot of other stuff that helps Elements be as efficient as it can.

Although Elements' backup process can be a lifesaver, it's not the same as a regular Windows or Mac backup. With Elements, the backed-up files are referenced in a completely different way to those that are simply copied to a different hard drive – which is why if you open the Elements backup file, everything appears scrambled (see the following screenshot). However, if you reinstate the catalog via the correct process, everything reappears in perfect order:

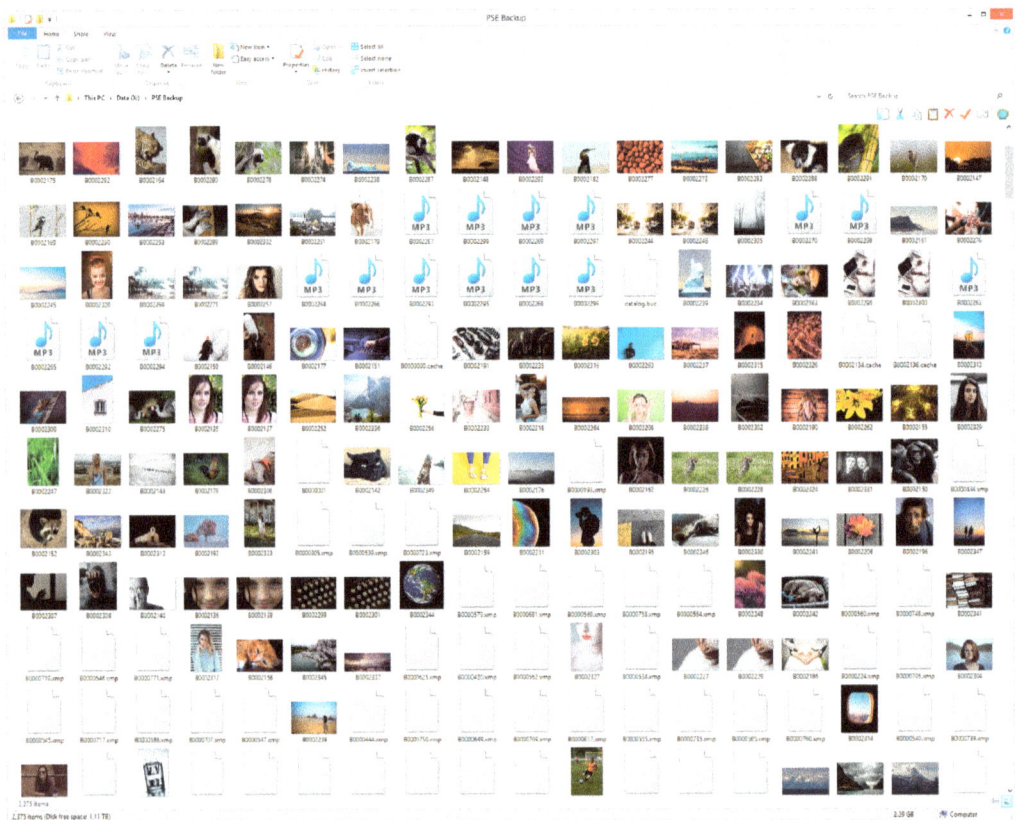

If you look at the backup once it's completed, you'll probably not recognize any of the original image file names because the **Organizer** renames the files with alphanumeric codes. Your proper names are reinstated once a **Catalog Restore** function is completed. Generally, we only access an Elements backup if the original has been compromised and you need to restore the entire catalog contents.

In an emergency, you can still open the `Backup` folder and pull out images, if need be. If you have issues with the current catalog, it's easy enough to choose **File | Restore Catalog** from the **Organizer** and reload the entire catalog from its backup location.

The logical way to perform a catalog backup is to choose **File | Backup Catalog** in the **Organizer** and follow the prompts. Make sure that the location of the backup is not on the local drive—put it on an external drive. Elements insists on a full backup to begin with, then a partial backup if you are just updating work as you go.

Working with plugins

A plugin is an additional bit of software produced by a third-party company. It's designed to either expand Elements' existing features, or to add new ones. Plugins are typically called Photoshop-compliant plugins, which essentially means that they will work with all Adobe programs, as well as a wide range of other editing programs (such as Corel PaintShop Pro).

My current favorite Elements plugin changes the look of any image from purely photographic to something very artistic at the click of the mouse:

Probably my all-time favorite plugin for Photoshop Elements is called Moku Hanga (a Japanese phrase for wood block printing). Now, I love these traditional Japanese prints, but I could never afford one because they are very expensive—however, I can reproduce the look of a real woodblock print using this amazing plugin from JixiPix. It takes a few minutes to create an effect like this but, because the plugin offers so many variants, it usually takes a lot longer just to decide which one to keep!

One popular plugin (from Topaz Labs) brings incredible **selection accuracy** to the Elements edit suite, refining Elements' already excellent selection tools further. You can also get plugins for the following:

- Sharpening
- Noise reduction
- Grunge looks
- Fine art effects
- Painting looks
- Cartoons
- Graphic effects
- Three-dimensional paper effects
- High Dynamic Range (HDR) effects
- Black and white conversions

Installing a plugin is a simple operation:

1. Download the file from the host website.
2. Double-click the installer.
3. Follow the onscreen prompts.
4. Restart the computer, launch Photoshop Elements, and open an image. To check that the software has indeed *plugged in*, choose the **Filter** menu and scroll all the way to the bottom. Plugins will be located at the base of the **Filter** menu, under **Other**.

> **Important note**
> Not all plugins work on both Mac and Windows operating systems, so it pays to check the specifications carefully before you part with any money.

Additional resources – keyboard shortcuts and working tips

It's a sad fact that all image editing is virtually worthless if the monitor on which you make all your creative decisions doesn't actually represent the correct color, brightness, and contrast accurately. Color management—the process of making sure that what you see onscreen is both accurate to life and will be correctly reproduced online and in print—is, I think, an unnecessarily complex operation. Although Elements' calibration is not nearly as controllable as that found in Photoshop, it's presented in a reasonably easy format that should work well in most situations. And if you are sending your work into a commercial print environment, you can always let them handle the finer complexities of color reproduction, which allows you to pay more attention to the editing process.

Color management options

One area where Photoshop Elements really cannot compete with Photoshop CC is in serious color management:

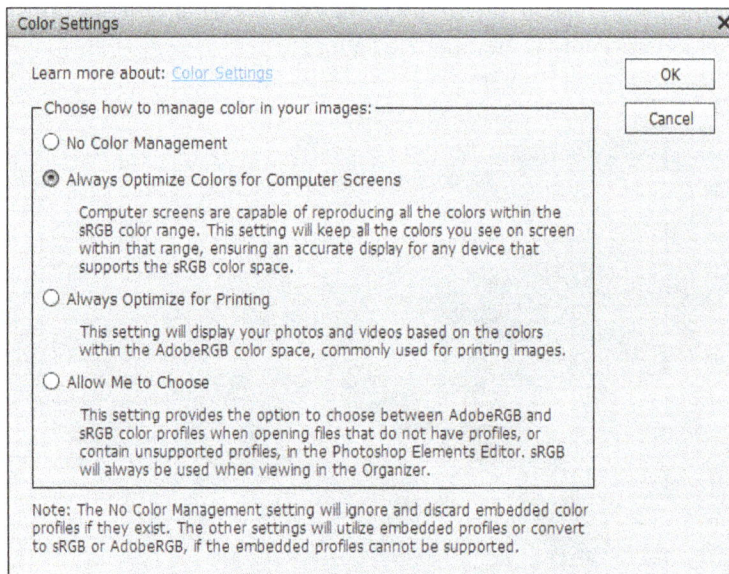

What you'll find in the program's **Color Settings** dialog box are four simple options:

- **No Color Management**
- **Always Optimize Colors for Computer Screens**
- **Always Optimize for Printing**
- **Allow Me to Choose**

Essentially, this means that if you choose to ignore any color management, Elements will discard existing color space settings, but if you choose to optimize colors, the color range will be kept within the existing sRGB color range.

If you go for the printing option, it would be best to set AdobeRGB (1998) as the color space in your camera. The **Allow Me to Choose** option permits the user to make a choice between sRGB and AdobeRGB (1998).

Screen calibration

Another important technique for ensuring that what you see onscreen is accurate is to calibrate your monitor with a hardware calibration device.

These third-party sensors plug into the USB outlet on the computer and hang over the screen. Run the associated software and the sensor will determine whether the RGB colors displayed onscreen really are 100% red, green, blue, white, grey, and black. If the screen is different to the known value for these colors, the software adjusts the brightness and color to make it display correctly. This is a far more accurate method of color management than using the human eye to gauge the settings. As a general rule, screens need calibrating every 6 months or so, especially if they are used a lot:

Calibration is done by attaching a USB-powered hardware calibrator to the laptop or desktop screen, as shown in the preceding image, with the *ColorVision Spyder 5*. This process needs to be done probably once every 6 months or so, just to ensure that what you see onscreen is a realistic representation of the original image.

Organizer keyboard shortcuts

I always provide my students with a list of 10-20 keyboard shortcuts. I can usually see that most are not happy with having yet more stuff to remember. But if you limit yourself to using some of these, instead of relying on the mouse all the time, you'll not only reduce the risk of RSI, but you'll find many repetitive tasks so much safer and faster to execute. Two hands are always better than one:

Here are some Windows/Mac keyboard shortcuts for specific operations:

- Undo last operation: *Ctrl/Cmd + Z*
- Redo last operation: *Ctrl/Cmd + Y*
- Copy: *Ctrl/Cmd + C*
- Paste: *Ctrl/Cmd + P*
- Select all: *Ctrl/Cmd + A*
- Deselect: *Ctrl/Cmd + Shift + D*
- Rotate image 90 degrees left: *Ctrl/Cmd + Left arrow*
- Rotate image 90 degrees right: *Ctrl/Cmd + Right Arrow*
- Adjust date and time: *Ctrl/Cmd + J*
- Edit in Expert Edit Mode: *Ctrl/Cmd + I*
- Edit in Premiere Elements Editor: *Ctrl/Cmd + M*
- Zoom in: *Ctrl/Cmd* + '+'
- Zoom out: *Ctrl/Cmd* + '-'
- OK: *Enter*
- Cancel: *Esc*
- Display metadata properties: *Alt + Enter*
- Add caption: *Ctrl/Cmd + Shift + T*
- Update thumbnails: *Ctrl/Cmd + Shift + U*
- Set photo as desktop wallpaper: *Ctrl + Shift + W (Windows only)*
- Open Color Settings dialog box: *Ctrl/Cmd + Alt + G*

Summary

Though setting up a computer isn't the most glamorous part of the image editing process, we have seen that if you can acquire at least some of the right gear, while adhering to a set workflow, the mechanics of editing will become both faster and easier. It should also greatly assist in helping to future-proof your skills for years to come.

We have seen that the process of organizing your media files is vital. If you follow even just a few of the suggestions in this chapter, you'll find that searching for and finding everything becomes so much easier. Misplacing images should become a thing of the past.

Coming up in the next chapter, we deal with the basics of image editing. Even the most basic tools and features covered in this chapter can be used to transform your work from the everyday to something quite special in just a single click. This is one of the real strengths of Photoshop Elements. The biggest issue facing any beginner is having to decide which of these editing processes to choose, but remember, most of them work in isolation, so if you find a couple of effects that really work for you, stick with them.

As we proceed through the subsequent chapters, you'll find the processes become more involved, but the important thing to remember here is that you don't have to know it all! If it's not of interest, or more importantly, not relevant to your creative direction, move on to something else and make it your own.

3
The Basics of Image Editing

To many, image editing, or more specifically, the word *Photoshop*, conjures up ideas of fantastical landscapes, or of portraits of impossibly beautiful people retouched to the brink of plausibility, and beyond.

If you are not interested in taking your creativity into the realm of photo illustration, or image composites, you'll use photo editing to make your digital files look exactly like they appeared when the shutter button was first pressed.

But why would we need this sort of artificial aid in the first place? It's a frequently asked question, and the simple answer is that **what we see is not always what our camera records**. This is because we have a brain that can be very flexible when it comes to processing the visual information it receives from any scene, whereas a camera simply responds to the light it is pointed at—with essentially a rather limited ability to translate that information into a faithful, realistic reproduction of any scene.

I'm always reminded of a quote by 1960s fashion photographer David Bailey, who said the following:

> *"It takes a lot of imagination to be a good photographer. You need less imagination to be a painter because you can invent things. But in photography, everything is so ordinary; it takes a lot of looking before you learn to see the extraordinary."*

These are wise words, spoken a long time before retouching software came into being.

One of the biggest drawbacks of image editing is its apparent complexity. No one wants to spend hours slaving over a keyboard with little to show for their toil. In this chapter, you'll discover the basics of making your RAW (and JPEG) files look just as they were when you first pressed the shutter button.

But you'll also learn how to generate some very cool effects and creative looks, all with very little time and effort. That might leave you with extra time to go out and shoot more great pictures!

By the end of this chapter, you'll be able to transform your RAW files into something that better resembles a perfect picture using the tools and techniques covered in this chapter.

In this chapter, we'll look at the following topics:

- The editing workflow and best practices
- Ten ways to open an image in Elements
- How to edit RAW files, including a brief overview
- Working with Camera RAW's basic tools
- Working with Camera RAW's sharpening and noise reduction tools
- The Camera RAW toolbar
- Understanding picture resolution
- Cropping for better composition
- How the Crop tool works
- Straightening horizons
- Resampling: making pictures larger or smaller
- Instant photo fixes using the Organizer
- Saving files and Version Sets
- Using the auto tone-correction tools
- Mastering contrast, color, sharpness, and clarity
- Adjusting contrast using Levels
- Adjusting color using Hue/Saturation
- Creating high-impact black and white images
- Perfecting skin tone color
- Smoothing skin tone
- Simple retouching using the Spot Healing Brush tool
- Modifying facial expressions
- Open Closed Eyes—AI is used to replace closed eyes with open ones
- Additional resources

The editing workflow and best practices

Nearly all digital camera images need some form of adjustment to make them appear as the scene did when the image was captured. What many might not immediately appreciate is that there will always be a visual difference between a RAW file and a JPEG file once they are downloaded to the computer.

This is because the former is neither compressed nor processed in-camera, while JPEG files are compressed and processed in-camera. However, they are also 8-bit files, which contain considerably less picture information than a 14-bit RAW file.

The following photos are a good example of how in-camera JPEG processing initially produces a significantly better-looking version of the same shot compared to the 14-bit RAW file on the left. That said, because this was shot inside a poorly lit church, there's some underexposure, but worse, a lot of overexposure in the highlights, most of which could be recovered from the RAW file in Elements. This most probably can't be recovered from the JPEG file, because it already discarded that detail in-camera when the file was reduced from 14 to 8 bits:

Best practices for editing files are as follows:

1. **Download** your images to the computer, if this is your default storage place. If not, download them to an external drive.

2. **Back up** the files on the computer to a hard drive, a second drive, and/or the cloud.

3. **Open** a file (see the *10 ways to open a photo for editing* section).

4. Crop the image to the desired shape or format (be aware that cropping removes pixels, which in turn reduces the printable size of the file—see the *Cropping for better composition* section coming up in this chapter).

5. Check and adjust the **White Balance**.

> **Important note**
>
> For RAW files, do this in the special **Camera RAW** editing window. It's possible to reset any camera's White Balance setting (that is, from 'As Shot' to **Shade**, **Cloudy**, **Indoors**, **Fluorescent**—to whatever setting you have on your camera). However, if the color is wrong in a JPEG file, you can also force it to open in the Camera RAW window (**File | Open in Camera RAW**), or just use one of Elements' seven color adjustment tools (**Enhance | Adjust Color…**) to make things appear better.

6. Check and adjust **Brightness** and **Contrast**.

7. Adjust color intensity using the **Saturation** and/or **Vibrance** tools.

8. Fine-tune the color using tools such as the **Adjust Color for Skin Tone** tool.

9. Apply **Retouching** where needed.

10. Add special effects, text, images, and so on.

11. Adjust the **Sharpness**, fine-tuning it to the file's ultimate usage: web or print.

And just as you thought the **File | Open** command was the only way to open an image in the editing part of Elements, here are nine more. All produce the same result—you choose which best suits your keyboard style.

Ten ways to open a photo for editing

You can choose one or more ways to get an image from the organizer into any of the three editing modes to start creating magic.

- Right-click any thumbnail in **Organizer** and choose **Edit with Photoshop Elements Editor** (highlighted in red in the following screenshot).

- Select a thumbnail in **Organizer**, then select the **Photo Editor** tab from the **Editor** button popup at the base of the page.

- Click/select a thumbnail in **Organizer**, then drag it directly into the edit window (in **Quick** and **Expert** modes).

- Click the **Open** tab (at the top left-hand side in **Expert** edit mode) and navigate to the image files. Double-click the file name/icon.

- Choose **File | Open recently edited file** in the **Quick**, **Guided**, and **Expert** edit modes.

- Drag an image (icon) from a Windows/Mac **Finder** window into the **Quick** or **Expert** edit window.

- Use the **File | Open** menu command.

- Use the *Ctrl/Cmd + O* keyboard shortcut.
- Click/select a thumbnail in **Organizer**, then press *Ctrl/Cmd + I* (opens in the **Expert** mode).
- Using *Alt/Opt + Ctrl/Cmd + O* (in the **Quick** and **Expert** modes), navigate to the appropriate RAW, JPEG, or TIFF file and click **Open** to bring it into the **Camera RAW** window.

Right-clicking any thumbnail in Organizer pops out a contextual menu, as shown in the following screenshot—choose **Edit with Photoshop Elements Editor** to take that thumbnail into the edit workspace. Watch that you don't accidentally hit the one beneath this—that's for the video editor:

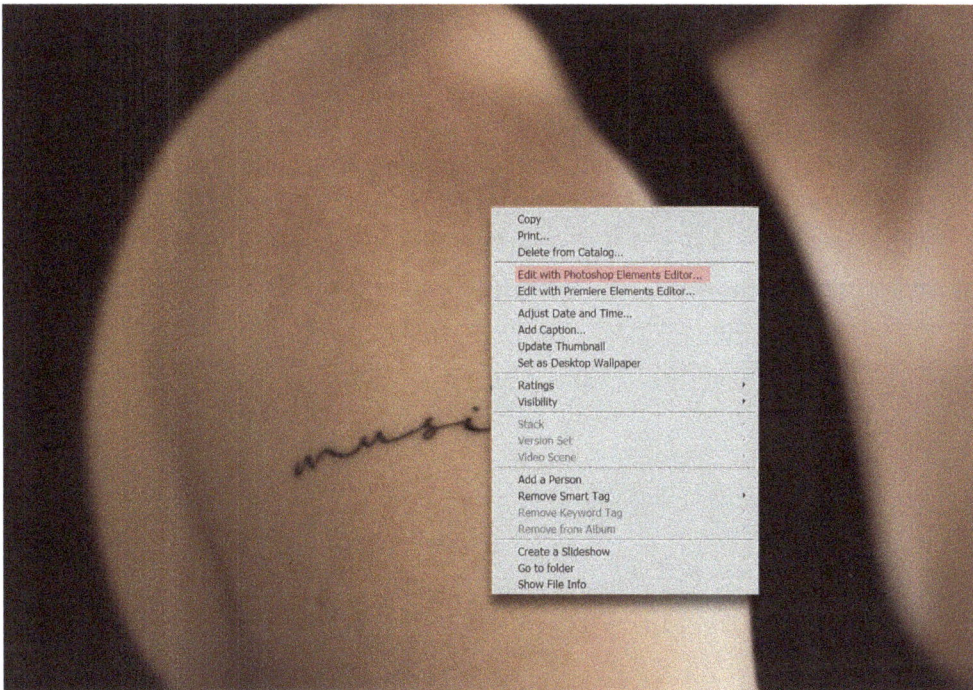

There are many different types of picture file formats. The most adaptable is the RAW file. Let's go ahead and look at how we can extract the best from these RAW files.

Editing RAW files

RAW files produce the best photo editing results because they contain about four times the image data of an 8-bit JPEG file. But this extra size can be annoying, as it uses up more hard drive space and means that the files can't really be emailed and, initially, they even look rather drab compared to a JPEG file. That said, some **light editing** in Elements' native Camera RAW utility will usually produce an image that looks a lot better than most JPEGs.

RAW files – a brief overview

One feature that might confuse beginners is that RAW files have their own special editing software utility separate to the **Quick/Guided/Expert** edit modes. This is called **Camera RAW**. It's a bit like having a specialist application within the parent application, Photoshop Elements. So, if you double-click any RAW file, you'll see it opening in the **Camera RAW** window within Elements, rather than opening normally inside the **Quick**, **Guided**, or **Expert** workspaces.

Double-clicking any JPEG, TIFF, PNG, or PSD file will open that type of file in **Quick** or **Expert** mode. If you want one of these file types to open in the Camera RAW window, it is possible, but you have to specifically choose **File | Open in Camera RAW** first, then go looking for the actual file. Double-click and it will open as if it were a real RAW file.

The following screenshot shows the Camera RAW utility opened inside Elements' edit workspace. Double-click any RAW file and this is what you will see—in fact, for some photographers, this is the only software that they need to use to make their images look good. Click the **Open Image** button (on the bottom right-hand side) to close the **Camera RAW** window and bring the file into the main **Quick** or **Expert** workspace where it can be further edited, or it can be saved in a more usable file format than RAW:

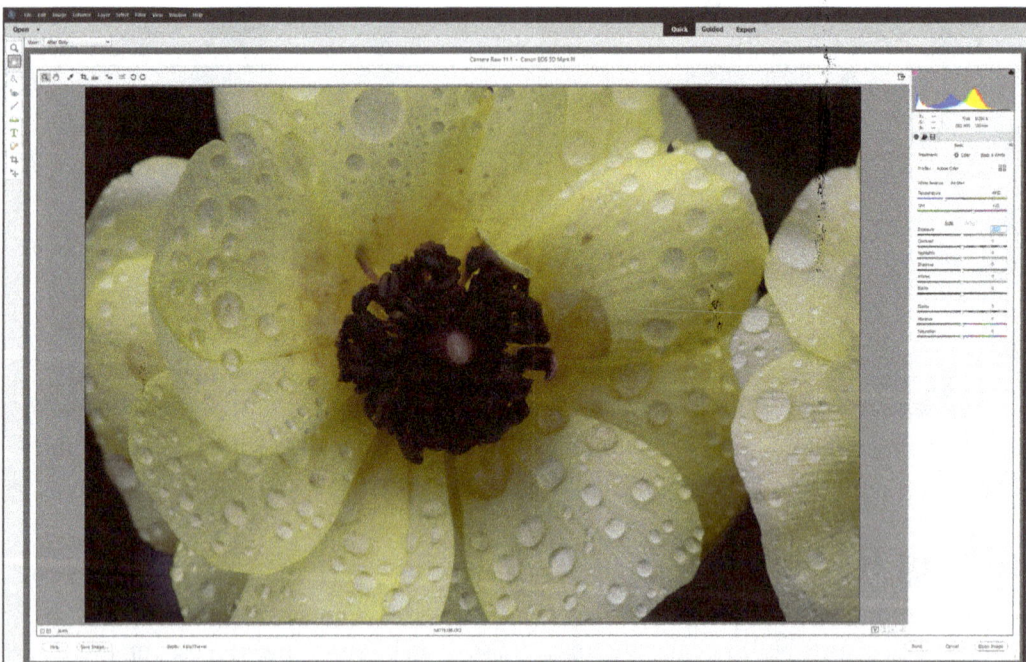

In Camera RAW, photographers can easily apply **White Balance** changes (color) and make adjustments to the **Exposure** (brightness) and the **Contrast**. Then, moving down the Camera RAW menu, as shown in the screenshot, you can single out tonal adjustments to **Highlights**, **Shadows**, **Blacks**, and **Whites** to produce a well-balanced, bright-looking result. Here's the same RAW file now processed using some of the tools on the right-hand side of the screen:

But it doesn't stop there. Camera RAW also offers image editors the ability to add a little **Clarity** (an increase of the mid-tone contrast levels), which can produce a significant visual boost in any file; **Vibrance**, which delivers a boost to weaker-looking colors in the file; and, of course, **Saturation**, a slider that boosts all the colors in the file across its entire spectrum. Set this to a negative value and the color will be leached out of the file until it eventually turns black and white.

Once you're happy with those processes, you can move on to the **Detail** tab in the **Camera RAW** edit workflow. This deals with **sharpening** and **noise reduction**. The reason these two features are at the end of the processing list is simple; there's absolutely no point in sharpening a picture if it's too dark or garishly colored because you won't be able to see the sharpening action effectively. Get the tones and color right first, then apply sharpening.

A second, equally important thing to consider, is the end result. **Sharpening for print** is more aggressive than if it's just being displayed on **social media**—unfortunately, there's really no *one setting that fits all* when it comes to sharpening photographs.

Here's the same picture in the **Detail** tab—used primarily for **sharpening** and **noise reduction**:

This should be the last step in the editing process and is essentially only undertaken when you know how the image is to be used. For example, different amounts of sharpening are applied to images that are to be printed or uploaded to social media. We generally add about 25% more sharpening to files that are to be printed because the print process of ink on paper produces a slightly softer-looking result.

And perversely, once the sharpening effect is added to the image, you might see more digital noise, which can be very annoying visually, so Elements incorporates not one, but two noise reduction filters, **Luminance Noise** reduction and **Color Noise** reduction, in the **Camera RAW** edit workflow.

> **Tip**
> Don't forget to keep your copy of Elements updated so that the RAW processor can read and edit RAW files from the latest camera models released. If you are not sure whether you have the latest version of Camera RAW, navigate to **Help | Updates** to check.

The following two sections deal with Camera RAW's editing features from the **Basic** and **Detail** tabs in much greater detail.

The Basic tab – RAW processing tools

This section includes a more detailed description of what the many Camera RAW tools offer the photographer.

To achieve significant changes and improvements to your images, concentrate on the following:

- **White Balance**: Using this, you can easily reset your shot's white balance setting to whatever you need (that is, reset from **Shady** to **Daylight**, **Tungsten**, **Flash**, or even back to **Auto**). It also allows you to refine colors using the blue/yellow or magenta/green sliders.

- **Exposure**: This is also called brightness. Use this to brighten/darken the initial exposure.

- **Contrast**: This is quite different from exposure. Contrast darkens the darker parts of the file while lightening the lighter parts of the image, resulting in fewer mid-tones. Use it to add a visual *punch* to your images. Too much contrast loses valuable details in the shadows and highlights—keep an eye on the RGB values in those marginal tonal areas.

- **Highlights/Shadows/Whites/Blacks**: Separate and adjust those tonal zones using these four sliders. They allow you to increase/decrease contrast and boost the appearance of sharpness without the need to create time-consuming masks or selections. These tools can make a significant improvement to almost any file. Double-clicking a .jpg file opens it in the regular edit workspace—to get it to open the Camera RAW utility, choose **File | Open in Camera RAW** first, then navigate to the .jpg file and either double-click or select it first and then click **Open** to bring it into the **Camera RAW** window.

- **Clarity**: This slider increases the mid-tone contrast and produces a **dramatic result** with little effort. **Warning**: too much *clarity* is not a good look; just enough can add a much-needed boost to the tones in almost any image, but too much and you'll lose valuable shadow and highlight details.

- **Vibrance**: This tool increases the richness in colors that are not so colorful, while, amazingly, doing little to enhance already bright colors in the rest of the file. It's a great color-boosting tool, especially for portraits (as in, skin tones) and landscapes.

- **Saturation**: This tool boosts the values of all the colors in the file, regardless of their current intensity, often producing what I call *candy-colored*, over-cooked results. A minus value reverts the color image to black and white. Use this tool with some caution.

Along with these, you also need to concentrate on all the other features in the **Detail** tab (sharpening and noise reduction). Everything else you see in the Camera RAW window is, essentially, of secondary importance and needs to be mastered only if you feel you need to push your understanding further. Most photographers are very happy using a combination of the aforementioned tools and nothing more.

The **Histogram** is often overlooked. This small window displays the distribution of tones in any image, with shadows and blacks on the left-hand side, and whites and highlights on the right-hand side, making it easy to see, at a glance, if the image is over- or underexposed.

I think it's rather confusing to see the tonal distribution displayed as RGB components, as well as all three together as a white graph. Use this readout to check the camera **shooting settings** (ISO, aperture, shutter speed, and the focal length of the lens).

An understated but really useful feature of the **Histogram** is its RGB values readout, here reading R: 92, G: 112, B: 51. Move the cursor over any part of the image to see how dark or light it really is as an RGB value. Zero means it's so black that you can't see any detail, while 255 means that it's so white (overexposed) that you can't see any detail there either. This measurement bypasses the accuracy of the screen display (which might be wrong if it's not properly calibrated—see the *Color Management Options* and *Screen Calibration* sections in *Chapter 2, Setting Up Elements from Scratch*). What it displays is an accurate measurement of what's in the file, and so it can be used to assess the influence of your editing on the file:

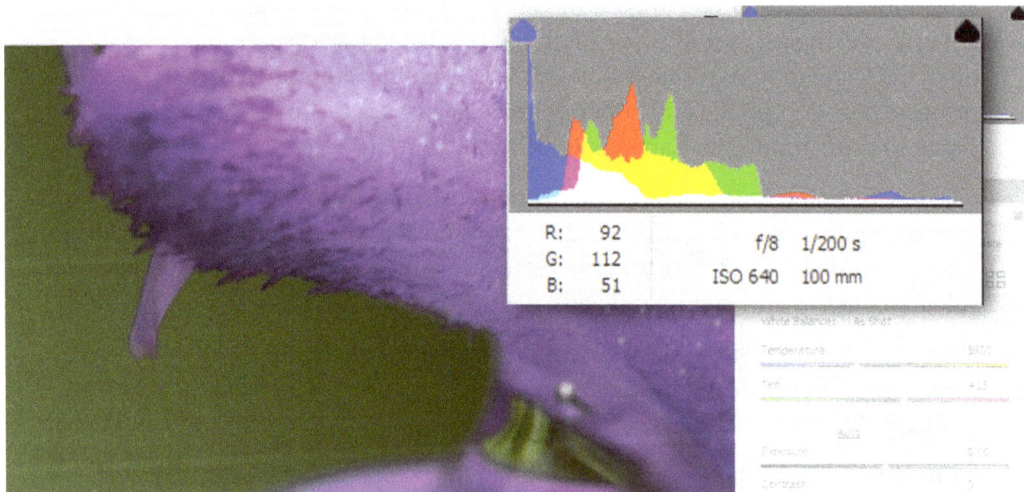

The **Histogram** feature keeps on giving—by clicking either or both of the triangles at the top left and top right of the Histogram window (the enlarged inset in this screenshot), you can switch on the **Shadow** and **Highlight** warning feature. If the image is over-brightened or over-darkened, you'll see a warning color highlighting the affected tones. In the example of the purple flower image, you can clearly see that the highlights are red, indicating dramatic overexposure. Like the RGB value display, this can be an invaluable quick feedback tool on a monitor that might not be properly **calibrated** (that is, what you see onscreen is not what you get in print):

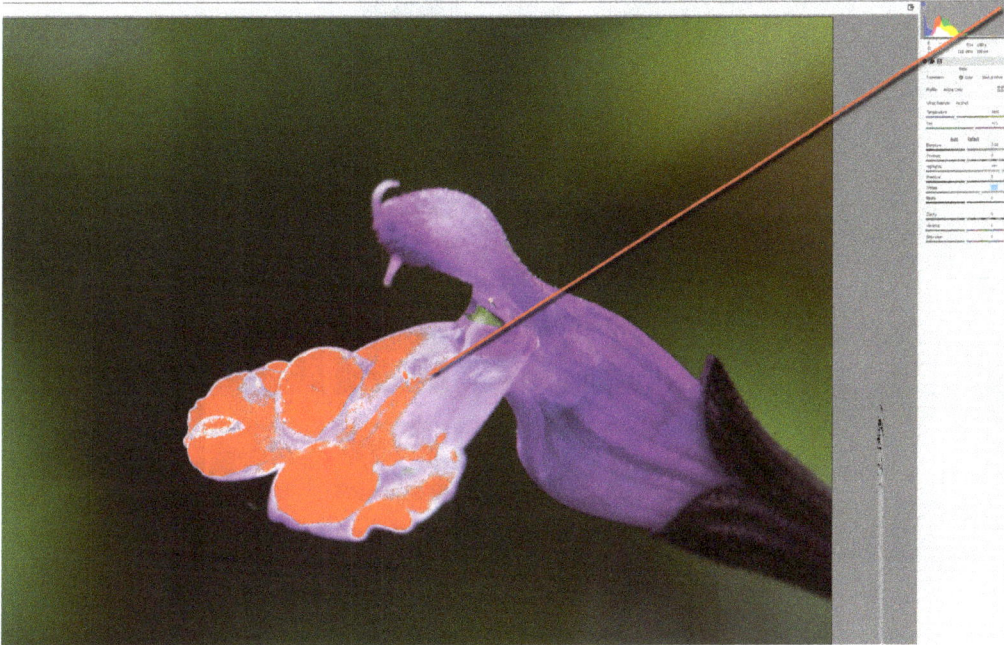

Treatment refers to different historical methods of converting RAW files as they are opened into the program. Most photographers have a **backup camera** that's an older model—even if it is the same brand, it might produce a differently colored file to a newer camera. This feature is what we'd use to match colors. But it's not just a choice between color and black and white. Adobe provides a base color and black and white conversion for all RAW files—but on top of that, you can choose, via the **Profile Browser** (see illustration on p.78), a wide range of legacy profiles (matching older digital cameras), plus a huge range of other color profiles with somewhat vague descriptions, such as artistic, black and white, modern, and vintage. Note that if this all looks too confusing, it might be best to leave it at the default **Adobe Color** setting, and make your creative changes using some of Elements' highly effective effect presets, which I will discuss later in this chapter.

Holding the *Alt/Opt* key down while sliding the **Exposure**, **Highlight**, **Shadow**, **Whites**, or **Blacks** sliders left or right displays the **gamut warning**, which highlights a loss of detail due to overexposure or underexposure. This is an excellent technique for assessing just how far to go with your brightening or darkening adjustments.

Camera RAW – profile browser

This is the expanded view of the **Profile Browser**, a comprehensive color management and special effects feature located in the Camera RAW window just beneath the Histogram window:

Click the tiny **Profile Browser** button, to the right-hand side of the **Profile** drop-down menu, to view the entire selection of RAW profiles in Elements. As we mentioned earlier, you might decide that this is too complicated and just go with the Adobe defaults. (Note that these profiles can also be applied to JPEG files.)

The next section deals with what I consider to be the more important part of Camera RAW—it's all about adding sharpness back into the image, plus learning how we can attempt to reduce or even remove the deleterious effects of high ISO digital noise.

The Detail tab – sharpening and noise reduction tools

Years ago, I used to get students very excited in my software classes when the subject of sharpening was raised. Students would pull out images that, in my opinion, were hopelessly blurred, and I had to bear their looks of disappointment when I gave them the bad news that we could sharpen already clear-looking images, but if it was out of focus, out of focus it stayed! That said, a little sharpening can make a slightly shaky-looking shot appear a bit clearer, and it can make an already clear image look really stunning.

Another important part of the sharpening process is sharpening for specific image usage. By this, I mean sharpening for print is different from sharpening for social media. It's even slightly different for different types of paper stock (that is, gloss or matt) because each has a varied absorbency characteristic.

Note that by pressing one of the three small tabs at the bottom right-hand side of the main window, you can view **before** and **after** versions of your labors, as seen in the screenshot here. Once you begin editing, you can move the already-edited display to the left by pressing the second tab. The third tab (outlined in red in the screenshot) allows you to transfer edits from the left to the right so you can carry on adding edits, or transfer the effects already added before carrying on with more changes:

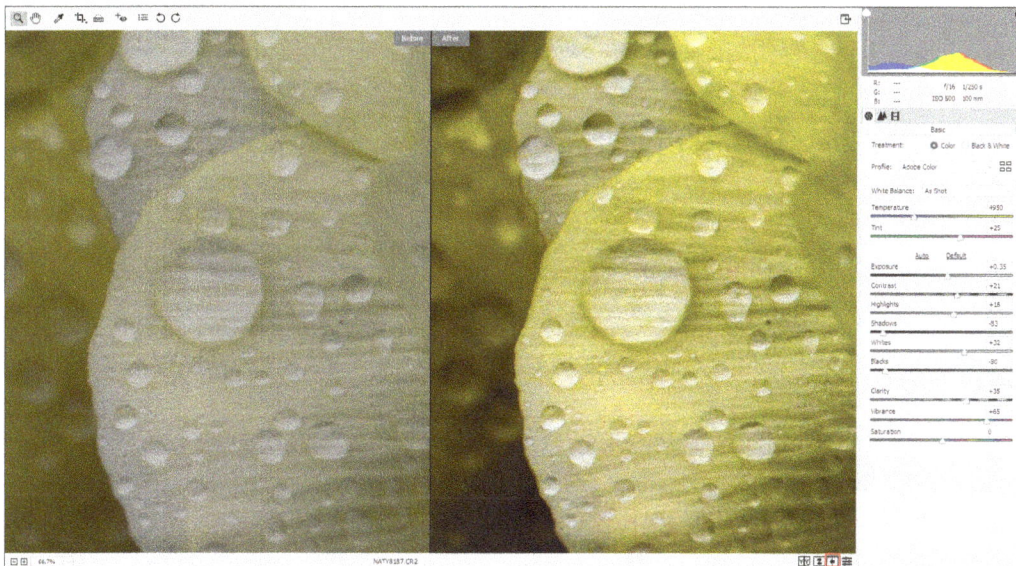

The following screenshot shows a slightly enlarged **Detail** (sharpening) panel with a very clear before/after preview of how the file looks once roughly sharpened:

The first task is to add sharpening—preferably using the **masking feature**, which gives more creative control—then to reduce any digital noise in the file. Unfortunately, sharpening may actually make any noise present in the file look a lot worse.

Let's move on to learn what these specialist sharpening tools actually do.

Sharpening tools

The **Detail** (**Sharpening**, or more correctly, **Unsharp Masking**) tab offers some adjustments that don't make a lot of sense until you understand how a sharpening *mask* actually works:

- **Amount**: Adds the amount of sharpening effect to the file. Set it to 100 and move on to refine the look by tweaking **Radius**, **Detail**, and **Masking**.

- **Radius**: The sharpening process looks for **edges of contrast** onto which it applies its effect. The radius dictates how far, either side of the found edge, it looks for that contrast difference. A setting of 1.0 to 1.5 pixels works well.

- **Detail**: This is used to emphasize the found **edge detail** in the image. Hold down the *Alt/Opt* key when shifting this slider to see the precise edge detail being added to the image.

- **Masking**: This feature should be under **Amount**, not at the bottom of this list. If you hold down the *Alt/Opt* key, then shift the **Masking** slider, you'll see a black and white mask appear onscreen (see the following screenshot). Anything that's black is *protected* or masked, so no sharpening is added. Everything white is not masked and therefore is sharpened accordingly:

By applying full strength to all these sharpening settings, you'll see a lot of grittiness in the skin tones, especially if the ISO setting is high (that is, over 800 ISO). Too much sharpening is never a good idea because it can make the subject appear older than they really area, as you can see in the left-hand portrait example here:

By adding a **mask,** in this case, set to a value of 86, I have limited the effect of the sharpening to the white areas in the mask only. The black areas in the mask are opaque, and therefore "protect" that part of the image from change.

This control is especially important when editing portraits so as to avoid sharpening and therefore highlighting skin imperfections, such as enlarged pores. If you control this masking feature correctly your subjects will love the results.

Noise reduction

Digital noise is the bane of any photographer's life. It's caused, mostly, by using **high ISO settings** while shooting in poor light. Ironically, high ISO in good, even lighting usually has negligible effects. Smaller sensor cameras are particularly prone to this deleterious effect. Sharpening can also bring the negative effect of added graininess to the front, so we have to use the **Noise Reduction** filters to limit its visual effect.

There are two kinds of noise: **Luminance** and **Color** noise. Both are horrible to look at, but perhaps color noise is worse:

- **Luminance** noise is essentially just graininess in the image, especially in the darker, underexposed parts of a scene, while color noise is made up of tiny green and purple dots, again mostly visible in the darker, underexposed parts of the file. The **Luminance** noise reduction slider essentially softens the texture of the picture—too much, and the image might take on a slightly surreal, airbrushed look. The **Luminance Detail** and **Luminance Contrast** sliders are there to help re-introduce sharpness without adding more noise, but in practice, you might agree that they have only a very limited influence on the end result.

- **Color** noise, I think, is significantly uglier than luminance noise simply because we, as photographers, are more aware of regular film grain—this was present in the super-fast films of only a couple of decades ago, but color specks in our digital pictures? This is a new, all-digital phenomenon that just never looks right, however you look at it. Shifting the slider essentially renders color noise into monochrome noise—it's converted into luminance noise—which can then be filtered to make it significantly less noticeable. Color noise reduction also features a **Color Detail** and a **Color Smoothness** slider, there to help render the noise removal process less obvious. Personally, I use the **Luminance** and **Color noise** removal sliders all the time, but find the other four to be almost too subtle in their actions to have a visual benefit for my images.

- Once the file is looking good, you can click **Done**—this automatically saves all the edits and closes the image down. Next time you open that RAW file, it reads the edit instructions that were automatically recorded previously (as an .XML file) and applies those edits to a copy of the RAW file. If you ever lose/erase the .XML file that lives in the same place as the original RAW file, your RAW file automatically defaults to how it was before you started editing. If you choose **Cancel**, it doesn't save any editing details and reverts to its original version.

As you can see in the following screenshot, noise reduction can produce some outstanding results, but if used too liberally, it can also produce a surreal result that might not please those seeking fidelity in their editing:

Noise reduction is the second part of the **Detail** panel and should only be used if you think the image requires it. Remember, any noise reduction filter action will end up softening the image. How much to add depends on your requirements and how the image is to be exported, be it online or in print.

If you choose **Open Image**, it opens the file in the **Expert** mode, ready to be either saved in a more appropriate file format or, possibly, for more editing before being saved. Even though you have edited a RAW file to perfection, because they tend to be large and often camera-specific (and therefore not viewable by all photo-editing applications), it makes sense to save the finished RAW file in another, more usable format, such as .jpg, .tif, .psd, or .png.

> **Tip**
>
> It's interesting to note that over the years, file types (for example, .jpg, .tif, and .psd) have not changed much—apart from one new format, HEIF (high-efficiency image format). This is supposed to contain twice as much image data as in a same-sized .jpg file with no loss of quality and is currently the go-to image recording format for Apple smartphones. This is a derivation of the HEVC (video) format that uses the highly successful H.265 codec. Adobe Photoshop Elements 2020 is fully compatible with HEIF and HEVC files.

The Camera RAW toolbar

Along the top of this handy utility, you'll find a bunch of **additional tools** that are designed to assist in navigation, as well as to make the job of improving the look of your pictures easier. You could elect to use these tools or move on to process the file in Elements' **Quick** or **Expert** modes. Personally, I use the navigation tools all the time (**Hand** and **Zoom**), the **Crop** tool, and occasionally the **Straighten** tool. Everything else is done in the **Expert** window. Try them for yourself and see if these are easier to use than some of the tools described later in this chapter.

The following screenshot shows the **Camera RAW** toolbar:

The **Camera RAW** toolbar is often ignored by photographers because it's small and positioned in the upper-left part of the main window, away from the very obvious bunch of adjustment tools on the right-hand side. Even so, despite its remote location, it does offer a few neat features (going from left to right on the toolbar):

- **Zoom** (*Z*): Allows you to click and enlarge the image in the main window. Holding *Alt/Opt* while you do this sends it into reverse, to reduce the size of the image. (*Ctrl/Cmd* + "+" and "-" also zooms in and out.)

- **Hand** (*H*): Once an image is enlarged larger than the main window, use the Hand tool to drag the picture left, right, up, or down.

- **White Balance** (*I*): Click anywhere in the image to adjust or reset the white balance (that is, the color values). If this doesn't work, try clicking somewhere else in the frame. When this works, it's a good feature, but if it changes the color detrimentally, you might have to reset (*Ctrl/Cmd + Z*) and use the white balance settings on the right-hand side of the RAW panel.

- **Crop** (*C*): This is a great tool. Use this to recompose your initial framing. Click anywhere in the main window, hold the mouse down, and drag to draw a **cropping marquee**. Let go and press *Enter* to execute the crop. When you release the mouse, if it's not in the right position (which it usually isn't), simply grab one of the marquee edges and reposition before pressing *Enter*. Note that because this is a RAW file, Elements never discards the cropped pixels. So, the next time the same image is opened, if you choose the **Crop** tool, you'll immediately see the entire shot, with your previous crop marquee in its last position. Grab it again and fine-tune its position, if needed.

- **Straighten** (*A*): A fantastic tool for making wonky horizons level or for tilting buildings to the vertical. Click on the real horizon, hold the mouse button, and drag a line along the horizon or up the side of a vertical building. When the mouse is released, the image is rotated to bring the horizon in the photo 100% flat, or a building 100% vertical. Most photographers always shoot slightly off-level, myself included, so this is a very handy tool. (That said, the **Crop** tool in the **Quick/Expert** mode is better because it can automatically fill in the white edges that are added to the image when it rotates.)

- **Red Eye** (*E*): Because camera technology has improved so much recently, red-eye is a receding problem. If it happens, drag the cursor around the offending red eye and watch as it turns the red eye into a gray eye.

- **Preferences** (*Ctrl/Cmd + K*): Use preferences to change how this program works with its sidecar files (**Advanced**).

- **Rotate Image** (*L*): Rotates the image 90° counter-clockwise. (*Alt/Opt* + click to flip the image horizontally.)

- **Rotate Image** (*R*): Rotates the image 90° clockwise. (*Alt/Opt* + click to flip the image vertically.)

The best file formats to save an edited RAW file are as follows:

- **JPEG**: These are used the most. They're good for emailing, for use in digital photo books, and for social media.

- **TIFF**: A robust file format designed for more aggressive editing or high-end printing.

- **PSD** (Photoshop): An excellent format if you are creating masks, selections, multilayered edits, adding text, and more.

- **PNG**: Perfect for any project where you need a transparent background.

Photoshop Elements' **Save Image** panel is one of the least used features because it offers few real benefits for most users—unless, of course, you need to rename files or save the RAW data in the *DNG format:

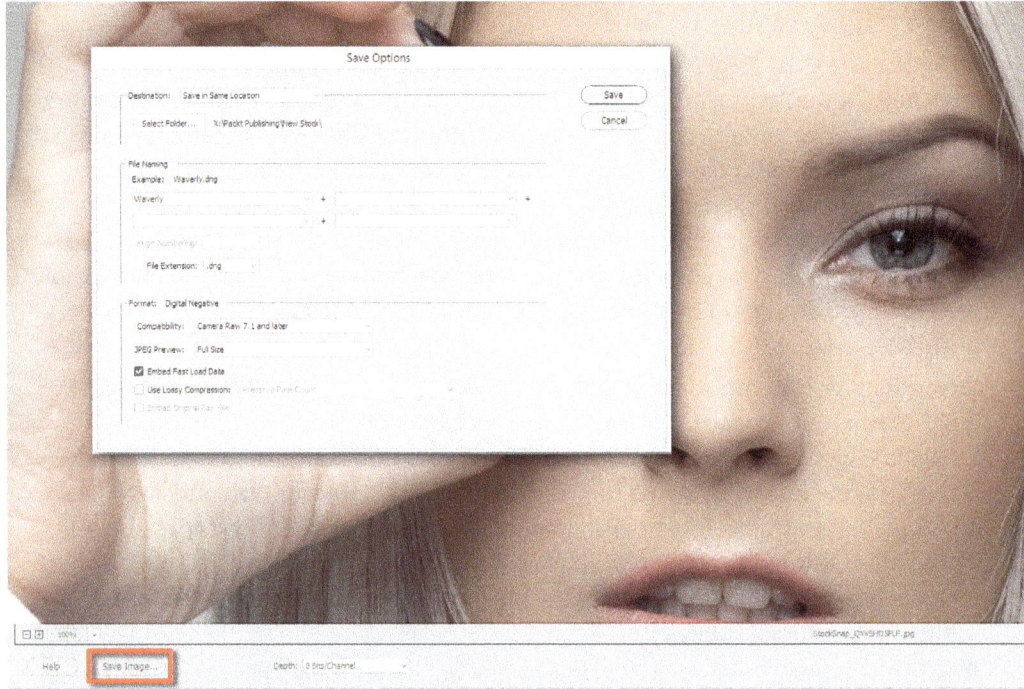

At first sight, this lesser-known feature appears relatively simple—starting with the **Save Image** command (at the bottom of the left-hand side, highlighted in red). This function is for advanced users wanting to save a different version of their work. Elements allows you to do this, converting the RAW file into Adobe's universally readable .DNG (digital negative) format. Tools in this space include the ability to rename the file, limit its file size, and add compression (to make the file smaller).

> **Important note**
>
> Incidentally, if you have just bought a new camera and discover that Photoshop Elements will not recognize the camera's RAW files, don't panic. There's always a lag between the release of a new camera (and therefore a new RAW format) and the updating of third-party software capable of reading such new files. If this happens to you, simply download the free DNG converter software from Adobe's site, and convert your as yet unreadable RAW files to the DNG format, then open them in Elements.

Understanding picture resolution

Resolution, and in particular, **photo resolution**, is a feature that confuses many beginners. This shouldn't really be an issue because the resolution of a camera is a **fixed quantity** and will only change when you choose a different image size in the camera menu, or if you **crop the file** on a computer. But to be pedantic, resolution is not only to do with the number of pixels in the camera, or in a file, although this is important. Resolution is also connected to the quality of the **glass elements** in a lens, the camera's image stabilization technology (indirectly), and the camera technique employed by the photographer. The biggest point of confusion comes with the way the number of **pixels per inch (ppi)** can vary widely from camera to camera. Note that, in the printing world, **dots per inch (dpi)** is the same as ppi, which in turn is the same as **lines per inch (lpi)**.

Because so much work is displayed onscreen these days, it is hard to accurately illustrate the finer points of resolution other than by showing the size restrictions imposed when a file has insufficient pixels to display correctly:

Demonstrating resolution using a medium such as an e-book can be daunting because the web is a low-resolution medium and is unsuitable for exhibiting very high-resolution files. That said, look at the two identical photos in the preceding composite image. The only difference is one contains fewer pixels than the other. And because it contains fewer pixels, it appears, at a resolution of 72 dpi, a lot smaller. The big image is 4,032 x 2,691 pixels, which is 10 megapixels (MP). The small image is 500 x 334 pixels, which is 0.16 MP. If we look at the smaller image sized to 500 pixels wide onscreen, it appears as a smooth **continuous tone** picture with as much detail as the larger one. But as soon as I enlarge that image onscreen to 4,000 pixels wide, because it doesn't have enough pixels to produce continuous tone, it begins to look pixelated and soft, or just out of focus.

As a general rule, if an image appears to be out of focus or fuzzy, it might still be sharp but enlarged beyond the capabilities of the number of pixels it contains. Most software and viewing devices cleverly blur low-resolution images—a process called **dithering**—to try and give the impression of continuous tone, rather than just presenting an image as jagged pixels:

In this example, I have sized the small image to the same size as the larger version—and you can clearly see the pixelation on the right-hand side, plus a general loss of sharpness and quality. If I performed this operation using Elements, the program would automatically **resample the pixels**—this adds in the number of pixels needed to display such an enlargement. In this example, there's no resampling, so what you see is what you get; a sharp image on the left and a soft image on the right!

If we look at files from a 24 MP Nikon, a 24 MP Canon, and a 24 MP Sony camera, we might find that once opened in Photoshop Elements, the program's **Image Size** feature (**Image | Resize | Image Size**) displays the Nikon files set as 72 dpi, the Canon as 180 dpi, and the Sony as 300 dpi. So, what's going on here? The fact is, that number, the dpi value, just describes how close together the pixels are arranged by factory default. The closer together, the finer the detail, but also the smaller the surface area they will cover when displayed or printed.

All three cameras are 24 MP and contain the same number of pixels so their resolution is ultimately the same. The different default dpi measurement is nothing more than a number programmed into the camera's operating system.

When printing images, you need all the pixels you can get. The 30 MB RGB file, on the left in the following image, when set to 200 dpi, prints to A3 (420 mm x 297 mm), while the small sub-megapixel file, on the right, prints to playing card size. If I were to **resample** the small file, I could print it larger, but because the original is small, the resampling quality would suffer—it would look larger, but also softer:

If I print a file from each camera to A3 size (420 mm x 297 mm), making sure that the printer software's **Fit to Page** function is checked, all three files will be rearranged to approximately 300 dpi. The Canon and Nikon files will be reduced in size, while the Sony file, already set to 300 dpi, will not change, so it fits into the A3 format without the need for the **Fit to Page** option to be checked. If I print the same three files in A4 dimensions (fit to page—210 mm x 297 mm), each file will be made smaller by pushing the pixels closer together, producing an approximate file resolution for each of 600 dpi (because A4 is half the physical size of A3). Since most printers produce a smooth, continuous tone at 300 dpi, there's absolutely no benefit to setting the resolution higher than this because the printer cannot do any better. In fact, sending a 600 dpi file to a printer will take longer simply because the file is larger.

If you want to make 100% sure that your files are a **specific resolution** for printing, open the program's **Image Size** feature (**Image | Resize | Image Size**), uncheck the **Resample Image** checkbox, type your desired resolution into the **Resolution** field, and note that the overall dimensions of the file (if it was originally lower than 300 dpi) will shrink. Then, click **OK** and save.

> Tip
>
> There's little to no advantage in printing an image at a resolution higher than 300 dpi because, at that setting, the pixels reproduce the look of *continuous tone* (that is, no pixels are actually visible). Once it is a continuous tone print, adding more pixels does not increase quality—it just has the effect of slowing down the print process (because the file is much larger and takes longer to transfer from computer to printer). When resampling, software such as Elements can also add dithering, a process where pixels are blended into each other to give the effect of smooth tone—inkjet printers are especially good at this. You don't necessarily choose it; it's just part of the process. Although a 300 dpi file produces a smoother, continuous tone, because of this dithering process, even files set to 100 dpi can look very good.

Cropping for better composition

Cropping is an editing feature that allows you to trim off parts of the image that you don't like—essentially, it provides you with the opportunity to **recompose the shot after it has been taken**. One vital thing to remember when cropping is that it **discards pixels** (and therefore lowers the resolution). I love photographing birds, but unfortunately, they always tend to be too far away, even with a 400 mm telephoto lens, so I have to crop the file to make the subject appear larger. If I crop 50% from a photo, it then looks as if I have an 800 mm lens, not my regular 400 mm lens.

Cropping has saved me a lot of money in not having to buy an even more powerful (and thus expensive) lens, but in doing so, I lose half the pixels in the file; therefore, effectively, I can only hope to print it half as large.

The following screenshot shows what the **Crop** tool looks like in Camera RAW—its main advantage over using the **Crop** tool in the **Quick** or **Expert** modes is that it never discards the cropped pixels, allowing you to change your mind multiple times while never losing pixels or compromising on quality. That said, cropping this image to the proportions seen here would take it from being a 30 MB file to one that's a lot less than 20 MB, seriously limiting its potential print size (at 300 dpi), but not affecting its display quality online (at 72 dpi). Besides its easy drag-and-crop operation, if you right-click the screen, you'll see a list of preset crop ratios—alternatively, you can make up your own **custom crop ratio** in the box seen here:

How does the Crop tool work?

This is one of the easiest tools to use. Let's get started:

1. In **Quick** or **Expert** mode, press C on the keyboard to engage the **Crop** tool, or select it from the toolbar (highlighted in red).

2. Click and drag the cursor over the image. This draws a rectangular **Crop Marquee**. When you press the green check mark at the bottom of the marquee, the parts of the image inside the marquee are kept while the outer pixels are discarded. Clicking the red *No Entry* symbol cancels the cropping operation, as does pressing the *Esc* key.

3. If it's not the shape, size, or rotation you want, simply release the mouse and grab one of the edge handles (the little square tags in the center, or corners, of the marquee) and adjust the proportions of the crop edges. Note that if you slide the cursor over the edge of any corner to the outside of the marquee, the cursor changes from a **diagonal shape** to a **curved shape**, meaning that you can now **rotate** the entire crop marquee. Use this to crop and rotate at the same time, for example, to get a horizon level. If you find this fiddly, try the **Straighten** tool first (see the *Straightening horizons* section), then crop it.

This is what the **Crop** tool looks like in the **Expert** edit space—very similar to the same tool in **Camera RAW**, except for the fact that its tool options, along the base of the screen, are a little easier to understand and use:

Elements has a number of excellent additional cropping features to help the compositional process, such as a **Rule of Thirds** (being used in this example) and a **Grid** overlay. These are included to help you recompose your shots as more dynamic-looking compositions. There are also four **preset crop shapes**—click the thumbnails in the **Crop Options** panel to find them. I don't find these to be very useful at all because they rarely put the crop in the right place, so I do it faster by hand.

If you intend to crop your files to a specific print dimension, use the preset drop-down menu in the **Options** panel. It offers classic print sizes such as 4 x 6 inches, 5 x 7 inches, 10 x 8 inches, and so on. This is very handy when you have a lot of images to crop to the same size. But if you are cropping to a size that's different to the presets, type the dimensions into the fields seen in this panel, making sure you add cm, px, or, in (for centimeters/pixels/inches, respectively), after the width and height measurements; then, when you crop, it also resets the resolution at the same time. And if the file happens to be smaller than what you have chosen to crop to (that is, a file from a low-resolution camera or smartphone), Elements adds pixels to the image to bring it up to size using a feature called **Resampling**. It might make the end result appear a bit softer, but it works pretty well.

A feature that most will miss is the small resolution field (just above the **Grid Overlay** option in the **Crop** tool options panel, not the two fields under the preset drop-down menu). You can enter your ultimate resolution here (in dpi) so that when you're free-form cropping, you can maintain the file resolution, irrespective of the crop shape.

The **Crop** tool panel also features the **Cookie Cutter** tool, which I will deal with in *Chapter 6, Advanced Editing Techniques*.

Straightening horizons

Alongside the **Crop** tool, I rate the **Straighten** tool very highly. Why? Very few photographers can shoot a landscape, for example, and get the horizon 100% on the level. Many photographers, myself included, also have serious problems getting verticals, well, 100% vertical. Here's how this tool works:

1. Open an image that needs its horizon corrected to be 100% on the level.

2. Choose the **Straighten** tool (cunningly, its symbol is a builder's spirit level).

3. Click once on the horizon and, while holding down the mouse button, drag the *elastic* line that appears from that first click point across the horizon and let go. You do not have to stretch the line along the entire horizon—a few inches is enough. The program immediately rotates the image to make this line the new horizon. If you get it wrong, **Undo** (*Ctrl/Cmd + Z*) and try again.

4. Using the regular crop tool, trim off any white edges introduced by the rotational shift in the image alignment. It also works well for correcting vertical lines. This is a clever and very well-designed feature:

The **Straighten** tool is straightforward. Drag the line, in this example, across the river's surface, let go, and the image will rotate to give you a level horizon. So far, so good, but as you can see here, because it has been slightly rotated, it has added white pixels around the edges (monitors can only display horizontal rectangles onscreen—it's a digital display thing...). Your options are to then go back with the **Crop** tool to trim off the added pixels, or, before you use the **Straighten** tool, ensure **Autofill Edges** is checked in the **Option** panel. This is an effective software widget. Drag the "string" across the image and watch as it not only rotates/levels correctly but also fills in those white edges using an auto clone process. When this works well, it's brilliant. In the image seen here, **Autofill Edges** was not checked, so you can see the rotation/straighten effect as a white border around the photo. Sometimes, the image structure is too complex for the algorithm to work. If this is the case, undo it, level the horizon again, and crop manually.

Resampling

As we mentioned in the previous section, **resampling** is the process of adding or subtracting pixels to any file to make it larger or smaller.

Now, you might think, if this is the case, then your dreams of producing very high-resolution files have just been answered. But there's a catch. Resampling is a mathematical algorithm that can be used to up- or down-sample files quite effectively, providing that the original is of the highest quality. This means that if you download a 1 MB file off the internet, then resample it to print it as a poster, it's not going to look very good. But if you start with a lot of image data—let's say, a 24 MP Canon file—this can be resampled nicely to 30, 40, or 50 MP with almost no loss of quality. It could go as high as 200 MB before it really looks soft. Further sharpening after the resampling process will help to alleviate the softening that adding extra pixels to a file might create. Also, bear in mind that we might hold an A4 print at arm's length to appreciate its quality, but for a poster, you'd probably stand 6 feet away to get the best view, and therefore would not be so aware of any softening due to resampling. Viewing distance is very important when calculating these features.

How can we enlarge (or reduce) the size of a file? Follow these steps:

1. Open the file in Elements' **Expert** mode.

2. Open the **Image Size** feature (**Image | Resize | Image Size**).

3. Check the **Resample Image** box, at the bottom of this panel.

4. Select the resampling method from the drop-down menu at the base of the panel (see the following explanation to learn what each resampling method should be used for).

5. Click **OK** and watch as Elements resizes the file.

6.   Save the file:

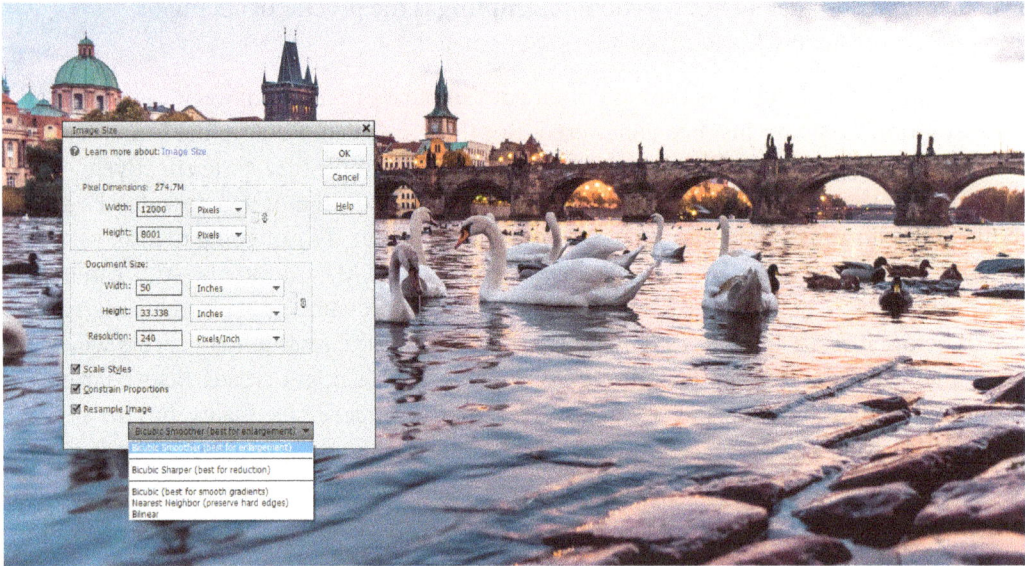

There are several types of resampling offered:

- **Bicubic Smoother**: Best for enlarging a file

- **Bicubic Sharper**: Best for reducing the size of a file

- **Bicubic**: Good for producing smoother tonal gradients

- **Nearest Neighbor**: Perfect for upsizing hard-edged graphic images, such as the screen captures used in this book

- **Bilinear**: Far better than **Nearest Neighbor,** but still not quite as good as bicubic resampling

> **Tip**
> While Elements' default resampling method (Bicubic) generally works well when increasing or decreasing pixel-based images, choosing the specific Bicubic Smoother or Bicubic Sharper should produce a better-looking result. Care must be taken, however, to reset your Resample method in the Image Size panel if you move on to resample hard-edged graphics. Resampling with the wrong choice of (resample) method can lead to very poor quality—usually in terms of overall sharpness. As this feature does revert to the default setting, it pays to check before you resample the image.

I'm taking a bit of visual liberty with the following illustration of a large-format inkjet printer. However, if you start resampling with a very high-resolution file (let's say, something shot with a Nikon D850, producing a 45 MB file), it's entirely possible to resample the file to be several times larger, up to 1 GB and higher, to produce a file capable of printing massive prints:

Here are some tips for best results:

- Make sure the image is well exposed (that is, not too dark or light) and clear (that is, not blurred).

- Leave the sharpening process until after you have resampled the file.

- Upsampling works best if you keep the enlargement to between 10 and 50%. Any more than that and you'll notice it becoming softer.

- Once resampled, make adjustments to the brightness, contrast, and sharpness, if needed.

Instant photo-fixing in Organizer

The **Instant Fix** feature found in Elements' Organizer is a very good way to produce quick and highly visual effects without the need to transfer the file from **Organizer** to the **Quick**, **Guided**, or **Expert** modes.

Here's how:

1. Find an image in **Organizer** that you'd like to edit.

2. Select it (click once).

3. Click the **Instant Fix** button, at the bottom of the page.

4. Use one or more of the tool or process icons that appear on the right-hand side of the screen.

In reality, you will find that not all of them are *instant*. The **Crop** tool, for example, requires you to choose a crop ratio first, then position it over the appropriate part of the image, then resize it, if needed, before clicking the green check mark to execute the process. But I'm being pedantic.

Other effects, such as the impressive **Smart Fix** tool, just require a single click to *fix* the shot. You might not like the **Smart Fix** result, so try the **Effects** tab first—this has 30 preset effects *recipes* to choose from. It functions just like an iPhone app or an Instagram filter in that you choose a style—let's say, *Coral*—and click it. The color, contrast, and vignetting in this particular recipe is applied in one go to give you that instant visual gratification. It's simple, effective, and looks great.

Because this process is so fast and varied, it's a great place to experiment with creating your own specific style—all without the need to open the image in the more complex **Quick/Guided/Expert** modes.

Instant Fix also has a **Red Eye** fix, plus **Lightness**, **Color**, and **Clarity** adjustment menus to choose from. Once you are happy with the result, click the **Save** button at the base of the page to apply your awesome edit to the file. I tend to save my files with a different name (that is, `cherryblossomFinal.jpg`) so that, months later, when I am looking for that very file, I can recognize it easily from its name.

Saving files and Version Sets

It's important to note that, when saving JPEG, *TIFF, PSD, or PNG files, if you choose the **Save** option (**File | Save**), some software applications simply write the new file on top of the old one, effectively deleting the original and saving the (hopefully) improved new version on top. This isn't the case with Elements, as it always asks if it's **OK** to overwrite the previous version of this file.

But if you are in a hurry, or just go **OK**, click, **OK**, click, without really looking, you might accidentally overwrite the original. If you choose either the **Save** or the **Save As** command (**File | Save As**, or *Shift + Ctrl/Cmd + S*), the window that opens offers a swathe of different file-saving options:

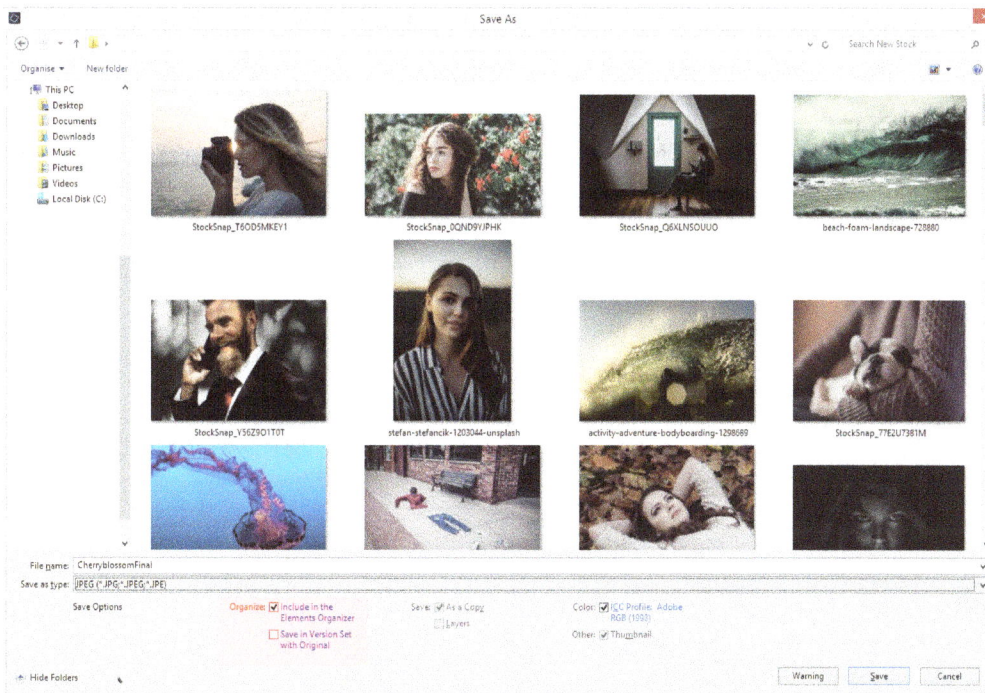

Note that when you choose **File | Save As** (*Shift+ Ctrl/Cmd + S*), not only can you choose a different file type (that is, `.jpg`, `.tif`, `.psd`, or `.png`) but, by checking **Include in the Elements Organizer** (highlighted in red), the new file automatically appears in the Organizer—no need to import it.

Other things to note in this dialog window are the **Save in Version Set with Original** and **Save as a Copy** checkboxes. What these do is pack the new version of your cherry blossom shot with the original for safe-keeping. In the Organizer, you only see the original image, but if you right-click it, you can choose to view the different versions of the same file, saved as a **Version Set**, as single files:

A **Version Set**, therefore, is a bit like a **layered Photoshop file** that contains several versions of the same image packed into the one file.

The following screenshot shows the saving options:

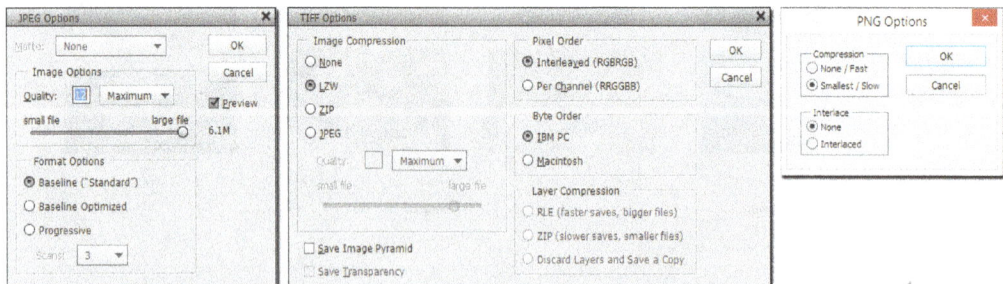

Different file formats offer different saving options, some of which can have a radical impact on the quality of the resulting saved file. Save a JPEG and you'll see the **JPEG Options** panel (on the left in the preceding screenshot). JPEGs compress their data—too much compression damages the file, making it look softer, blocky, and less colorful. Always choose the largest number (12) where possible, as this is the least compression. The figure under the **Preview** checkbox indicates how much it has been compressed—it updates each time you change the settings. I generally recommend a compression amount of between 10 and 12 (that is, Maximum), but if you really need to make the file smaller for email or storage reasons, you can go as low as 7. Anything smaller than this and you'll see serious compression damage in the saved file. (See also *Chapter 2, What's the Difference between File Formats?*).

JPEG format options

Baseline is the most often used compression option. **Baseline Optimized** produces a slightly smaller saved file using a different compression algorithm. **Progressive** is used specifically on larger web images. Rather than waiting a long time for the image to load, **Progressive** slowly displays the image, building it up with a number of scans (set through the menu). This was designed a long time ago when the fastest modems available were 28.8 kb/s.

TIFF format options

Similar to the **Progressive** option in the JPEG panel, many of the options in this panel are redundant because the internet is lightning-fast and storage drives are incredibly affordable. I generally use the **None** option for compression, but if you really need to save on space, use the **LZW** compression option. This is lossless compression that reduces the file size by about 25%, with no loss of quality. ZIP and JPEG compression is no longer supported in some applications. **Pixel Order** needs to be **Interleaved** as **Per Channel** is not supported in Organizer.

Byte Order is also not relevant anymore, as Macs and PCs can work seamlessly with each other's files.

PNG format options

This is one of my all-time favorite formats. I create a lot of irregular-shaped files that need to blend into different backgrounds so PNG's transparency-saving capability feature allows me to create irregular orientations (you can see an example of this in *Chapter 1, Photoshop Elements Features Overview*):

- **Compression**: **PNG** files are lossless; therefore, **None** is a fast way to save a file, but it is larger than a JPEG. You can add compression without losing quality, but it takes longer to create.

- **Interlaced**: Keep it set to **None**. Because the internet is so fast, **Interlaced**, just like **Progressive** for JPEGs, is redundant.

Using autocorrection tools

If you don't like the **Instant Fix** effects, Elements has a stack of other automated editing tools found inside the **Quick** and **Expert** modes. Both sets of effects are designed to make your picture-editing day go a bit faster and with less stress. Some, I think, are nothing short of beautiful, while others might not work at all. There are hundreds of visual possibilities achievable with these features and if some don't work, there will be many others that do. Remember, these are created using specific photos as test examples. If you are living in a different hemisphere from the one in which the filters were created, it's possible that they might not be as effective simply because the light in your country has a totally different look to it. Effects designed in Europe, for example, might not be so effective in Australia. Or they might be better!

Here's a screenshot of the correction tools in the **Quick** edit mode, set to a *warmer* color temperature on the right:

Elements' tone correction tools fall between the **On** and **Off** characteristics of the Organizer's **Instant Fix** function and the myriad variants to be found in the **Expert** edit mode. Here's how to use the autocorrection tools using the **Quick** edit mode:

1. From **Organizer**, select an image and press *Ctrl/Cmd + I* to open that file in the **Editor** window. It opens in whatever edit space you were last using. If this is **Expert**, click **Quick** at the top of the window, and it will switch into the easier-to-use **Quick** edit space.

2. At the bottom-right, you'll see the **Adjustment, Effects, Textures**, and **Frames** tabs. Click the **Adjustments** tab to open that panel and note the **Smart Fix, Exposure, Lighting, Color, Balance**, and **Sharpen** tools that slide out of the right-hand panel. To use these effectively, start at the top (**Smart Fix**) and click **Auto**. If this doesn't *fix* the shot the way you'd like it to, simply slide the cursor over the tiny thumbnails to select another strength of the **Smart Fix** effect.

3. Then, move on to the **Exposure** setting and repeat the same process if needed, or simply jump ahead to fix one of the other features on offer.

I usually find that these **Auto** effects work 25% of the time. When it clearly makes little or no impact, move on and try something else.

I always joke that some of these effects in Elements were designed on a Friday night, just before everyone went home for the weekend. This is my way of saying I'm not happy with the design or the look of the end result. Auto Smart Tone is one such design—but I also get why it's presented like this. If you are the sort of photographer that eats, sleeps, and breathes cameras and computers, nothing will be too hard to grasp in terms of techniques. But there are a lot of beginner photographers and plenty of folk who are still intimidated by computers, so this is a good way to see, immediately, how your mouse actions change the image. The trick to learning this kind of software is to try a bit of everything. Never be scared to experiment!

Autocorrection in the **Expert** edit space is quite different. Some of the features offer no adjustment, while others, such as **Auto Smart Tone**, are not really *automatic* at all because it's fully adjustable.

Here's how to use the autocorrection tools using the Expert edit mode:

1. Open an image from **Organizer** in the **Expert** window.

2. Starting at the top, click the **Enhance** menu and try the **Auto Smart Fix** or **Auto Smart Tone** features. (Note that **Auto Smart Fix** might not do much, but if its effect is too strong, use the **Adjust Smart Fix** feature, which, weirdly, is located 11 items further down the menu. In my mind, this should be part of the top-level **Smart Fix**.) **Smart Tone** has its own integral adjustment window.

3. **Auto Levels** will adjust both contrast and color.

4. **Auto Contrast** will adjust only the black and white tones in the frame (not the color):

5. **Auto Haze Removal**, as the name suggests, is ideal for hazy days, dust, fog, mist, and sea spray. It adds clarity while sometimes making the image darker with more contrast. Often, this action is too harsh—be careful not to overdo it!

6. **Auto Shake Reduction** sounds too good to be true, but it can reduce the appearance of blurriness quite effectively. Note that the **Shake Reduction** feature, second from the bottom in this menu, gives you greater control over how this tool works and might prove to be the most effective way to go with not very sharp pictures.

7. **Auto Sharpen**, amazingly often, hits the spot nicely, adding just a bit more *snappiness* to the edges of your subject and making it appear crisper than it was before. Like all the **Auto** tools, though, **Auto Sharpen** can often leave you wishing for a stronger version—which, of course, you will find with the **Adjust Sharpness** and **Unsharp Mask** tools seen further down the menu.

See how the **Haze Removal**, **Shake Reduction,** and other sharpening tools work in greater detail in *Chapter 8, Advanced Drawing and Painting Techniques.*

Mastering contrast, color, sharpness, and clarity

Contrast, or more specifically, the lack of contrast, is often the most noticeable fault in many pictures. This is partly because cameras are designed to capture images in a slightly lower contrast than we perhaps remember—and in doing so, they capture a slightly wider range of tones than if they were recording higher contrast from the get-go.

I equate this effect with the difference between **professional film** and film bought over the counter in a supermarket. The supermarket products always looked superficially really good because they were super-colorful and quite contrasty. But they were no good for commercial photographers because they would not be able to record valuable detail in the sensitive highlights—such as a white wedding dress.

Professional film is typically low-contrast and captures a wider range of tones for which the contrast could be increased if and when needed. JPEGs, and specifically RAW files, are similar, which is often why, when you look at your shots from a day's photography, many features, including the brightness and the color, appear underwhelming in your RAW files while JPEGs of the same scene might look better.

It's our job as photo editors to increase the color, brightness, and contrast until we reach a point where we think the image has been done justice. And that can be a tricky path, simply because it's so easy to lose valuable detail by over-brightening or increasing the contrast too much.

Adjusting the contrast using Levels

The best tool to begin editing any image (a JPEG, TIFF, PNG, or PSD file) has to be **Levels** (*Ctrl*/*Cmd* + *L*). This is used to adjust the tonal distribution in any image. You'll recognize this when you see the **Histogram**—this is the same display that you'd see on the back of your camera's LCD screen when replaying a file (to make the histogram appear, press the **Display** or **Info** button on the back of the camera). Some cameras do not display the shooting information by default—it has to be turned on via the **Camera** menu:

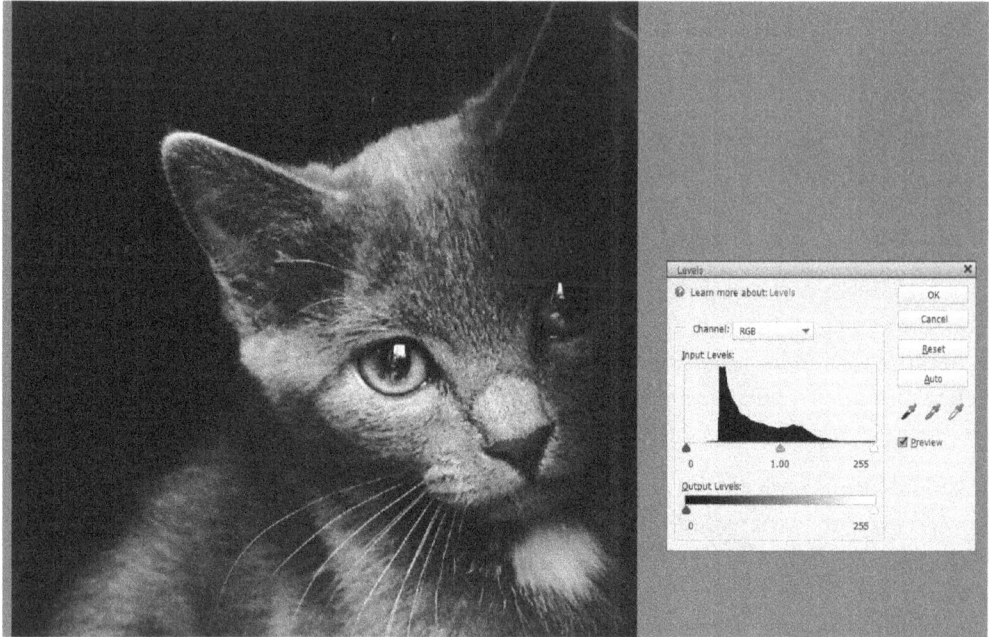

Digital files typically display in low contrast (that is, the black tones usually look a bit washed out). Although this is a very cute-looking kitten, its tones are a little washed out or low-contrast. In the **Input Levels** panel, if you see a flat area to the left or right of the tone *mountain* shape, it most likely needs *fixing*:

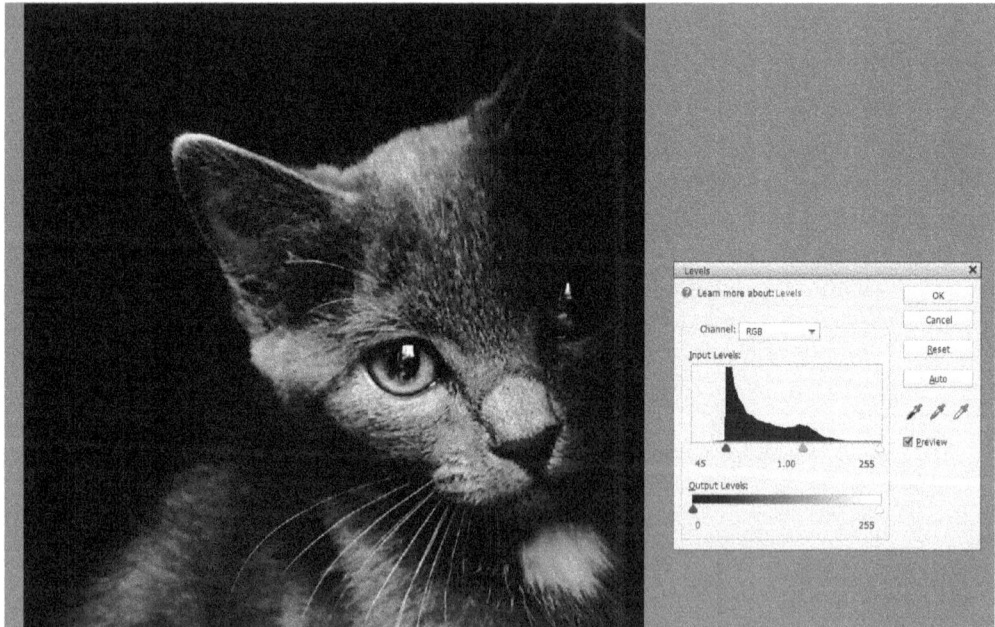

As soon as the shadow slider is shifted to the right (in the **Input Levels** scale, in the previous screenshot), the darker parts of the image go even darker and might lose detail, even though it actually appears clearer and sharper. To maintain the tonal range in the file, restrict yourself to stopping at the edge of the tonal mountain, as you can see here:

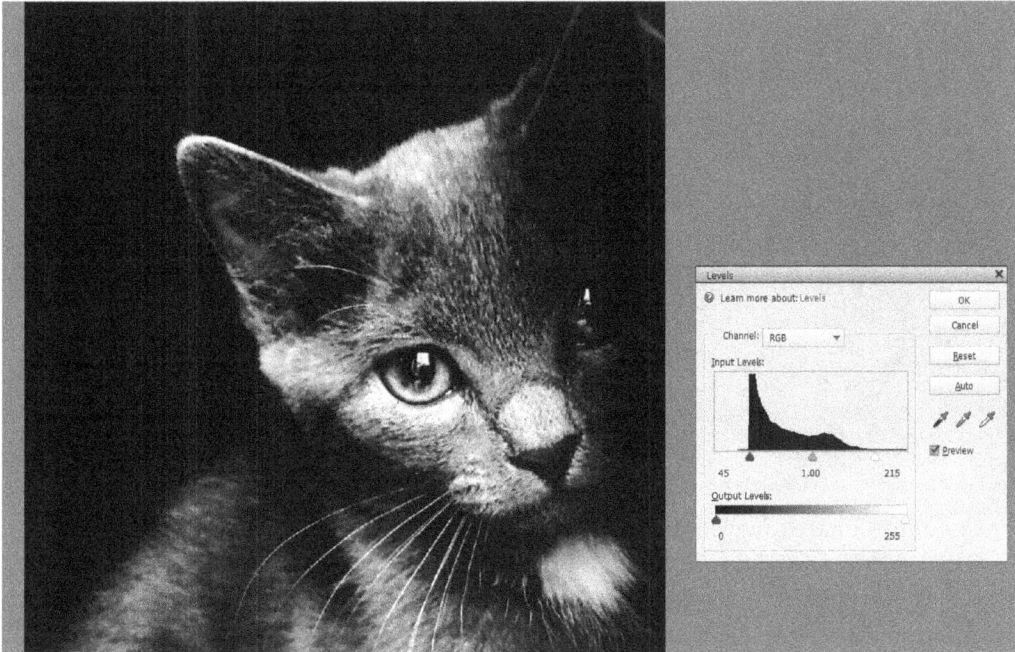

In this third step, I have shifted both the shadow and the highlight sliders to the right and to the left, respectively, stopping just at the edges of that central mountain shape. Both the shadows are darker and the highlights are brighter. In general, this is all you really need to do to a file to make it pop off the page. Interestingly, the shape of the tone mountain doesn't make any difference to the result—other than indicating whether it's a darker shot (with the mountain slumped to the left-hand side) or a lighter shot (with the mountain slumped to the right-hand side):

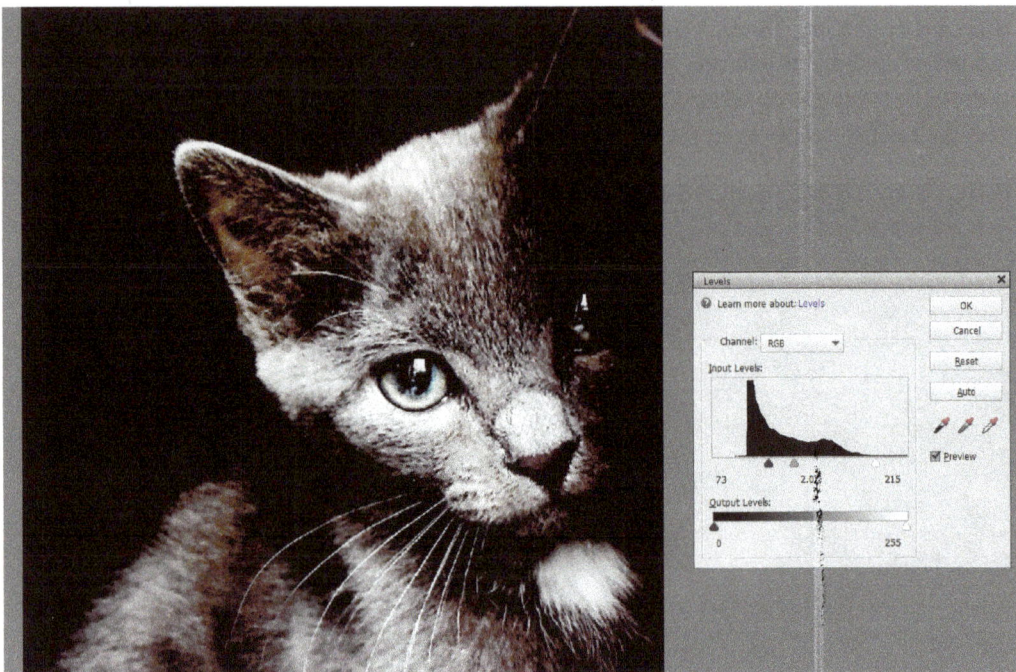

In this example, I have dragged those sliders too far toward the center of the **Input Levels** scale. This produces a significant contrast boost (which has also affected the color values). The black is not jet black and prevents you from seeing any detail at all; the whites are also a bit too bright. Note that the **Output Levels** scale is used to lower the brightness of the shadows and highlights, which in turn drops the contrast.

In general, an **Auto Levels** adjustment works quite well—but it adjusts both contrast and color in the one action, which might not be what you want. I advise against using **Auto Levels** because what do you do when this doesn't work the way you want it to? You have to come up with a **Plan B**—and this requires more time and effort.

It's far better to do the following:

1. Open an image.
2. Open the **Levels** panel (*Ctrl/Cmd + L* or **Enhance | Adjust Lighting | Levels**).
3. Move one or a combination of the three small triangular stops to make the image lighter/darker (using the center stop) or more contrasty, using one or both of the end stops, as seen in the cat images.

4. If there's a flat area where the tone 'mountain' doesn't extend to the left, and right hand sides of the scale, drag one or both of the triangular stops across the flat 'beach' to where the tones start. Remember, the shadows are on the RHS while the highlights are on the LHS.

5. If the contrast looks better, but the image remains too dark, move the middle stop, controlling the brightness, left or right to darken/lighten the tones.

6. Sliding the shadow or highlight stops past where the tone mountain starts can lead to a loss of highlight and shadow details, so be careful not to shift them too far.

Let's move on and see how Levels can be used to fine tune the image's color:

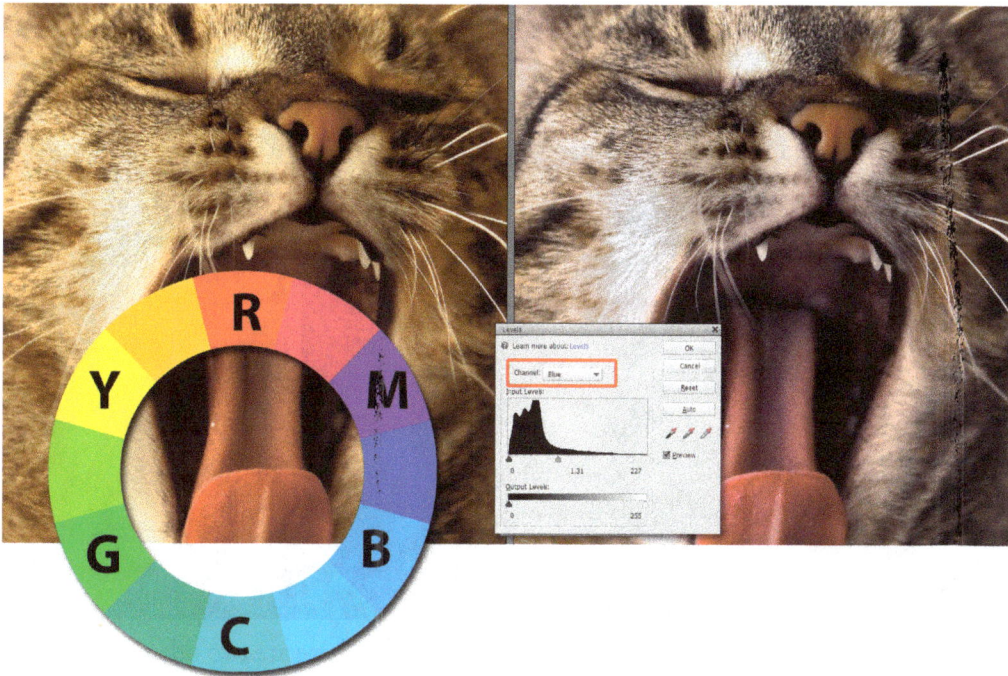

As you can see in the preceding screenshot, the **Channel** drop-down menu now reads **Blue**. The blue histogram is a different shape to the three-color RGB histogram. Move the slider to the left to add blue and to the right to add the opposite color: yellow. The color wheel displays RGB and their opposite colors: cyan, magenta, and yellow.

General adjustments using **Levels** are good for perfecting the contrast range in any file. These are global adjustments that are applied to all three channels (red, green, and blue) at the same time. If you make adjustments to just one color channel, you can shift the image color quite considerably. I'd use these color channels to add a **warm tint** to any shot, to correct a **color cast** (that is, from a white balance mistake), or just to add a **color accent** to the image.

Levels has a second scale, **Output Levels,** which is used for reducing the **black density** and the **highlight brightness**, as you can see in the following dramatic black and white image. The original is on the left, while the right-hand version shows distinctly lowered brightness in the highlights, essentially dulling the image significantly:

You'll note that under the **Enhance | Adjust Lighting** menu, there are two other tools worth mentioning: **Brightness/Contrast** and **Shadows/Highlights**.

The former does exactly what **Levels** does, but without the benefit of being able to see that tone mountain, which for most photographers is enough encouragement not to use this feature. It's also regarded as being a destructive form of editing—too much use might damage the pixels irreparably, so I'd not recommend using it.

The **Shadows/Highlights** tool can be very useful for rescuing tones that might appear lost in the highlights and the shadow areas. Remember that if you are doing this on a JPEG file, it has already been processed in-camera, so if there appears to be no tone in the lighter parts of an image, you might not be able to recover them at all, but it's certainly worth a try. You'll have more luck using the shadow-recovering part of this slider, revealing details that might be hidden in an over-darkened part of the file. Although the photographer deliberately hid some of the darker details in this striking portrait, it's interesting to see how the image can change radically just by lightening the shadows only (on the right-hand side):

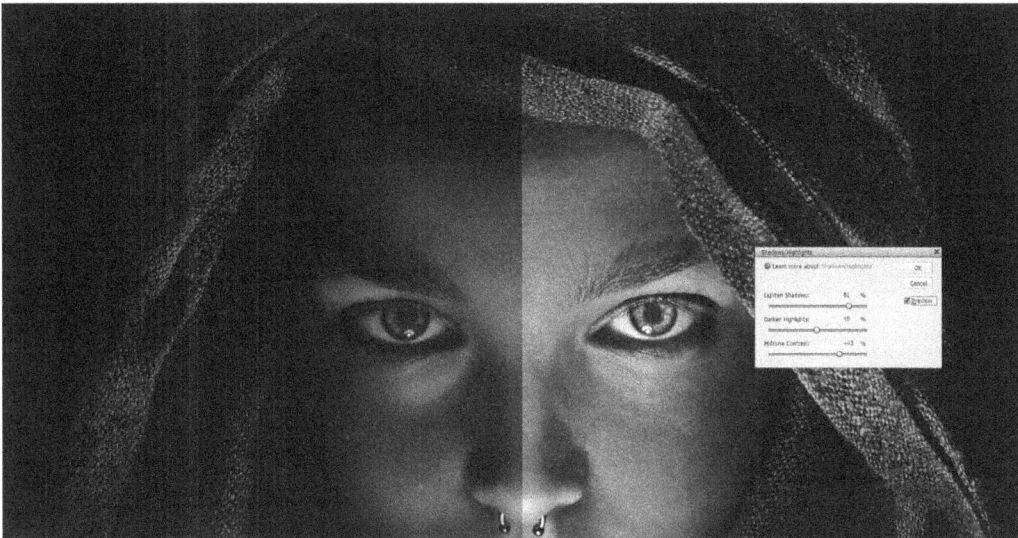

Adjusting color using Hue/Saturation

Elements comes with several color adjusting tools, the most commonly used one being **Hue/Saturation**.

Hue describes the color values of the pixels—with this slider, you can reassign different color values to what's in the file, such as changing red to yellow. Used on its own, it operates **globally**, so not only do the red tones change to yellow, but all the other colors shift as well, often producing wildly surreal and not very useful color results.

The **Saturation** part of this feature controls the intensity of the color value in the pixels. So, if you set the slider to a minus amount, it begins to lose color, or *desaturate*, eventually turning black and white, while shifting it to the right increases the color values, making the image appear richer in color. Again, this is a global change, so everything in the file gets more colorful.

> **Tip**
>
> **Warning**: When using the Hue/Saturation feature, if you push the (Saturation) slider value beyond 30 or 40, the color might well become incredibly intense. And while this might look great on your screen, it most likely will not reproduce in any kind of print format, commercial or inkjet. If the file is destined for print - it's best to make a test proof first before committing to an expensive print run.

The third part of this tool is one that, in my opinion, isn't very useful—and that's **lightness**. Moving this slider adjusts the maximum and minimum black levels in the file, essentially helping you fine-tune the global contrast in the file. It does the job, but I find using the **Output Levels** scale of **Levels** to be a more efficient tool to use if I need to lower the contrast. But you can decide for yourself.

All these effects are **global** which, most of the time, is exactly not what we want to happen. For example, an image might just need the red tones to be brighter; nothing else. Elements has the answer:

1. **Open** the image.

2. Choose the **Hue/Saturation** tool (*Ctrl/Cmd + U* or **Enhance | Adjust Color | Hue/ Saturation**).

3. From the **Master** drop-down menu, choose the color that you'd like to adjust (that is, reds, yellows, greens, cyans, blues, or magentas). Note that these are Adobe colors—to make your color selection more accurate, move the cursor off the **Hue/Saturation** tool and over the picture, then precisely click the color you want to change. You might see the color bars along the bottom of the panel shift as you specifically sample the color in the photo, rather than picking the canned Adobe *red*.

4. Moving the **Hue** slider now reassigns red to another color. (**Note**: You can also make use of the eye droppers at the bottom of the window to fine-tune a color selection. Use the left-hand dropper for a general color selection, then either the minus or plus droppers to add/subtract different tints from the initial selection.)

5. Move the **Saturation** slider to minus 100 and anything red in the image will turn black and white; move it to a plus value and just red will increase in intensity. It's a fantastic tool, enabling photographers to quickly and easily make radical changes in a shot without the need for time-consuming masks or selections. Its only downside is that, in this example, everything that has a red value changes color, not just the red-colored subject (that is, the red reflection in the yellow building is also affected). To limit the color change to just one (red) item in the picture, you would need to make a rough **selection** around that item first, then adjust the **Hue/Saturation** sliders. More on selections in the next chapter.

You can make all the colors in an image **more colorful** or **saturated**, or you can select just one color from the **Master** drop-down menu (in this case, I have chosen yellow) and boost that.

In the following screenshot, I then selected red and removed the color, shifting the slider to the left, rather than to the right, so now the red tones have no color value and appear black and white (or rather, gray):

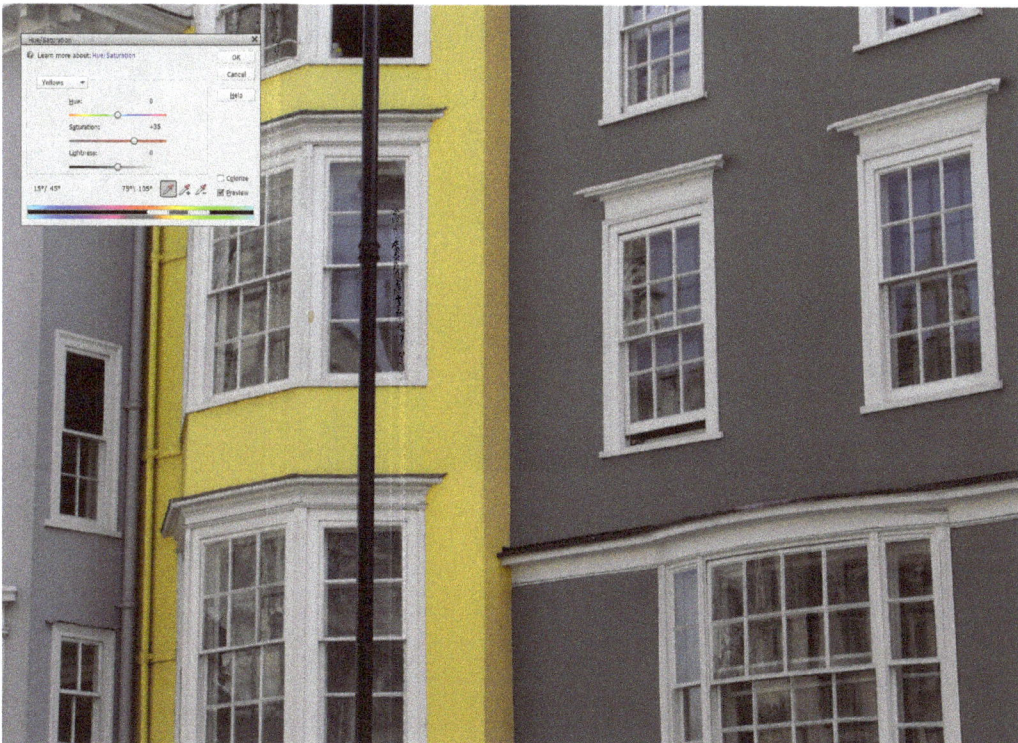

With the same image, by choosing a specific color (red), then clicking in the image to select that exact shade of red, I can target just that tone. This works really well, providing that the subject for which you are trying to change the color is the only thing colored red. If there are multiple red objects in the frame, you will have to make a **basic selection** using one of Elements' excellent selection tools to limit your color changes to just one object. Using this tool will also teach you a lot about the components of specific colors—how much the color yellow is a part of the color green, for example:

Having fine-tuned the precise selection of the color red in the panel by physically clicking on the photo, shifting the **Hue** slider creates an almost perfect color change, from red to dark blue. To make this selection process even more specific, you can try shifting the tiny white pins along that rainbow-colored color picker located at the base of the HSL panel. The two inner pins limit how broad the color selection is—the narrower these are, the more specific the color choice. The gap between the inner and outer markers fades the initial color selection from that specific color (as seen in the top bar) with the new color, blue (as seen in the lower bar). The further apart these pins are from each other, the softer the gradation from the chosen color to the color that's next to it. This sounds more complex than it really is. Move the pins to see how they affect fading from one color change into another in your image:

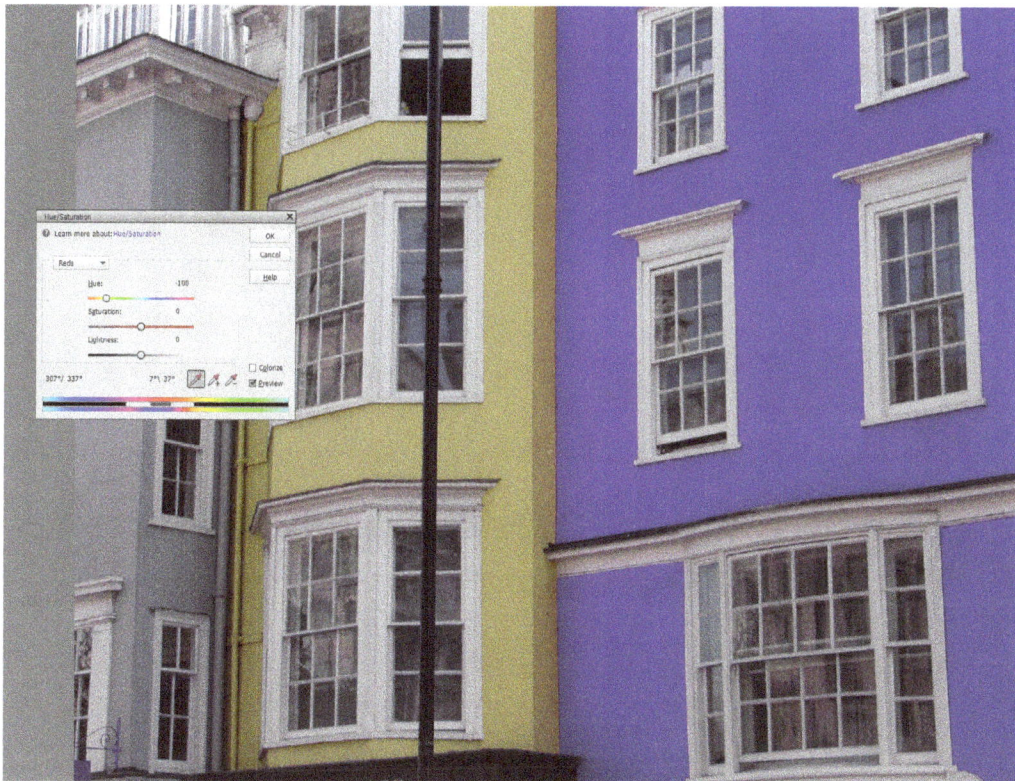

A final tip is to use the **Colorize** feature (check this at the bottom right-hand side of the tool). This instantly renders any color image as a monochrome file with a colored tint—the color (hue) is controlled using the **Hue** slider (naturally). Its intensity can be adjusted with the **Saturation** slider:

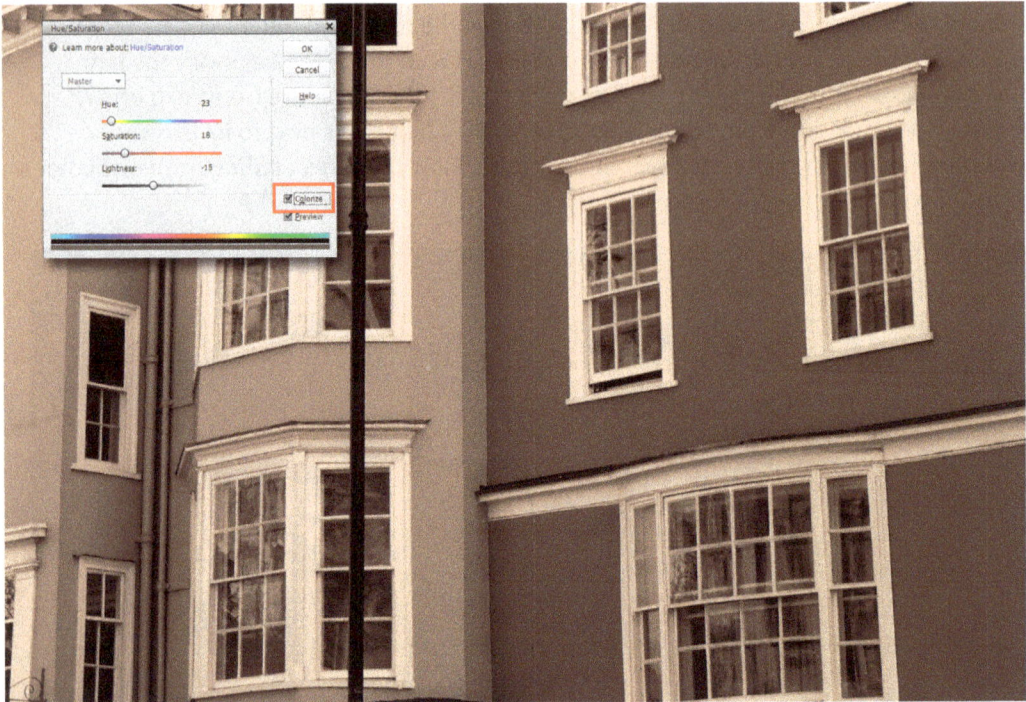

Creating high-impact black and white images

Black and white images are favored by a lot of photographers—they evoke feelings of antiquity, style, and artiness in many different scenarios.

The trouble is, if you ask a bunch of photographers how to convert a file into black and white, they'll come up with multiple different ways of doing it—some good, some great, some too complex.

Elements makes this process a little easier with a specific **Convert to Black and White** tool. Here's how it works:

1. Open an image.

2. Choose the **Convert to Black and White** tool (*Alt/Opt + Ctrl/Cmd + B* or **Enhance | Convert to Black and White**).

3. The **Convert** window opens and the image in the main edit space automatically converts into one of the black and white *recipes* on offer. With the introduction of higher-resolution monitors, the fixed-shape preview before and after windows are less relevant than the main image behind them.

4. Choose from one of the recipes on offer, that is, **Infrared effect**, **Newspaper**, **Portraits**, **Scenic Landscape**, **Urban Snapshots**, or **Vivid Landscapes**.

5. Adjust the **intensity** of the black, white, and mid-tones using the sliders to the right of the recipes.

6. When satisfied, click **OK** and save the file.

Personally, when it comes to using this specific tool, I prefer to use the least contrasty conversion first (for me, this is usually **Urban Landscape**), click **OK**, then finish editing the contrast using **Levels**. Everyone has their own *best* way to make a black and white shot pop off the page:

Seven other black and white conversion techniques are as follows:

- In the **Hue/Saturation** tool, set the **Saturation** slider to -100.

- Convert the color mode from **RGB** to **Grayscale**. (**Image | Mode | Greyscale**).

- Use the **Remove Color** tool (**Enhance | Adjust Color | Remove Color**, or *Shift>Ctrl/Cmd + U*).

- Use the **Black & White Effects** thumbnail in **Quick** edit mode.

- Use the **Black and White Conversion** tool in the **Guided** edit mode.

- Use the **Monotone Color** menu from the **Expert | Effects** panel.

- Use a **Hue/Saturation** adjustment layer.

Perfecting skin tone color

Portrait photographers should love the **Adjust Color for Skin Tone** tool because it's simple and fast to use. Let's learn how to use it following the steps given here:

1. Open the image.

2. Choose the **Adjust Color for Skin Tones** tool (**Enhance | Adjust Color | Adjust Color for Skin Tone**) and follow the on-panel instructions. Basically, just click on the face and if it corrects the color nicely, either click **OK** and save, or make further tweaks using the **Tan**, **Blush**, and **Ambient Light** sliders. Remember that although your subject might look like they have a slightly tanned complexion, the skin tones themselves are made to look as they do by blending pixels of different colors from yellow to ochre, brown, grey, and even red pixels, in various amounts, and with a specific but complex distribution.

3. So, one random *click* might hit on the wrong-colored pixel and give an instantly disappointing result. Persevere! As with most aspects of image editing, adjustments to tone and color values can be wasted if your computer monitor is not correctly calibrated. If the screen is not displaying accurate color, then you'll risk poor results once the image is output to another device such as a printer (see *Chapter 2, Setting Up Photoshop Elements from Scratch*, specifically the *Color Management Options* and *Screen Calibration* sections).

You could also use the **Remove Color Cast** tool to achieve a similar result, although this feature is not quite as flexible as it lacks those **Tan**, **Blush**, and **Ambient Light** sliders:

Essentially, any tool designed to adjust the color by taking a sample from the image itself is based on the **White Balance** feature. Because we are making a reasonably inaccurate sample by clicking in the image, the information that Elements receives might not be accurate enough to allow it to work properly. To average your sampling, consider changing the **Point Sample** method from a single point to an average 3 x 3 sample or 5 x 5 sample in the **Color Picker Options** panel and you might get a more accurate sample, and therefore a more useable result.

Skin smoothing

One highly effective new feature in Elements 2020 is called Smooth Skin—no guesses what this does.

Open an image, apply the feature (**Enhance | Smooth Skin**), and make a quick adjustment in the (smallish) window that appears onscreen (see the following screenshot). This feature works very well; using artificial intelligence, it can identify a face in the picture. It does not work so well for profiles or shots where the subject is not looking more or less at the camera. It does work with pictures that feature multiple faces:

Simple retouching – spot removal

I clearly remember when the **Spot Healing Brush** was first announced by Adobe. It was at the launch of Adobe Photoshop 7.0 in 2002, and once the presentation was over, there was a stampede to the back of the auditorium to buy the product (which was *the thing* to do in those days), such was the impact it had on all those portraitists, wedding shooters, and retouching gurus. Overnight, their lives had changed, because no longer did they have to make careful selections, feather that selection, then copy and paste the selected area from one part of the shot to another, then line it up directly over the skin blemish, before blending the copied pixels into the background using **Layer Opacity** settings:

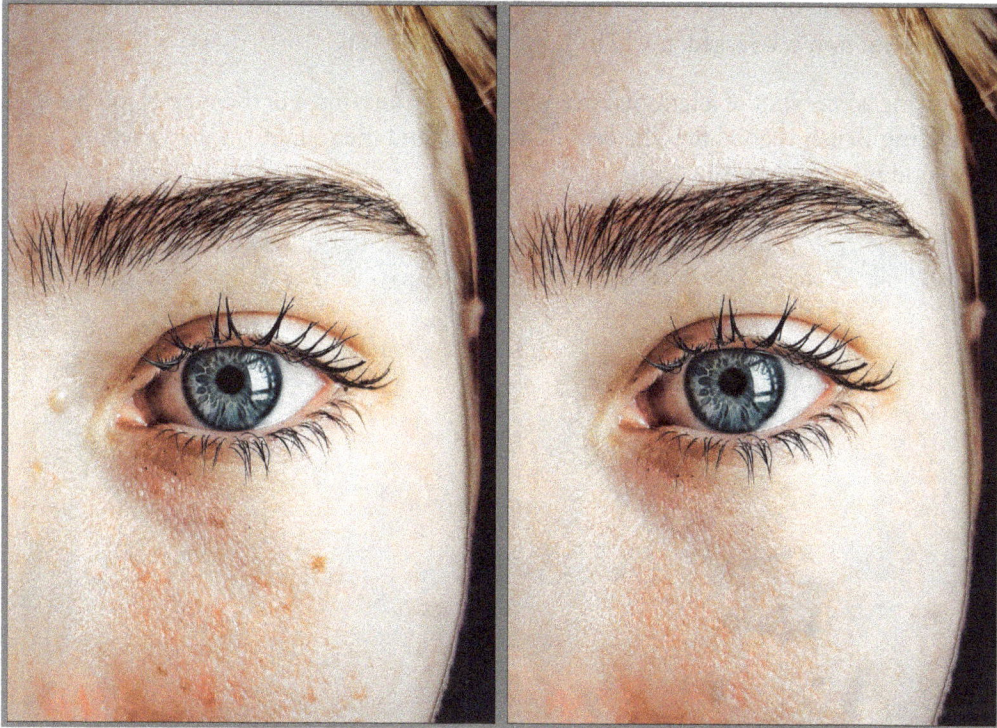

All that's needed with the **Spot Healing Brush** is to set the brush diameter a little larger than the target area, click it once, and the blemish disappears. It seemed like magic at the time, but now this tool is totally synonymous with retouching and can be found in a huge range of photo editors, including Photoshop Elements.

How does the **Spot Healing Brush** work? It couldn't be simpler:

1. Open a file and enlarge the image so you can clearly see the blemishes onscreen (*Ctrl/Cmd* + "+"), or use the **View** menu to zoom in or out.

2. Select the **Spot Healing Brush** and enlarge the brush size to just a bit larger than the blemish itself. Do this using either the **Size** slider in the tool's **Options** panel or using the handy keyboard shortcut *[* (to make it smaller) and *]* (to make it larger (square brackets)). Click on top of the blemish. It will instantly vanish.

3. For larger areas, you can either make the brush bigger, or simply click, hold the mouse button down, and drag the brush over the entire blemish area. When the mouse button is released, it will be removed/covered up.

The following screenshot of a tattooed person is a perfect example of the type of job the **Spot Healing Brush** is good for. The *blemish* is small, and the source, the area used to sample good pixels, is large:

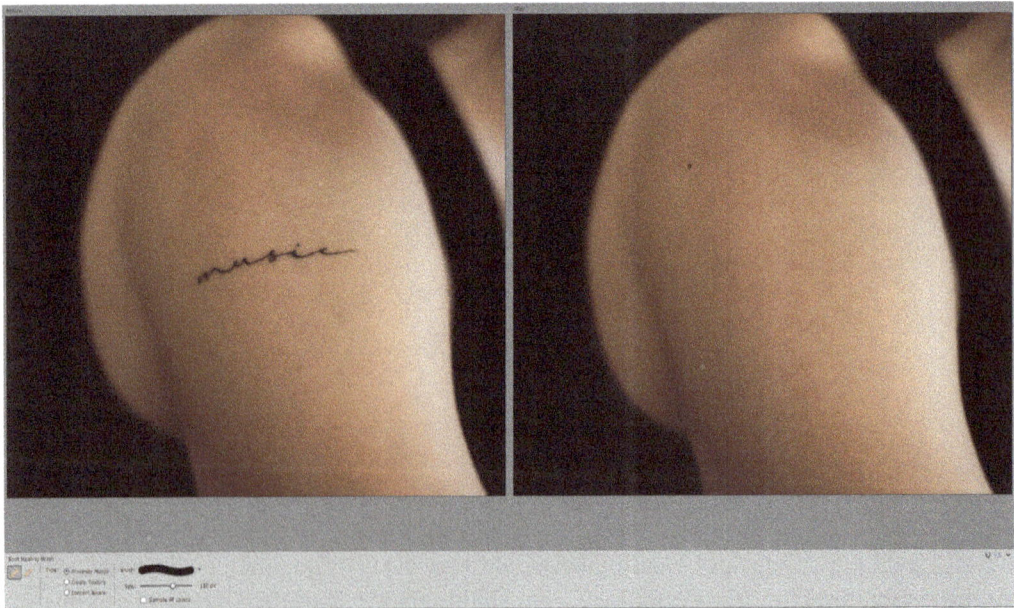

Despite being a fantastic tool, the retouching process doesn't always go to plan. It can smudge the image, blur out details when it is not supposed to, and even copy and paste inappropriate bits of the image back into the frame rather than out of it!

So, if the result is not what you were expecting, here are some troubleshooting suggestions.

This is an easy and effective tool for removing small to medium blemishes (tattoos are removed painlessly). But if the area being retouched is very large, you might find it cannot find enough good pixels around the damaged area to complete the repair.

Release the *Alt/Opt* key, move the brush over the target (that is, the area needing to be covered up), and click again. This copies pixels from the **Source** to the Target area. How much is transferred is controlled by the **Opacity** of the brush. For instance, if it's set to 50%, you'll have to click twice on the Target area to transfer all the pixels from the Source area to cover the damage up entirely.

Although the healing brush does an incredible job of blending tones from the Source area into the pixels in the Target area, lowering the brush Opacity might also be helpful to make your retouching skills become both efficient and invisible. Clicking multiple times on a lower opacity state might take a lot longer, but you can use it to blend mismatched tones together more convincingly. Although the tool does an amazing job of blending regular tones to match the area it's being pasted into, you might also notice that textures do not blend—so hair and skin blemishes, although blended to be the same tone as the Target area, never lose their texture. In this case, care must be taken to pick the right Source areas.

Reselecting the Source area again and again from different parts of the image is one way to work with a limited Source area. Another way to do so is to check the **Aligned** check box in the tool's **Option** panel. What this does is leave the Target exactly where it was first clicked. Clicking and dragging makes the Source move with the Target, but just clicking repeatedly does not.

The following section highlights a reasonably new feature using Adobe's artificial intelligence (AI), a technology that's increasingly employed to make quite complex processes far more accessible to novice photo editors. AI is also applied to the new Colorize feature in Elements 2020 (see *Chapter 1*, *Photoshop Elements Features Overview*, and *Chapter 5*, *Easy Creative Projects*).

Modifying facial expressions

This appeared in Elements a few versions back. At the time, I didn't give it a second thought, but when I tried it, I realized how amazing it was. (Warning: your family photos might never look the same after trying this tool.)

The clever **Adjust Facial Features** tool somehow identifies the facial area in a portrait and, using artificial intelligence, isolates key facial elements such as the eyes, nose, lips, and mouth so they can be masked and edited separately. These sections can then be changed using a number of distortion techniques—Elements treats the pixels as if they were elastic, allowing you to stretch, expand, push, and contract features accordingly. To get started with modifying the facial features and expressions in a portrait, here's a brief overview of how to get the best from this innovative feature:

1. Open a suitable image (note: this works best with a **single portrait,** with the subject more or less looking directly at the camera).

2. Choose the **Adjust Facial Features** tool from the **Enhance** menu.

3. The tool should automatically isolate the face in the picture, ringing it in blue.

4. Use the sliders on the right-hand side of the screen to make your changes.

5. Click **OK** when you are happy with the edit and save the file. It's that easy!

Once opened, using the **Enhance | Adjust Facial Features** shortcut, the software automatically identifies the facial features inside the blue circle. It's like magic and, I suspect, involves some very clever programming and the use of artificial intelligence technology on the part of the Adobe software engineers:

Work your way down the sliders on offer along the right-hand side of the window to improve or change the character of your subject:

I can't get over how effective this tool can be, provided that the portrait is taken relatively straight-on, facing the camera. Another consideration is its resolution—the more pixels there are in the file, the better the response and a cleaner-looking final result you'll get. Images taken off the internet might also present issues as they typically don't have enough resolution and if there are any distractions elsewhere in the image, it might not lock on to a face and refuse to work. When it does work, it can be great fun!

Eyes wide shut

Another seemingly impossible editing feature that you'll see in Elements is its impressive **Open Closed Eyes** tool.

Sure, now I've heard it all—a software application that opens the closed eyes of your portrait subject? Well, it works, and in most examples that I have tested, it works very well indeed, provided that you can find a pair of eyes that match the portrait sitter's eyes reasonably well. Why is this feature needed? If you have a bunch of portraits but the one composition you really like has the subject blinking in it, you can use this feature to copy and paste good eyes from another shot over the blinking eyes. You can also use it to replace one set of eyes with a second, different set of eyes. How good is that!?

Here's what you have to do:

1. Open the shot in **Quick** or **Expert** mode.

2. Choose the **Enhance | Open Closed Eyes** tool and wait for the utility to open in the main window (see the screenshots here).

3. If no replacement eyes are visible in that window, search for other portraits of that same person and bring them into the window by accessing **Folders**, **Organizer**, or the **Photo Bin**. You can bring in any number of samples—even pictures of different people—to try, but clearly, you need to match the ethnicity, skin color, eye color, and possibly the sex of the subject to make this feature work optimally.

4. Simply click on one of the thumbnail faces on the left-hand side to see those eyes being pasted over the eyes of your subject instantly. The utility softens the edges of the selection so, providing the skin tone is roughly similar to the target, the process ends up being almost seamless. Brilliant fix!

The example in the following screenshot has two portraits in the right-hand panel. These are quite different women, but even so, the digital surgery worked quite nicely using the portrait on the far right of the screen:

Clicking the sample thumbnail automatically selects, **feathers** (an edge-softening process), **copies**, and **pastes** the eyes from the sample across to the main image. This happens in the blink of an eye; it's an amazingly quick process:

When casting around for a pair of fresh eyes, be careful to choose faces/eyes that are clear of stray hair, spectacles, or jewelry, as these might be accidentally copied into your portrait by mistake. The algorithms that make this work are pure genius:

Additional resources

Using keyboard shortcuts has several significant benefits for photographic editors, regardless of their skill level. Firstly, they take the pressure off your mouse hand. If every function is performed using only the mouse, you will tire more easily. It can also lead to greater physical strain, which in turn could lead to all sorts of medical issues (such as stiffness, arthritis, and even carpal tunnel problems).

Therefore, using a few keyboard shortcuts will not only help to alleviate the physical stresses of just using one hand to edit images, but it'll also significantly speed up the editing process and make your actions more efficient. Elements has a huge range of possible keyboard shortcuts—far too many for most of us to remember, let alone to use effectively, so to keep things as simple and as practical as possible, here are a few of the most **relevant shortcuts** for this chapter:

- Create a new, blank file: *Ctrl/Cmd + N*
- Auto Smart Fix: *Alt/Opt + Ctrl/Cmd + M*
- Adjust Smart Fix: *Shift + Ctrl/Cmd + M*
- Auto Smart Tone: *Alt/Opt + Ctrl/Cmd + T*
- Auto Levels: *Shift + Ctrl/Cmd + L*
- Auto Contrast: *Alt/Opt + Shift + Ctrl/Cmd + L*
- Auto Haze Removal: *Alt/Opt + Ctrl/Cmd + A*
- Auto Color Correction: *Shift + Ctrl/Cmd + B*
- Auto Redeye (removal): *Ctrl/Cmd + R*
- Convert to black and white: *Alt/Opt + Ctrl/Cmd + B*
- Haze Removal: *Alt/Opt + Ctrl/Cmd + Z*
- Levels: *Ctrl/Cmd + L*
- Hue/Saturation: *Ctrl/Cmd + U*
- Open a file: *Ctrl/Cmd + O*
- Close a file: *Ctrl/Cmd + W*
- Close all open files: *Alt/Opt + Ctrl/Cmd + W*
- Save As (that is, to give your edited file a proper name): *Shift + Ctrl/Cmd + S*
- Open in Camera RAW (used specifically if you want to open a non-RAW file in this editing window): *Alt/Opt + Ctrl/Cmd + O*

Summary

In this chapter, we have looked at introducing you to the **best editing practices** in Elements so as to streamline your creative photographic workflow, which in turn will make your output more efficient, giving you more time to shoot pictures. It's also been a comprehensive introduction to the use of **RAW files**, and most importantly, how to edit them using Elements' **Camera RAW** utility—an important step if you are to develop and maintain a high level of professionalism in your creative careers. We should also now have a good understanding of **image resolution** and file **resampling** when it comes to reducing or enlarging image files.

We have also seen how easy it is to come up with a stunning look for your images by editing them using one of Elements' many instant-preset **special effects** and **image fixes**, just as you might when applying an Instagram filter online. It's important for beginners to see how easy it is to produce beautiful effects with no previous experience. These effects not only work with very high-resolution images but also provide a far greater depth of choice. We have also made ourselves familiar with the all-important tasks of controlling **brightness**, **contrast**, and **color** using two of Elements' most important non-RAW editing tools for **Levels** and **Hue/Saturation**, plus some of its more esoteric—but nevertheless useful and fun—features, including changing facial expressions and opening closed eyes. They might sound gimmicky, but they actually do the job surprisingly well.

In the next chapter, we will show you how to assess an image for its creative potential— that is, what it could become if you had the knowledge and the skills. Then, you'll learn exactly how it's done with a complete **image makeover**.

4
Image Makeover

One of the most important aspects of good picture editing is also very simple: you need to have a plan. And to have a plan, you need to have an idea or a vision of how you want your picture to look after it has been edited. Having a logical plan, therefore, is almost as important as knowing how to execute that plan in order to create great results. Not surprisingly, this requires some forward thinking and a reasonable knowledge of the tools at your disposal.

At a basic level, this plan might simply be to see your picture appear brighter and more colorful than the underwhelming drab-looking RAW file that you see in Photoshop Elements's **Camera RAW** window.

Because of its relative simplicity, this kind of plan is relatively easy to accomplish quickly and effectively using any of the amazing Photoshop Elements' global tone-changing tools or instant-effect presets that we looked at in *Chapter 3, The Basics of Image Editing.*

In this chapter, we will look at specific examples where an image needs editing and describe the processes used to make it appear more impressive. The chapter begins with a relatively simple brightness and contrast makeover that escalates to more ambitious levels of complexity, culminating in the last example, which involves bringing together multiple images and text into one document

In this chapter, we are going to look at several quite different image makeovers:

- Basic and creative workflows
- Makeover one: brightness fixing
- Makeover two: brightness, contrast, color, and simple retouching

- Makeover three: fixing incorrect color and simple retouching
- Makeover four: perfecting a portrait using the skin-smoothing tool
- Makeover five: heavy portrait retouching
- Makeover six: combining three images and adding text to create something from nothing

Basic edit workflow

Editing any image requires us to follow a certain process. Here, I will explain the steps that are needed when you're converting an unedited image into a final product:

1. A good portion of the editing process can be applied in Camera RAW, but if you're editing a non-RAW file, such as a `.jpg`, `.tif`, `.png`, or `.psd` file, I recommend the use of the **Levels** tool (*Ctrl/Cmd + L,* for Windows or Mac respectively) because it's used to improve the contrast and brightness first. Once the file is closer to being perfect, you will get a better idea of how the color and sharpness might appear.

2. The second step is to adjust the color, again using one of the many enhancing tools that are available, if you think the image requires it.

3. The final stage is to sharpen the image according to how it's going to be used. Images destined for **social media** are somewhat easier to sharpen because what you see on your computer monitor screen is similar to what you see once the file is uploaded to Facebook, Twitter, 500px, or Flickr. And besides, if it's uploaded and that media channel's preferences change the resolution or the compression, thereby producing a poorer version of what you edited, it's quick enough for you to re-edit the file and apply a different amount of sharpening to suit that particular host's display particularities. In print, this is a little more complex as the sharpening benefit can be lost somewhat through the printing process. Experience can help a great deal here, especially in a commercial printing environment, but if you are printing at home on an inkjet machine, make a test print and re-edit where needed.

Creative edit workflow

Once you have gained confidence in being able to control the **color**, **brightness**, **clarity**, and **sharpness** of your image output, it's time to consider something a little more creative.

Once the tones in the file are looking the way you want them to, it's also time to consider the onerous task of cleaning up the subject using one of Photoshop Elements' amazing **retouching tools**. This might be a simple operation of **perfecting skin tones** by covering up tiny blemishes, scratches, or color inconsistencies using the **Spot Healing Brush** or it might be something a little more ambitious where objects in the foreground or background need removing or at least covering up to prevent them from dominating the subject.

Before you get too involved in this kind of advanced retouching, it's important to ask yourself if, by removing a certain object, the composition will change noticeably. If this is the case, you may want to camouflage that object by simply dulling it down, rather than removing it entirely.

Sometimes, these questions are very hard to answer before you actually start the editing process, which can lead you into unnecessary complexities. This is why we're going to learn to develop a structured editing workflow—a plan might save you heaps of time and, more importantly, frustration.

Makeover example one

In this example, we are just going to use Elements' basic brightness and contrast tools to make this underexposed image appear more appealing.

Problem: There are dark, gloomy tones and poor color reproduction.

Solution: The best tools to fix this issue are **Instant Fix** in **Organizer** or **Effects** in **Quick Edit** mode.

Outcome: I want to make the highlighted flower image as light and as colorful as it was when I took the snap:

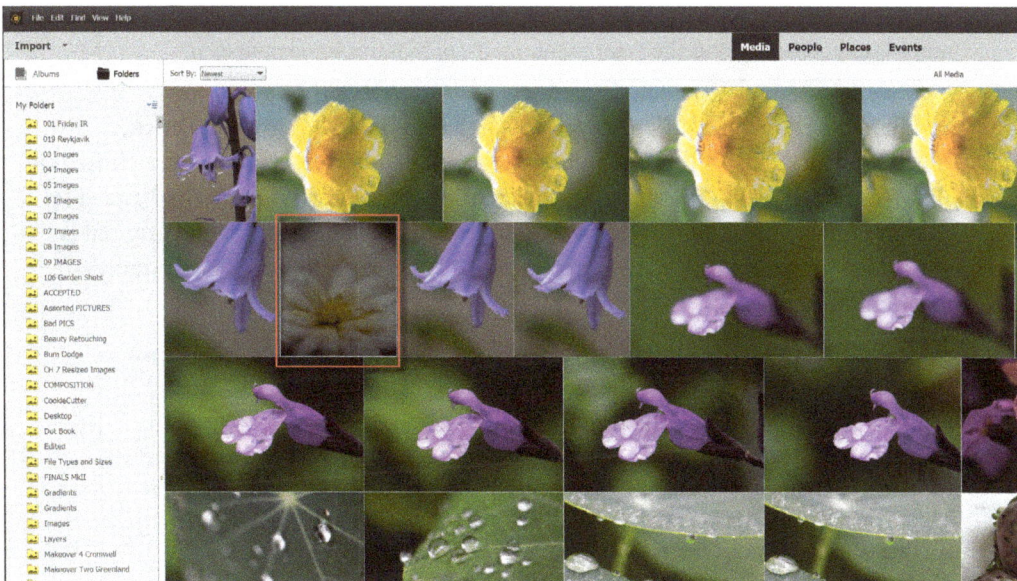

It's often a bit disappointing when you open an image for the first time in any application and discover that the snap you thought was pretty good looks dull and murky (there's an entire row of them in this screenshot).

Though this is frustrating, it's certainly normal. What we see on the camera's LCD screen is rarely what we see on a computer monitor, more's the pity. Why? This is partly because we are not necessarily paying a lot of attention to the screen when we're in the field, plus looking at an LCD in bright light is hard at the best of times, which is why reading the histogram is so much better. It might also be because the monitor is not calibrated (see the *Screen calibration* section in *Chapter 2, Setting Up Photoshop Elements from Scratch*, for information on how to calibrate your screen).

> **Note**
>
> A quick word about **calibration**. Although I have covered this topic in *Chapter 2, Setting Up Photoshop Elements from Scratch*, it's very important to state that not all computer screens are the same—in fact, there can be a huge brightness and color difference between one model of display and another. Many monitor models are designed for gaming, widescreen movies, or other confusing preset viewing modes, or they might just be very hard to calibrate. It's especially tricky with smaller devices, such as laptops and other mobile devices, or when you're trying to balance the output from a **PC** with the output from an **Apple Mac**. For most younger photographers, accurate color displays might not be such an issue because everything might be published online, but if you ever wish to move into publishing and the print medium, it's of massive importance.

Photoshop Elements provides numerous ways to *fix* a dull file like this in its **Quick**, **Guided**, and **Expert** modes. In the example of the grossly underexposed flower, I chose one of Elements' excellent range of presets from the drop-down menus on the right-hand side of the screen in **Quick Edit**. These are very easy to use and fast, and unless the original is disastrously under- or overexposed, they produce good results at the click of a button—two clicks if you want to save it.

> **Note**
>
> A preset is really like an editing recipe. It usually involves several changes to the image, such as brightness, color, contrast, and sharpness, all wrapped into one easy button click. Some presets can be modified while others are designed to be a like-it-or-leave-it option. There are usually plenty of others to try if the one you initially chose does not take your fancy.

We have all taken images like this flower shot—it's too dark for any practical use, but help is at hand using Elements's **Quick Edit** mode presets:

The makeover in this first example is simple: to make the file look how we remembered it in the field. In practice, these presets are sometimes a bit hit and miss, but as you can see, there are plenty from which to choose.

Makeover example two

In this example, we will move on to editing a RAW file that is very dark and displaying poor color. It will also require some very basic retouching to remove a series of sensor spots in the sky area.

Problem: As in the previous example, this **RAW file** is very drab, so much so that I pretty much ignored this shot for months. On closer inspection, I realized it has a great deal of creative potential. The reason I snapped this massive iceberg was, well, because it was massive and had an amazing inner blue color. The weather was cold and heavily overcast with a hint of color in the far distance, just above the horizon.

Solution: Use the **Basic** and **Detail** sliders on the right-hand side of the Camera RAW window to edit the picture back to perfection.

Outcome: I wanted to brighten the entire scene and really bring out the color in the ice, the tone in the sky, and the details in the iceberg. Essentially, I wanted to add some more **drama** to the following seascape:

Here's a good example of why I really don't like to rely on Camera RAW's **Auto Correction** tools.

Sometimes, these instant-fix type tools work well, but I find that a lot of the time, they never do quite enough—or they might do too much—which means that you have to find an alternative fix, and that wastes time. It's far better to use the tools that are going to get it right from the start—then, everyone should be happy.

Here's my version, edited using the workflow that was described in the previous section:

Adding brightness and contrast will always give the image a boost visually—it's going to stand out 100% better than not adjusting it at all (but only if it needs adjusting in the first place). In this example, I brightened the highlights and whites, then darkened the shadows, which usually gives an image a greater feeling of depth.

Because the tones are now *cleaner* (with less murkiness and more brightness), I can now appreciate any color enhancements that are made to the frame using **Saturation**, or perhaps the **Vibrance** slider.

Most would be happy with this result, but I went on to adjust the **sharpness** and **reduce the noise**, as shown in the following resulting screenshot:

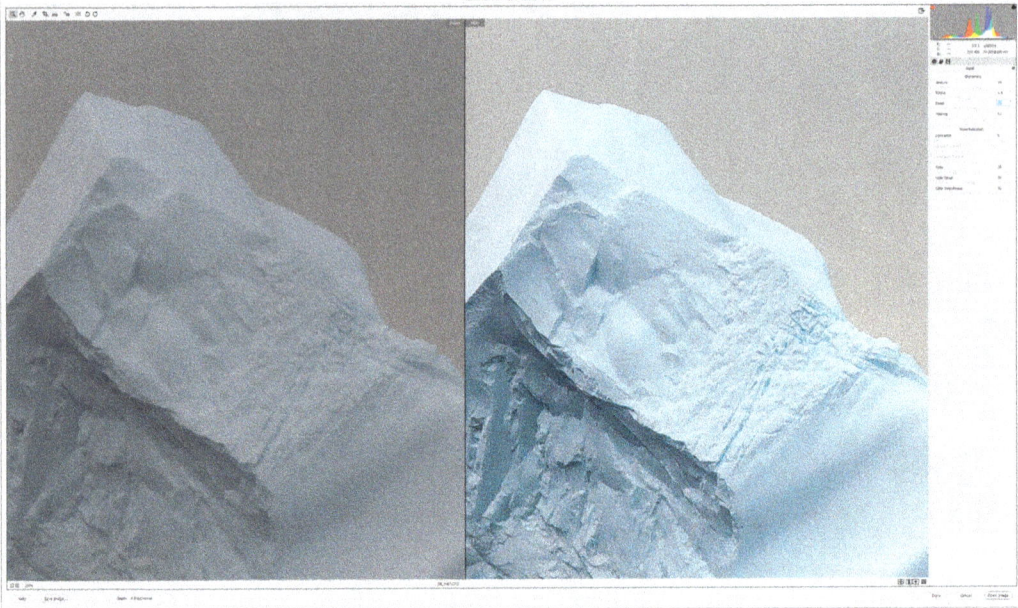

This is a sharpened version (RHS). What usually happens in a file that's both underexposed (as this was) and shot using a relatively high ISO setting is that you see more noise. The more it's sharpened, the more the noise becomes noticeable.

This frame shows my choice of **sharpening**. The noise is still noticeable, but, with the **Unsharp Mask**, is restricted to the edges of contrast in the shot.

To activate the mask, hold the *Alt/Opt* key when moving the Masking slider—it displays the black-and-white mask on screen. Note that **everything that turns black is protected** (not sharpened). Everything that's **white in the mask** takes on the sharpening that you add via the sliders. It takes a bit of getting used to, but once the right setting is chosen, you can limit the negative side of too much sharpening by limiting the sharpening effect to just the bits that are important.

Unfortunately, once the image has been sharpened you might see more digital noise appear in the shot. It's an annoying part of digital photography, but Elements has the tools to remove or at least minimize the deleterious effects of this visible noise. Let's move on and take a look at how the **Color** and **Luminance** noise reduction filters work.

To temper the often very aggressive-looking sharpening action, I have added both **Luminance** and **Color** noise reduction to this example.

Like most things digital, how far you go with these sliders is controlled by what it looks like on screen, but also by what it might look like once it's output. Concern about publishing the image online is a no-brainer because once the image has been uploaded to a website, blog, or social media, it gives instant feedback. If you've done too much sharpening or noise reduction, you can simply redo the sliders and upload again.

Printing poses a slightly stickier problem in that the print process itself literally absorbs some of the harshness of the **Unsharp Mask** because it's ink being sprayed onto an absorbent surface: paper. Images that are destined for print therefore require a little more sharpening—almost to the point where it looks like too much on screen—in order to get a satisfactory result. I generally advise sharpening about 25% more than you might be comfortable with to compensate for this softening effect. To make matters even more complicated, different paper stocks produce quite different sharpness results because they absorb ink at different rates. Always test your prints when you can before committing to a commercial print job.

Often, it's a good idea to walk away from the computer to give your mind a rest before finalizing any edits. When I took a good look at this particular image file, I realized that I'd gone a little too hard on the colors:

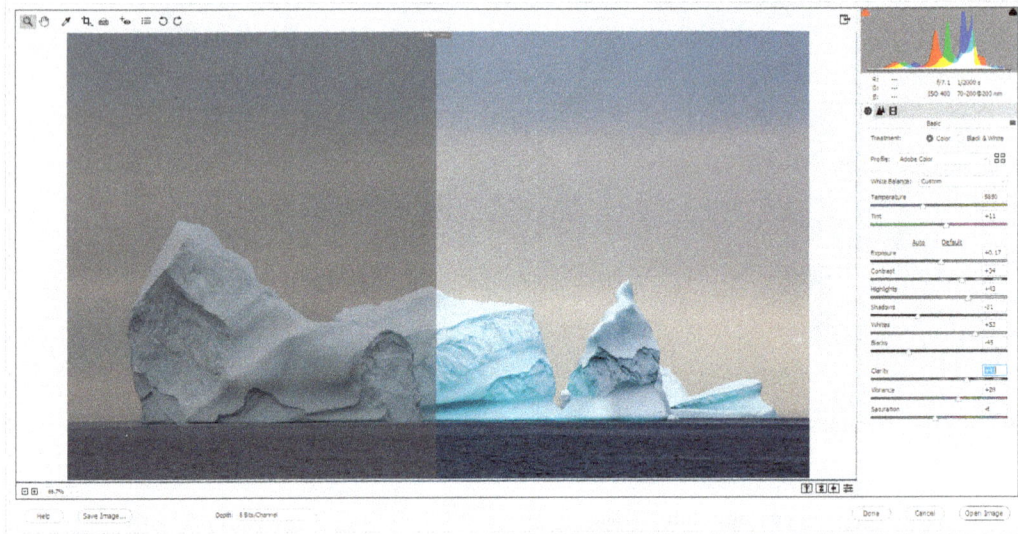

The following image shows my final *look* in Camera RAW. I think the color is a little *hot*, so I can either reduce the intensity using the **Saturation** and **Vibrance** sliders here or do it once the retouching has been finished in Elements's **Expert** edit mode:

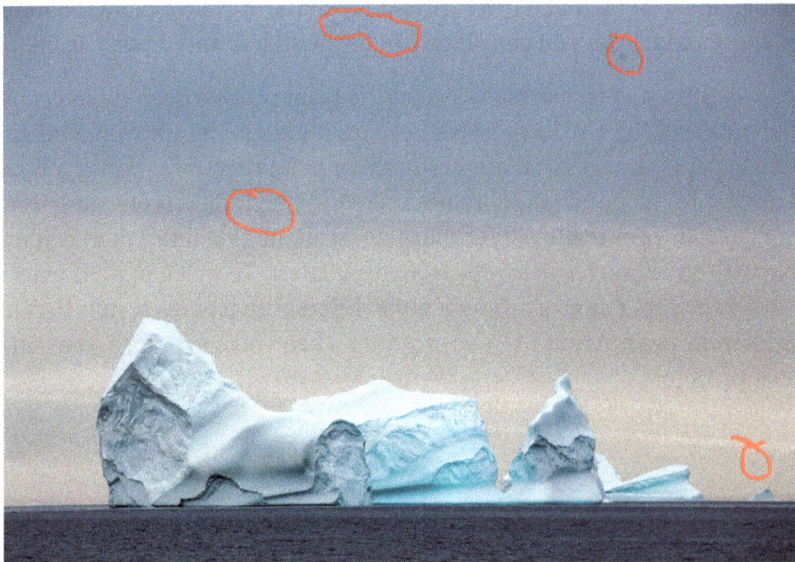

Interestingly, Camera RAW doesn't have any *local* retouching tools (it does in Photoshop CC). So, once the editing was completed in **Camera RAW**, I clicked the **Open Image** button on the bottom right-hand side of the **Camera RAW** window to bring the now-edited file into Elements's **Expert** mode.

What you can see in the previous screenshot, circled in red, are **sensor spots**, which are out-of-focus blobs that are created by dirt or, more likely, moisture on the filter that covers the sensor. They are a part of the digital process and are sometimes not noticeable until the image contrast has been edited (increased).

I could spend $60 and get my Canon to the nearest service center for a clean or I could use the **Spot Healing Brush** to get rid of these eyesores.

This click-and-move-on brush tool is awesome as it replaces the blemish with new pixels copied across from the adjacent image area. It's like magic—all you have to remember is to keep the brush size approximately the same or a little larger than the problem areas and bingo, one click and the problem is gone, as you can clearly see in this final edited example here:

The **Spot Healing Brush** is a legendary tool, one of the best features to arrive in photo editing software for years. It's ideal for removing specks of dust, dirt, and blobs, all with the click of the mouse. It's easy and very effective:

The **Burn** and **Dodge** brushes control local brightness. They allow the user to *paint* in darkness or lightness, respectively.

What's more, each of these tools can be set to operate in a specific tonal zone only, namely **highlights, midtones,** and **shadows**, making them the perfect tools for adding local contrast (burning the shadows a bit darker and making the highlights a bit lighter). I also used a very large-sized **Burn** brush in the sky to darken the already (slightly) dark sky a bit more in order to give it a more stormy look.

To make a final decision about the accuracy of what I have edited, I find it a great help to come back to the edited file after a few hours, or even overnight, to see if I still feel the same way about what I have changed.

In this example, I felt that the color had been increased too much, so I used the **Hue/Saturation** feature to reduce the intensity of the blue/cyan tones, and I am now happy with the result.

Makeover example three

Example three takes on the task of perfecting the color of an image, along with a slight brightness and contrast tweak.

Problem: Oftentimes, once an image's brightness has been improved, the contrast looks a bit *flat*, and so that too requires attention. But in this example, it's the color cast that's the most unflattering aspect of the image.

Solution: We shall use the **White Balance** tools to fix the inaccurate color, as well as the contrast-fixing capabilities of the **Levels** tool.

Outcome: Recreate the lighting and the color to give the image a more natural feel.

Skin Tone Fixing: The following is a press shot of **Dr Angela Merkel**, one of the world's most recognizable global leaders, sourced from Wikimedia. The color is wrong; it has a green-cyan color cast:

I'm not sure if this is the photographer's fault (perhaps the **White Balance** is set incorrectly), but this is unlikely if you have the credentials to be so close to someone so important. It's more likely a result of **environmental color**. Merkel looks as though she's standing in a room that's tinted in this color, so it's affecting everything else, including the skin tones. Note that incorrect color tends to be most visible in the mid-tones, so if the mid-tone grays are not 100% gray, you'll know there's a color-cast issue. Whatever the reason, it's not a very realistic color, and it needs to be fixed.

Possibly the hardest thing for beginners starting out in the confusing world of image editing is deciding what exactly it is that's wrong with any image, if anything.

I spent several years as a color printer in a commercial lab, so I find it relatively easy to identify color problems, while others don't. It's a complex process that requires experience. What's important to remember is that Photoshop Elements is an **RGB application** (displaying a mix of red, green, and blue). The opposite colors to red, green, and blue are **cyan**, **magenta**, and **yellow**, so if the image is a bit greenish-cyan, I'd need to add the **opposite colors** to correct it. In this case, adding a bit of magenta and red should do it.

One shortcoming of Photoshop Elements is that it doesn't have as many specific color-tuning tools as you'd find in Photoshop CC. That said, we can first try to fix the problem using the **Auto Color Correction** feature. As you can see in this screenshot, it didn't work—in fact, it made the image a lot worse:

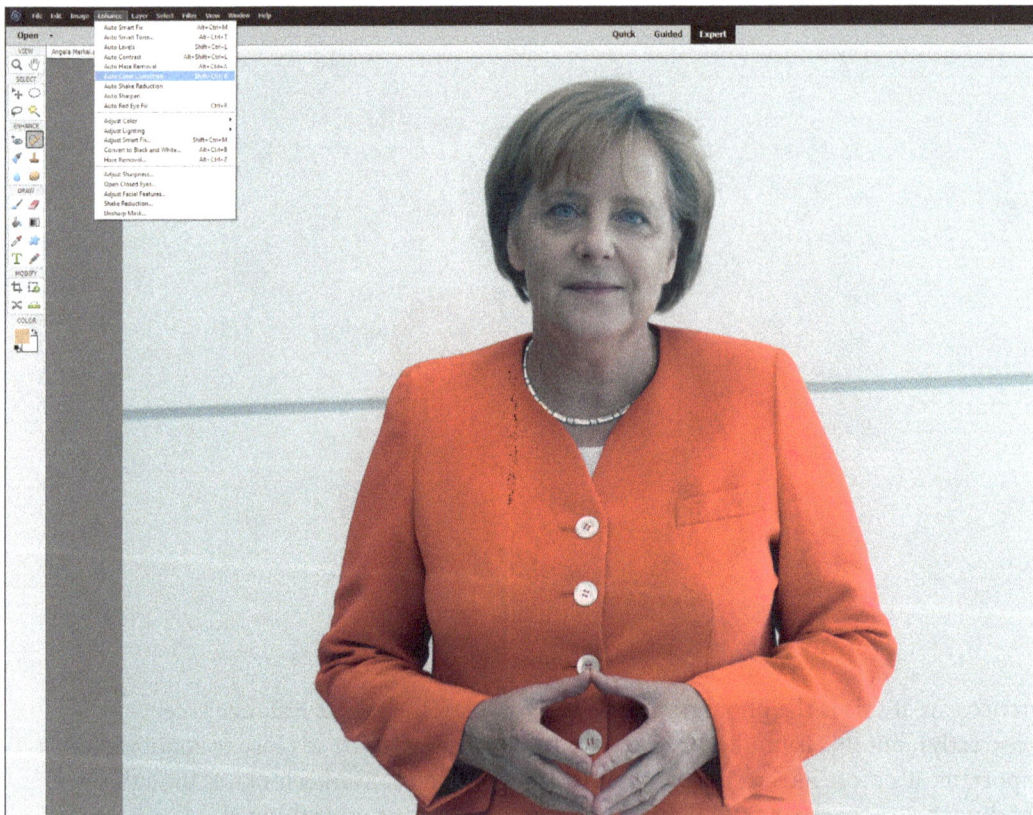

Dr Merkel will not be amused!

On my second attempt, the aptly named **Remove Color Cast** tool did a good job of making my subject's color appear a lot more realistic. One click on something that is supposed to be white, mid-gray, or black in the image and the cast is gone—mostly.

This feature is essentially the same tool as the three **White Balance** eye-droppers we sometimes use in the **Levels** tool, but instead of white, gray, and black eye-droppers, there's only one. Your job is to identify one of those three tones in the image and click it. In this instance, I clicked on the chancellor's (white) tee-shirt and the color immediately looked significantly better. Because this process works by resetting the pixels to white, gray, or black (depending on which color is clicked), I also tried clicking in the shadows up her sleeve to see if it might produce a better result. Because the shadows are not 100% black, the color correction was not as effective as the tee-shirt sampling.

Having locked that result away as a win for this semiauto tool, the image now needs a tiny contrast adjustment (darker shadows) to make it perfect:

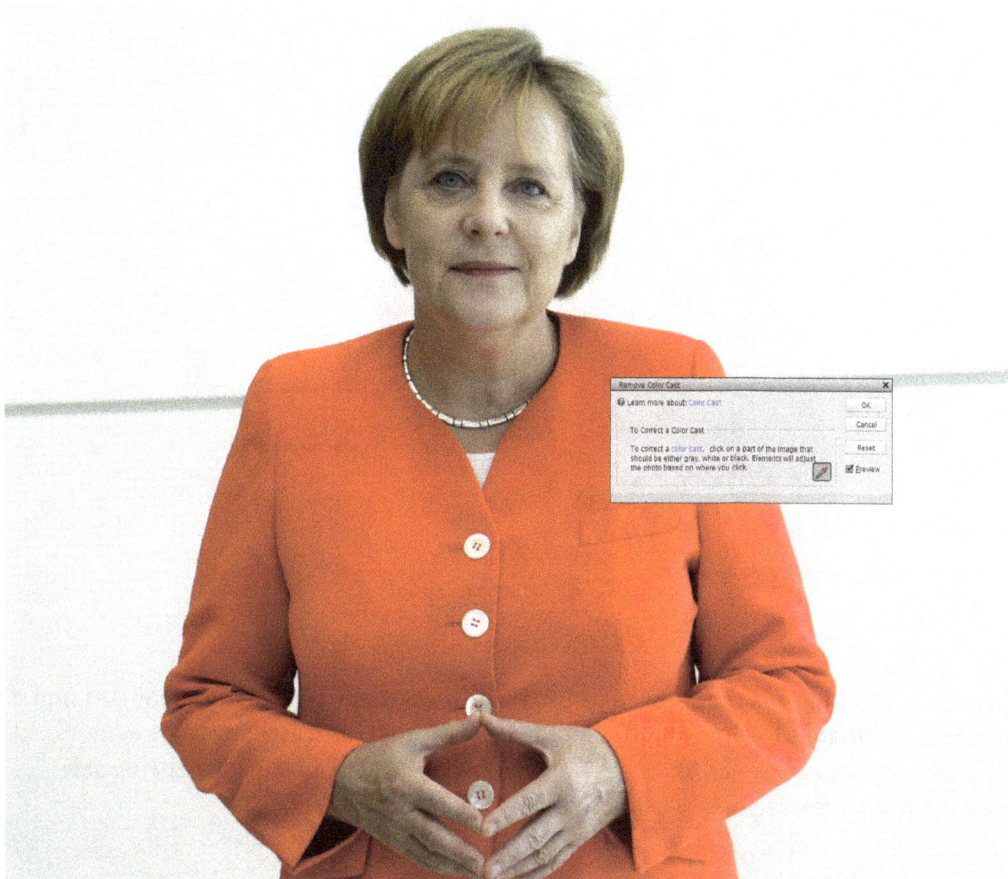

As I thought, on closer inspection, although the **Remove Color Cast** tool has done a good job of removing most of the greenish-blue tint, the image now lacks a bit of contrast. The whites in the image are not really very white, but more to the point, I can see that the black areas are not really true blacks either, making the image appear a bit flat, or lacking in contrast.

For contrast, **Levels** (as shown in the following screenshot) is certainly the go-to tool for fixing this (don't bother wasting your time trying **Auto Contrast**) as it is so easy and immediate. As you can see in this screenshot, in its **Input Levels** scale, I merely pushed the shadow slider a little to the right (outlined here in red) to darken the shadows, effectively boosting the contrast:

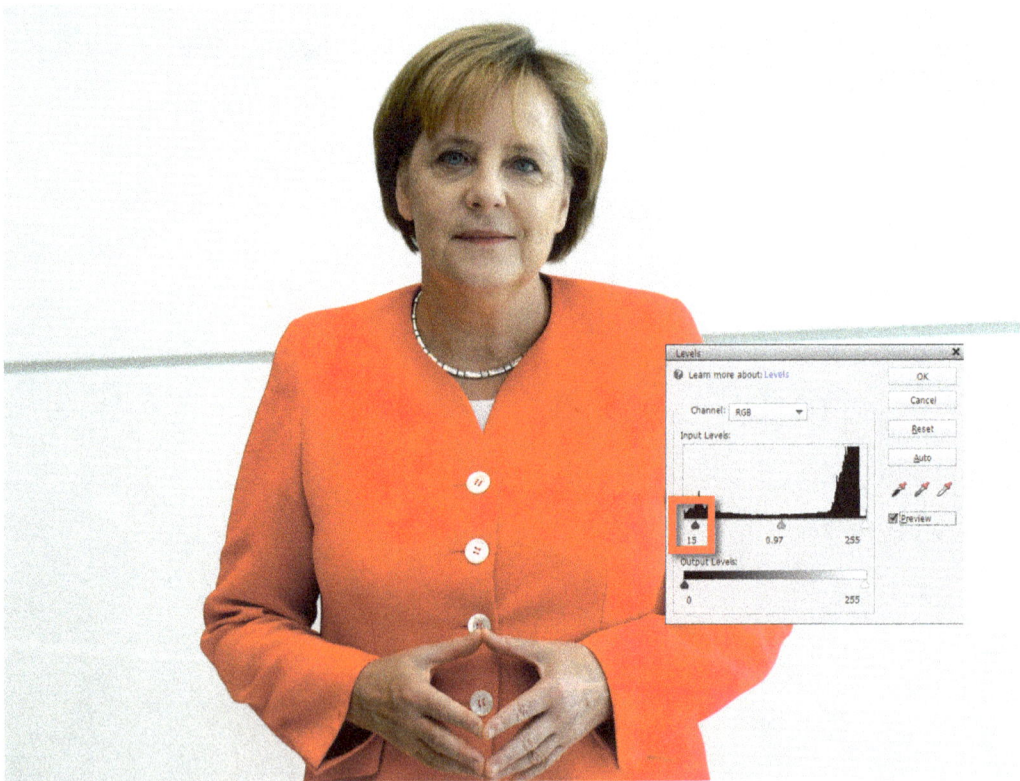

An alternative to **Levels** is the simpler-to-use **Brightness and Contrast** tool (you can find it by going to **Enhance | Adjust Lighting | Brightness and Contrast**) but while being quite effective, it's just a slider, and does not give you the added advantage of being able to read the histogram, as you are using **Levels**:

Having got the color close to realistic, I can now examine the rest of the shot for possible **problems**. The only thing I can do now is remove that background line that seems to cut right through the figure.

To remove this line, I can do either of the following:

- Paint it out using a similar color that will be selected from the wall.

- Use a retouching brush to select, copy, paste, and blend pixels from the immediate vicinity of the line.

The drawback of using the **Brush Tool** is that you'll have to select the exact color to cover up the line, much as you would if you were in the same room armed with a tin of paint and a brush. This technique will work perfectly in this example because the tones in the wall are all the same. Let's get started:

1. Choose the brush from the **Tool Bar** (press the *B* key or locate it in the **Draw** section of the **Tool Bar**). Make sure it's the **Brush Tool**, not the **Impressionist** brush or the **Color Replacement** brush.

2. Hold the *Alt/Opt* key and click in the picture to select a matching color, and then paint over the line to cover it up. To get a smooth result, use a **soft-edged** brush that is set to a **lower opacity** (such as 45%). You'll have to use more brush strokes, but as it's effectively watered-down paint, your brush marks will be invisible. As you get near the hard edge of the red jacket, change the brush tip from soft to hard to avoid bleeding color into the figure, as you can see in the preceding screenshot.

Probably the best option is to use the **Spot Healing Brush** (that's the band-aid symbol on the **Enhance** section of the **Tool Bar**):

Note that there are two versions of this: the **Spot Healing Brush** and the **Healing Brush**. I used the former, with its options set for **Proximity Match**. Funnily enough, the tool works best with a hard-edged brush. Even when I dragged the cursor over the edge of the red jacket, it painted the wall the right color and ignored the red. It's a brilliant bit of intelligent software.

Elements's **Healing Brush Tool** is also a great retouching/blending tool; its main difference from the **Spot Healing Brush** is that you have to specifically elect where it copies from by holding the *Alt/Opt* key and clicking in the source area first. The **Spot Healing Brush** simply copies from the pixels immediately around the brush edges.

Makeover example four

In this example, we are going to see how easy it is to smooth over a person's skin tones, basically making them look 100% better using nothing more than a feature new to Elements 2020 called Smooth Skin.

Here's how easy it is to get a great look in only a few seconds:

1. Open the image.

2. Find the **Smooth Skin** feature under the **Expert Edit | Enhance** menu.

3. Add the desired amount of smoothness to the portrait.

4. Use the **Before and After** slider to judge how much smoothness to apply to the picture, then click **OK** and your portrait is done (see the following screenshots for image comparisons).

Because this tool employs Adobe's artificial intelligence algorithms, something that's way above my pay grade, I can only sit and watch this amazing feature produce impressive results. Exactly how it works remains a mystery to me, although it's clear that the feature first analyzes the picture to check whether there's a face it can isolate. Angled portraits and side views don't work—your subject or subjects must be more or less facing the lens, as they are in this family group:

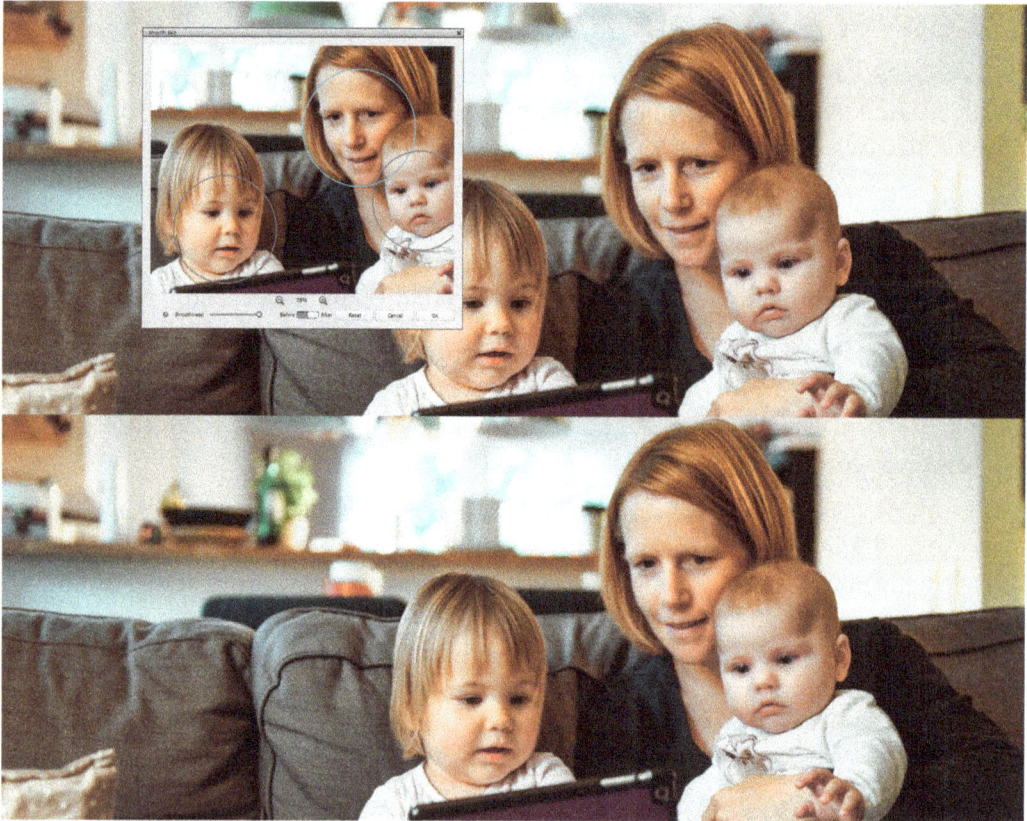

In the preceding comparison, you can clearly see that the before and after examples (the top and bottom screenshots respectively) present a big difference—the setting was pushed to maximum softness in all three faces. Smooth Skin can also be used to reduce the grittiness of excess noise.

This is a good new feature, enabling you to add softness to more than one face in each snap. Click the circle to make it active, set the softness value, and move on to the next face. It's a good new feature in my opinion, but it lacks a few features:

- The preview window's size is not adjustable.

- The softening effect is only visible in the preview window, so it's hard to be precise.

- You have no control over the exact bits of the portrait that are softened.

As you can see in this female head shot here, the softening effect (on the right) is an effective look that's easily created with the least amount of effort:

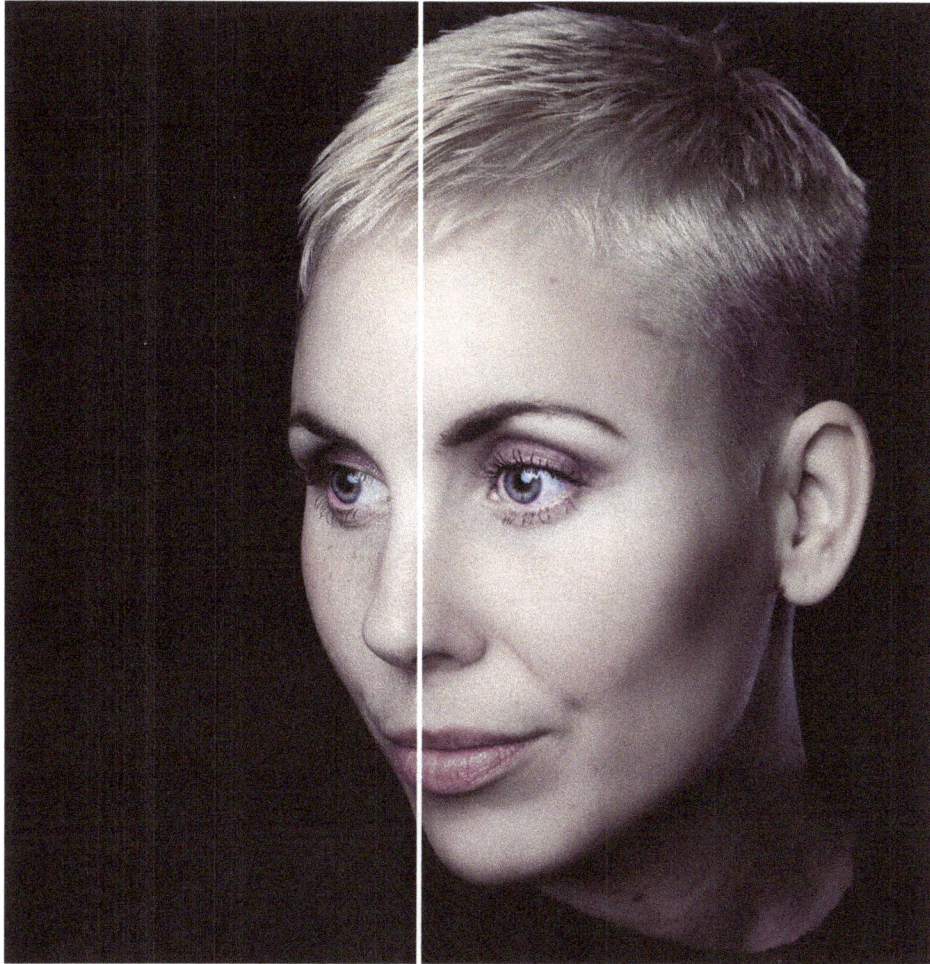

Interestingly, this technology is also incorporated into the **Perfect Portrait** feature located in the **Guided Edits | Special Edits** section. This feature has gone from strength to strength with the **Skin Softening** look, but also **Contrast Increase**, **Remove Blemishes**, **Whiten Teeth**, **Brighten Eyes**, **Darken Eyebrows**, **Adding a Glow**, and **Slimming Down**, if there's a body in the shot:

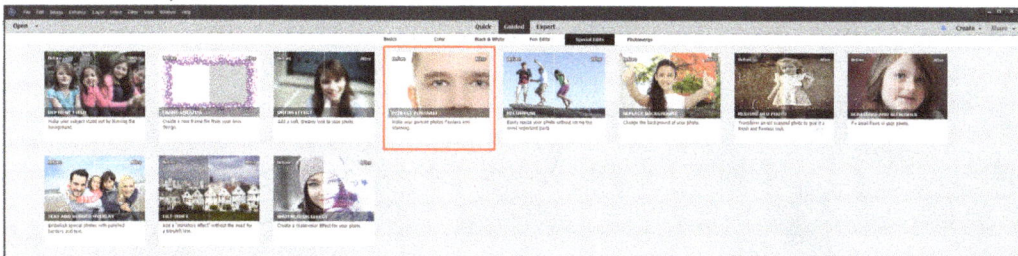

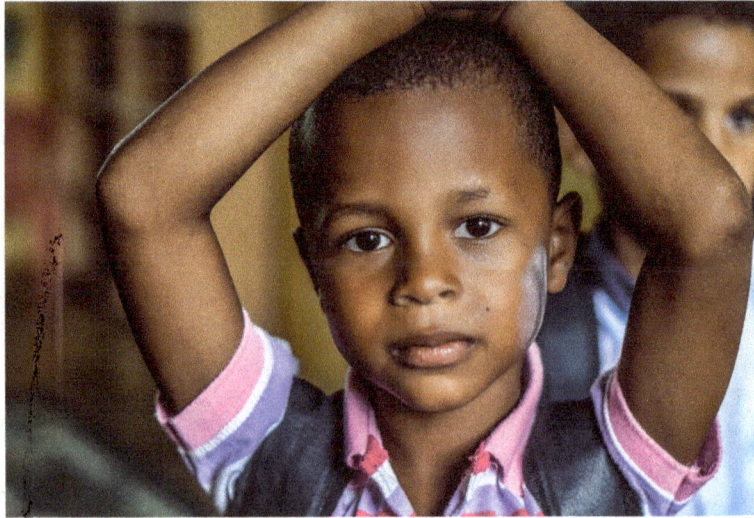

In the example of the young lad on this page, I used most of the tools on offer in the **Guided Edit** window, including **Remove Blemishes** (that's the **Healing Brush** tool), mostly to remove some of the scarring on his forearms to produce this cleaned-up version that you see here:

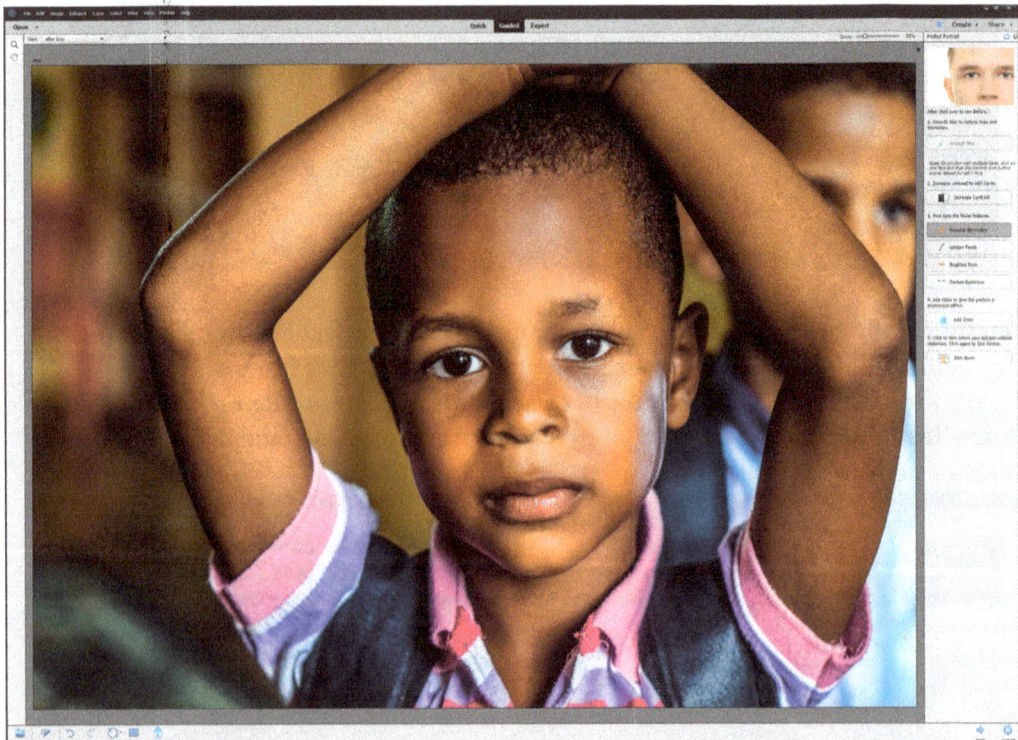

Makeover example five

In this exercise, we are going to attempt to create perfect-looking skin tones by retouching a portrait using the **Spot Healing Brush**.

Problem: The client has poor skin (acne) and needs good publicity head shots for their new job.

Solution: Use the **Spot Healing Brush** tool and the **Healing Brush** tools to remove all signs of skin imperfections.

Outcome: Produce a professionally retouched portrait.

Photoshop Elements has two **Healing Brushes**. The **Spot Healing Brush** effectively copies pixels from just outside of the brush shape (called the **Source area**) and pastes them into the brush area (the **Target area**) while blending and matching the tone of the outside pixels with those on the inside. It's simple, easy to use, fast, and very effective.

For the best results, try to keep the brush about the same size, or a little larger, than the affected area. Too big and it will copy unwanted detail into the target area, as well as *good* pixels:

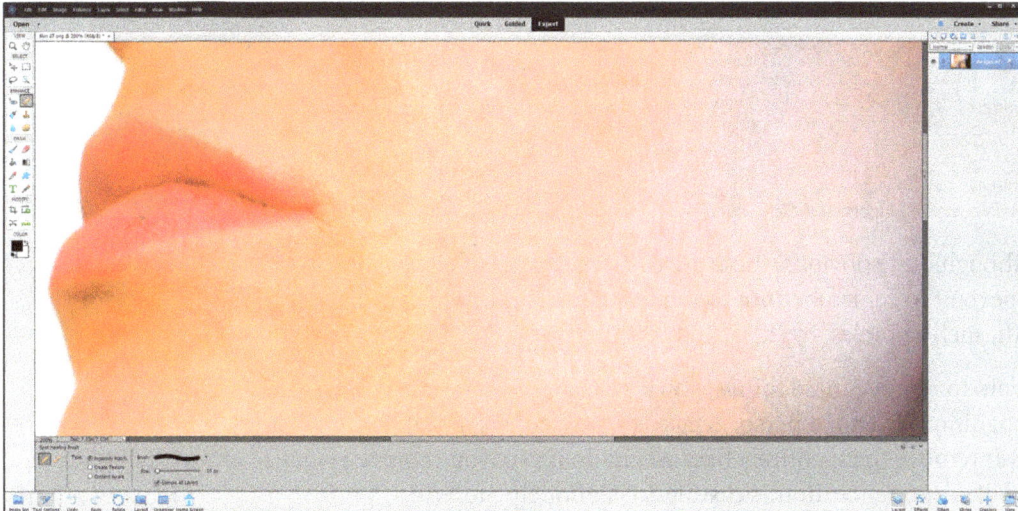

The **Healing Brush**, on the other hand, has very similar actions to the **Spot Healing Brush**, but you have to select the source area first. You can do this by holding the *Alt/Opt* key down, clicking in the source area (where the good pixels are), then moving the cursor over the damaged area (in this example, the acne damage), and clicking again to paste and blend the **Source** pixels over the **Target** pixels.

Because it's essentially a blending tool, it matches the tones in the target area, even if the source area is much darker. But it also copies texture, so if you select hair, for example, and then paste the pixels over a smooth skin tone area, although the tones are matched, the hair texture remains. Avoid doing this for obvious reasons!

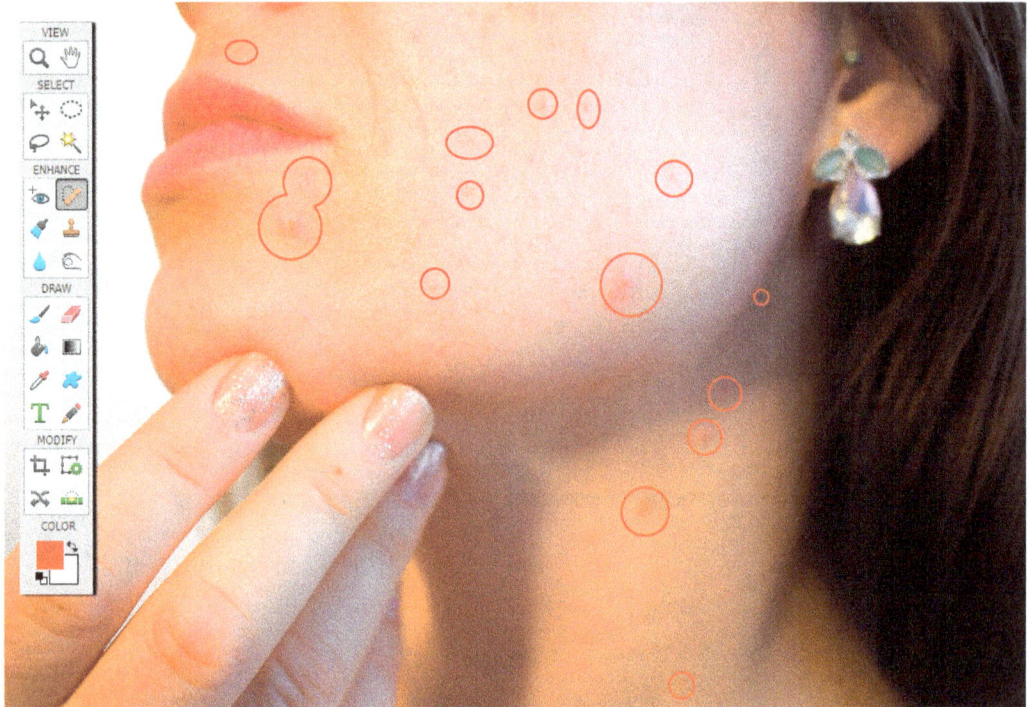

Although quite obvious, these are the target areas of concern. When retouching, it's important to remember not to remove marks and skin areas that the subject was born with, such as moles, freckles, and birthmarks.

If you do remove these things, you'll be changing the character of the person beyond recognition. Even if a person's face is wrinkled, it's usually best to soften the wrinkles but never remove them entirely because, in doing so, you remove evidence of their fallibility and life experience. In this case, less is definitely more.

In the following screenshot, I have highlighted the **Spot Healing Brush** mode in the **Options** panel. From here, you can set the tool options, choosing from **Proximity Match**, **Create Texture**, and **Content Aware**:

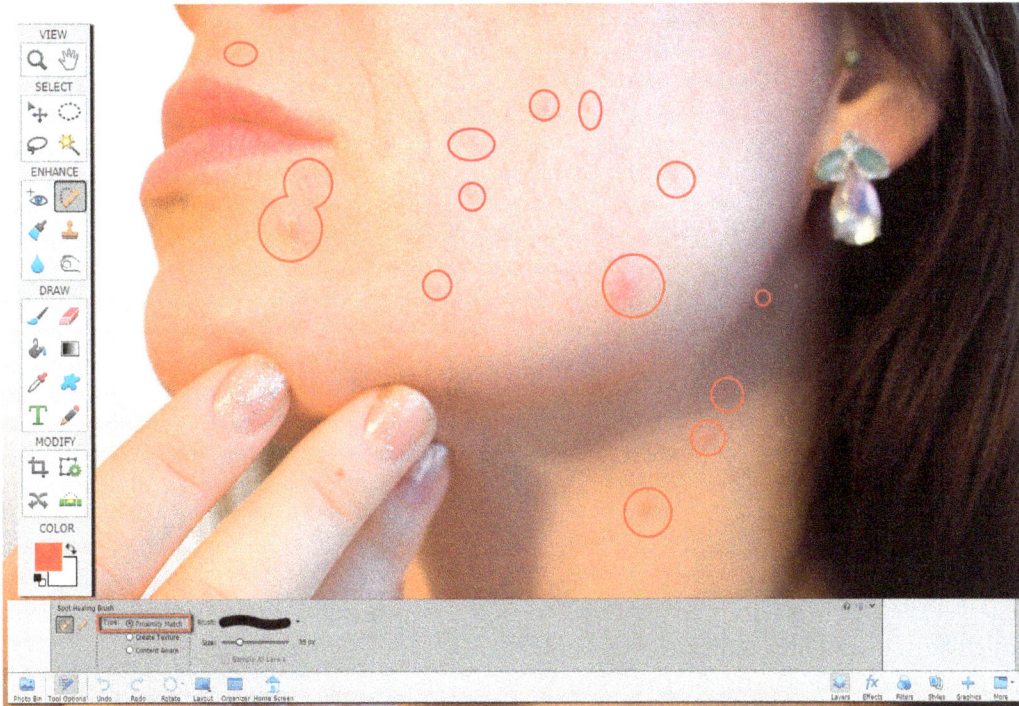

Proximity Match analyzes the pixels around the area being retouched, identifies the best pixels to be sampled, and uses those to cover up the pixels in the damaged area. This is software black magic, but it works. Use a small brush where possible.

The **Create Texture** mode generates a texture by creating new pixels with which to cover the blemishes. In this example, it doesn't work because the retouched pixels are too smooth and look retouched.

Content Aware is an intelligent mode where Elements tries to reproduce the shadows, lines, and shapes that have been sampled from around the brush shape. This sounds more like software black magic, but in reality, it functions more or less perfectly. Whoever came up with the algorithm for this feature is a genius as it has revolutionized the effectiveness of this program's retouching tools.

As you can see in the following screenshot, the black blob is actually the **Healing Brush** being moved across the blemish area. It remains dark like this until the mouse is released, and then the magic happens. You should use the click, drag, and release technique on all irregularly shaped areas that need a retouch:

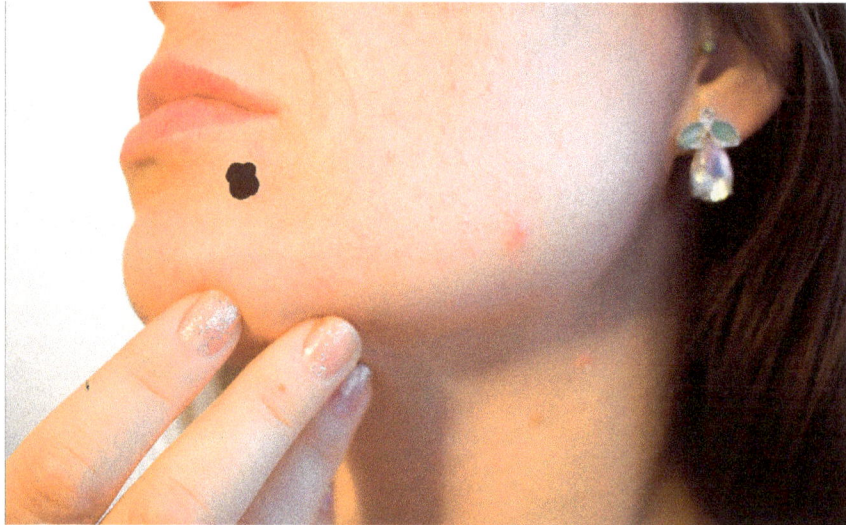

The larger the area that's dragged over, the longer the software and computer takes to calculate the sampling and pixel retouching:

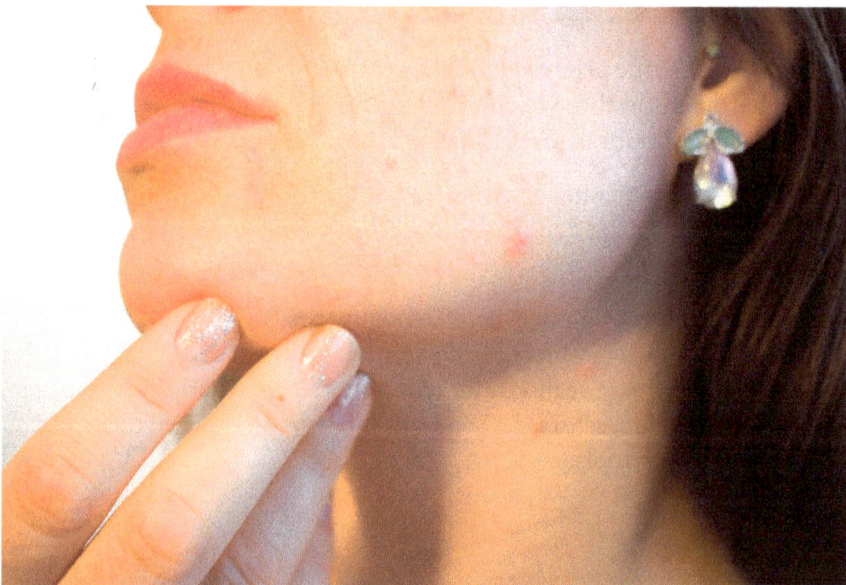

Release the mouse and the **Spot Healing Brush** does its thing. This is the easiest of all of Elements's retouching tools to master, and once you've done it, you'll be happily retouching everything!

Larger objects are much harder to remove from images than small ones with this tool. For the big stuff, you'd need to use the **Clone Stamp Tool**, or even make a large **selection**, and then copy, paste, and blend it into position (this is difficult).

Another click-and-drag action produces a dark area, which identifies the area covered in this one action so far. Release the mouse button and the skin damage is mostly gone:

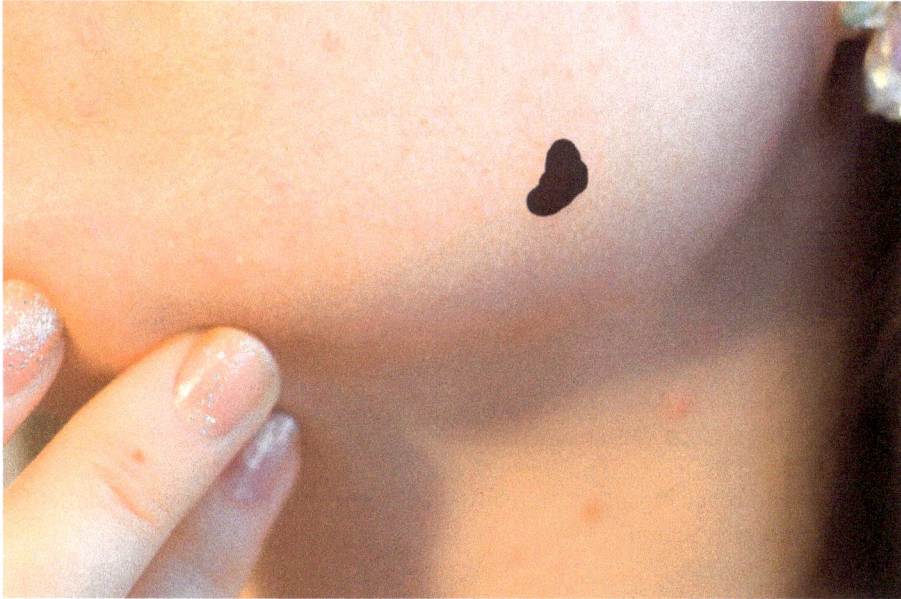

Operating tips

If you try to repair an area that's too close to something totally different in nature (such as jewellery against skin tones), you'll find that Elements might blend the hard-edged metal with the skin tones. If this happens, either use the **Healing Brush** and direct the **Source** area well away from the problem pixels or use the **Clone Stamp Tool**.

Retouching is almost impossible with the image sized to just fit the main edit window. Get into the habit of enlarging the screen image to 100% or higher so that you can see what you are doing. Use the handy keyboard shortcuts of *Ctrl/ Cmd* + + or - to zoom in and out.

Here's the final version. I healed all of the major blemish areas, then went back over the entire image magnified to 400% (hold down *Ctrl/Cmd* and press + to enlarge the image. Use *Ctrl/Cmd + -* to reduce the image size and *Ctrl/Cmd + 0* to fit the image in the window) to retouch some of the color inconsistencies that were created by the skin condition and the mixed lighting sources:

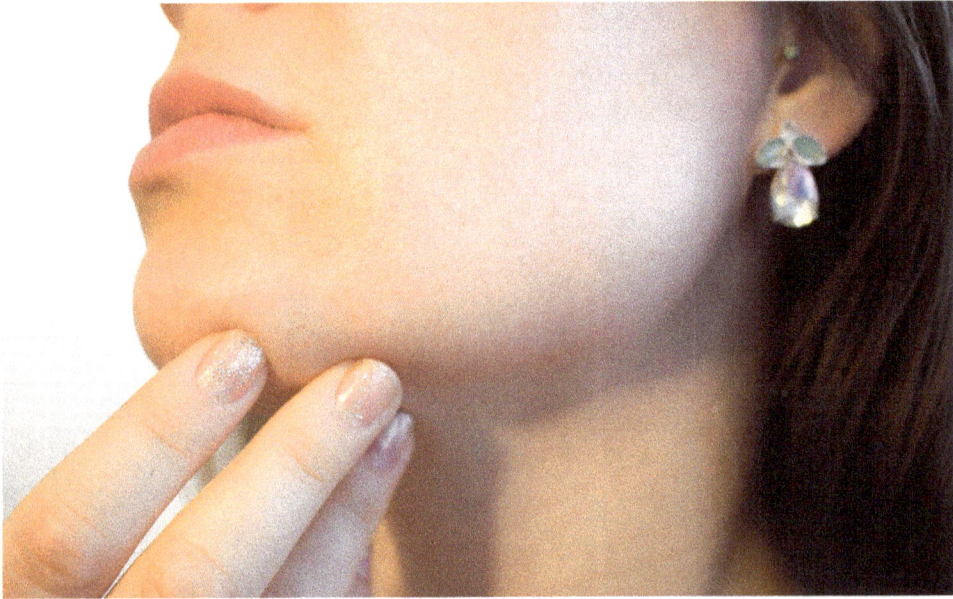

By going in close and repairing all of the really small blemishes (and we all have them), you create a far smoother overall effect:

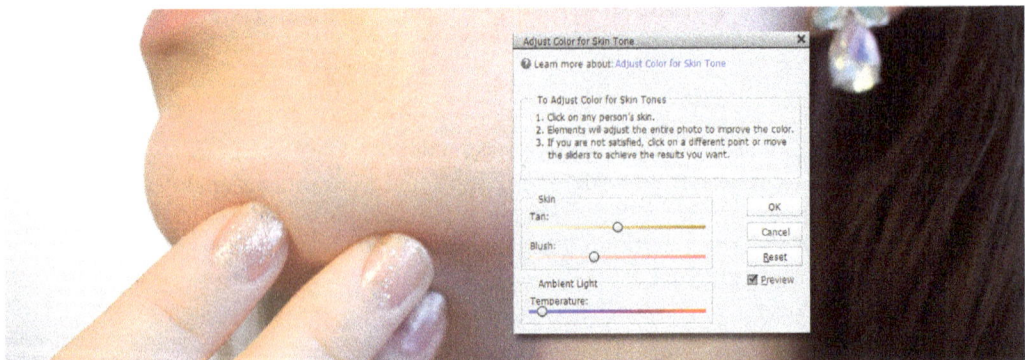

Tip

Another way to fix up color inconsistencies is by going to **Enhance | Adjust Color | Adjust Color for Skin Tones**. Use it to warm up or cool down the color, then apply a degree of tan or blush to the image.

Makeover example six

This example is more of a re-creation than a retouching exercise, taking three different images and blending them together using the **Spot Healing Brush**, the **Eraser Tool**, and the power of **Layers**.

Problem: Combining different images can be problematic.

Solution: Exploit **Layers** (including **Layer Blend Modes**, **Layer Opacity**, and **Simplifying Layers**) to combine the images and text, and use the **Eraser Tool** and various brush settings to help to blend the images' pixels together convincingly.

Outcome: Blend three images and some text together to make it look like a professional promotional TV poster.

In this example, I wanted to combine several images to make up a **digital illustration**, something that only works if you combine the *right* elements together:

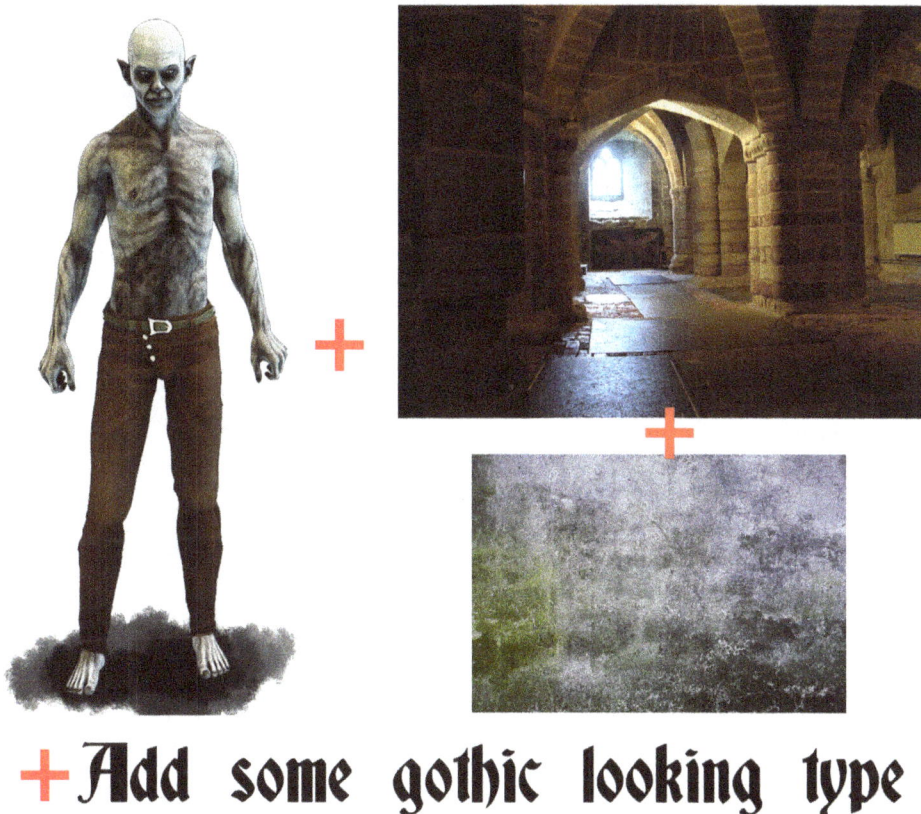

We'll look at adding two images together, then manipulating how they interact by simply erasing bits from the upper image in the layer stack (in this case, it's a free stock illustration of a vampire). You'll learn how to work with **Layers**, **Layer Blend Modes**, and **Layer Opacity**, and how to use the **Type Tool**. On top of that, you'll be using the now-familiar **Levels** and **Hue/Saturation** features to make the two layers appear the same color and Contrast so that they look like one image, not two different pictures sourced from entirely different places.

Open the images—in this example, I have three: a medium resolution illustration of a vampire; a picture of a cathedral crypt in the UK; and a textured plaster wall saved to my ongoing **textures library**. You can see all three images by clicking (to open) the **Photo Bin** (arrowed). It really pays to also have the **Layers** panel open at all times so that you can monitor which layer it is that you are currently working on:

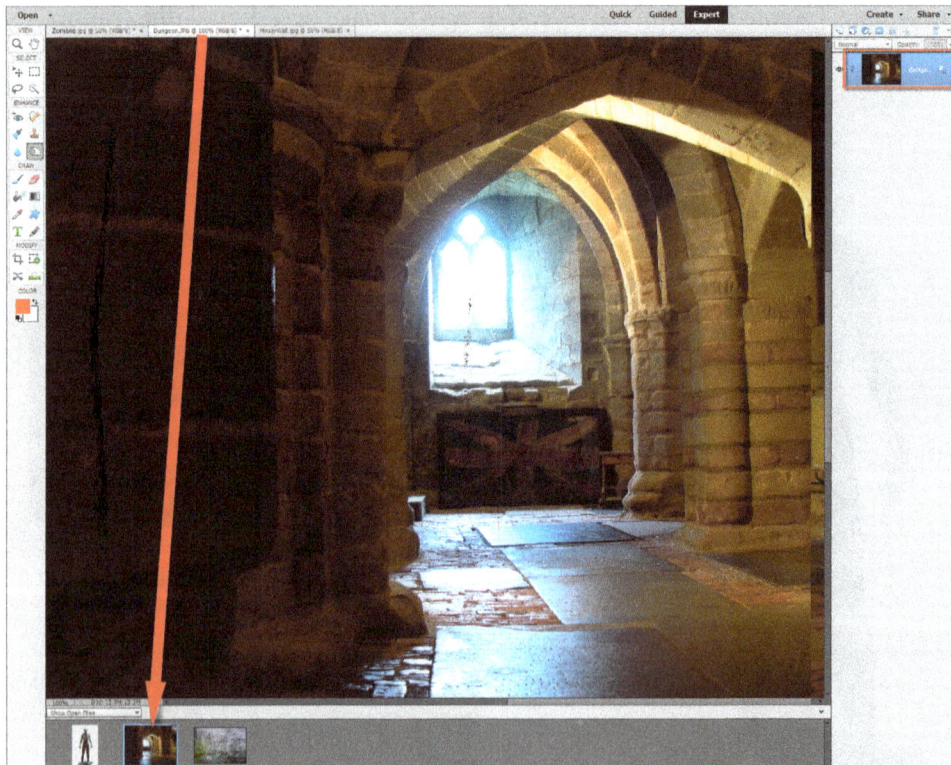

Open images are always **tabbed** at the top of the screen (as indicated by the arrow in the following screenshot). The lighter-colored tab indicates that that image is the one currently at the front, and is therefore obscuring the other two open images. You can bring a different image to the main window by either clicking another tab or by clicking its thumbnail in the **Photo Bin**.

To add one picture into another, **select it first**, copy that selection, then find the host image and paste it into that file. It's a simple process; however, if you have never done this before, there's a faster way. With the picture that's to receive your pasted image open in the main screen (that is, the crypt image), use the handy **Move Tool** (press the *V* key or click the tool icon in the **Tool Bar**, which is in the top left-hand corner in the **Select** part of the **Tool Bar**) and click, hold, and drag the thumbnail from the **Photo Bin** into the main window (marked with an arrow in the following screenshot):

If the resolution of both images is the same, then the one being pushed into the *base* picture might cover it entirely. Use the **Move** tool to click and drag it slightly to the left-hand side of the main screen. Note that the image has little squares called *handles* in the corners and midway along each edge. Click and drag one of these corner *handles* to resize the transferred image so that it's larger or smaller. Clicking the midpoint handles doesn't work as it will only distort the proportions.

When you push one image over a second like this, Elements creates a **Smart Layer**. If you want to apply any kind of color or tone change to that layer, the Smart Layer has to be **simplified** first. You will be obliged to do this by Elements as soon as you try to make a tone change anyway, or you can simply right-click the layer panel and choose **Simplify Layer**. It's easy:

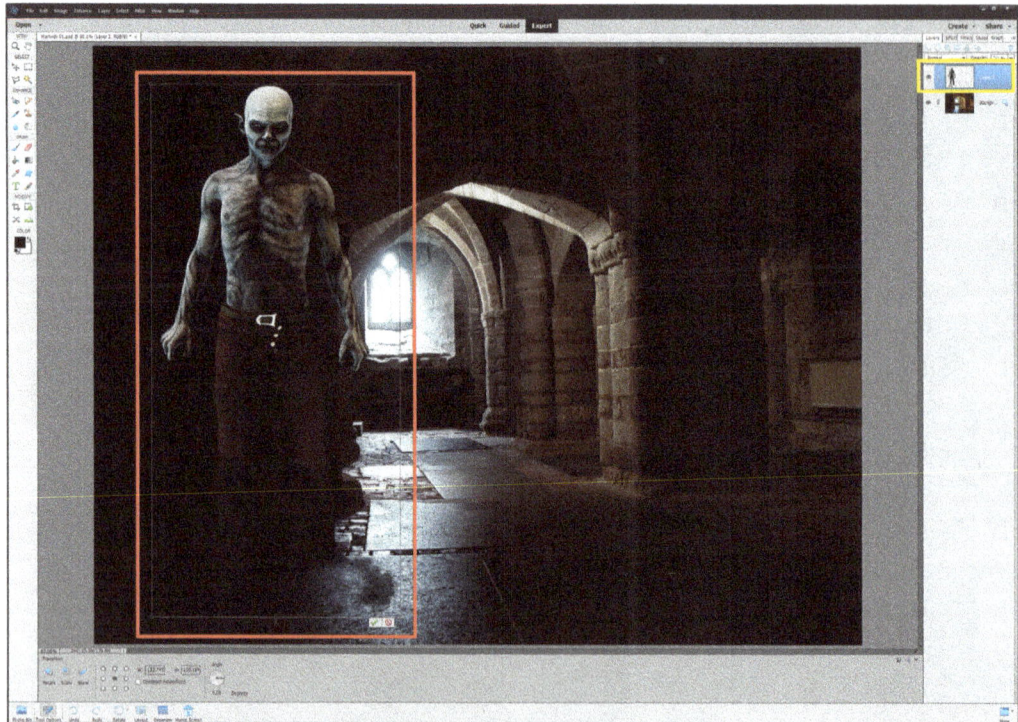

To check whether this automated copy-and-paste operation has worked, look at the **Layers Panel** (highlighted in yellow in the top right). You should see **two layers**. The top layer is the image just copied into the base layer—it's highlighted in blue. This indicates that it's currently the **active** layer. If I were to open and use **Levels**, for example, then any tone change made would only affect that layer. As soon as you click, hold, and drag one of those corner handles (outlined in red in the main window) to stretch the active layer smaller or larger, the **Accept/Reject** symbols appear. If you like the new size, click the green symbol to accept the change. If it's not right, click Cancel or click, hold, and stretch the handles again. In the Layers Panel, you'll see the image thumbnail change shape as you resize it in the main window. I wanted the figure to be mostly on the left-hand side of the composition so that we could still see the vaulted ceiling and the window at the back of the base image. Lucky for me, the vampire illustration already had most of its background removed.

Brushes play an important part in any retouching process, however simple or complex. Photoshop Elements ships with around **300 different brushes**—these range from hard-edged brushes to brushes with fuzzy edges, square edges, ragged edges, and many more. You can also go online and download hundreds of special-effects brushes from Adobe or third-party websites and use these for special projects (see *Chapter 8*, *Advanced Drawing and Painting Techniques*, for more information on using custom brushes). These brushes work with all of the retouching, painting, drawing, erasing, and graphics tools. Besides having a mind-boggling range of brush types to choose from, Elements also allows you to change the brush **Opacity** and **Size**. With any brush-based tool engaged, right-clicking in the main window will open the brush menu):

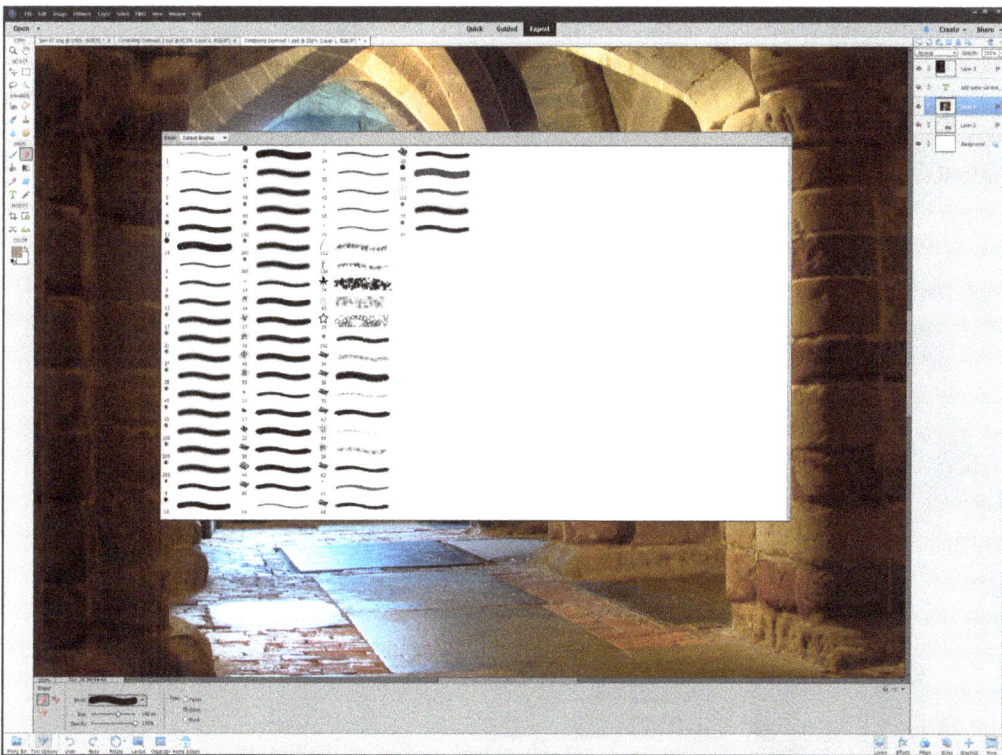

> **Tip**
>
> To choose a different brush tip, right-click anywhere on the image or head over to the tool's **Options** panel. This opens the screen we can see in the preceding screenshot. Grab a corner to stretch it to its full size. Note that there are different brush menus: **Default** brushes, **Assorted** brushes, **Calligraphic** brushes, **Square** brushes, and many more. Most Elements users never get past the **Default** brushes.

Choose the Eraser brush, then select a soft-edged brush tip (indicated by the long red arrow in the following screenshot) from the pop-out brush palette, move it over the image layer you want to work on (short red arrow), and click. It removes all of the pixels in that vicinity. If the **opacity** of the tool is reduced, say, to 50%, you'll have to click twice to remove all the pixels. Operating at a reduced opacity is one of the better ways to edit images because your actions become less obvious. Brush size can assist or hinder retouching. If it's a large, soft-edged brush, its erasing action will extend far beyond the apparent edge of your brush. Start erasing well away from important parts of the image first—in this case, the figure. I gradually removed the dark pixels of the shadow on the base of the vampire layer:

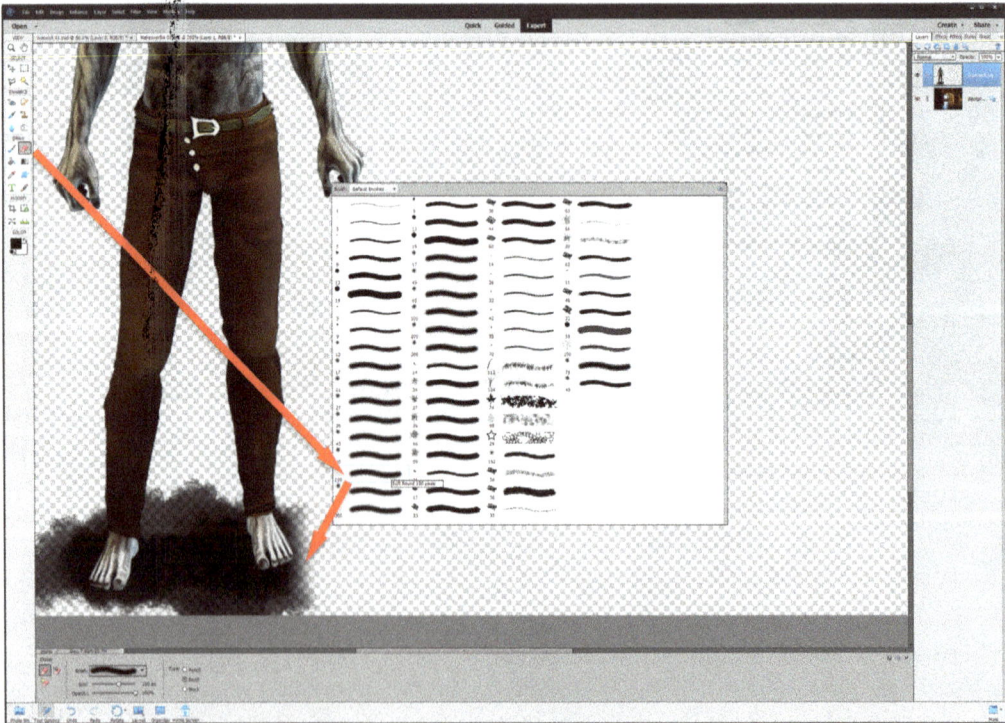

> **Tip**
>
> To make it easier to see what you are erasing, I suggest turning the bottom layer (the base layer) off.
>
> Do this by clicking the tiny **eye icon** located to the left of the layer thumbnail. When it's off, the eye has a red line through it, and if you can't see the eye, you can't see the layer either. Clicking it a second time removes the red line and the layer becomes visible again. The checkerboard effect that's shown in the background indicates **layer transparency**; it's still part of the layer, but there are no pixels in it.

Here, you can see that I have now turned the background layer back on by clicking the **eye icon** a second time. I also clicked the bottom layer in the panel, thereby making it the active layer (highlighted in blue). I think that the background layer is a bit too warm (yellow/red). Due to this, I thought the saturation needed to be reduced considerably so that it was closer to black-and-white than a realistic color. To achieve this, I simply used the **Hue/Saturation** tool (*Ctrl*/*Cmd* + *U*, or go to **Enhance | Adjust Color | Hue/Saturation**) and pulled the **Saturation** slider way over to the left-hand side, effectively reducing the color intensity by around 75%. The background now looks like it's closer in tone to the top layer, but it's still too light:

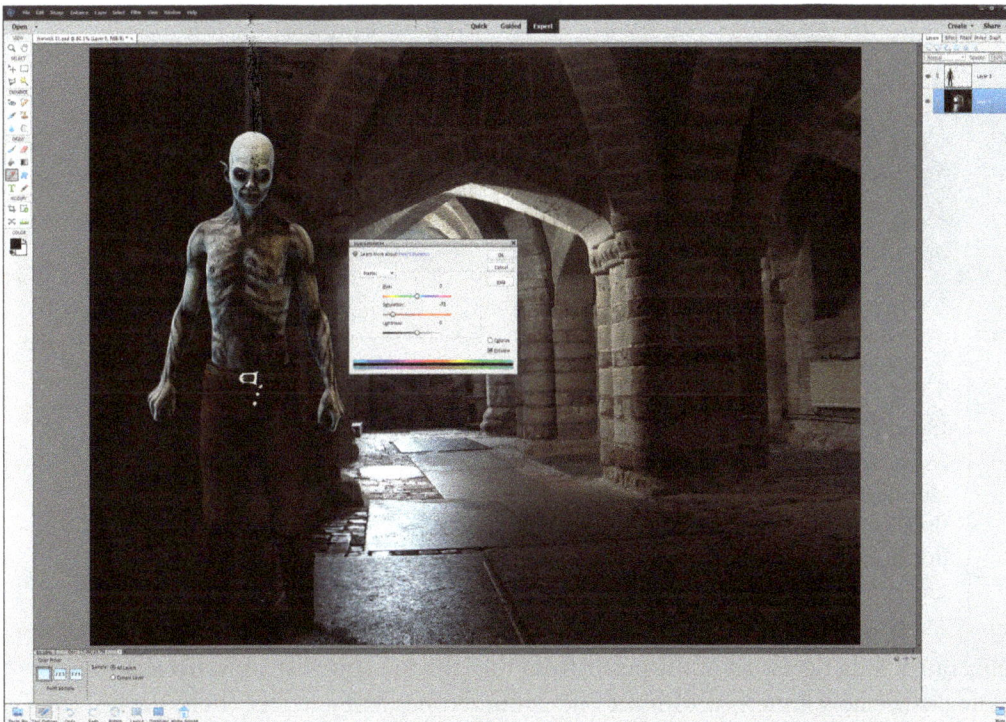

To make the background image appear closer in tone to the vampire image, I darkened it using the **Levels** tool, pushing the mid-tone slider to the right (pictured) to make all of the tones in the frame a little darker. Sometimes this simple action makes all the difference to the illusion that this is a single shot rather than an assemblage of different images cobbled together.

Now, the background and foreground elements are beginning to look like they were shot in similar light, which we know they weren't:

Tip

If you like the idea of creating your own multi-image art, special effects, and complex projects, it really pays to start your own collection of **textures**, **skies**, **clouds**, **fonts**, **brushes**, **masks**, and more. All of these can be used to refine the illusion that what you are looking at is not a collection of mismatched stuff downloaded off of the internet, but rather a complete image with synchronous and continuous tone.

I deliberately didn't erase all of the pixels from the vampire layer's shadow because I wanted to see how it merged with the background tones first—in fact, it's so dark that you can't see it at all. Problem solved!

I think the vampire layer, which is clearly an illustration, has more contrast than the background, so, by clicking from background layer to the vampire figure layer, I used Levels a second time to lower the highlight brightness. That's what the lower **Output Levels** scale is used for (shown with an arrow in the following screenshot).

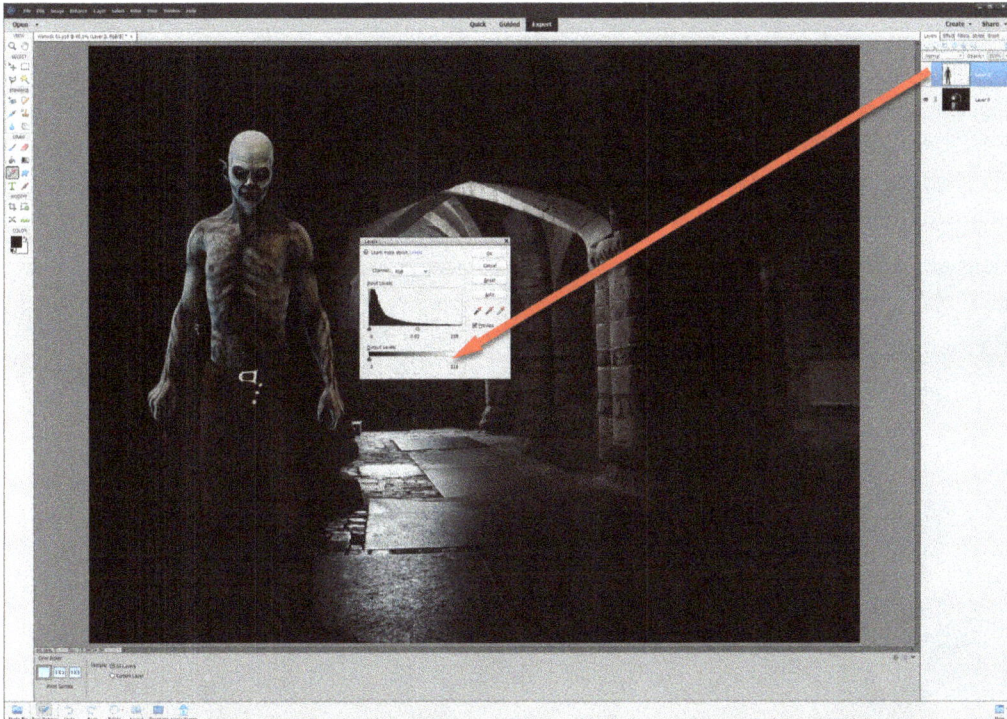

Shifting that right-hand slider to the left lowers the highlight density. The left-hand slider, when moved to the right, lowers the density of the black tones. Note that some care must be taken with these Output sliders. If pushed too far, the image loses all of its contrast and can appear flat and uninteresting. But used sparingly, it's a tremendous way to bring contrast back to acceptable levels.

> **Tip**
>
> Erasing, painting, drawing and retouching can be quite tricky because it's not easy to draw with a mouse—it's a bit like painting with a bar of soap—but if you practice, it will become easier. One option is to try drawing with a **graphics tablet**, a device that emulates your mouse actions, but with a cordless pen, which makes the process feel a lot more natural and easier to control. Most tablets can also be programmed to use keyboard shortcuts and perform other functions, making them a very handy accessory if you spend a lot of time and effort using the brush-based tools in this program.

Now that the background has been desaturated and the vampire layer has had the contrast lowered, the illusion is taking shape. Let's add **text**. Elements has a feature called the **Horizontal Type** tool, which is used to add text to any image. Press the *T* key to access this tool or mouse over the **Tool Bar** and click the **T** symbol.

It's not the easiest of tools to use. Click once anywhere in the image and you'll see a blinking **text insertion point**, like any normal word processing program. Clicking once adds the text insertion point, while typing immediately after puts the text into the document to the right of that point; however, if you click, hold, and drag the cursor across the image first, a **text box** is drawn (highlighted in red in the following screenshot). If you let go and start typing, the text entered will be restrained by the box edges. Click-and-drag one of the text box corner handles to make the box smaller/larger:

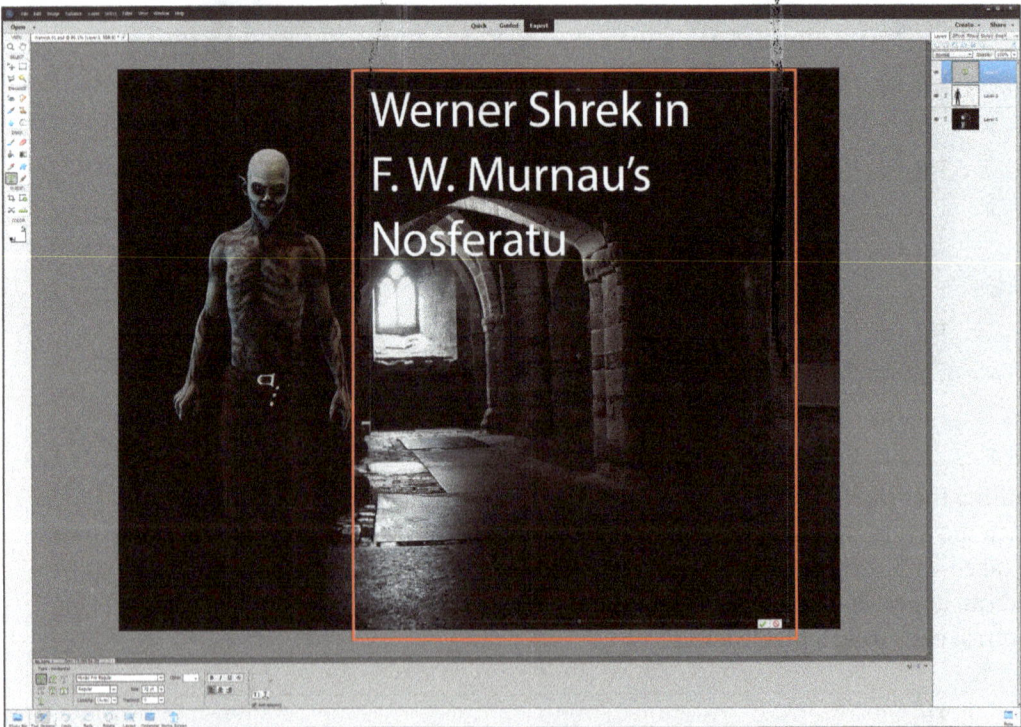

Tip

You will also note that, as soon as you type in the document, a special **Text Layer** appears in the **Layer** panel. By default, it picks up the Foreground color, black, but if you need a different colored text, a different point size, leading, or style, then all of this can be changed from the **Type Options** panel.

Text, by default, starts as black - or whatever was previously set in the **Foreground Color Picker** (the upper square of color at the bottom of the **Tool Bar**). If that color is not what you require, select the text first (double- or treble-click inside the text to do this), click the color palette, and choose a more appropriate color:

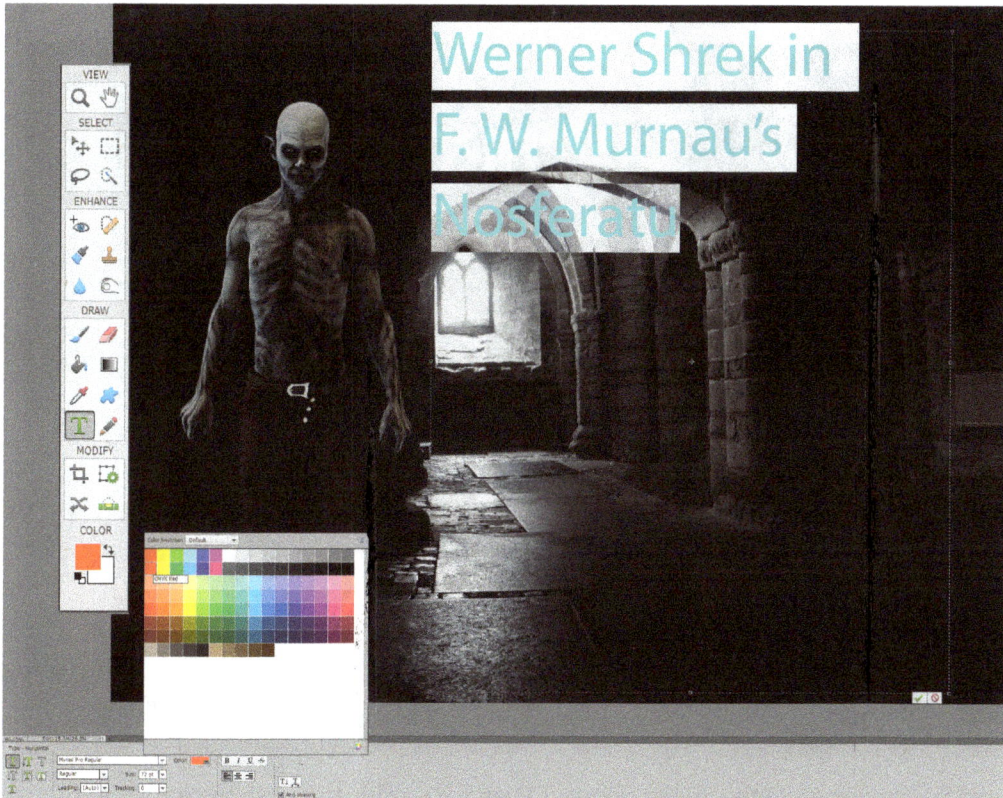

Tip

Note that, if your picture is sized to 72 dpi (as many files are when they come straight out of the camera), then when you click on the image, the text insertion point might be very small and hard to see. Open the **Image Size** feature and, without resampling the entire file, change the resolution to 300 dpi, click **OK**, and save before trying the text again. At 300 dpi the text should appear at a more reasonable size. Note that there's little to be gained by setting the resolution higher than this (to make the text larger) because 300 dpi is the default print resolution.

When text is selected, its color—in this example, red—**inverts**, which is why it looks a bit weird in the previous screenshot. Note that everything you can do with text in a regular word processor can be done in Elements. It's a little fiddly to get right at first, but you can use features such as left/right/center justification, leading, and point size to add to the design of any individual text layer:

I ended up choosing a gothic typeface called **Deutsch Gothic** to match the mood of this 1922 silent movie classic. It seems to fit the mood of the illustration nicely.

> **Tip**
>
> Sometimes, text becomes unreadable when laid across an image. Changing the font color is one quick way to make it more legible. Another technique is to add a drop shadow. It's easy to do this in Elements. Select the text layer, click the **Styles** panel, and choose the **Drop Shadow** option from the drop-down menu. Select a drop shadow style and click once to add the effect to that layer. To modify those shadow characteristics, choose the layer; note that it now has an FX icon added to it. Click this to open the **Effects** panel and make your adjustments from there (that is, adjust the height of the shadow, its density and size, and so on).

Note

If you don't have this font or anything that closely resembles the style that you might want to emulate in any project, one suggestion is to use a free font, downloaded off of the internet. I use a site called www.dafont.com to source special fonts when I want to make a bit more of a statement than just using Helvetica or Times New Roman. The fonts on this site seem to be very reliable—most are put there by designers who have used them in commercial projects and no longer care if they are in the public domain. Most of the fonts on this site are available for personal use. Some can also be used commercially. Check the small print carefully before you use someone else's font without their permission. Fonts, on macOS or Windows, are stored in the communal **Font** folder, so once your new font has been downloaded, it can be copied and pasted into that folder. Restart Elements and it should magically appear in the **Font** drop-down menu in Elements and every other application that uses text.

I'm sure you are now wondering why I had that **texture layer** at the beginning of this section. I occasionally add a **texture layer** to image projects if I want to create the feeling of age, deterioration, or grunge (one reason why I shoot interesting textures while I am out and about with a camera—I can use them for projects later on):

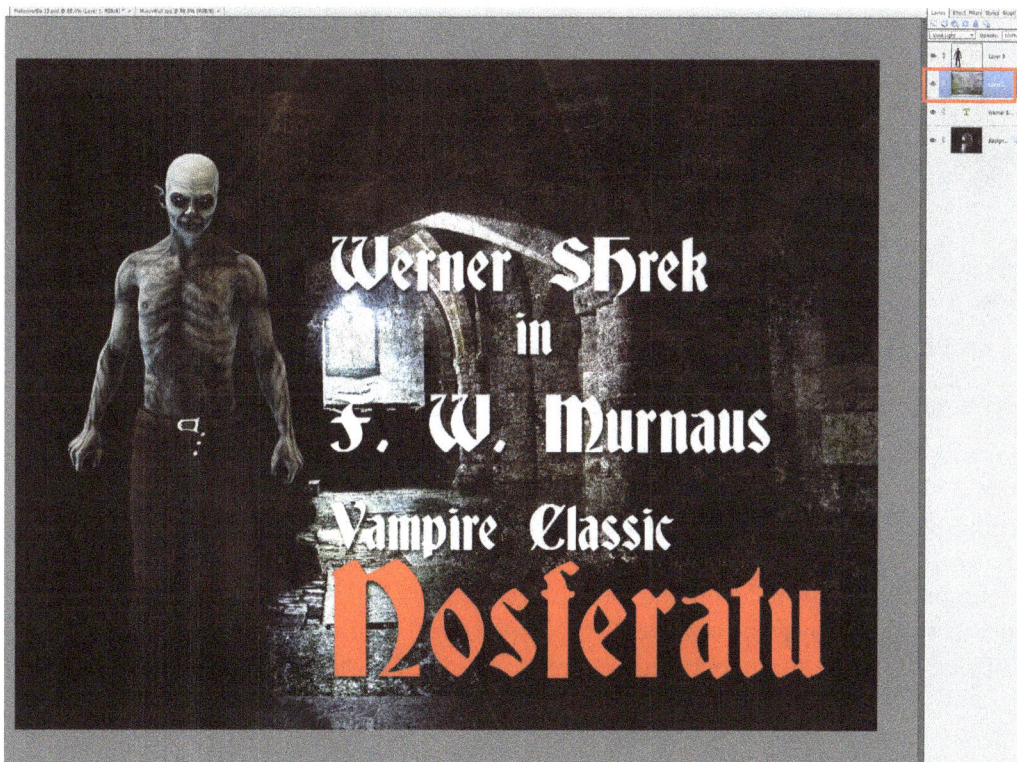

In this example, I dragged that texture image from the **Photo Bin** into the Document; you can see it sitting in-between the top layer and the background layer (highlighted in red in the previous screenshot). If it lands as the top layer, because it's opaque, it will cover the entire image. So, to move that layer, click, hold, and drag it from the top to the center of the layer stack; let go when you see the lower layer highlighted in blue. Treat it like shuffling a deck of cards; it takes a little trial and error to get it in the right position because, if you release that layer too soon, it flips back to where it came from. Drag it until you see the line separating the two lower layers lighting up with a blue line (between the two layers), and then let go:

With your **texture** layer in place in the **Layer** panel, change the layer's **Blend Mode** from **Normal** (the default setting) to **Soft Light** or **Hard Light** and note that the texture now becomes see through, blending with the bottom layer only. The vampire layer remains untouched, but the cathedral crypt now looks 200 years older. If the aging effect is too abrupt, adjust it by reducing the texture layer's Opacity. If it is not strong enough, duplicate the layer (by going to **Layer | Duplicate Layer**). You can read about Layers and Blend Modes in greater detail in *Chapter 6, Advanced Techniques: Layers and Masking*.

> **Important note**
>
> What's a **Blend Mode?** Blend modes can befound in both the **Tool** options and the **Layer** palette. Elements has 25 different modes in this drop-down menu, most of which might not seem to do anything to the image at all. They are there to change how the blend-mode layer interacts with the layer underneath it, which is why there's never a **Blend Mode** accessible on the bottom layer. (See *Chapter 6, Advanced Editing Techniques*, for more information on using blend modes).

Summary

In this chapter, we moved through a series of makeover exercises designed to demonstrate the power of Photoshop Elements. Starting with a simple brightness problem, we then stepped it up to include fixing underexposure in a RAW file and simple spot retouching in a sky scene, to full-blown color correction and contrast enhancement and detailed skin repair, before finishing up with an assemblage of images brought together to make a digital illustration.

It was a bit of a rollercoaster of experiences, so don't feel bad if the more advanced makeovers felt too hard at this stage; you have learned that you can fix everything from basic brightness and contrast issues to removing stuff that is inappropriate for the shot. You are now well on your way to becoming an accomplished image retoucher and photo editor!

In the next chapter, you'll learn how to work with some of Elements's excellent project-based tools. Essentially, these comprise a number of fairly complex actions that have been semi-automated to both make the learning curve less steep for the user and to make the results appear more professional. You'll love how they are both easy to use, yet allow you to produce awesome results with very little prior experience.

5
Easy Creative Projects

In this chapter, you'll find a wide range of interesting special effects, most of which can be applied to your images with speed and ease.

I have always liked Elements' slightly alternative approach to image editing, specifically because it includes a lot of project-based editing skills rather than concentrating just on the pure skills of image editing. However, over the years, this has changed—Elements now boasts some of the most sophisticated editing features that you'd normally expect from the top end of town—while still retaining awesome features such as panorama stitching, calendar making, and scene cleaning.

This chapter highlights the sort of features anyone can use to produce great results without having to climb that steep learning curve—that's coming in *Chapter 6, Advanced Techniques: Layers and Masking*!

In this chapter, we will cover the following topics:

- Finding inspiration on the Home Page
- Discovering easy-to-use artistic effects
- Creating widescreen panoramas
- Panoramas using the Guided Edit workspace
- Advanced panorama-shooting techniques
- Making a jigsaw panorama
- Using Photomerge Scene Cleaner
- Making a simple slideshow
- Creating custom calendars
- Creating custom greeting cards
- Making a custom Facebook page
- Keyboard shortcuts

Finding inspiration on the Home Page

How many times have we opened Elements, let's say, from a recent trip, and just stared at the page not knowing where to start?

This type of editing block happens for a number of reasons: we shoot a lot of images and are often overwhelmed by the sheer volume of visual information collected, and sometimes we just don't have the experience to come up with new ideas about how to use them creatively.

This is the **Home Page**. Initially, it might not look very interesting, but take a closer look. The thumbnails along the top of this panel refer to web-based sources of inspiration, much the same as the eLive page did in Elements 2018. The three buttons in the lower right-hand side are shortcuts to open **Organizer**, **Photo Editor**, and **Video Editor**, and below that, there's links to recently opened files. In Elements 2020, you'll see a couple of additions in the Auto Creations area (lower, left). The following screenshot is one of five panels suggesting creative projects using photos that have been taken directly from the **Organizer**—the idea of presenting creative themes using your own images carries more impact than using someone else's:

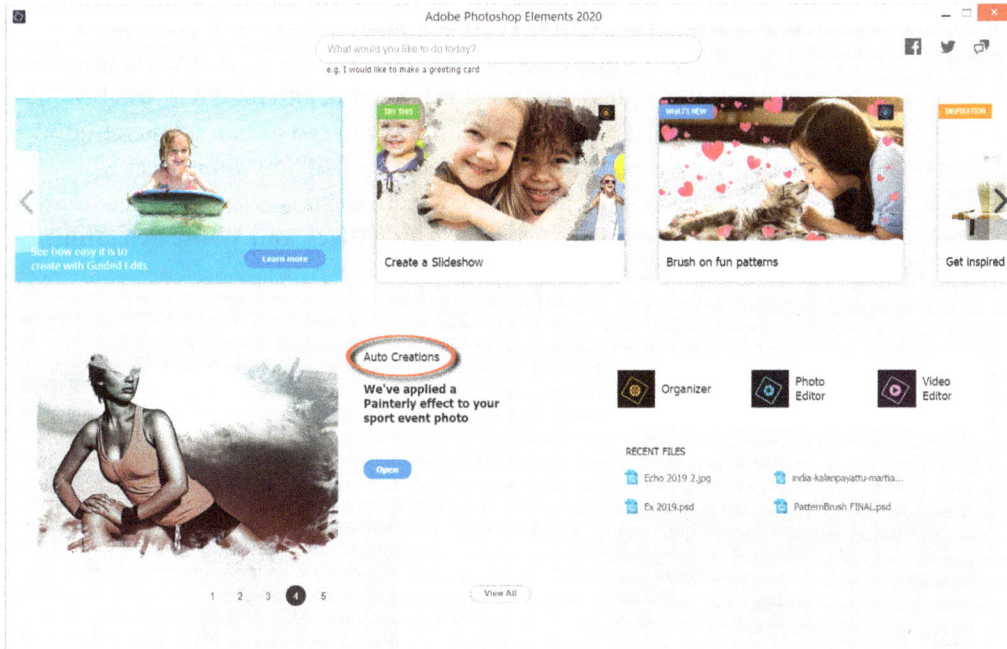

Editing and just leaving the images in a folder somewhere on a desktop is not being very creative—you have to get out and show the world, or at least your family, what you can create with all of those amazing pictures you shoot. You need inspiration!

It might take a few hours or days to populate the Auto Creations pages with your stuff (it depends on how many images you have in Organizer, and how long they have been there). Either click through the numbered pages (from **1-5**) or click the **View All** button to see everything at once.

These are not just illustrations of what Auto Creations might look like—if you click the **Play** button for the slideshow, for example, it actually plays a slideshow of your images, complete with a backing soundtrack. It's a very neat feature and, although it inevitably chooses the wrong images for a collage or video slideshow, you can click the **Open** button alongside each preview to bring the project into Elements, so that you can perfect what it started, adding different images, sound, and so on. Creatively, this is a good place to start. New Auto Creations appearing in this version include **Black and White Selection**, **Painterly**, **Depth of Field**, and **Pattern Brush**:

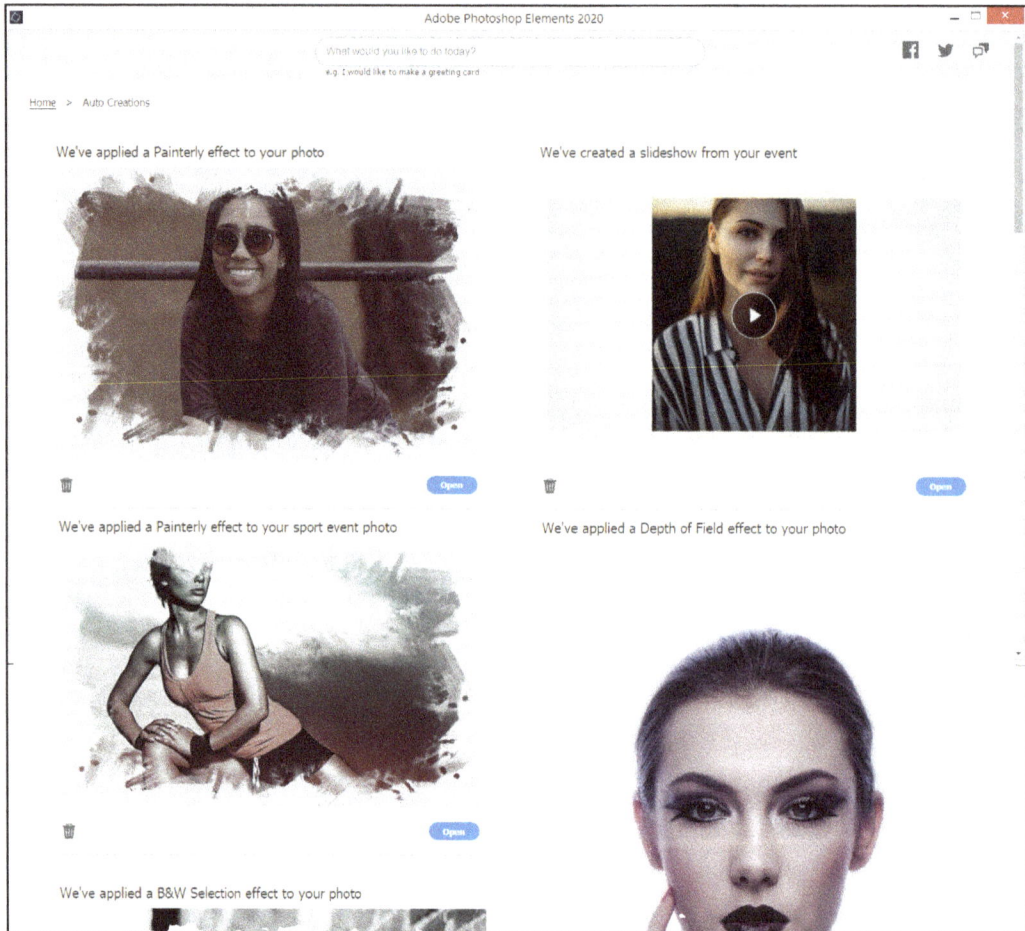

Adding artistic effects

Elements 2020 is heading the way of the smartphone. By this, I mean that the visual effects are increasingly thumbnail-driven. You open a file, have a look at a range of special effects on offer, choose one, and apply it to your snap by clicking on the thumbnail. Nothing could be easier, and while doing this doesn't educate you on how the effect is really achieved, it makes the process of enhancing your work simple, fast, and approachable for the majority of camera users, who don't want to spend hours in front of a screen.

A *look* is essentially a style that defines how a set of pictures might appear as a group. For example, they could all be **sepia-tinted** to give them an *aged look*, or they could be converted into **black and white** to give them a slightly different *arty* or even a *documentary* look.

Elements 2020 has a surprisingly wide range of **image presets**. These are best described as automated software *recipes* where, at the click of a button, a file is converted into black and white, texturized, or color toned. In some cases, this involves a very complex series of actions that produce a suitable WOW! visual moment. You then save that version and move on to the next edit.

Some of these presets come from Photoshop CC, a program that allows you to actually record, save, and use your own custom presets—these are called **Actions**. Elements also contains a few basic **Actions**, but we are not going to look at them here because they aren't very good. The supplied **Actions** in Elements haven't changed in the last 10 years. Don't get me wrong, it's possible to import Photoshop-created **Actions** into Elements, but this can be problematic because if the action includes a feature that's not shared by the two programs (which is quite possible), it won't work.

The illustrations here are a few different *looks* that have been created using some of the older special effects found in Elements' **Expert** edit mode's **Effects Panel**. Some of these are decidedly dated in their looks, but being able to apply such a range of effects in a few seconds is a great way to add pizzazz to your shots.

You might not like all of the looks created here but don't forget, if one appeals, you can then edit it further to modify what the automated process throws at you to be more to your taste:

That said, if we look at the **Effects** panel in Elements' **Quick** Edit window, you'll see 11 preset *looks*. All have five versions of the main theme so, in reality, there are 55 different and, I think, fantastic *looks* to play with:

Let's say I like the **Lithograph** effect; I could describe how to make this using the **Expert** edit mode and a number of different processes. This would entail at least one page of instructions so that I can run through the techniques that are needed to make something similar. You might tune out halfway through the page, so clicking on one button to achieve the same is a vastly more attractive proposition. Give it a go and see for yourself how easy it is to get a great look with only a small investment in time.

Because presets are generic, they might not work on all images. Alternatively, you might find that you need to lighten or darken your shots before or after the preset is applied to get it to look just right, but it's still a great starting point. The following are some more preset samples from the excellent **Quick** mode's **Effects** panel:

Here's a selection of some rather racy Andy Warhol-type looks (**Effects | Textures | Rubber Stamp**). The process to create such an effect is really quite complex, but as with many cool things in this application, all you do is click a button and it does the hard work for you:

Interestingly (or confusingly), the **Expert** edit workspace features preset effects that are mostly legacy features from previous versions of Elements, most of which I don't consider as useful as those in the **Quick Edit Mode**. There, you'll find 11 different categories, which include: **Smart Looks**, **Tint**, **Seasons**, **Pencil Sketch**, **Toy Camera**, **Black and White**, **Lithograph**, **Cross Process** (one example of this is seen below), **Split Tone**, **Vintage**, and finally, **Light Leak**.

Exploit the easy stuff

One of Photoshop Elements' main strengths is its ability to add or create neat-looking "looks" in your images without you having to complete a degree in applied physics. As you have seen in the previous section, it's so easy to choose an effect from the Quick Edit mode and apply it to any of your image files in seconds, and for the most part, the results are pretty good:

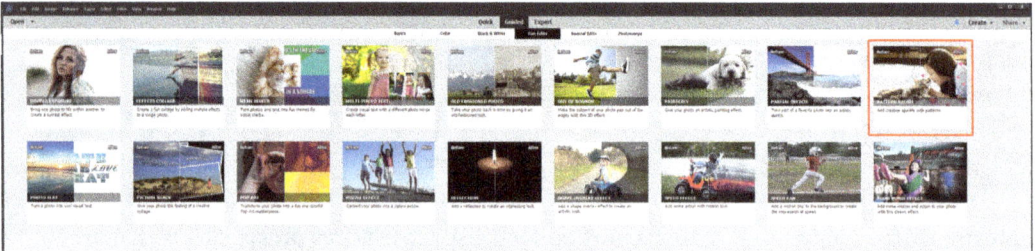

But don't miss out on exploiting the Guided edit mode either as this is packed with very cool and creative material. A recent addition to the stable of effects is a feature called the Pattern Brush. I mentioned in *Chapter 1, Photoshop Elements Features Overview* that I suspect this is a serious reworking of the old Pattern Stamp tool from Photoshop CC, but in a refined and fully functional format. The Photoshop version never really offered much in terms of practical application to the photographer. The new Elements 2020 version works like a dream: select the subject of the image first (using its new subject selection AI), then lay a pattern of graphics around and behind the subject, but not over it, unless you click that option:

There are 15 different graphics to choose from. Each can be drawn at random by adjusting the **Size**, **Scatter**, and **Opacity** settings. You can also click **Fill** to spread that graphic right across the canvas, including the subject, or just keep it under control using the (supplied) brush tool. It's easy, fast and effective. In truth, the Guided edit mode provides some very useful special effects, which are, for the most part, quick, simple, and easy to apply; here are three neat looks that took me less than five minutes to create: **Black and White>B&W Selection**, **Special Edits>Watercolor Effect**, and **Fun Edits>Partial Sketch**:

Colorize – AI-driven creativity

You might not like all of the looks, and you might think that they aren't really that much different from the previous versions. To an extent you'd be correct, but one feature that caught my eye was called Colorize Photo—you'll find it under the **Enhance** menu in the **Expert Edit** window.

Initially, I was drawn to this effect because I have actually spent many years hand-coloring black and white images for sale around the city I live in. It's great fun, but involves a lot of printing, coloring in, erasing, ripping up prints, and starting again. The oils used added a permanence to the print, so they naturally lasted a long time—I'm sure you might find the odd hand-colored photo among your family albums. Before color photography was an affordable thing, this was the only way to get a color print!

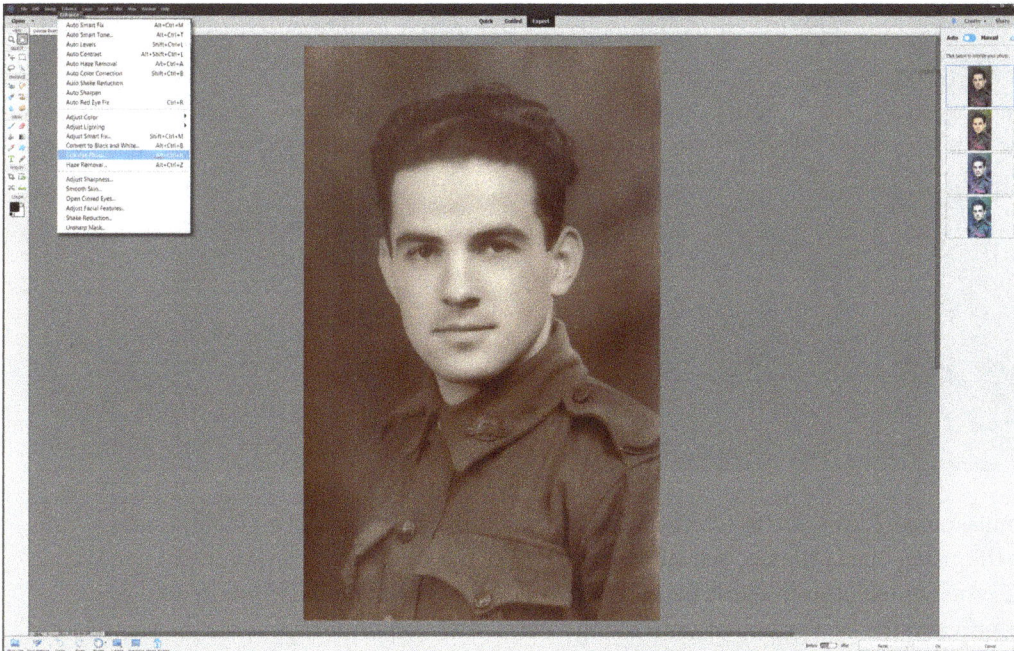

To use this, all that's needed is a black and white image (OK, OK, in this example, I started with a sepia picture) and you choose one of the colorized looks from the panel on the right-hand side of the window. Nothing could be easier! I was excited about this because I thought of all the hours I'd spent physically painting, then correcting and repainting prints, and was secretly hoping this would at least be as impressive as the example touted by Adobe. Sadly, this example was a bit of a disaster, even once I converted it to a black and white file and tried again. It just did not look real.

Then I noticed that Adobe has included a manual override mode in this new AI-driven feature. Brilliant, because this result was not looking good:

Manual mode allows you to select different bits of the image for a color change one at a time. Do this using one of the two selection tools offered: the Selection Brush or the Magic Wand. The problem with this image is that there's no distinct separation between the soldier's uniform and the background, thus making a clean selection near impossible. As you select one object in the photo, add a droplet—this means that any tint chosen floods the selected area with color. You choose the tint and the depth of color from the drop-down color checker and it adds automatically. If it is too light or dark, just choose another color then move on to select another part of the image, then add a droplet and another color.

I found that the Selection Brush was the most effective tool for this picture, but as you might be able to see in the next screenshot, the selection worked well for the skin tones because they were so bright, but the uniform color bleeds into the background a bit. It's not really an accurate result, but I think it looks like a genuine hand-colored vintage photo.

This is a brilliant tool because with most of the other examples you see here, the automatic AI-generated select-and-color process actually works beautifully:

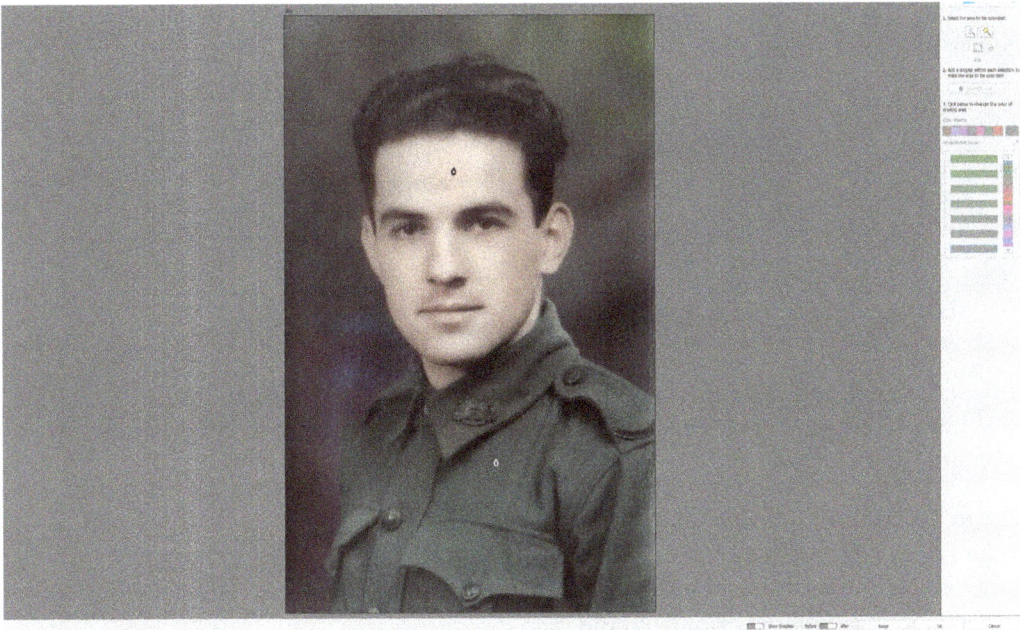

I tried using this tool on this beautiful Hollywood promo shot of Jean Simmons, and all four AI-driven examples worked perfectly.

I then tried to improve what Adobe Sensei had produced in its auto mode with my own manually painted version. It took around 20 minutes and, although it is certainly a lot cleaner in terms of painting accuracy, unless you blow it up to 400%, you'll probably not appreciate the added work - see the comparison with the original image overleaf:

In this screenshot, you can clearly see the different droplets, each one denoting a differently selected part of the image. The active droplet, the one currently being colored in, is highlighted in blue.

In the final version, I was able to add small areas of color to her lipstick, earrings, and necklace (that's a lot of diamonds!). The combination of using a quality picture and the colors selected produced a result that looked as though it really was a professionally made hand-colored promotional print from the thirties:

The previous and following images show how well this automated coloring-in process works with no user intervention required. It worked fine on the two old family snaps (scanned files) as well as the more recently created landscape. And as this last example is so simple in its structure, the light coloring effect is particularly apt.

Don't forget that to get the best from this effect, use the **Sponge Brush** tool (in both its **Desaturate** and Saturate modes) to remove color that has spilled over into the wrong areas, as well as to boost color in other areas that might need help. If the effect still does not work, I'd **Revert** the image to its original state (**Edit | Revert**) and try adjusting the contrast using Levels (*Ctrl/Cmd + L*) and try again.

Creating widescreen panoramas

Everyone likes a panorama, which is why smartphones and compact cameras have an automated panorama feature. These usually work well—I find myself using my iPhone for this all the time because it's so convenient. The following is a photo I took in Ait Ben Haddhu, Morocco:

This was a five-frame panorama, complete with a black border and Arabic style text. We all visit beautiful places on our travels, many of which are too large or too majestic to warrant just one snap. A panorama is the perfect answer. The following is a photo I shot of Himeji, Japan's best-preserved castle:

I still create panoramas using a DSLR camera and Photoshop Elements because the image quality is far better than one that's produced with a smartphone—plus, if Elements makes a mistake stitching the different sections, I can usually fix it. Smartphone panoramas are convenient, but their tiny image sensors are unable to cope with high contrast scenes and fast subject movement.

This panorama was taken at the Imperial War Museum, Duxford, one of the UK's best aviation museums. There were about 10 aircraft, some on the ground, some suspended from the ceiling. Getting a clear shot of just one plane was hard enough, but the entire hangar? The best option was to shoot five frames, then use Elements to stitch them together:

Here is a smartphone panorama taken in Ethiopia. It's OK, but there's a lot of *smudginess* in the sky where the software hasn't blended the tones together correctly:

Unfortunately, most of us are quite lazy (myself included), so we find the attraction of shooting panoramas with a smartphone irresistible. And if you only ever look at the results on the smartphone's small screen, you might never get to appreciate the technology's shortcomings.

But save the file and display it on a computer screen and you'll begin to appreciate how much better multiple high-resolution sections assembled using Photomerge can be. It's a very powerful software feature.

Panoramas the easy way

Because panorama stitching is not an automated process, you have to do a bit of preparation work to set up a panorama. Here's what I suggest:

1. With the camera set to **Program** mode, point the camera at the scene you want to make into a widescreen panorama and take a **test snap**. Use the **Exposure Compensation** feature on the camera to make the image lighter/darker if needed.

2. If you are happy with the look of the exposure, delete that test and take a snap of your left foot.

3. In your mind, divide the scene very roughly into five vertical sections and start snapping (use more sections if necessary).

4. Start at the left-hand side and take a shot, shift the viewfinder to the right, overlapping the frame by up to 20%, and take a second shot, then repeat this process until you have covered the entire width of the scene.

5. Finally, take another picture, this time of your right foot. This should help you when it comes to finding those panorama sections from among all of those other images shot at the same time, which might be months or even years later.

6. Open just those sections in Elements.

7. Navigate to the **Guided** edit workspace.

8. Choose the **Photomerge | Photomerge Panorama** option from the menu at the top of the screen:

9. Select all of the panorama sections through the **Photo Bin** first, and then click the **Create Panorama** button on the lower right-hand side of the Photomerge window. Elements goes into action, selecting all of the images and then matching edges, then arranging all of the sections into one widescreen image, blended together using a series of clever black and white masks:

10. Photomerge will ask whether you want the blank edges filled. If you click **Yes**, Elements uses its **content aware intelligence** to fill the empty spaces with pixels. If you elect not to do this, then you'll have to crop the image to remove any unevenness around the edges:

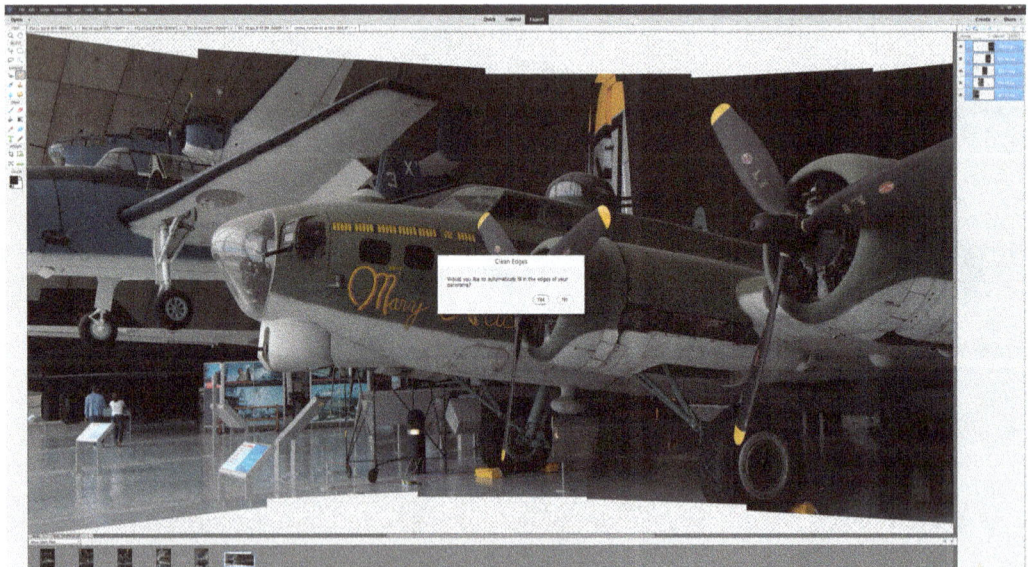

11. Save the entire panorama as a Photoshop (.psd) file in case you need to come back to it to make final edits. Alternatively, to make it smaller, **flatten** the multiple layers (**Layer | Flatten Image**), then save it as a JPEG file. In this screenshot, you can clearly see the dotted selection lines that delineate where Elements has added pixels to the composition. In this panorama, the **Auto Fill** process has worked well, but it doesn't work on every image, especially if it contains a lot of detail. If this is the case, you might just have to crop off the rough edges:

The port of Sur in Oman looked like it was the setting for *Sinbad the Sailor*. This was a big, wide scene, 12 sections in all, but here the width had to be cropped by 50% to fit the page:

Another massive, wide landscape with an incredible amount of detail from the front to the back proves an easy task for Photoshop Elements' Photomerge. In this example image, which was photographed in Oman's Jebel highlands, there were six frames stitched together. Once that was done, I added a little more contrast with the **Levels** tool (*Ctrl/Cmd + L*) and boosted the color slightly with the **Hue/Saturation** command (*Ctrl/Cmd + U*) before finally adding some sharpening using the **Unsharp Mask** filter (**Filter | Sharpen | Unsharp Mask**):

Working tips

However, like all things to do with software, the process can go wrong. Here are a few practical tips to make your panorama stitching more successful:

- Always shoot vertically; that way, if you have to crop the image because the sections were not shot on the level, it isn't so problematic in terms of the overall proportions of the panorama.

- Use a tripod, making sure that the panning head is 100% level (most tripods have a bubble level built into the tripod head).

- Choose subjects that aren't too close. Close subjects, especially ones that contain a lot of detail, make it harder for the software to align.

- Zoom in with the lens slightly. It's better to take more shots than fewer wide-angle shots. Wide-angle shots will be distorted so the verticals will not be 100% upright, making it tricky to line up in Elements.

- Shoot JPEG or RAW. RAW will always be better but, because they are much bigger, it will take longer.

Advanced panorama techniques

For a greater level of control over your panorama-making process, I suggest the following camera and software processing tricks:

- Shoot in **Manual Metering** mode. Take a test shot in the approximate middle of the proposed scene and use that as your base exposure.

- Shoot with the **Auto Focus** turned **Off**. Manually focus on the scene and leave it off for the entire sequence.

- Use a leveled **tripod**.

- Some professionals even create a custom **White Balance** setting for the panorama because, in some situations, the light, and therefore the color, might change between section one and section five.

- If you think that you have forgotten to include one bit of the scene, it's fine to **reshoot an area** that you think you might have missed. The sequence isn't important. I have actually mixed verticals with angled and horizontal images in one panorama and it still finds the edges and stitches them together perfectly.

- If the **Automatic** function doesn't pull everything together correctly, try again and use one of the other options: **Perspective**, **Cylindrical**, **Spherical**, **Collage**, or **Reposition**. One of these is bound to work!

These **Settings** options can also be useful to experiment with:

- **Blend images together** should always be used, unless you want to reposition each section manually and then adjust each layer's tone manually (time-consuming).

- **Vignette Removal**: Some lenses tend to be darker at the edges than in the center of the lens. Merging two vignetted sections together makes this look even worse. This feature lightens the edges and gets rid of the problem.

- **Geometric Distortion Correction**: This helps when there's optical distortion in the image, typically when you're shooting things such as architecture and straight lines.

- **Content Aware Fill Transparent Areas**: Even panoramas shot meticulously, with a tripod, might not end up looking 100% rectilinear. When this occurs, Elements creates a space to fill in the unevenness, leaving you with the options of either cropping it to a proper rectangle, leaving it as is, or filling it with the AI feature.

Considering that you are effectively combining multiple high-resolution files into one panorama, don't be surprised if the final version is hundreds of megabytes in size. Elements will automatically save this new creation as `Untitled_panorama1.jpg`, unless you specifically give it a *real* name.

Making a jigsaw panorama

One of the problems you will encounter when stitching a panorama is that if it's too wide, it's nearly impossible to print. Although it might be 48 inches wide, it might only be eight inches high, especially if all of your sections were shot horizontally. One fun and creative answer to this is to zoom in slightly and shoot multiple *decks* so that, even after cropping, the image isn't compromised. The following is a photo I shot in Fes, Morocco:

Don't think that you have to shoot on the level all of the time. This is a **jigsaw panorama**, a random shoot of 37 sections, shot in three decks, from left to right. I really like the fact that although Elements does an amazing job of lining up all of the images near-perfectly, it's not put off by having images at an angle, horizontally, vertically, zoomed in, or in wide-angle settings. It handles such a challenge with ease (although this took 20 minutes to put together). If you think you have missed a section while shooting the sections, it's easy enough to go back over the scene and shoot a few extra frames to cover any possible bald patches. I love the randomness of the edges in this technique, so I'm quite happy to leave the edges uncropped for effect.

The final version was well over one gigabyte and could print over two meters wide. As a working tip, try reducing the file size, either while shooting in the field or using Elements so that it does not over-tax your computer.

Using Photomerge Scene Cleaner

Elements started out offering the Panorama stitching utility on its own, but within a few versions, the engineers over at Adobe came up with a number of other very useful applications for Photomerge, including the ability to remove people and moving objects from a scene with absolute ease.

How can you do this? We have all visited places in our travels that are very beautiful but, when we get there, it seems there's barely any standing room because, of course, everyone else wants to visit that same place too:

Busy or clean? The **Scene Cleaner** is an efficient automated copy and paste feature that's designed to produce less populated shots with the least amount of hassle.

Like the process of shooting panorama sections to stitch later, the trick with the **Scene Cleaner** is to remember to shoot the raw material while you are still on location. However, unlike panorama sections, the idea here is to position yourself quietly in one place and take between three and five shots of the same scene over a short period of time. Having a tripod, or a wall on which to rest the camera against, will really help the line-up process:

1. Set yourself up in front of the scene and take a **test shot** to get the exposure to 100%.

2. Take your first image, then wait a short time for those people walking past to move to a **different position** in the scene and take a second shot. Repeat this process a few times.

3. Start Elements and open the images that were taken at the busy location:

4. Click the **Guided** edit mode and choose **Photomerge | Scene Cleaner**. It will ask you to choose two or more images from the **Photo Bin** to use in the technique. In this screenshot, I have four images to work on:

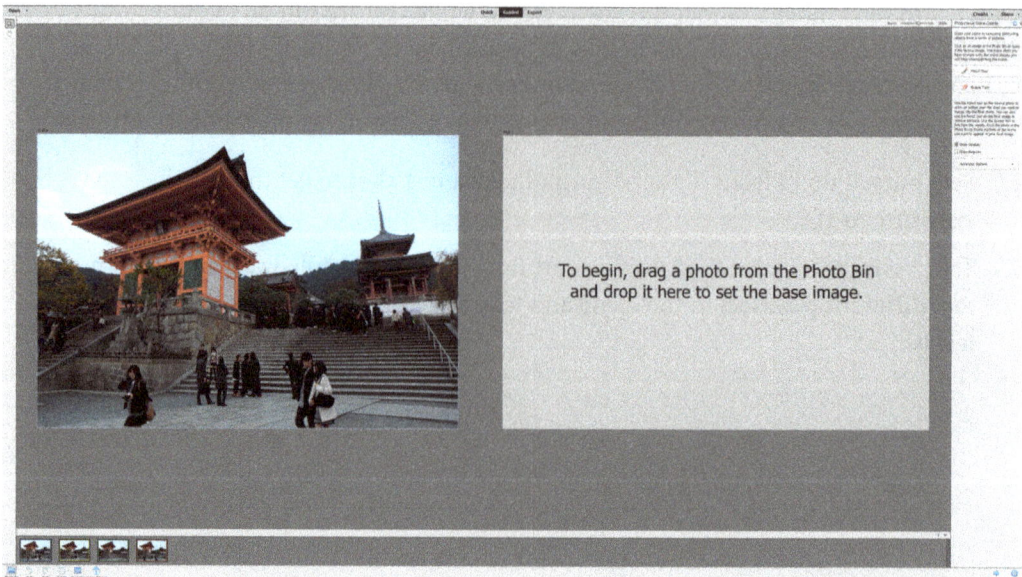

5. In the twin windows that open, the **Target** (final) is the right-hand pane, while the **Source**, that is, the image where the *clean* pixels are being copied from, comes from whichever image is loaded in the left-hand pane. Choose the image with the fewest people in it and drag it up into that right-hand pane as a start point:

6. In this screenshot, I pushed the yellow highlighted image thumbnail to the right-hand side main window. The idea is to then note where people are standing in the right-hand image and choose a different shot for the left-hand pane in which no one is standing in the same place as the people in the right-hand pane. Here, they just happen to be identical, so I need to grab a different one to put into the left-hand pane before we can work the magic:

7. You have a **Pencil** tool. Make sure this is active (click the **Pencil** tool button in the top-right and draw around an (unpopulated) area in the left-hand image that roughly corresponds to the area that's populated in the right-hand pane). This sounds complex, but you only have to do this a couple of times to see exactly what it's doing: automatically copying the pixels marked out by the pencil tool and pasting them into the same location in the other image, on top of and (hopefully) covering the people in the right-hand image. The wider a shape you draw, the more real estate it copies and pastes over to the opposite image.

Use the **Eraser** on your pencil marks if the process has copied too much. Trim off a slice of the pencil's thickness to see whether it's enough to replace fewer pixels, hence making the copy process more accurate.

> **Tip**
>
> Remember to shoot the base files while still on location! Be patient—you might have to wait more than a few minutes, especially if you are in a popular location. Wait until people move, then shoot again and again. You might not **clean** the entire scene of people, but at least you can thin them out.

8. Find a second **Source** image by double-clicking the thumbnails in the **Photo Bin** and repeat the process to see whether you can rid the scene of all visitors:

Adobe has combined a rather complex select, feather, copy, paste, and blend operation into this easy-to-use, fun, and very effective feature. You'll note that all of the images are cleverly color-coded, making it easier to identify which bit comes from which file.

Refine the transfer process by choosing to use **Pixel Blending** from the **Advanced** options menu.

9. Once you're happy with your **cleaning**, click the **Next** button at the base of the page—this allows the software to fully process the images together as a high-resolution file and save the resulting magical transformation.

If this is shot hand-held (not recommended, but often unavoidable!), Photomerge has an amazing **Alignment** tool, which can be found in its **Advanced** options menu:

Drag the three tiny registration crosses (either the ones in the left- or right-hand image) to three different points in the frame. In this example, I lined them up just on the apex of the three different temple roof points. Then, match the position of the corresponding registration points in the other window and click **Align Images**. If your registration marks have been placed accurately, it will do a very neat job of aligning both shots. Note that if there's subsequently a noticeable shift in the rotation of the file, you will have to crop it once the processing has finished.

Making a simple slideshow

A slideshow in Elements is not quite what I was used to as a child, when my parents would drag out the Kodak projector and the old screen to go over the various snaps that were taken that summer holiday. A slideshow these days is a multimedia event, normally presented as a video file that can be replayed on a computer or uploaded to a range of social media sites.

If you already have images in your **Organizer**, and you look at the all-new Home Page, chances are you'll see that Elements has already created a slideshow through its **Auto Creations** section. Click **Open** to view and edit this or, better still, create your own slideshow from scratch.

Making a slideshow in Elements 2020 is quick and easy. Previous versions featured a far more sophisticated slideshow-making utility, but it was both complex and very time-consuming to use. This version has been almost dumbed down a bit too much—if you want a greater level of creativity, you'd have to go to a specialist slideshow package such as **Pro Show Gold**. This utility is not very sophisticated, but it's easy and fast:

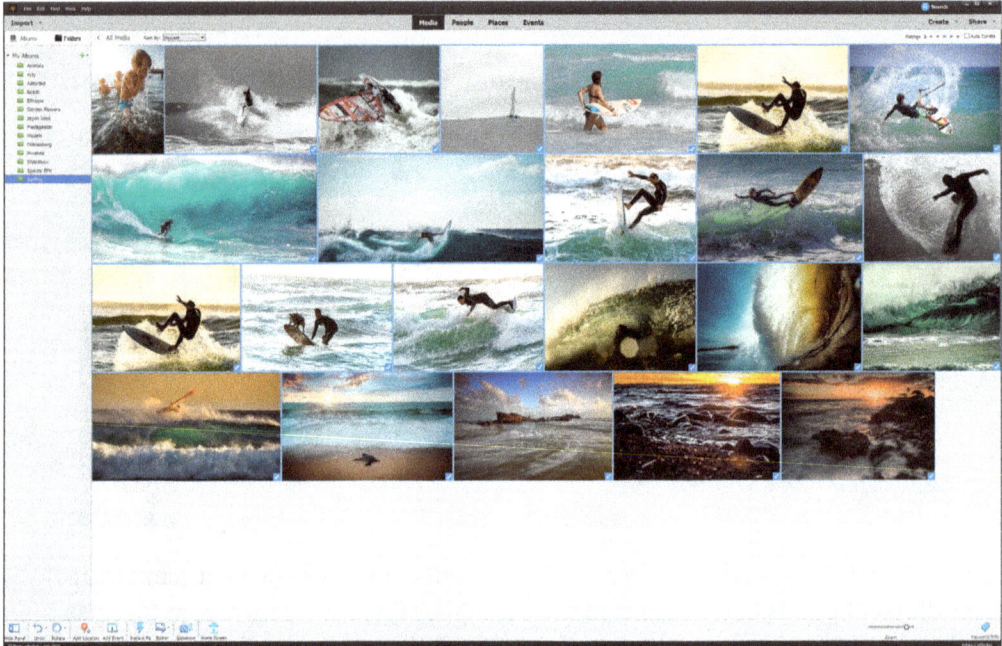

Here's how to knock up a slideshow in a few minutes:

1. Select the pictures you want to include—because of its final video format, it's best to choose horizontally-orientated images. The best practice would be to create a specific **Album** in the **Organizer** for your slideshow images.

2. Select all of the images (you can always add or delete images later).

3. With the images selected in **Organizer**, click the **Slideshow** button at the bottom of the page or go to the **Create** menu (top-right) and choose **Slideshow** from there—it's the same process.

4. The slideshow renders immediately for a preview. You might have to wait a minute or so, depending on how many images you have included. Once it's rendered, it then automatically plays:

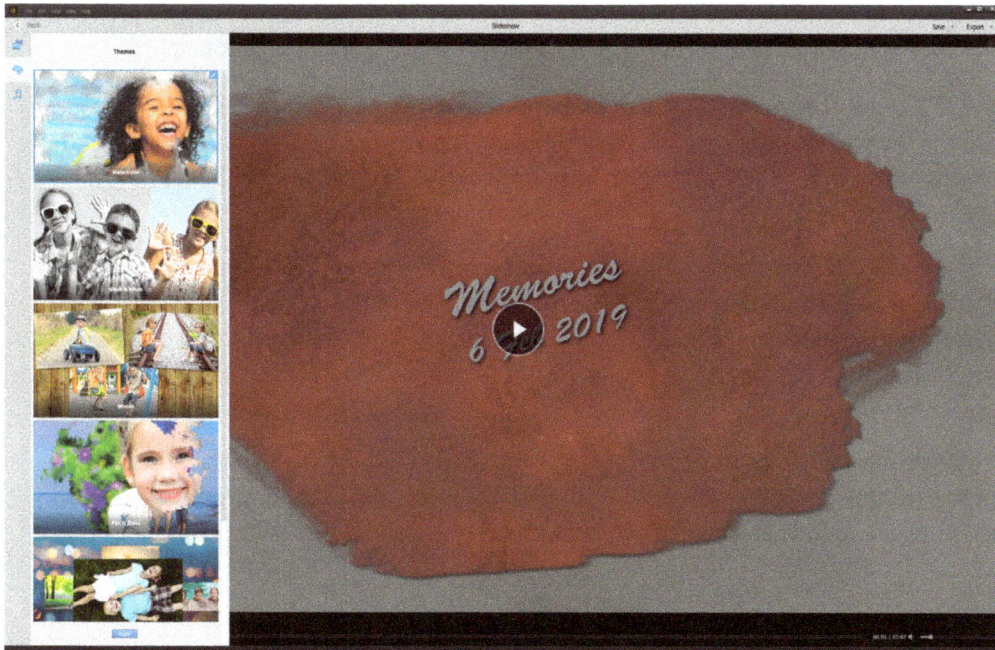

5. If you don't like the **music** or the **theme** Elements starts with, pause the slideshow and access the tiny menu at the top left-hand side of the slideshow screen. There's a range of eight different themes to choose from and several copyright-free music tracks to select:

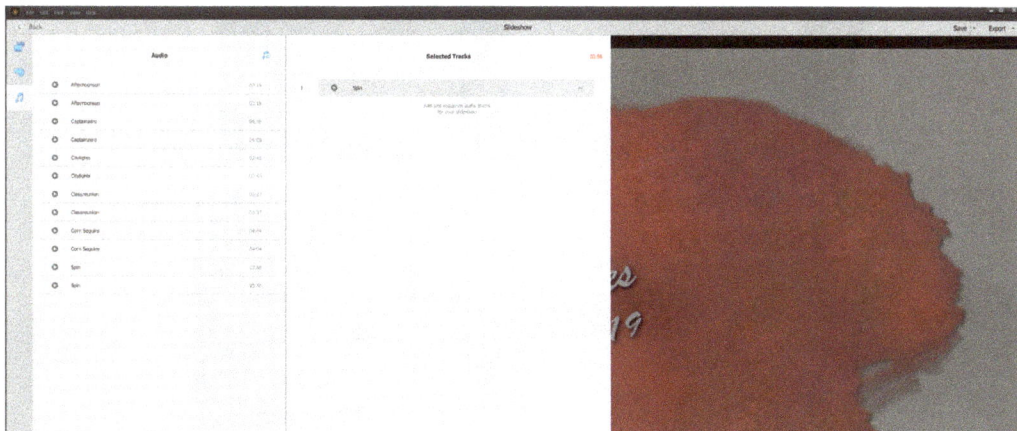

6. You can also use this menu to import more images, video, and sound clips where needed. Right-clicking any thumbnail allows you to remove or rotate that particular slide.

7. There's also a tiny checkbox for adding **captions** to each slide. When you play the slideshow, these captions animate into the frame, which is a nice touch.

Save and Export: The menu on the right-hand side of the slideshow screen allows you to save the file with a unique name. Next to that is the **Export** option—use this to send the video to a folder somewhere on your computer (such as **Export to Local Disk**) or upload directly to Vimeo or YouTube.

Copyright alert: If you plan on publishing the slideshow video into the public domain, note that it shouldn't contain any images, music, or video that are not your own. There are plenty of free image and music sources online where you can download completely copyright-free material for use in personal, and in some cases, commercial projects. It always pays to check first!

Here's a selection of slideshow styles to give you an idea of how it all works. It took me about five minutes to make all five slideshows—they only have 12 pictures in each, but, because this is a simple automated process, it's very, very fast:

Creating custom Photo Calendars

A calendar is a marvelous gift for family, friends, and even work colleagues. What's more, it's also a great way to show off your prowess as a photographer, and creating a calendar has never been easier. Once again, Adobe has packed some incredibly complex imaging actions into a simple-to-understand, single-click operation, and it works very well.

My only niggle with this particular offering is that the available templates haven't really been updated for several versions of the application—I'd like to see more variety; maybe in the next version release? Anyway, let's get started:

1. Like most creative projects in Elements, it pays to sort through your work and create an **Album** in **Organizer** for your calendar pictures:

2. Then, it's just a matter of choosing **Photo Calendar** from the **Create** drop-down menu at the top right-hand side of the **Organizer**, and checking out the range of calendar styles presented in the next stage.

3. Choose a **design style**. I think this is one of the weak points of the calendar-making process. It's very hard to see exactly what you get with each of the designs because they are so small. Monitor resolution has steadily climbed over the past five years, but the preview window remains tiny!

4. Choose one of the 31 layouts, set the start month and year, and click **OK**, making sure that the **Auto Fill with Selected Images** checkbox is unchecked. It's simple enough to load the right pictures onto the correct pages later:

5. You might have to wait a while as the templates for that particular design physically download from Adobe:

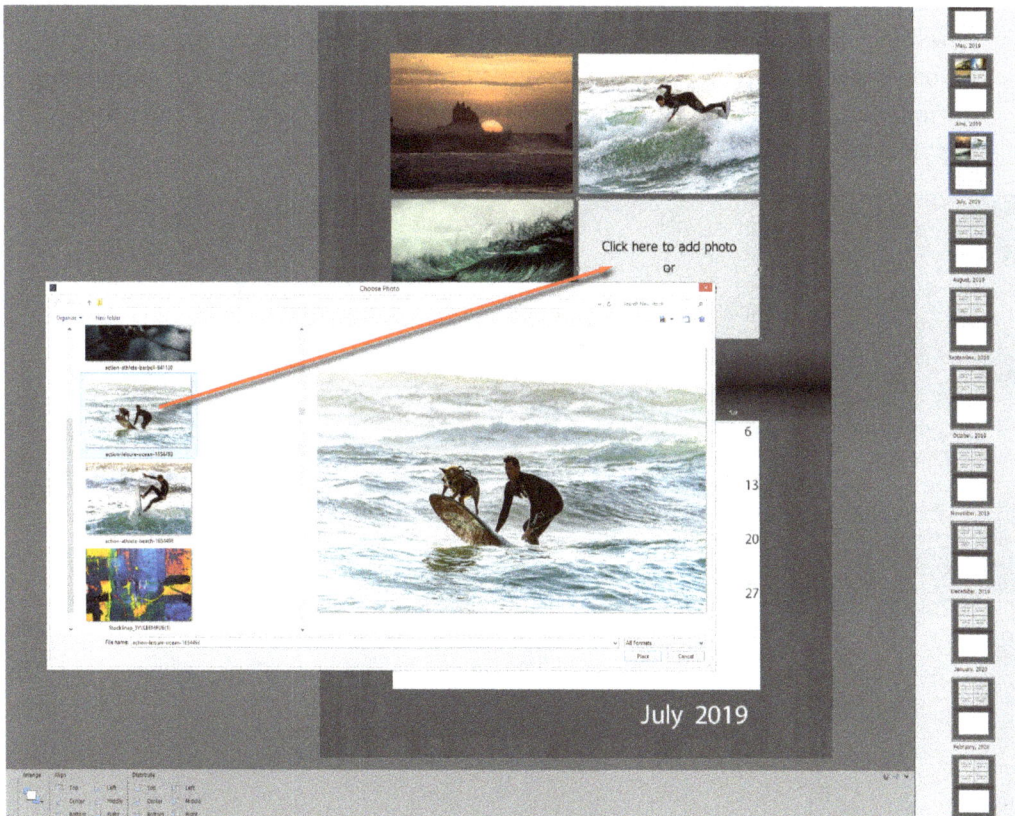

6. Start by navigating to the front cover if it's not already in the main screen. If you have taken the time to put your calendar-bound images into an **Album**, you'll see the images at the base of the page in the **Photo Bin**. Click-hold and push an image into the gray image holder. It automatically resizes and rotates to fit whatever shape the image template is for that calendar design.

7. Double-click in the text box and type in your title and subtitle. Click the green **OK** button to confirm what you wrote is OK. If there are typos, go back to the page, double-click on the text again (to make it active), and correct the text.

8. Repeat the click-hold and push operation for the other monthly images.

9. Note that if you don't like the **number of images** on a particular page or the **image orientation**, it can easily be changed by opening the **Layouts** panel, in either the **Advanced** or the **Basic** window. Once there, simply replace what's being used with a new design by double-clicking the thumbnail in the panel. It's easy. You can do this for one image or all of them. You can even get into the complexities of manipulating the individual layers in the **Advanced** mode but that's, well, advanced and not for this chapter:

10. Once the calendar is complete, save the file; it's ready for printing. You can do this on a regular photo inkjet printer—12 pages, plus a cover page—then take it down to the local office supplies shop to get it **spiral bound**, ready to send off to your friends or family.

Creating custom greeting cards

To make a custom greeting card, the process is almost identical to that of the calendar, except that you are making 1 page instead of 12:

1. Select or arrange a few possible images into an **Album**.

2. Select one, two, or three images from this album (depending on how many images you'd like to put into the card).

3. Choose **Greeting Card** from the **Create** menu.

4. From the tiny design menu that opens (on the left), choose a style and click **OK**. It's actually hard to see exactly what you are getting from this tiny menu, so it might be more a case of trial and error until you hit on a design that you can work with:

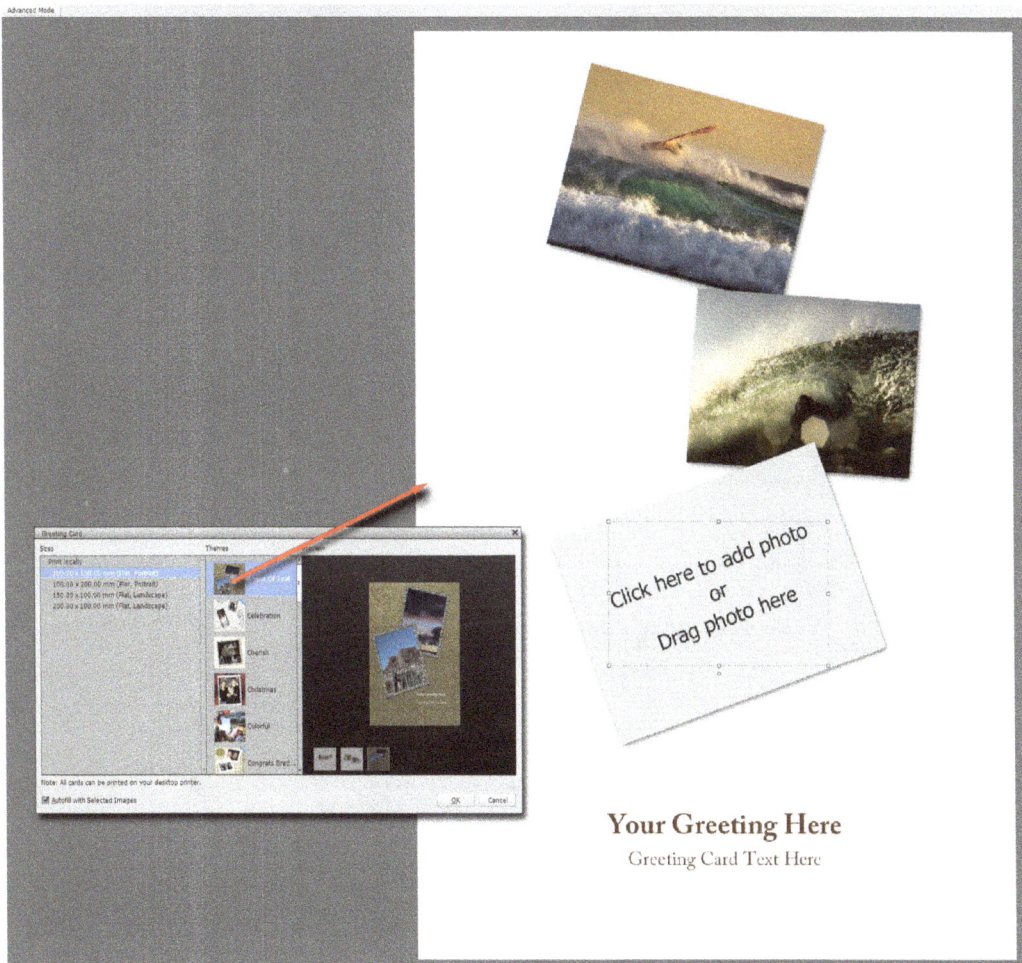

5. Once this design has downloaded, I usually shuffle the images around if they have auto-loaded into the wrong part of the card. Do this by right-clicking the image itself and either choose **Replace Photo** or **Delete** and go find a replacement:

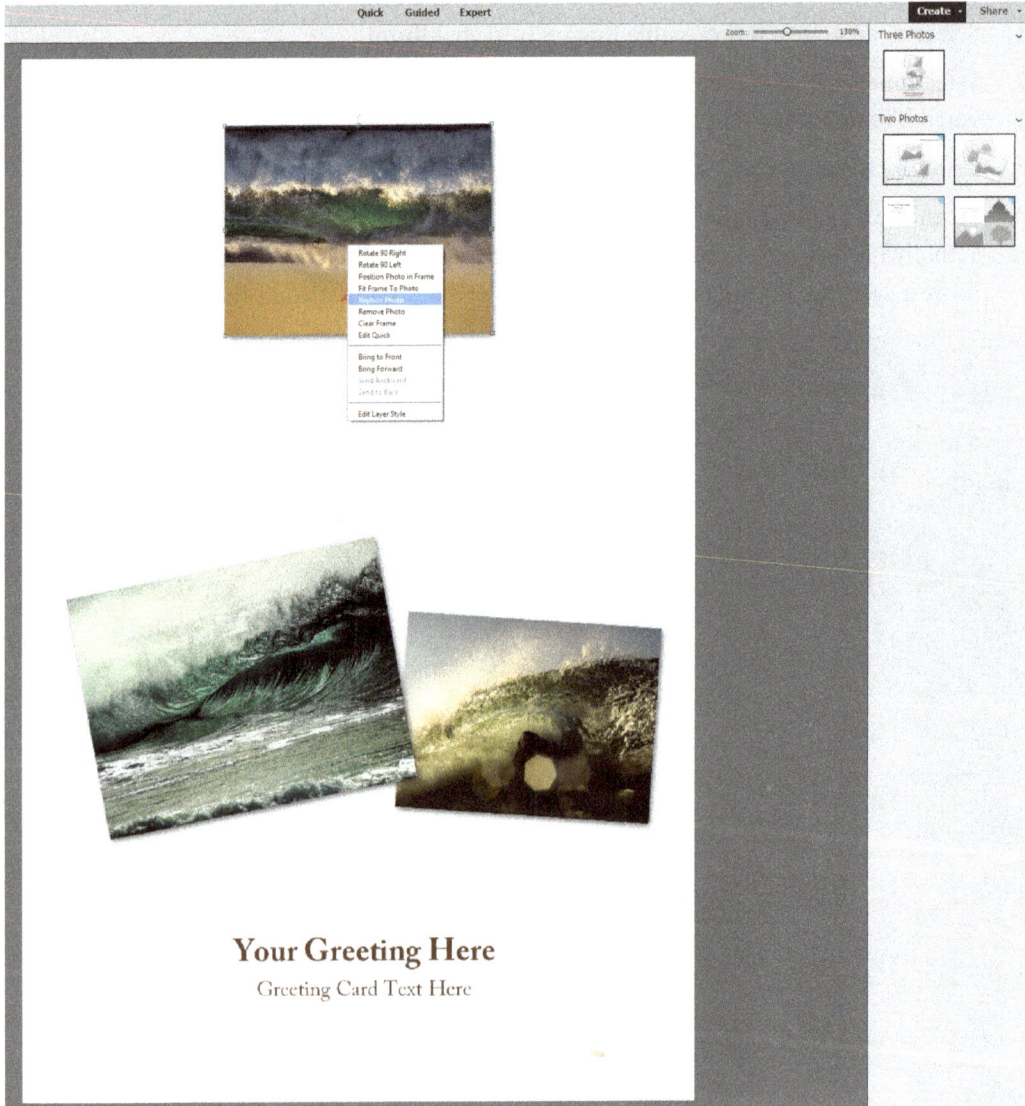

6. Move the image holders to the best position. If you're printing these at home, you need to bear in mind the **fold line** through the center. A lot of the Adobe designs run over the middle of the document, which can be annoying if you want to fold it in half. Using the **Move** tool, click and drag the image, in its holder, to a better position. Note that if you move the mouse just to the outer edges of any image, the double-headed arrow changes into a **rotating arrow**—meaning that you can click, hold, and drag the orientation of the image to a different rotational value. Use the green tick (check) button to confirm your image movement before moving on:

7. Once this is done, fill in the text boxes and save the file so that it's ready for printing.

Making a custom Facebook page

Users of past versions of this excellent software will know that, from time to time, features sometimes get removed or updated in Elements. This can be annoying if it's a feature you particularly liked:

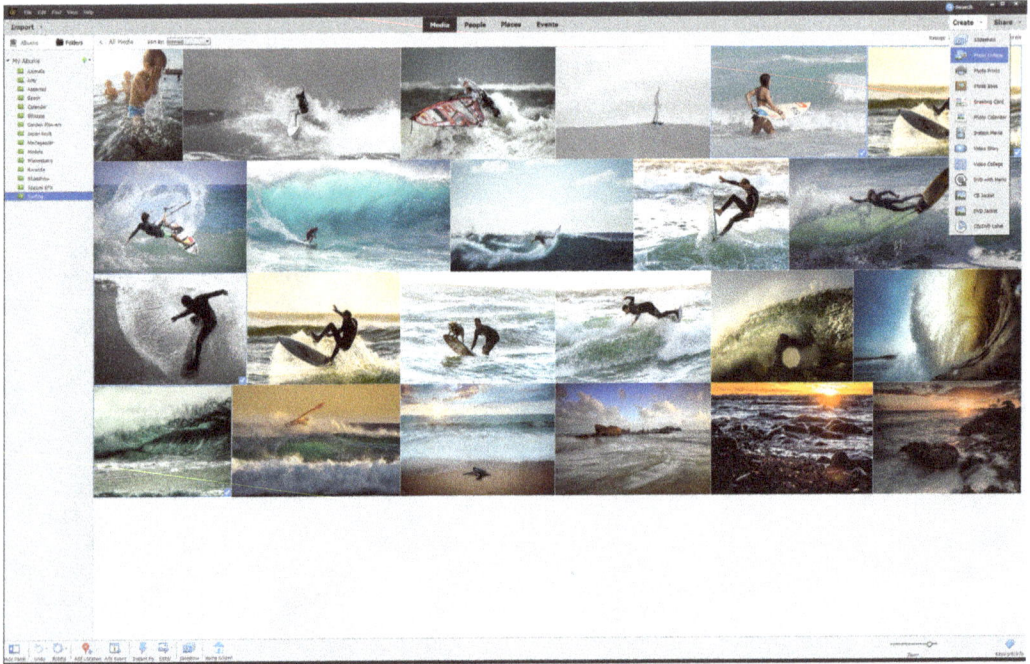

Elements' Facebook page auto design and layout tool is just one of those features that has migrated from its own spot on the **Create** menu into the **Photo Collage** section. Here, you'll find a bunch of collage templates, including four for **Facebook** and four for **Instagram**; it's not a huge selection, but they are very efficient in their delivery:

1. Choose a few images for the page design (for example, four shots).

2. Navigate to the **Create** menu and choose **Photo Collage**:

3. Choose a design from the panel on the right-hand side of the screen and double-click on it. It might take a few moments to download. Sit back and watch as the software loads the images into the preset windows and resizes everything to fit. This is a brilliant bit of software programming because it's so fast and yet it encompasses a range of very complex editing processes:

> **Note**
>
> Note that if the images load OK but the subject in that image is not ideally positioned in the window, you can use the **Move** tool to click and drag that image around in its frame to a better position.

4. When you're working on these collages, you'll also note that there's a **Graphics** panel visible. Use this to add or change the backgrounds of these Facebook pages where needed. As with all of Elements' massive library of assets, these background textures have to be downloaded first:

Keyboard shortcuts

Where will you find all of these amazing projects? Under the **Create** menu—but watch out, the list is slightly different in the **Organizer** than it is in the **Editor**.

The **Create** menu (**Organizer**) contains links to the following:

*   **Slideshow**
*   **Photo Collage**
*   **Photo prints**
*   **Photo Book**
*   **Greeting card**
*   **Photo Calendar**
*   **Instant Movie**
*   **Video Story**

- **Video Collage**
- **DVD with Menu**
- **CD Jacket**
- **DVD Jacket**
- **CD/DVD label**

The **Create** menu (**Editor**) contains fewer links:

- **Slideshow**
- **Photo Collage**
- **Photo prints**
- **Photo Book**
- **Greeting card**
- **Photo Calendar**
- **CD Jacket**
- **DVD Jacket**
- **CD/DVD label**

Summary

Adobe Photoshop Elements started life as very much a scrapbook-type, project-based photo editor, and while that feel has been somewhat replaced by an increasing number of hardcore image editing features, it continues to surprise with the types of clever, instant, and automated features we discussed in this chapter. But for many, these automated processes, while extraordinarily useful, also have finite practicality—you can only go so far with them.

In the next chapter, we'll be looking at the **advanced editing features** that can be found in this application: **Layers**, **Selections**, **Adjustment Layer Masks**, **Layer Masks**, local tone control with the **Burn**, **Dodge**, and **Sponge** brushes, and more.

Once you've grasped these features, you will be able to significantly power up your editing skills.

6
Advanced Techniques – Layers and Masking

This is the chapter where you'll move up a notch, from practicing the basics of good but essentially quite basic image editing, to learning the art of greater creative control over your work output.

That said, for many grappling with the concepts of layers and masks, this might seem counterintuitive. Indeed, when I first started to learn Photoshop Elements, it took me months of self-persuasion before I was ready to make an assault on the concept of layers, such was its perceived complexity.

I was lucky in that, at that point, I had always worked in photography—from commercial audio-visual production to printing in a pro lab, so the concepts of **dodging**, **burning in**, **masking**, and **exposure** were all familiar.

Even so, I still found layers somewhat tricky, but after a few weeks of messing about, it became one of my all-time favorite features simply because it opened my eyes to a completely new range of creative possibilities.

Hopefully, this chapter will do the same for you...

The chapter begins with an introduction to layers—what they are, their features and options, and of course, how to use them. We then explain blending modes—a way of making images sitting on different layers blend together to produce often startlingly vibrant effects.

Then it's time to practice non-destructive editing using adjustment layers. This section, along with the following pseudo masking section, introduces you to the technique of layer **masking**—controlling precisely where in the file the edits work and where they won't.

We also look at the image transformation process, a very powerful feature used to resize, reposition, or reshape images on layers to make flyers and posters and ultimately to correct perspective and other types of optical distortion—a perfect technique for all those photographers with a passion for architectural photography.

Plus you'll find a bunch of handy information on using Elements' range of eraser brushes and the fabulous Gradient tool.

In brief, the techniques that you will learn about in this comprehensive chapter include the following:

- Introduction to layers
- Layer panel features
- Layer blend modes
- Merging layers
- Adjustment layers
- Adjustment layer masking
- Pseudo layer masks
- Combining pictures – posters and flyers
- Correcting perspective with transformations
- Other transformation modes
- Correcting skewed perspectives
- Full-layer masking
- Erasing brush tools
- The Gradient tool

Introduction to layers

Layers are a feature found in Elements that I think will dramatically change the way you edit your pictures. More importantly, they will also significantly expand your *creative potential*.

Layers are used when we want to include more than one element in a file (image, text, or graphics) or when we want to edit individual parts of an image without affecting the rest of the picture. The following illustration shows a depiction of how layers work in an image:

The preceding illustration is a rather scary 3D representation of a regular multilayered Photoshop file. This collage contains 50 different components, sitting on 40 separate layers. Each component can be moved, resized, and edited using any of Elements' tools independently of everything else.

Perhaps the best way to understand how layers work is to start at the beginning.

A single photo, irrespective of its dimensions, resolution, or color mode, occupies a **single layer**. It's usually made up of pixels. The following illustration comprises far more than 40 pixel-based images—some are on their own layers, while some are grouped together on one layer:

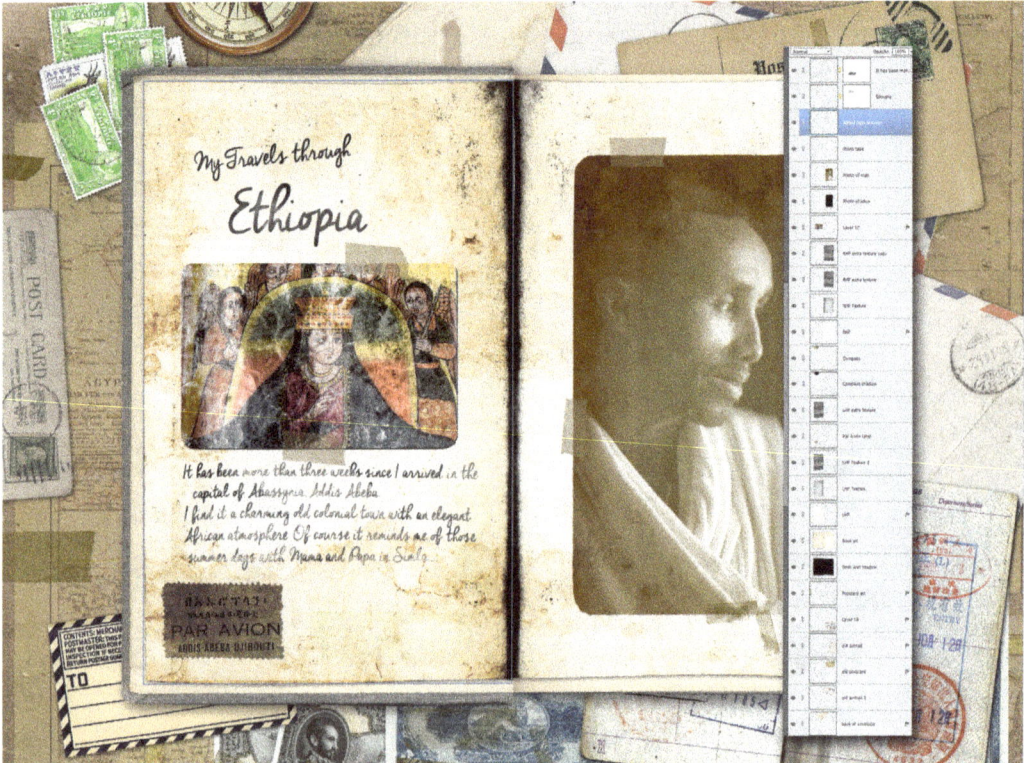

This is an illustration depicting a hand-written travelogue and a scrapbook from the end of the nineteenth century. Some of the images were shot by myself, though the majority were sourced from a range of copyright-free clip art sites, texture libraries, and online scanned originals. I have deliberately left the Layers panel visible to give you an idea of its complexity. The more layers there are in the image, the larger the file becomes, and the more complex it is to edit.

To get the best understanding of the power that layers bring to the photographer and graphic artist, let's start by looking at the layer components and how they can be employed to jump-start your creativity...

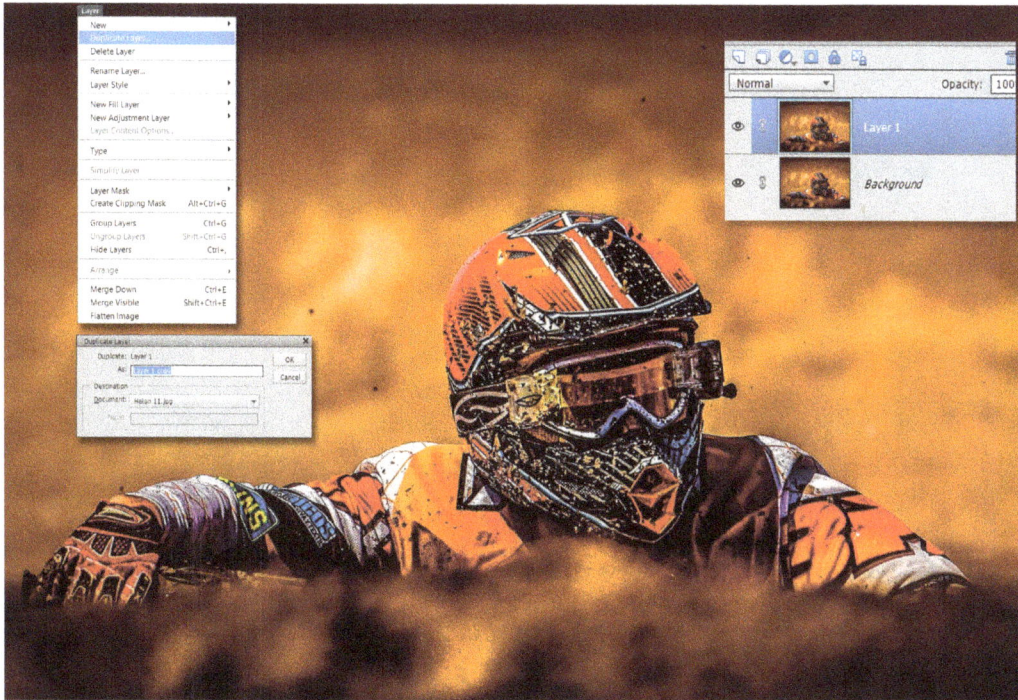

If you hover your cursor over the **Layer** menu at the top of the screen, choose **Duplicate Layer**, and then click **OK** in the **Duplicate Layer** panel that opens (there's no need to give that new layer a special name), you'll see that you now have two identical layers in the **Layer** panel. One is highlighted in blue—this means that it is the **active layer**, so anything done to this file (changes to the color or contrast, transformation, or retouching) will only appear on this layer, not the ones beneath it.

When duplicating a layer, nothing changes in the main screen in front of you because you have simply replaced the original picture with a copy of the original, and since it's identical, you won't see any changes.

The duplicated layer will always sit above the original layer, which is always called the **Background Layer**. Also note that the **Background Layer** has a small **padlock icon** to the right of its name. This means that that particular layer is partially locked and cannot be moved or made smaller unless the padlock is removed (clicking the padlock will remove the padlock icon and rename it as Layer 0—then, it can be moved).

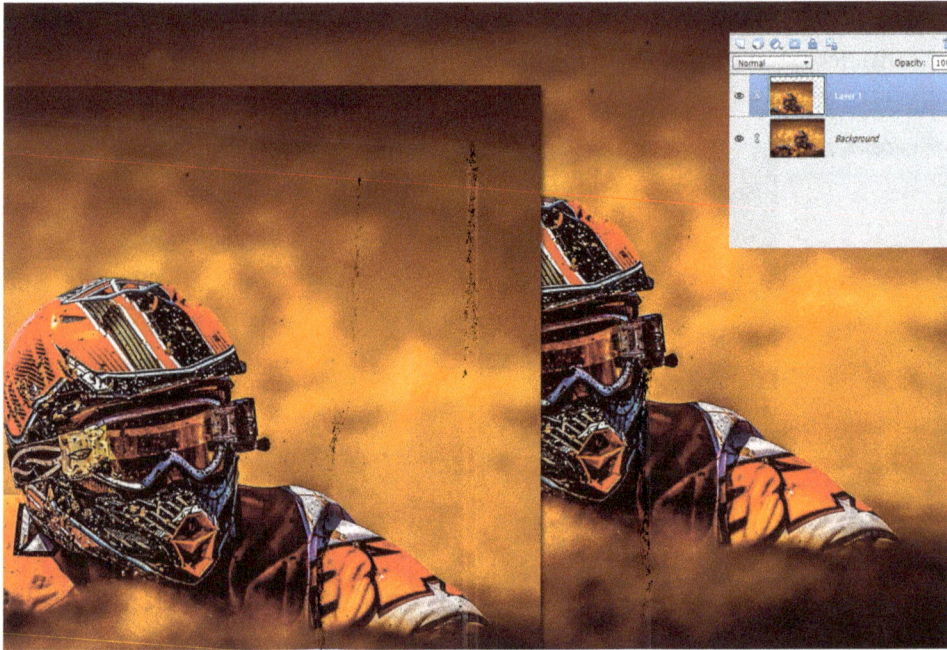

When it comes to layers, I always use the analogy of a garden shed sitting on a concrete slab. The **Background Layer** acts like the concrete slab, while any layer above it represents the lightweight tin shed, which of course can be moved around on its base (provided that you have enough people to help you!).

I generally recommend that everyone should have the **Layer** panel visible at all times so that you can keep an eye on which layer it is that you are currently working on. If you are trying to change something like the color or contrast, but nothing changes on screen, it's usually because you are trying to add the effect to a layer that's hidden beneath other layers. The tiny *eye icon* indicates the **Layer Visibility**. If you can see the eye, then that layer is also visible. Click the eye to make that layer, and all its contents, invisible until that crossed-out eye icon is clicked again, which makes it visible once more.

To get a better idea about layers, if I select the **Convert to Black and White** feature from the **Enhance** drop-down menu, then click **OK** (no need to spend any time choosing the black and white style), you'll see that the active layer turns black and white (as well as the tiny thumbnail in the **Layer** panel).

However, although the **Convert to Black-and-White** feature shows it turning black and white, the main image remains in full color. Why is this happening? Because the active layer is the one *underneath the color layer*. Since the color layer is 100% opaque, it effectively stops us from seeing what's going on in the layer stack.

But we can always see what's happening if we look at the layer thumbnails. To view the B/W version, I need to make that top layer invisible by clicking the tiny *eye icon* to the left of the thumbnail in the active layer. Turning the visibility of that layer **Off** means that we can now see the content of the layer directly below it, which is the newly converted B/W version.

The newly converted black and white version is on the bottom of the layer stack, while the color version is on the top. Knowing which layer you are actually working on can be a bit confusing, but as long as you keep an eye on that **Layer** panel, you should be fine.

To make the color layer smaller, I can use the **Transform** tool (*Ctrl/Cmd + T*) and push one of the square photo corners inward to shrink it down. As you make that upper layer smaller, it reveals the original color version behind it. When transforming any object on a layer, Elements needs you to confirm or cancel the action by either clicking the green checkmark (**OK**) or the red symbol (**Cancel**) before you can proceed with more editing.

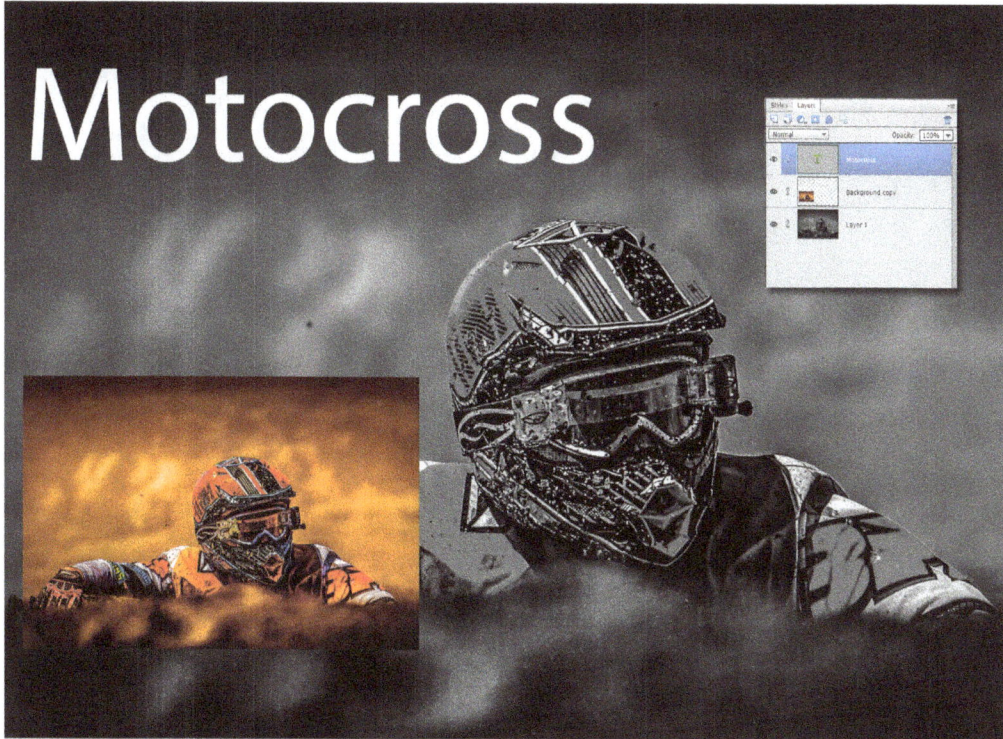

If we add *text* to an image, it will create its own unique *text layer*, which is made up of *vectors*, not pixels.

The main difference between a vector and a pixel layer is that the former is essentially nothing more than a *mathematical formula*, and can be enlarged to any practical dimension, with no loss of quality (because it's just an algorithm), while the latter—the pixel-based layer—has a very finite range of enlargability that it can move through before it loses quality.

When you shrink or enlarge an image on a layer, Elements uses clever interpolation or resampling algorithms to calculate how many pixels are needed to make the image larger or how to remove them to make it smaller. It's an excellent process, but it also involves a lot of **dithering**, a process that softens the edges of pixels (to avoid obvious pixelation), which makes the resulting resized image softer.

After spending some time practicing with layers, you'll find that adding text is a relatively easy operation, and can then embark on a range of text-based creative projects, from posters to flyers and even business cards. I changed the regular **Myriad Pro** font to something a little rougher to match the texture of *Motocross*—a font I discovered on my computer called **Soul Mission**—then added a drop shadow from the **Styles** panel.

Other vector layers that you'll find in Elements include **Custom Shapes**, such as **text boxes**, **copyright stamps**, and other graphic **symbols**, which can be combined into any document. Like all the pixel-based photo layers, text can also be edited independently of the rest of the image, which makes it a great feature if you're as bad a typist as I am.

Layers can also be shuffled like a deck of cards so that, if you find during the design of a multi-image poster that one picture is partially hidden by another, that picture's layer can be dragged up the stack so that it appears above, and not below the problem area.

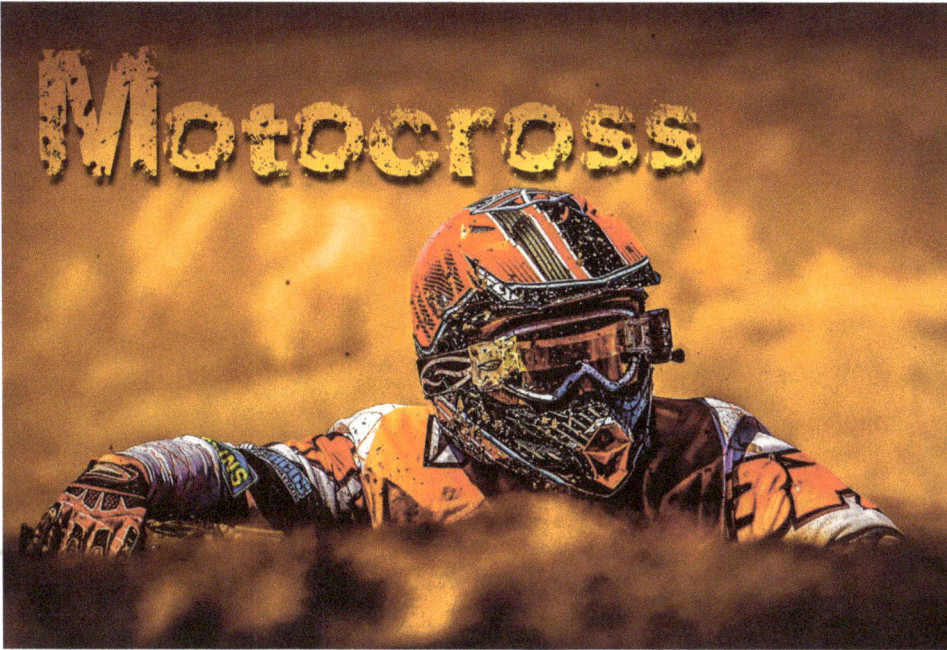

Drop shadows do a great job of lifting text off the surface of the image. They add *depth* as well as *legibility*, which is particularly important when adding text on top of an image. The *busier* the image is, the harder it might be to read.

Font choice is also vital to the success of any multimedia document that might incorporate text. Understanding how **font choice**, **font style** (bold, italic, and so on), and **point sizes** work can make or break a good project (refer to the next section on custom fonts). As we'll see in the section on graphics coming up in *Chapter 7, Advanced Drawing and Painting Techniques*, you can also add textboxes behind the text itself to make the typeface 100% legible. You can also reduce that textbox's opacity so that some of the image shines through so that it's not a solid block of color on the image.

Other features on the Layer panel

The **Layer** panel (on the right-hand side of the main window in the **Expert** edit modes) features a number of useful shortcuts in the form of buttons along the top of the panel. From left to right, these include the following:

- **Create a New Layer**: Click this to add a new layer to a document. It has nothing on it, so it appears totally clear.

- **Create a New Group**: When you are working with a lot of layers, you might want to group similar layers together into a (**Group**) folder to help compact the **Layer** panel (**Advanced**).

- **Create a New Fill or Adjustment Layer**: Use this to add functionality to a specific layer.

- **Add a Layer Mask**: Layer masking is described later on in this chapter. Masks add tremendous control over different parts of any layer simply by using a black or white brush to hide or reveal different parts of the image (indicated with an arrow in the preceding image).

- **Lock All Pixels**: Use this feature if you want to prevent further changes to the layers.

- **Lock Transparency**: As the name suggests, this prevents you from accidentally losing the transparent sections of the document.

- **Delete Layer**: Take out the trash! I think this is self-explanatory. You can also delete a layer by right-clicking the layer itself and choosing **Delete Layer** from the pop-up menu.

Blend Modes

Underneath the **Layer** panel's row of buttons sits another drop-down menu with 24 settings—these are the blending modes. The default setting is **Normal**. It's very hard to provide a clear description of what blending modes do other than to say that different blending modes affect the way the top layer *blends* with the one below it. Some appear to do nothing, while others have a radical effect. In the following images, I have duplicated the layer so that there's an identical layer on top of the original, and then I changed that top layer's blending mode (note that those that made no difference to the image have been excluded):

As a practical example of how to best use blending modes, for example, if I add a text layer to the document and then change that layer's blending mode from **Normal** to **Overlay**, then the effect that's produced looks as if I have sandwiched two bits of film together to create a ghosted-out effect, with the textures of the background layer showing through the text layer. Sometimes, this works spectacularly; sometimes not so much. Note that I also added a drop shadow to the text layer to make it stand off the page. It can produce some very creative looks, especially if you have two different images in the mix. Note that it can also produce very underwhelming results. Every image produces a different look. We'll look at blending modes in greater detail later in this book.

- Two identical image layers; the top one is set to **Multiply**

- Two identical image layers; the top one is set to **Linear Burn**

- Two identical image layers; the top one is set to **Darker Color**

- Two identical image layers; the top one is set to **Screen**

- Two identical image layers; the top one is set to **Color Dodge**

- Two identical image layers; the top one is set to **Linear Dodge**

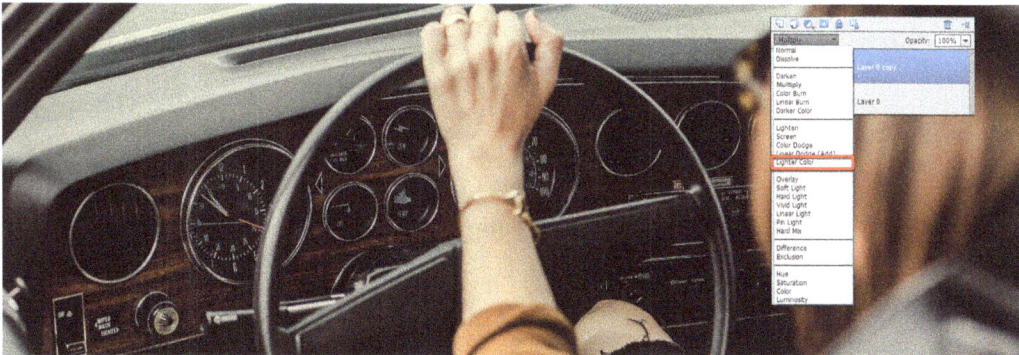

- Two identical image layers; the top one is set to **Lighter Color**

- Two identical image layers; the top one is set to **Overlay**

- Two identical image layers; the top one is set to **Soft Light**

- Two identical image layers; the top one is set to **Hard Light**

- Two identical image layers; the top one is set to **Vivid Light**

- Two identical image layers; the top one is set to **Pin Light**

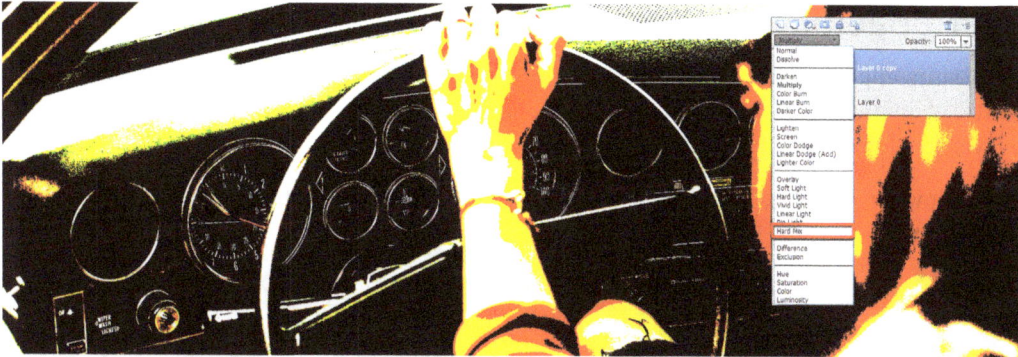

- Two identical image layers; the top one is set to **Hard Mix**

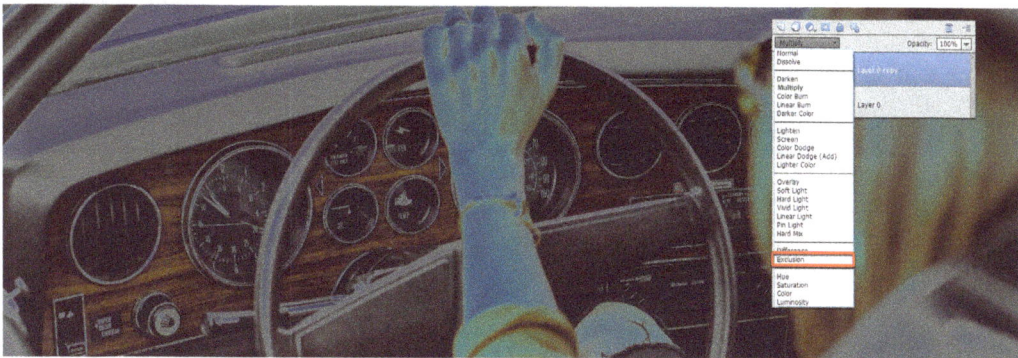

- Two identical image layers; the top one is set to **Exclusion**

So, blending modes can make radical changes to two layers, or not. It depends on the blending mode used and the relationship of the tones and colors in the top layer with those of the base layer. The best advice I can give is to try them yourself, and then decide whether they are improving your edit.

Most of Elements' brush-based tools can also be set to operate in a specific blending mode. If you take a paintbrush and set that tool's blending mode to **Exclusion**, for example, any subsequent brushing will produce a similar reversed-out color to the one you see in the preceding image.

Layer opacity

As the name might suggest, you can use the **Opacity** feature to change the density, or **opacity**, of an individual layer. One way to blend one layer into another is to change the top layer to a lower opacity.

In the following example, I lowered the **Opacity** of the MAGAZINE text layer to 50%:

You'd also use a lower opacity value to see what's underneath that layer if, say, you needed to position that top layer precisely on top of an object in the layer underneath it. Once done, the layer opacity is returned to 100%.

Merging layers

Apart from the physical buttons and menus on the **Layer** panel, if you right-click the tiny icon to the right of the trash can, a pop-up menu offers the same features in the **Layer** menu at the top of the main screen, including the ability to integrate one (active) layer with the one underneath it, which is a process called **Merge Down**.

Merge Visible is slightly different as it flattens all the visible layers into one layer. The more useful **Flatten Image** command merges all the layers into one layer. If you try to save a multilayered Photoshop format file as a JPEG, watch the **Layers** panel as Elements automatically flattens the layers, saves the JPEG, and then unflattens the layers as it returns to its multilayered .psd format file state, leaving you with the original .psd file, plus a flattened .jpg file, as shown in the following screenshot:

Adjustment Layers

On the surface, an adjustment layer behaves somewhat like a *ghost layer*. We use them to make nondestructive tonal changes to regular images. The clue here is in the term *nondestructive*. Regular editing on JPEG, TIFF, PSD, and PNG files can be *destructive*, especially if it's done over-enthusiastically, repeatedly, or just not very well. In such cases, the image begins to lose quality, unless it's a RAW file, which is always a copy of the original. I may add that, although this nondestructiveness claim certainly looks impressive on paper, it's actually hard to quantify with real-life examples, when compared with some so-called destructive forms of editing.

Even so, for many photographers, one of the huge advantages of using an **Adjustment Layer** is that it can also be used as a **mask**. A mask is a Photoshop feature that can be used to limit the effect of any change, tonal or otherwise, on specific parts of the picture. They are an incredible way to lighten, darken, saturate, or desaturate specific bits of an image while leaving the rest of the image untouched. What's more, a mask is a relatively simple feature to create.

An **Adjustment Layer** can be added to any image via the **Layers** menu at the top of the main window, or via the **Layers** panel as shown in the following image:

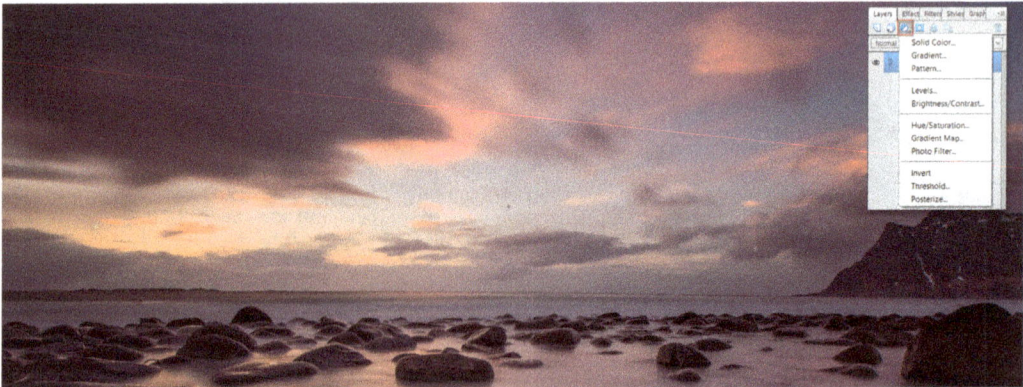

> **Tip**
> For my style of editing, the Adjustment Layers I use the most would be **Levels**, **Hue/Saturation**, and **Photo Filter**, and nothing else, but it's up to you to try them out and decide for yourself.

When you choose one of these special tone-altering Adjustment Layers, you must decide what it is you want to achieve with the image. Your choices are, in order: **Solid Color**, **Gradient**, **Pattern**, **Levels**, **Brightness/Contrast**, **Hue/Saturation**, **Gradient Map**, **Photo Filter**, **Invert**, **Threshold**, or **Posterize**.

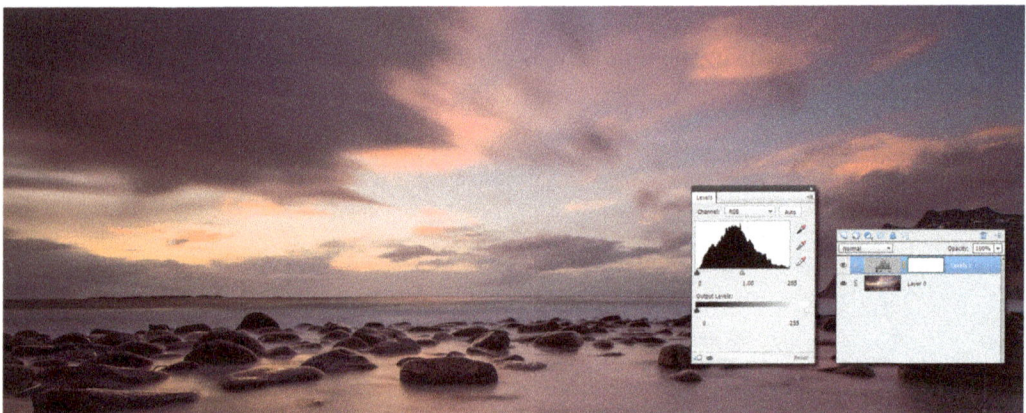

Once selected, you'll note that a new layer has appeared on top of the regular photo layer (which is called the **Background Layer** by default). This is the **Adjustment Layer**, and whatever tool it's associated with appears on the main screen. So, if it's a **Levels Adjustment Layer**, the layer appears along with the **Levels** tool, as shown in the previous screenshot.

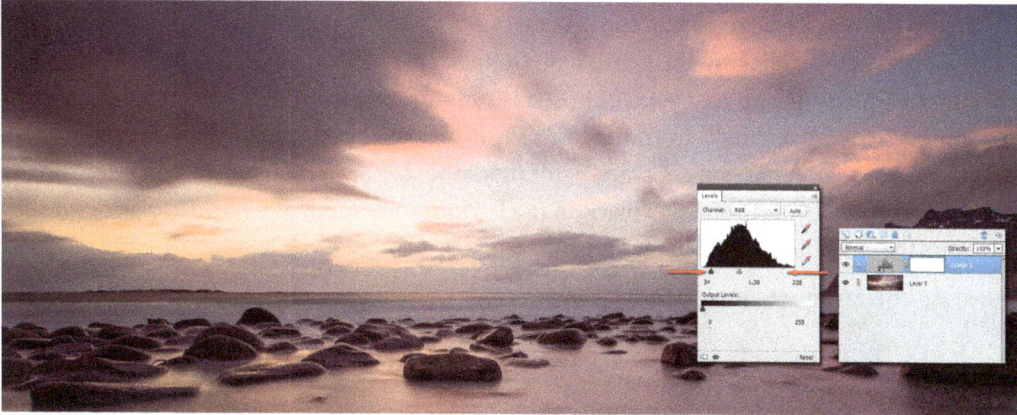

In this example, you then make a **Levels** adjustment, and to close it, click the **x** at the top right of the tool panel. If you want to do it again, simply click the gray tool icon in the **Adjustment Layer** to bring **Levels** back for more editing.

As I mentioned previously, *the difference* between making a **Levels** adjustment directly onto the layer and via an **Adjustment Layer** is very hard to detect visually unless it has been over-edited, in which case you might detect damage to the smoothness of the pixels, but this is unlikely. Where we can really make a significant impact on the editing process is when we modify the layer (mask) so that the **Levels** effect ends up only being applied to part of the image.

Adjustment Layer masking

Taking the role of the **Adjustment Layer** one step further, not only can we use this layer in a nondestructive editing fashion, but we can also apply those edits to specific areas in the image by using its attached **Layer Mask**:

1. When using the **Adjustment Layer**, you'll note that not only is there a **Levels** icon on the **Adjustment Layer**, but there is also a **white rectangle**—this is the **Layer Mask**. All Adjustment Layers have this feature. In its white state, it's see-through (fully transparent). Click this white rectangular thumbnail once to select it (rather than having the **Levels** icon selected). A light-blue (highlighted) line will appear around that white mask rectangle. This indicates that it's now the active part of the Adjustment Layer (and not the **Levels** part of the Adjustment Layer).

2. Here's the very creative part of the process. Choose the **Brush** tool from the toolbar (by pressing *B* or clicking the brush icon in the **Draw** section of the toolbar). Make sure that the brush tip that you've chosen is suitable for the process (that is, a hard or soft brush, large or small) from the tool's **Options** panel and that the chosen color is **Black**. To ensure that you get black paint (and not some other color), press *D* (for the default color setting), which is black in the background and white in the foreground. Press the *X* key to swap black with white. Press *X* again to swap it back to black.

3. With that white mask thumbnail highlighted, paint directly into the image in the main screen, and note that the brightness/contrast effect created by the **Levels** adjustment is removed as you paint black into the white mask. Black makes the mask opaque. Check the thumbnail and you'll see that your black brush marks appear in the thumbnail. The more you paint, the less the **Levels** adjustment appears in the main image. If you make a mistake and paint black into the mask where you shouldn't have, simply press the *X* key (to swap black with white) and paint over the black paint to make that bit of the mask see-through again. The amazing thing about this technique is that you can go backward and forward, fine-tuning the position and accuracy of the tonal change, as many times as you like. It is infinitely editable.

The previous image clearly shows a comparison between the original (as an overlay) and the improved version on the right-hand side, sporting a lighter, brighter, and more colorful foreground where the sky remains relatively untouched, such is the creative control provided by adjustment layers and layer masks (more on layer masks later in this chapter).

Quick facts:

The following are some facts to bear in mind when using adjustment layers:

- Adjustment layers can be stacked on top of each other, should you need to add contrast to one part of an image and add color to another part.

  Adding adjustment layers to a file doesn't increase the size of the file.

- An **Adjustment Layer** effect—for example, **Levels**—will only affect the layer beneath it. However, you can make it apply to all layers beneath it by clicking the **Clip to Layer** icon, next to the (eye) visibility icon, at the bottom of the (**Levels**) layer.

- You can add another **Adjustment Layer** by opening the pop-up menu that's just below the tiny **x**, to the top right of the (**Levels**) panel.

- You can cancel your adjustment layer action by clicking **Reset**.

One of the main benefits of using adjustment layers is that they are nondestructive. They operate like virtual tools, making the same tonal adjustments as a regular tool—but with the advantage that they come with an attached mask for additional accuracy. But to be honest, it's virtually impossible to see the quality difference between an image edited with a **Levels** adjustment layer and the same image edited using **Levels** directly—but having that mask attached is a very handy bonus...

Pseudo layer masks

Before we get into describing the use of true masks in Photoshop Elements, let's have a look at a feature I call **pseudo layer masks**.

A true mask is one that is attached to an image thumbnail in the **Layer** panel. Its default color is white, which means that it is **see-through**, but as soon as you paint black onto that mask, it becomes opaque, therefore blocking whatever effect that particular layer is displaying, to reveal what it looked like before it was changed. For a beginner, this might seem complicated.

Masks are designed to isolate parts of the image in order to make changes without affecting everything in the picture; for example, to change the depth of field "look" in a landscape. To replicate this slightly complex action using a **pseudo mask layer** (this is my name for the technique), simply duplicate the layer, then add some diffusion (that is, using a **Gaussian Blur** filter) to the duplicated layer so that everything goes blurry, and then erase everything but the main subject (in this example, the foreground flowers) to reveal the unchanged original underneath it. The technique is basic, but it's easy to make a significant local change this way. Its main disadvantage is that, unlike a true mask, once the pixels have been erased, the process is relatively irreversible, so I'd recommend simple edits to begin with.

Firstly I'd duplicate the layer, then apply blurriness using one of Elements' many blur filters (the best one to use is called **Filter | Blur | Gaussian Blur**), before carefully erasing the subject from this blurry layer to reveal the original, sharp version underneath. This can give you an almost instant shallow depth of field look with very little work on your part. Once done, it's a simple matter of flattening the top layer with the **Background Layer** before saving it and moving to the next project:

Making what I call a pseudo layer mask is easy. Duplicate the layer you want to change—you can clearly see the copied or duplicated layer in blue in this screenshot—in the **Layer** panel inset. You also need to be reasonably accurate at drawing with the Eraser tool, which can be tricky because the mouse is not exactly an easy-to-control device. Look at the following image:

With the new, duplicated layer selected (active), choose the **Gaussian Blur** filter from the **Filter** menu at the top of the screen (**Filter | Blur | Gaussian Blur**).

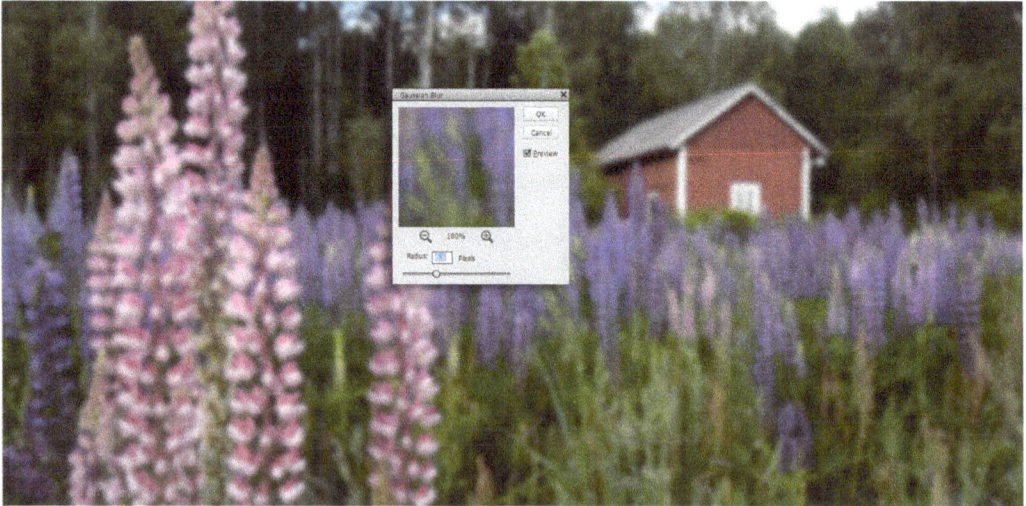

The **Filter** panel pops into the main screen, and you can choose from a tiny bit of fuzziness to all-out blurriness. The idea in this exercise is to make the background of this landscape image appear as if it were shot with a wide aperture—for example, f2.8—rather than at the mid-range setting of f5.6 that was chosen at the time it was exposed. How much fuzziness or **Gaussian Blur** you add is dependent on the effect you'd like to create and the overall resolution of the original picture. The more megapixels, the more filter effect you have to add to get a good effect. It's easy enough to experiment with duplicated layers. Undo this if it is wrong and try a different blur setting. Look at the following image:

So, having got the blurriness more or less at the right amount, select the **Eraser Brush** from the toolbar. Like every painting, drawing, and selection tool in this program, the brush tip can be varied. Do this by right-clicking inside the main image to access the Brush pop-up menu or by going to the **Options** panel at the bottom of the page.

In this screen grab, note that I have turned the bottom layer **Off** (by clicking the eye icon next to that layer's thumbnail), so once I begin erasing the blurred layer, it reveals transparent pixels (that's the weird checkerboard pattern seen here) and gives me a better idea of how to be more accurate with my erasing.

To easily regulate the size of the brush tip, you can use the **Size** slider in the **Options** panel, but an easier method is to use square brackets. Next to *P* on the keyboard, press the left *[* to make the brush tip smaller and the right-hand *]* to enlarge it. This keyboard tip works for all brush-based tools in Photoshop Elements and Illustrator.

This is my progress so far. Although I started this technique by stating that this process was easy, I omitted to say that it does take a bit of time, depending on the complexity of the edges of the area being erased, of course. I set the brush opacity to 90% to make the erasing process a bit smoother, but it does take longer to erase *all* the pixels because you'll have to go over everything twice!

When retouching, you really cannot see small details with the main image fitting the screen—it needs to be enlarged to get into the nooks and crannies. If you take care of the fine detail, then the illusion of a fabricated depth of field will appear that much more realistic. Use *Ctrl/Cmd + +* and *Ctrl/Cmd + -* to zoom in or out when erasing, respectively. Look at the following image:

Here's another screen grab, full-frame, with about 95% of the top layer's pixels removed. It's time to turn the bottom layer back on to get a glimpse of how realistic the fake depth of field effect has turned out.

I could spend a lot more time erasing some of the tiny pixels around these colorful lupins to make everything appear a bit more realistic, but I think 15 minutes was enough to get this to work nicely.

> **Tip**
> It's worth bearing in mind how much time you spend fine-tuning the editing process. In this example, the tall flowers can be regulated by how large the image is that will be reproduced. If it's only ever going to be posted online as a small 480 x 640-pixel image, for example, then there's no need to spend hours on retouching because no one will see your errors. But if it's to be printed as a front cover for a digital photo book (as an example), then it's worth investing more time in the editing process because mistakes, poor masking, and inaccurate selecting will more than likely be visible.

The point of using a duplicated layer is that if you mess up the erasing process, even though it's not always effective to go back to a previous version or change the blurriness, it's easy enough to duplicate the **Background Layer** again and give it another go.

Note that *real* layer masking involves a fluid selection process that can go forward and backward an infinite number of times. You'll find more on layer masking toward the end of this chapter.

Combining pictures – posters and flyers

The best way to understand how layers work in Photoshop Elements is to create a **multi-image poster**. By adding multiple pictures to a single file, you can then resize those pictures and move them so that they sit side by side rather than sitting on top of each other.

1.　First off, open the pictures you want to incorporate into the project. Note that their thumbnails appear in the **Photo Bin** at the bottom of the screen:

2.　Then, create a new document to the dimensions of your poster by going to **File | New | Blank File**. This is where it's a good idea to research your printing options. Check on the lab's printing dimensions (and cost).

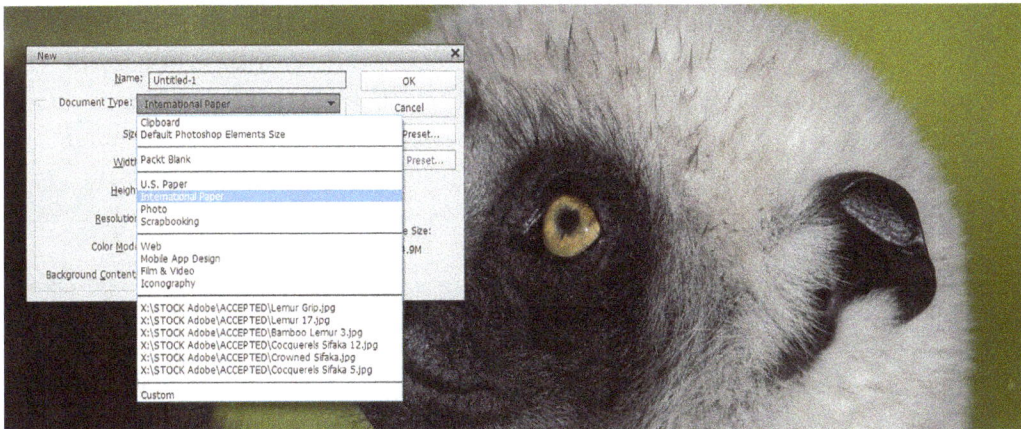

3. The **New** panel that subsequently appears on screen allows you to type in the vertical and horizontal dimensions of your new document, along with its base resolution. You can also quickly choose one of the preset document dimensions from the **Document Type** drop-down menu (such as **A4, A3, US letter**, and **HD Video**). If the poster is to be printed, I suggest setting a resolution of 200 or 300 dpi. Click **OK**. The new, white **Background Layer** will appear on screen, as shown in the following screenshot:

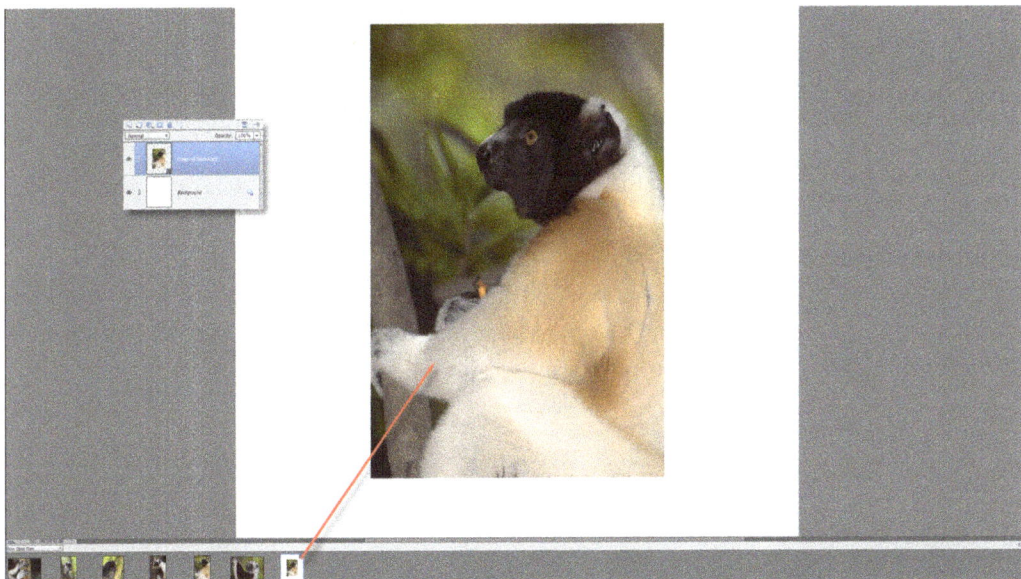

4. With the white new document displayed on the main screen, push one of the image thumbnails from the **Photo Bin** into the main image. You'll see it appear on top of the white document. Check the **Layer** panel when you do this to confirm that there is indeed a new layer containing your photograph on top of the white background later. Save the document in either Photoshop (`.psd`) or Tiff (`.tif`) file format. Remember that JPEGs cannot contain any extras, such as selections, layers, or masks.

5. Follow the same process with the other images that you want to include in the poster, checking every time to confirm that the new image being pushed into your master document appears in the **Layer** panel. Inevitably, each image being copied into the master document will cover up the previous image (as you can see in the following screenshot), but don't worry about this because we are about to reposition everything for a better design. Save your work and move on to the next stage.

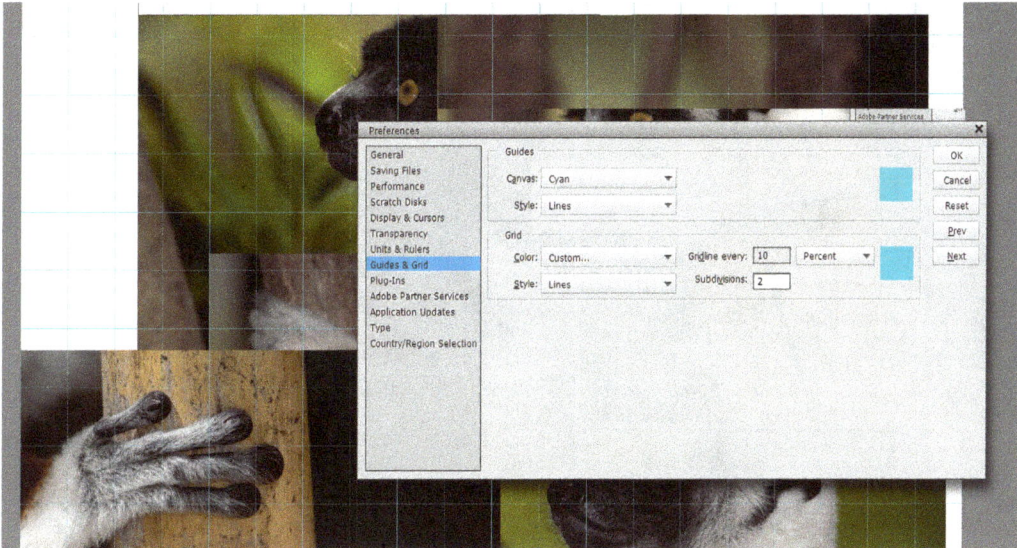

6. As a great working tip, use the **View** menu to open either the edge **Rulers,** or better still, use the **Grid** (we will deal with the **Grid** later in this chapter). Note that the default Elements **Grid** is far too busy (too many lines) to be of any practical use, so open **Preferences** (*Ctrl/Cmd + K*) and change the line spacing to something like 10%—you'll see fewer lines, which makes it significantly easier to use correctly. You can also change the grid color. Note that all the design and line-up **Grid** *helpers* are only visible on screen; they do not print.

7. The easiest technique for changing the proportions of any item on an individual layer is called a **Transformation**. To begin this process, choose **Image | Transform | Free Transform** (use the keyboard shortcut *Ctrl/Cmd + T*, or just click and push the corner of the selected image). Once this is selected, you'll notice a grid appear across that single image with what Adobe refers to as *corner handles*. If you click one of these handles, then drag the mouse inwards. You'll reduce the size of that image proportionally. Dragging any of the midpoint handles—there's one on each side— will shrink the size of the image while also distorting it. Avoid doing this. Once the image has been resized so that it is smaller on screen, you'll see a green checkmark appear at the bottom right-hand side of that image. Click this if you're happy with the resizing operation or click the red icon if you want to cancel. You can always try *Ctrl/Cmd + T* again to modify your resizing if necessary.

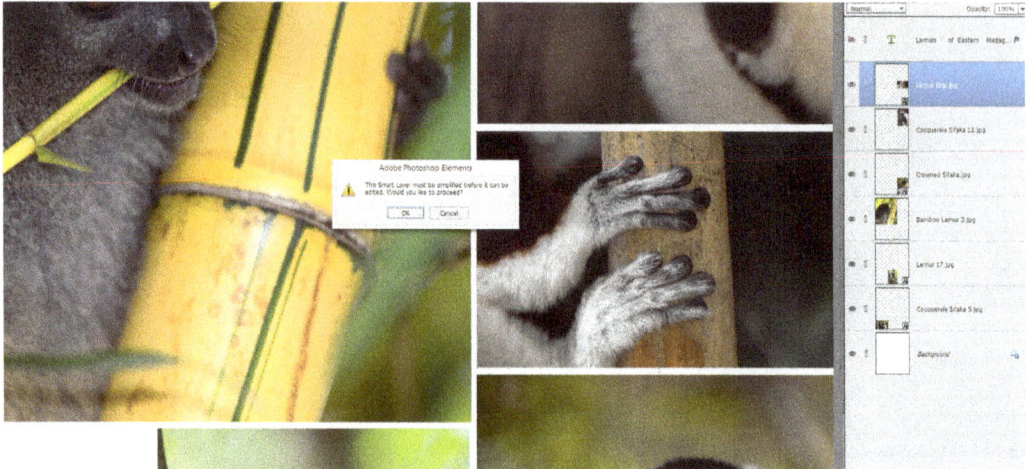

8. It's important to note that the process of click-pushing an image from the **Photo Bin** into the (new) master document converts a pixel-based image into a feature called a **Smart Object**. Smart Objects are essentially nondestructive layers. You can't perform operations that alter pixel data (such as painting, dodging, burning, or cloning) directly on a **Smart Object** layer unless it's first converted into a regular layer, a process called **Simplify Layer**.

Although there is nothing wrong with this process, if you want to continue editing those images, the Smart Object must be converted back into a pixel-based layer before you continue. To do this, navigate to the relevant layer in the panel, right-click, and choose **Simplify Layer** (you can also do this from the main **Layer** menu). Alternatively, as you can see from the following screengrab, if you try to access a tool such as **Levels** (*Ctrl/Cmd + L*) to make a contrast change, Elements automatically asks whether it's OK to simplify that layer.

When you simplify a layer, note that the tiny **Smart Object** icon in the layer thumbnail disappears and that you're now ready to make tonal adjustments to that image.

Repeat this transformation process for all the other images, resizing them so that they fit together in the design of your choosing. Whenever an image is resized (larger or smaller), Elements waits for you to OK that action before allowing you to move on. This is a good feature, but if you are not paying attention, then getting stuck without knowing why can be a bit frustrating. Either click the green **OK** button, cancel the operation by clicking the red no entry symbol, or press *Esc* to cancel most operations in this application.

Remember, the huge advantage of working with layers means that, once everything in the document sits on an individual layer, it remains individually editable, which is a huge bonus, especially if you are working with a client that changes their mind frequently…

9. Click a layer to make it the **active layer**, and then fine-tune the brightness, contrast, and color of **each of your** layers using Elements' regular tone-correction tools, such as **Levels**, **Brightness/Contrast**, **Hue/Saturation**, or **Unsharp Mask**.

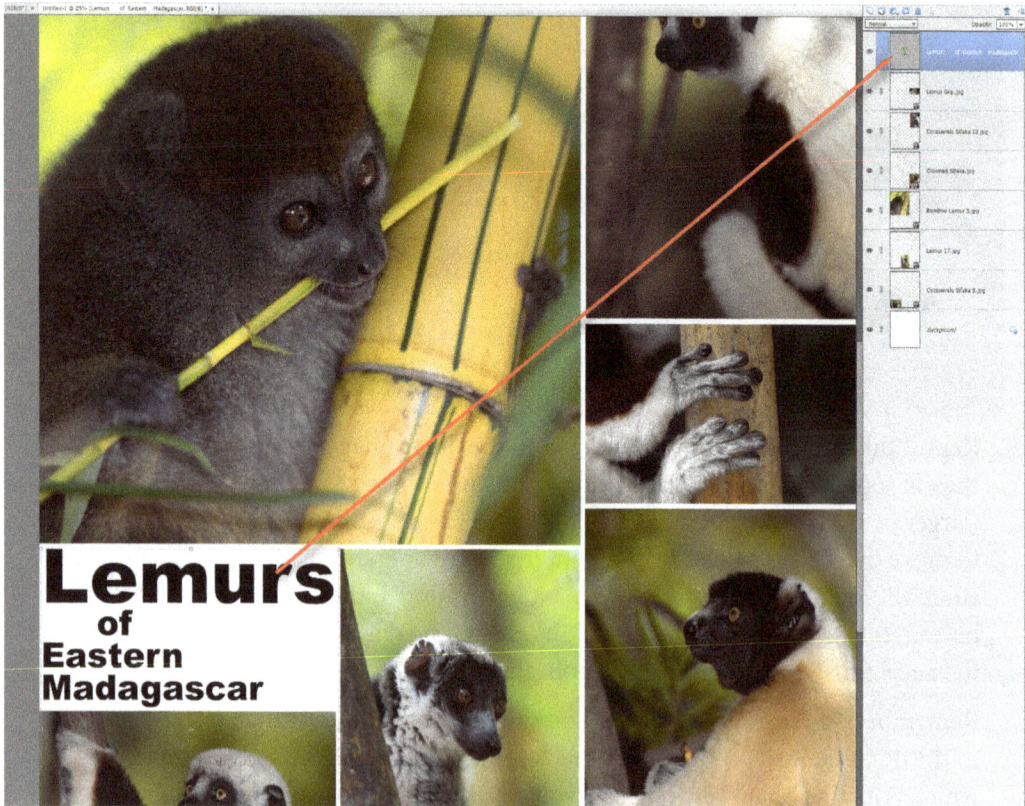

10. To add text to your project, choose the **Horizontal Type** tool from the toolbar (or press the *T* key), and then click once in the document to automatically create a new text layer (check the panel to confirm); note the type insertion point blinking just where you clicked in the image. Begin typing and the program will probably pick up the font and point size that were selected the last time the **Type** tool was used. Note that, by clicking once in the document to engage the **Type** tool, it will allow you to type a sentence.

If you want to add a block of text, the technique is slightly different. Instead of clicking once in the document, click, hold, and drag the cursor across the image to draw a textbox. Don't worry if it's in the wrong position or it's the wrong size or shape—both these things can be changed later. Now, if you begin typing, the word spread is restricted by the edges of the box. If the box isn't big enough, simply drag one of the corner handles to make it larger or a different shape.

Out of sheer habit, if a new text layer lands halfway up the layer stack, I usually drag it to the top so it's easily visible above the pixel-based layers. It's not necessary, but it might help you better organize any file that contains multiple layers.

Another way to work with text is to create your document in a standard word processing application (such as MS Word), and then simply select, copy, and paste that text directly into a Photoshop Elements textbox. Once the text has been added, you can select and then format it by changing the font, the color, the typestyle, and even the leading (that's the space between lines of type).

A really easy way to add text to any image is to use one of the text presets found in the **Graphics** panel. For more information on getting the best from the **Type** tool, check out the *Adding text to images* section later in this chapter.

Correcting perspective with Transformations

When shooting in cities, most photographers take pictures of architecture, grand old buildings, historical monuments, and even architecturally relevant new stuff. Architecture is a great subject, but because most of us photograph from ground level (and therefore point the camera upward), our pictures often suffer from **optical distortion**. By packing more information into a small frame using a wide-angle lens, the optical system cannot help but distort some of the vertical and horizontal lines. Shooting horizontally, from an upper floor opposite a tall building, means that you're likely to suffer less optical distortion because there's less reason to tilt the camera up to get everything into the frame. The following image shows one way around the problem of extreme optical distortion:

In the days before software applications such as Photoshop Elements, photographers had to spend upward of $3,000 to buy a **perspective correction lens** (also called a **tilt-shift lens**). These lenses typically come in 24 mm and 35 mm focal lengths and are physically split in the middle, allowing the user to slide the front section up or down, which, in turn, corrects vertical lines that happen to be leaning in. These products are beautifully efficient, but cost a lot of money.

Don't worry, because with Photoshop Elements, we can correct most cases of perspective distortion using the **Transformation** function (which we just used to resize pictures for our poster). Here's how it works with a typically distorted architectural shot:

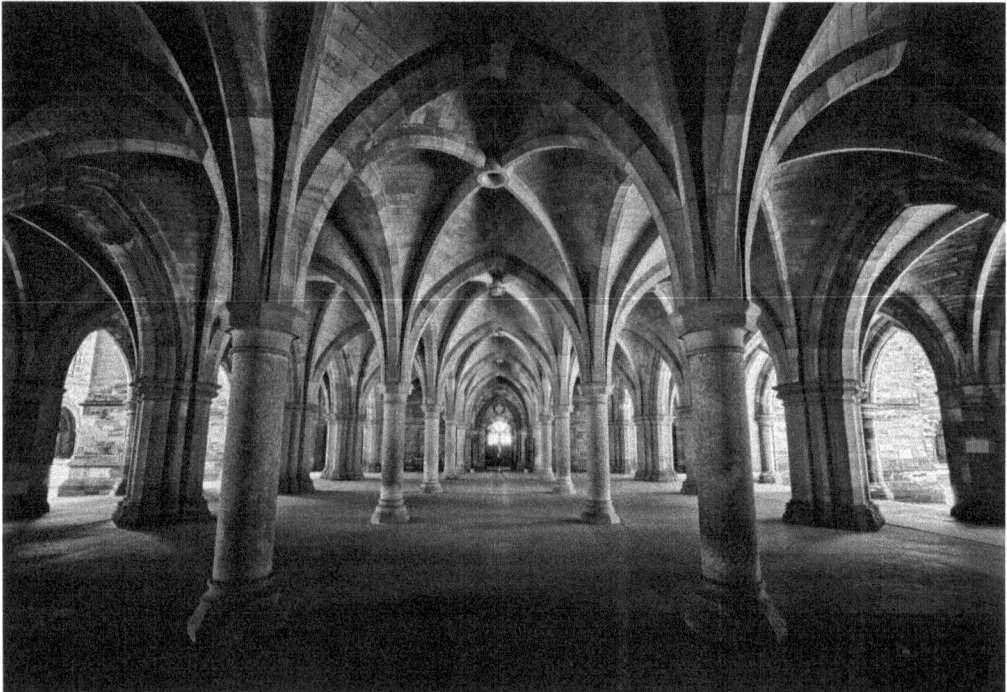

Open the offending picture. In this case, it's a magnificent vaulted ceiling supported by plenty of stone columns; you can clearly see that the wide-angle lens has added a fair bit of optical distortion to the columns, which we need to fix.

I use the **Grid** feature (**View** | **Grid**) on all images like this as it gives me a more accurate idea of what's vertical and what's not. If the **Grid** is too busy, reduce the number and color of the gridlines displayed via the program's **Preferences** (**Edit** | **Preferences** or *Ctrl/Cmd + K*):

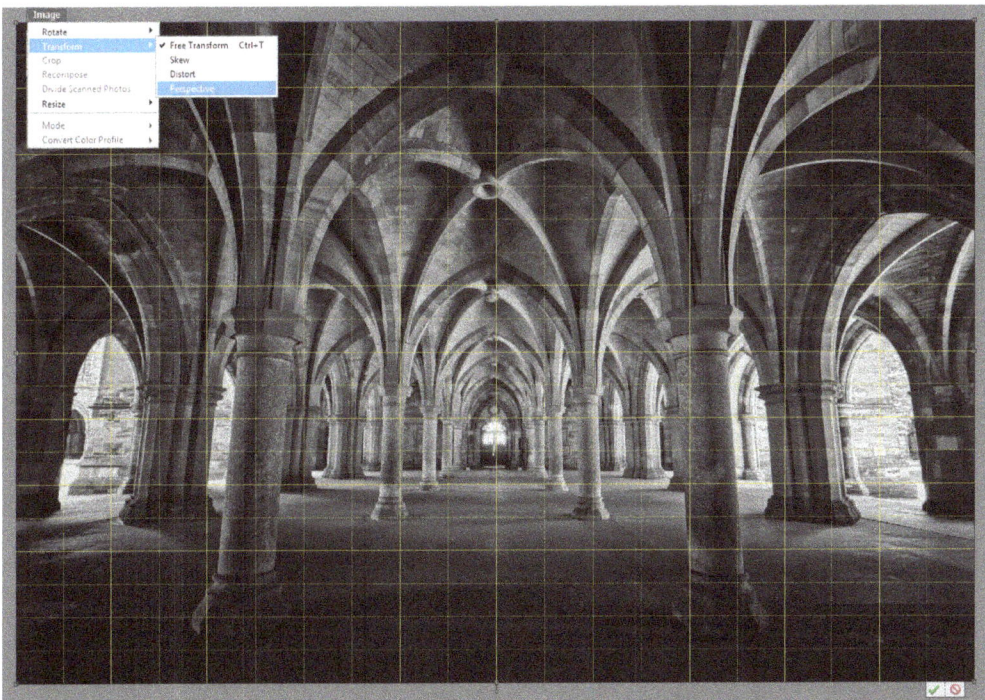

Here's the magic bit. Turn the **Transformation** feature on (*Ctrl/Cmd + T* or **Image** | **Transform** | **Perspective**). The typical corners of the **Transformation** tool appear at the edges of the image.

Grab one of the top corners and drag it outward, away from the image, and note that in doing so, the opposite corner is also dragged out, mirroring your movement. Essentially, you are making the top of the image wider. Keep an eye on the **Grid** to make sure everything is as symmetrical as possible.

On paper, this technique must read like a dream because all those architectural shots with the building looking as though it's leaning backward can now be corrected. One of the downsides to this technique is that, if the correction is fairly dramatic, you'll also lose a fair amount of the original image as it drags the edges off the picture. Next time you're out shooting architecture, take a few steps further back to encompass more of the surrounding area so that, once edited in Photoshop Elements, you won't lose so many vital details in the transformation process.

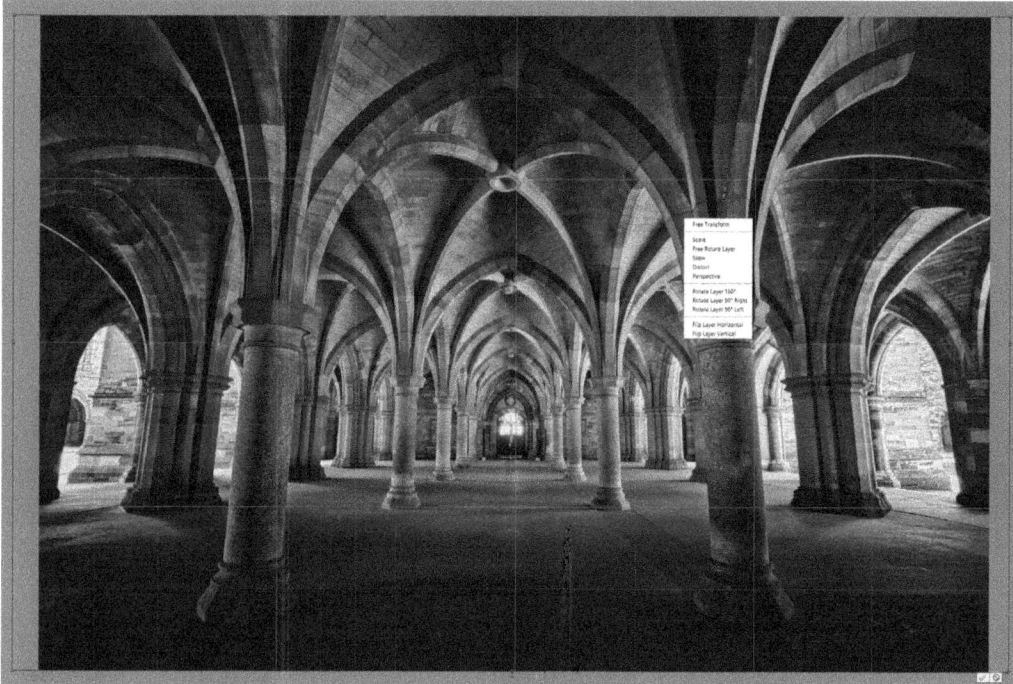

You'll note that the process of widening the top of the image not only loses a few pixels off the side of the rectangular photo, but it also makes it appear to be squatter. I usually finish off by resetting the **Transform** feature from **Perspective** to **Scale**, and then drag the top center handle upward to make the image higher, and therefore closer in proportion to the original, but without the added distortion. You will lose more of the image when doing this, but that's inevitable bearing in mind the pixel manipulations. Click the **OK** button and it's done.

Other Transformation modes

By right-clicking inside the transformation rectangle, you'll notice other modes, including the following:

- **Free Rotate Layer**: As the name suggests, if you move the cursor to one of the corners, you can click and rotate the entire image or image layer.

- **Skew**: This is an interesting distortion. In this mode, if you click and move any one of the central handles (not the corners), you'll see that they only move (skew) left or right. This is the perfect mode to make buildings appear to be leaning more vertically. That tower in Pisa, Italy, needs to lean no longer.

Let's take a look at how the **Skew** transformation mode works in practice.

Correcting skewed perspectives

Another thing to consider is that, when shooting architecture, we rarely stand 100% in front of the subject. Invariably, you'll find that all your pictures are shot slightly off-center, from the side, from the corner—in fact, at almost any angle but dead-center. What this means when you transform the perspective is that the left-hand transformation might not need quite as much distorting as the right-hand corner of the picture. The edited version will always look a little bit better, but if you want to be more accurate in your architectural reconstruction, you can always use other transformation modes, such as **Distort** and **Skew**. Look at the following image:

Here's a very typical example of a wide-angle lens distorting a tall building. I was standing as far back as I could get in St Mark's Square in Venice to get this shot (the further you stand back from the subject, the less the optical distortion will show), but it's still not 100% correct. In this example, I also (accidentally) shot the scene without the camera being vertical, so the top of the bell tower is tilting to the left.

To access this menu, you really don't need to use the menu at the top of the screen—just right-click anywhere inside the transformation boundary that sits around your photo, and from the menu that pops out, choose **Distort**.

Distort works in a similar way to **Perspective**, although grabbing one handle and pulling only affects the pixels immediately around that handle. This means that if your perspective-fixing works but is too strong on one side, you can jump from **Perspective** mode to **Distort** mode and correct the part of the image that needs more or less distortion to make it look more realistic.

As a photographer that shoots with a wide-angle lens, I find the **Skew** mode particularly useful in correcting distorted elements in my images. Let's now look at how to use the **Skew** mode:

Open the offending shot and use the **Grid** to keep an eye on the efficiency of your distortion corrections. Use *Ctrl/Cmd + T* to activate the **Transformation** tool.

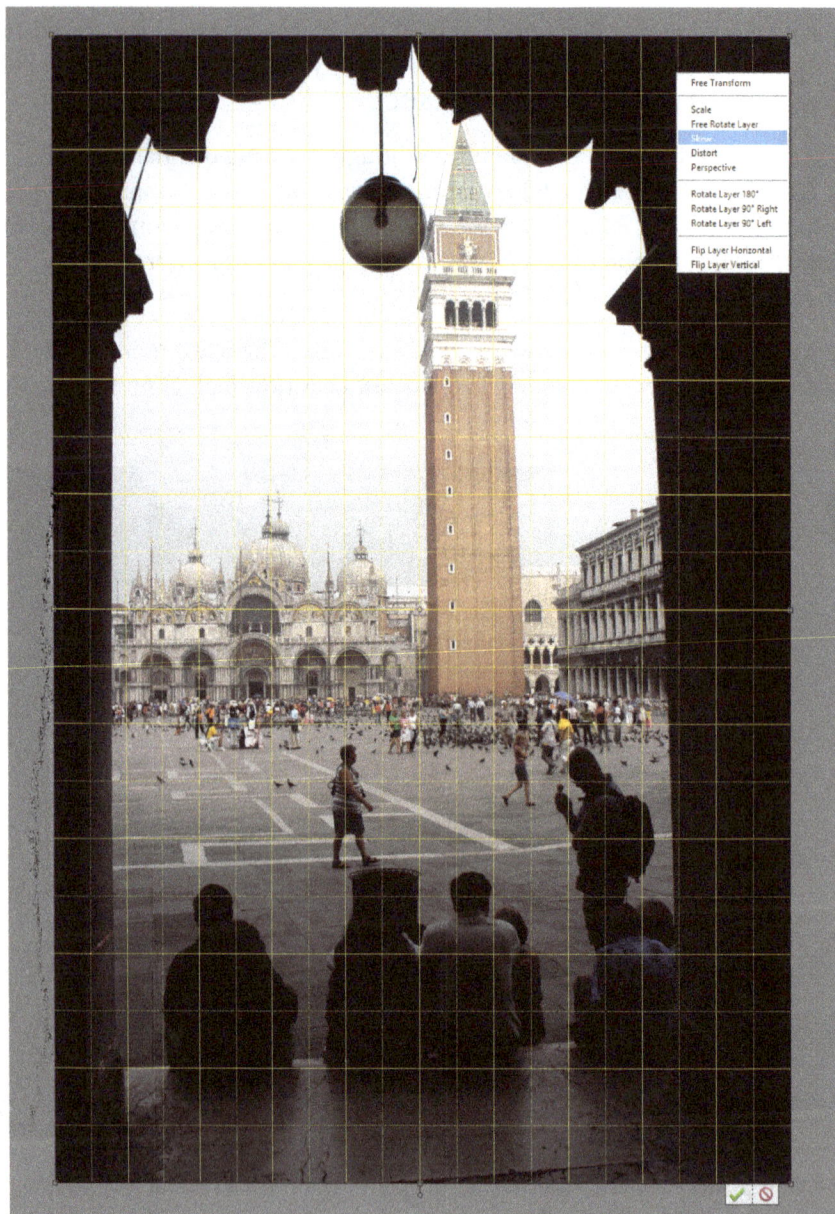

Once you see the tell-tale corner edges appear, you can right-click anywhere inside the image to set the **Transformation** mode—in this example, I need to choose **Skew**.

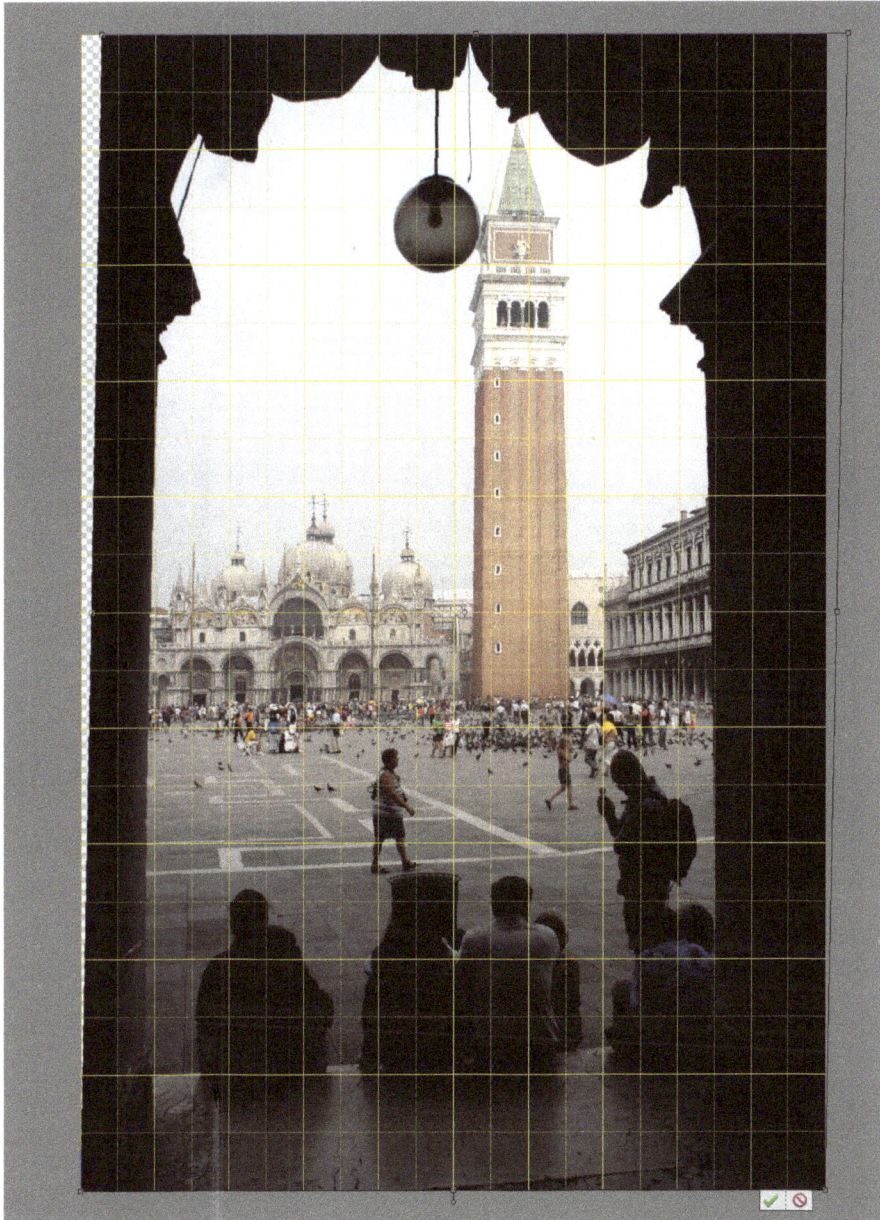

Skew will only work if you use the center handle. In this example, I want to swing the leaning tower to the right to correct its left-leaning distortion. As you do this, note that some transparent pixels appear on the left-hand side of the image because the pixels have been skewed to the right. If they remain there after the edit is finished, you will have to crop the final image.

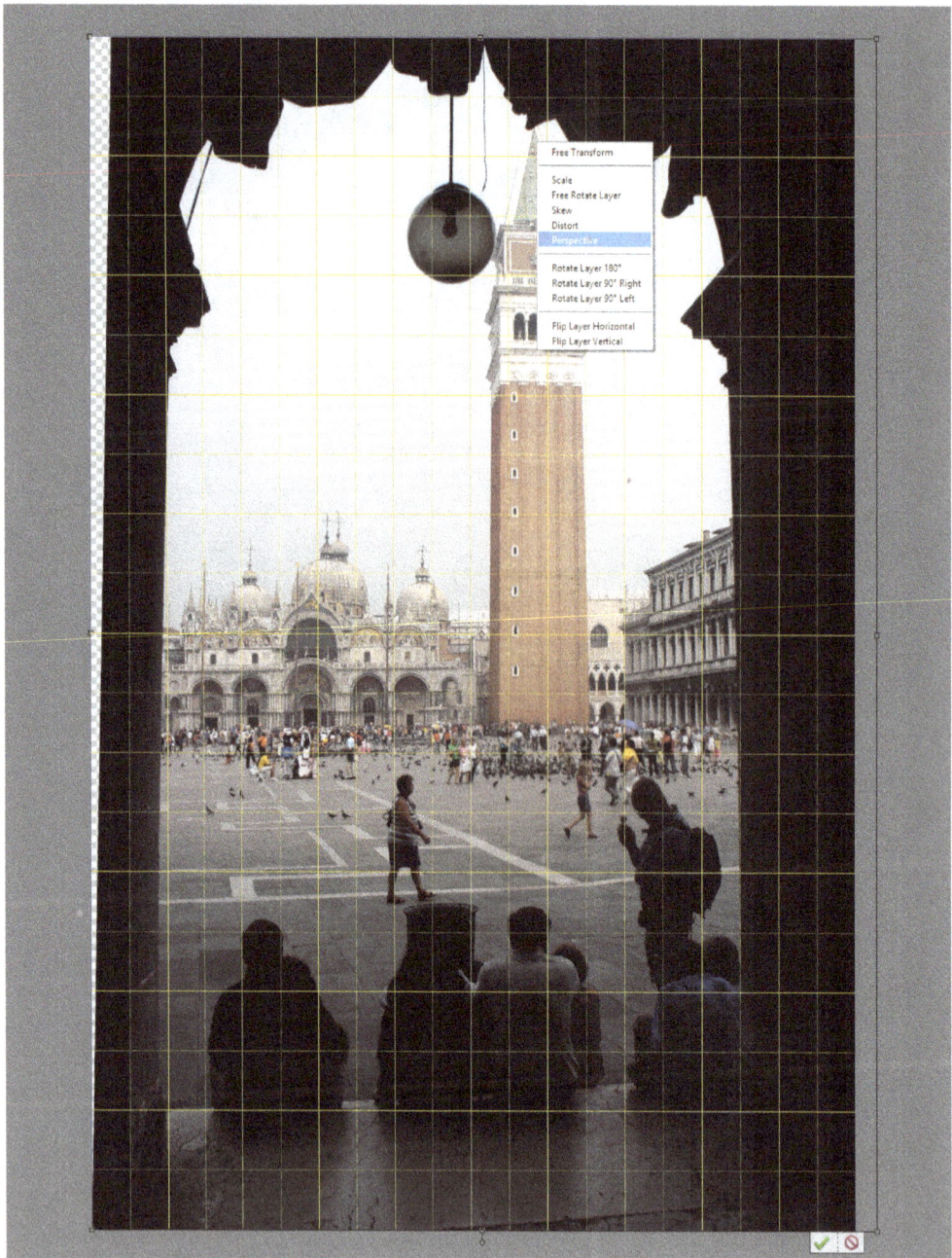

Now that I am happy that the tower is vertical, I can change from **Skew** mode to **Perspective** mode and try to widen the top of the frame to reduce or remove the optical distortion my lens has added to the frame.

This is the final version. But I think the lower left-hand side isn't 100% vertical, so I used the **Distort** mode to drag the doorframe back into vertical alignment.

This is the final result, having used the **Skew**, **Perspective**, and **Distort** modes to correct and largely remove the previous optical distortion. Don't forget that **Distort** mode allows you to move just one small edge or corner part of the image, so it's a perfect tool for adding the final tweaks to the file.

Working tips

When you are using Photoshop Elements, if you rotate a single image, you'll note that, because it's no longer vertical or horizontal, the application doesn't fill in the resulting gaps around the image, leaving transparent spaces. This is OK if you're saving the document in Photoshop, Tiff, or PNG file format (all of which can preserve transparency), but if it's saved as a JPEG, those transparent pixels are replaced with the foreground color—by default, this is white. As a working tip, I tend to duplicate my layer first so that, if the transformation on the **Duplicate Layer** reveals some of the image on the **Background Layer**, it's far less noticeable than transparent or white pixels.

As an alternative, once rotated, you can always **crop** the image to trim off those transparent or white edges, thereby making the entire image a little smaller.

Transformations can also be used to *add perspective distortion* elements in a multilayered composition—to emphasize perspective to create a **vanishing point**.

Layer Masking

To be honest, layer masking was a Photoshop Elements feature that I dreaded trying out because I thought it looked overly complex. It took me a few days to get my head around the idea of painting with a black or white paintbrush directly onto the picture to create a mask (), but once I realized why you needed to do this, it (almost) became the easiest thing ever. So, if at first, you don't succeed, try again, because once mastered, layer masking will provide you with the ultimate editing control.

Let's have a look at how this works.

Most photographers, I'm sure, will agree when I say that you can only take your editing so far using Elements' excellent **global tone-changing tools**. In this book, we have seen how effective the **Levels** and **Hue/Saturation** tools can be, but sooner rather than later, you'll realize that you need to develop special skills in order to edit small parts of your picture rather than the entire thing at the same time. This is one reason why I like the idea of painting in **lightness**, **darkness**, or **saturation** using the **Dodge**, **Burn**, or **Sponge** tools. Let's look at what we can do with these features by going through the following steps:

Setting up a **Layer Mask** is easy. Begin by opening the image that you'd like to work on; I'll use the preceding image to illustrate what we're doing. Duplicate the layer; this stage is not vital to the editing process, but out of habit, I've always kept the original layer intact and operated on or edited a duplicate so that I can easily go back to the original in the same file by switching the editing layer's visibility to **Off** (by clicking the eye icon)

Make sure that the **Layer** panel is fully visible and check that the top layer – the duplicated layer – is the active layer (highlighted in blue). Above that layer sits a row of buttons that are very specific to layer editing. The feature that we are interested in here is the fourth icon from the left, called the **Add a Layer Mask** button. Click this and note that a **white thumbnail** appears to the right-hand side of that layer's photo thumbnail. Congratulations! You have just created your first layer mask on your own. A white layer mask is totally transparent, so it serves no purpose.

The next step is to edit that particular layer. As an example, let's brighten the image using **Levels** (*Ctrl/Cmd* + *L*). Before you do this, it's important to make sure that the photo thumbnail, and not the white mask thumbnail, is **highlighted**. Double-clicking the thumbnail selects it, and you'll see that the thumbnail is highlighted in light blue. Now, adjust the image. Everything looks 100% normal; the white mask is still fully transparent, so all we see on screen is the adjusted version. Some parts look good, while others appear a bit too bright.

Now comes the magic. Clicking the white layer thumbnail will make it highlighted around the edges in **light blue**. This is now the **active** part of that layer. Select the **Brush** tool (making doubly sure that it is the real paintbrush and not the **Impressionist Brush** or the **Color Replacement Brush**), and choose black from the **Color Picker** (the two small color squares under **Modify** at the bottom of the toolbar). A quick way to do this is to press the *D* key, which sets a default of white in the foreground color and black as the background color, and then press the *X* key, which automatically flips the foreground to the background (to give you black paint). Now, paint over the object in the image that you want to be brought back to the original brightness, and as you paint onto the image (but it's actually onto the mask) with a brush loaded with black paint, you'll note that the original brightness and contrast return. Release the mouse and note that the black paint appears not in the main image but in the mask thumbnail.

Releasing the mouse reveals the painting on the mask, so if you keep an eye on this feature while you create your mask, it will keep updating.

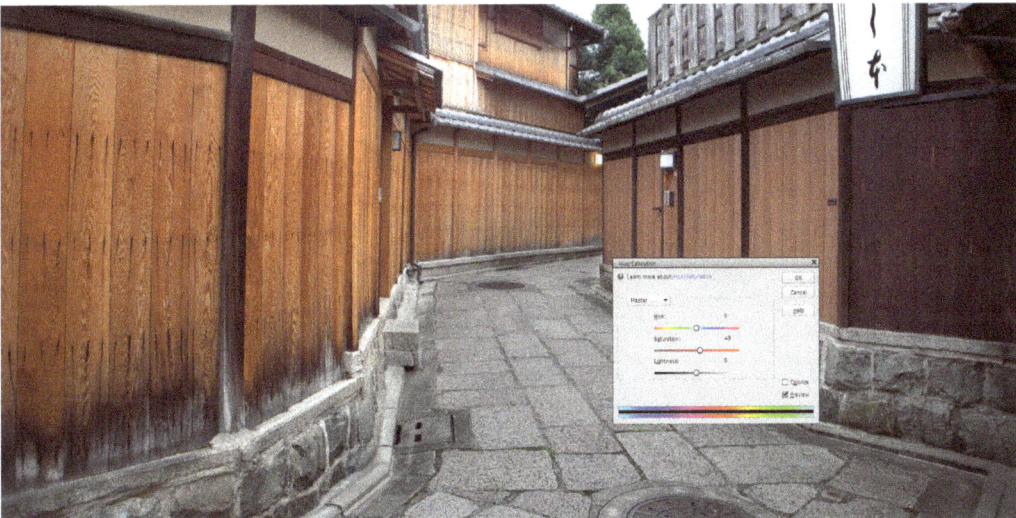

You are not restricted to just using **Levels**; any tool that can be used to change the tonal properties of the image can be used to change the tones in the masked areas. I added more color intensity to the wooden walls to emphasize the character of these very old Japanese buildings with **Hue/Saturation**.

I think what concerned me when I first started masking was the concept of physically painting into the photograph on the main screen and yet seeing no black paint appear. Instead, it magically reveals the original state of that picture. If you don't select the white mask before you start painting, you will just paint black onto the main image—you'll know it's wrong immediately. If this happens, **undo** the brushstroke, select the white thumbnail, and start over.

The magic of this technique becomes apparent if you make a mistake and paint over something in the mask so that a part of the image returns to the original tone when you really wanted it to remain as per the enhanced look. If this happens, tap the *X* key to flip the background to the foreground so that the brush is loaded with white paint and not black paint, and paint over your mistake. Magically, the mistake is erased with the application of white paint over black. The real beauty of this technique is that this backward/forward masking can be infinite. You can do it as many times as you need in order to get the balance just right.

> **Layer mask tips**
>
> Always make sure that the mask is active (highlighted in blue); otherwise, all your painting/masking will come to nothing. Use the *D* key to reset the color picker to a black foreground over a white background and use the *X* key to change between foreground and background colors.

Don't forget that you can further refine this technique by changing the size, shape, opacity, and softness of the brush that you're using. This gives the designer or photographer *infinite levels of control* in terms of adding subtle changes to any image.

Erasing Tools

Before computers, graphic-design studios used a range of drawing tools such as pens, pencils, brushes, and charcoals. They also used a range of *erasers* to remove mess, mistakes, and drawing errors. Photoshop Elements also has a range of eraser tools, the most commonly used being the **Eraser Brush**. Use this to remove excess pixels when blending images on top of each other, for example. The **Eraser Brush** works with all 300+ brush tips, and if you erase on the **Background Layer**, it will always erase back to the background color (which will be black by default). If you are erasing on a duplicated layer, it will reveal the pixels on the layer immediately beneath it.

Erasing has three brush modes: **Block**, **Brush**, and **Pencil**—although I think the **Brush** setting is the best for most retouching tasks as it's the softest and most controllable. The speed of the erasing process is controlled by the **Opacity** slider. Set it to 50% and you'll have to go over the layer twice to remove all the pixels.

The **Background Eraser** is a useful tool because it's based on the brightness of the pixels that are clicked. Click the background and drag the cursor through the image. It should erase only those that are close in color to the initial click, leaving other colors untouched. Use the **Tolerance** slider to increase/decrease how much latitude the color selection has. It's efficiency, like many tools in photo editing, relies on the type of image being edited as much as the capability of the tool used.

The **Magic Eraser**, as the name might suggest, automatically removes same-colored pixels once clicked. If the background is one color, it's an efficient tool to use. If the background is composed of many different colored pixels, you might find one of the other two eraser tools do a cleaner, more accurate job. Here's the Eraser Brush tool options panel floating on the image we will work on:

That said, this is the perfect tool for a small business, for example, that has a range of products carefully shot on a specific color background, like the preceding yoga image, making it easy to select and replace when and where necessary.

But in the next image, you'll see that the selection process is never as straightforward as one click that does it all. As the woman's arms form a perfect junction with her knees, the background between her arms and body has not been erased. Clicking in each of these white, unerased areas will finish off the background removal.

Another way to grab all similar colored pixels in an image is to set **Discontiguous** in the tool's **Options** panel (or just turn **Contiguous** off). This *tells* Elements to erase any pixels that match the sample taken when the image is clicked, regardless of whether they are adjoining.

In the final frame seen here, I added a random abstract background from the my backgrounds library to demonstrate the effectiveness of the **Magic Eraser** feature.

Tip

What's a background library? Many artists, designers, video editors, and photographers subscribe to online asset libraries where, for a small fee, they can use royalty-free images of things such as clouds, textures, patterns—you name it, and the library probably has it for rent or purchase. That said, it does no harm to start on your own collection of textures, colors, patterns, and so forth. Travel with a camera and pop off a few shots each time you go out and you'll soon build up your own, very convenient image library. But don't stop at images. You might also record video clips, live sound, sound effects and even clip art, depending on your creative requirements.

Gradient tool

Another greatly underrated tool in Elements is the **Gradient** tool. Those photographers among you who have used a graduated resin filter over the front of the lens from manufacturers such as **Cokin**, **Lee Filters**, and **B&W** will know what I am talking about.

Place the filter over the lens and position the darker part over the sky, with the clearer section at the base over the landscape. This effectively reduces the sky exposure, thereby balancing the often large exposure disparity that leaves us with an overexposed upper half and an underexposed lower half of the frame. Graduated filters come in different colors (for example, orange to enhance sunsets or sunrises).

This tool comes with 16 default gradients and eight gradient subcategories, giving you a choice of 83 in total. I have only ever used two or three.

> **Tip**
>
> Before you apply any gradient, create a new blank layer and apply the gradient to that. It works just the same, but since it is on its own layer, it can be moved and its opacity tempered according to the effect. Make sure that the layer's blending mode is set to **Overlay** before you start. If two gradients are too strong but one is not strong enough, reduce the opacity on the second gradient layer to 50%.

The **Gradient** tool can be used to completely transform an image in a range of different ways—from a simple color overlay, as shown in the following steps, to more localized effects when combined with selections and masks.

Here's a great-looking sunset shot, complete with two figures silhouetted by a bright sunset sky. Let's edit it. By clicking on the **Gradient** tool icon (toolbar) and then clicking the gradient thumbnail in the tool's options panel (highlighted in red), open the complex-looking **Gradient Editor**. Because my color picker is already set to its default black background color, you can see that the second-from-left thumbnail is black, fading to transparent (highlighted in red in the image). Click once to select, then hit **OK**, and you are good to go:

Before applying the **gradient,** you must change the blending mode for that tool; otherwise, you'll slap a pile of opaque black pixels onto the image, which will be a disaster! Choose **Overlay**, then, starting at the top-center of the screen, click, hold, and then drag the cursor south in a straight line. If you drag the gradient all the way to the base of the screen, the gradient effect will be long and smooth.

If you only drag the gradient a short way across the screen, the gradation will be very steep, and therefore quite noticeable, which is something you might not want. In this example, the **Gradient** is so steep it looks like a mistake—which it is:

Here's a before and after comparison. On the left is the original file, and on the right is the image featuring a gradient, applied twice, so that it's quite a dramatic color change compared with the original.

As a final thought regarding this tool, if you'd like to retain greater control, consider creating a new layer (**Layer** | **New Layer**) and applying the gradient to that so that it can be repositioned or the opacity of the layer can be adjusted. Make sure that **Overlay** is selected from the **Layer** panel drop-down menu; otherwise, it will look like the preceding screenshot, without any translucency:

Another way of getting greater control over where in the image the gradient actually falls would be to add a layer mask, and then paint black into the mask to modify the gradient—in this case, from the couple sitting on the bench, the ocean, and the foreground.

Keyboard shortcuts

As with most editing, you can lose sight of the image-making process and become too immersed in the more complex editing functions. Keyboard shortcuts are there to help spread the load, reduce RSI, and generally speed up your workflow. I use the first three all the time. It's also beneficial for you to memorize some of the tool access keys (letters) to make it easier to jump from process to process. Some of these are shown in the following list:

- *Ctrl/Cmd + J*: Duplicate the (active) layer.
- *Ctrl/Cmd + D*: Use this to deselect or remove any active selection.
- *Ctrl/Cmd + T*: Use this to transform objects on the active layer.
- *Ctrl/Cmd + E*: Merge down.
- *Shift + Ctrl/Cmd + E*: Merge (all) visible (layers).
- *O*: Burn, Dodge, and Sponge tools.
- *A*: Selection brushes (Quick Selection, Selection Brush, Magic Wand, Refine Selection, and Auto Selection).
- *L*: Lasso tools (Freehand Lasso, Polygonal Lasso, and Magnetic Lasso).

- *S*: Clone Stamp tool (also the Pattern Stamp).

- *J*: Spot Healing and Healing Brushes.

- *B*: Brushes (Brush tool, Impressionist Brush, and Color Replace Brush).

- *E*: Eraser brushes (Eraser, Background Eraser, and Magic Eraser brushes).

- *K*: Paint Bucket tool.

- *G*: Gradient tool.

- *Alt/Opt + Ctrl/Cmd + S*: **Enhance |Select Subject**.

Out of the hundreds of possible keyboard shortcuts published for this program, I consider those on this page and the previous one to be the most important. They sum up the most practical features in this program and, once learned, will advance your understanding and editing proficiency tenfold.

Summary

As you may well now be aware, it's possible to spend your entire working life immersed in the realms of commercial photography and professional retouching.

All the necessary tools are abundantly present in Photoshop Elements, but if you need to take the control you require to a higher level, this was certainly the chapter for you.

In this chapter, we ramped up the knowledge this book has explored so far by introducing you to layers—in their basic easy-to-use 'pseudo' form and then, in their most advanced guise: adjustment layers and full-on layer masking.

You have also learned how to enhance images and create powerful graphic effects using blending modes, layer opacity, layer transformations, and much more.

Learning to use layers like this will enhance your creativity tenfold. But that's not all; we also highlighted the power of its erasing tools, along with the often misunderstood but very useful Gradient tool.

Coming up in the next chapter are more extremely practical sections that will extend your experiences with layers: we'll take a close look at the intricacies of beauty retouching using the Clone Stamp and Healing Brush tools, as well as learning how to improve images with the amazing Burn, Dodge, and Sponge Brush tools. The chapter will also cover how to work with another powerful tool found in Elements—selection, which is used to limit the editing process to specific parts of the image only. The final part of the chapter takes you in the direction of graphic design with the use of text, and all its different applications, using special effects.

7
Advanced Techniques: Retouching, Selections, and Text

With the experience of understanding layers now safely in your repertoire of skills, it's time to look a little closer at developing your retouching skills. Elements 2020 has a range of very high-end tools with which to perfect your work— whether it's portraiture, weddings, or landscapes.

One of the big issues with regular photo-editing tools such as Levels and Hue/Saturation is that their effects are global—everything in the image is affected proportionally. To limit the spread of these effects to a specific part of the frame, we look at making **selections**, using a wide range of tools designed for isolating parts of an image for detailed, non-global editing.

And if this is not enough, the last section in this chapter is designed to ease you (slightly) in the direction of the graphic designer as we look at creating illustrations using Elements' range of downloadable graphics, and using text in all its forms, shapes, and effects. There's also a roundup of useful tools that often get passed over by some publications—for example, the excellent Custom Shape, Cookie Cutter, and Paint Bucket tools, and more.

In short, this chapter is designed to build on the lessons of the previous one, building up and focusing your editing skills so you can, with the right inspiration, create almost anything with the software.

Principal features in this chapter include the following:

- Beauty retouching
- The **Burn**, **Dodge**, and **Sponge** tools
- The selection tools
- Removing large objects
- Working with graphic elements
- Adding text to images
- Keyboard shortcuts

Beauty retouching

In this section, I will show you how to correct the tones, imperfections, and *look* of a simple beauty shot, step by step. In this process, you'll learn how to use the **Clone Stamp** tool, one of the original and incredibly powerful retouching tools in Photoshop Elements, as well as the amazing **Burn**, **Dodge**, and **Sponge** brush tools (but mostly **Dodge** and **Sponge**) that I consider to be among the many unsung heroes of this application.

The Clone Stamp tool explained

The **Clone Stamp** tool is one of the original retouching tools handed down from Adobe Photoshop in the years before it was Photoshop **Creative Cloud** (**CC**).

Essentially, this is nothing more than a **copy-and-paste tool**. If any of you have had the opportunity to copy and paste a paragraph of text from one part of a Word document to another part, you'll be able to use this tool. It's exactly the same principle, but because you are also dealing with color, texture, and tone in an image, the process is a little more complex than merely copying black-and-white text.

The important thing to remember with the **Clone Stamp** tool is that you need to identify a clear **Source** area first. This is the area from where the undamaged pixels are copied. If you can find a part of the image that closely matches the color, texture, and brightness of the area immediately around the damaged part of the image (called the **Target** area), it will make the process 100% easier and significantly more convincing.

One of the disadvantages of the **Clone Stamp** tool is that it copies everything and pastes everything, unless the opacity of the tool is reduced first. When we looked at the **Spot Healing Brush** tool, another copy-and-paste retouching tool, we saw that it also blends pixels in to the same color and brightness as those in the **Target** area, a huge benefit in many retouching instances.

So, why bother with the **Clone Stamp** if the **Spot Healing Brush** makes everything appear a lot smoother with its awesome blending capabilities?

The disadvantage of the **Clone Stamp** is its inability to truly blend pixels. So, if your **Source** area is a little more textured or darker/brighter than the **Target** area, any attempt at retouching seamlessly is going to fail. In fact, you'll discover that, in most examples, there simply might not be enough pixels of the same color/texture/brightness to make it work at all.

Although this sounds like a disastrous PR exercise for the poor old **Clone Stamp**, bear in mind that there might be a few occasions where copying precisely everything from point A to point B might just be what's needed. For example, you might want to move an object in the frame rather than removing it entirely, or you might need to cover up a tattoo. You can do this using a **Selection** tool (a process that's a little more involved), but you can also do this using the **Clone Stamp** tool. Copying and pasting an object onto a new (blank) layer gives you the added advantage that, once pasted, the cloned object (let's say it's a sheep) can be moved around the frame, resized, recolored, and so on.

Perhaps more commonly, beauty retouchers use the **Clone Stamp**, with its opacity set to a low number, to copy and paste pixels again and again and again, while moving the **Target** area slightly with each click, which effectively softens the **Target** area. This is brilliant for smoothing out skin tones to create a porcelain look that's impossible to achieve using Healing Brushes.

Retouching in practice

To familiarize ourselves with retouching, we will be using the following original unedited file as a practice example. It's OK, but as you can immediately appreciate, it's dark and murky, plus it has quite a few problem areas that are quite normal in a model shoot but that need to be fixed. When embarking on any editing process, I think it's vital to set out a plan—essentially, what you want to achieve and the order in which you want it done:

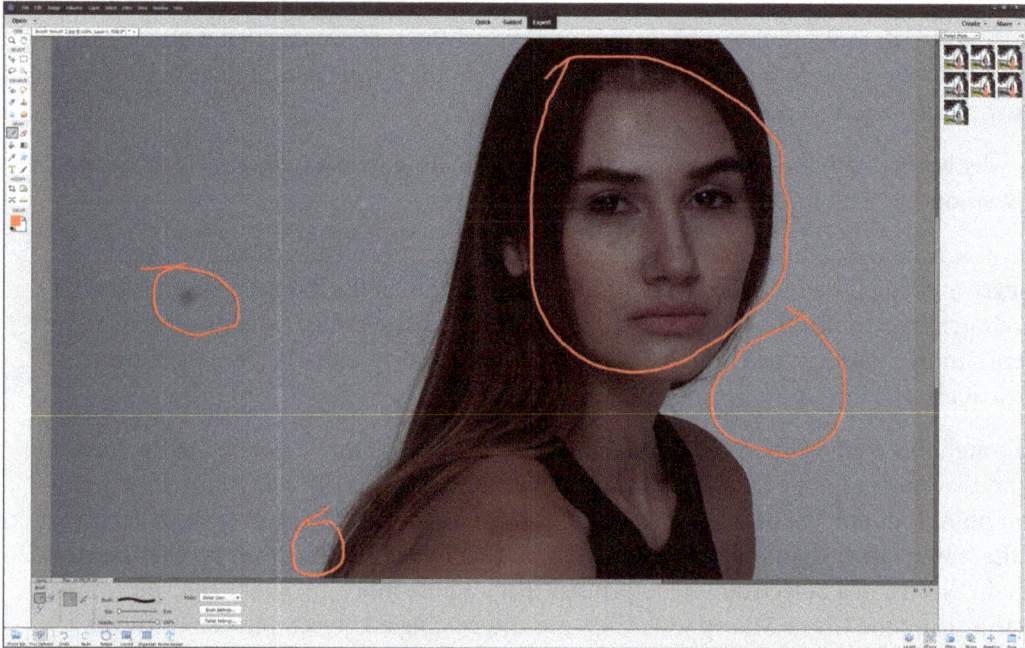

I have ringed most of the obvious errors that you might want to edit. The entire image needs brightening first. Then, the model's face could use a little pimple fixing, plus some skin smoothing and lightening. Her hair is a bit flyaway, so we can also remove some of the individual strands of hair on the face and against the dull-looking background.

In the following set of images, I will show you how to go about editing such a picture, and while the actions are specific to this model shot, the issues (that is, the dull tones, sensor spots, and skin imperfections) are common to many of our images. As a result of these actions, we should be in a position to radically improve the look of the sample image, as follows:

As with most editing projects, I like to *duplicate the layer* first. It's not essential, but I like to have the original handy so I can refer back to that—and other layers—as I proceed. To duplicate the layer, go to **Layer | Duplicate**. Also note that, because this is quite an involved edit, it's good practice to actually *name your layers* as you go (to name a specific layer, make sure that the Layers Panel is open then double-click the name tag for the layer you want to rename and type in your own description. By default new layers will be 'Layer 1', 'Layer 2', etc.). I used **Levels** to lighten the tones in the duplicated layer first (*Ctrl/Cmd + L*).

With the image now considerably lighter, you can clearly see more blemishes than were originally visible, not least the **sensor spots** - dark blobs on the background—these are caused by dirt or moisture getting into the camera, usually while a lens is being changed. You can have the sensor professionally cleaned for around US$45.

You could buy yourself a set of **sensor swabs** with which to clean your camera's sensor, but perhaps the quickest and most economical method of smoothing out and beautifying the skin tones would be to use either the **Perfect Portrait** feature (found in the **Guided edit** mode) or the new **Smooth Skin** feature that you'll find in Elements' **Expert edit** mode, the former of which is illustrated in the following screenshot:

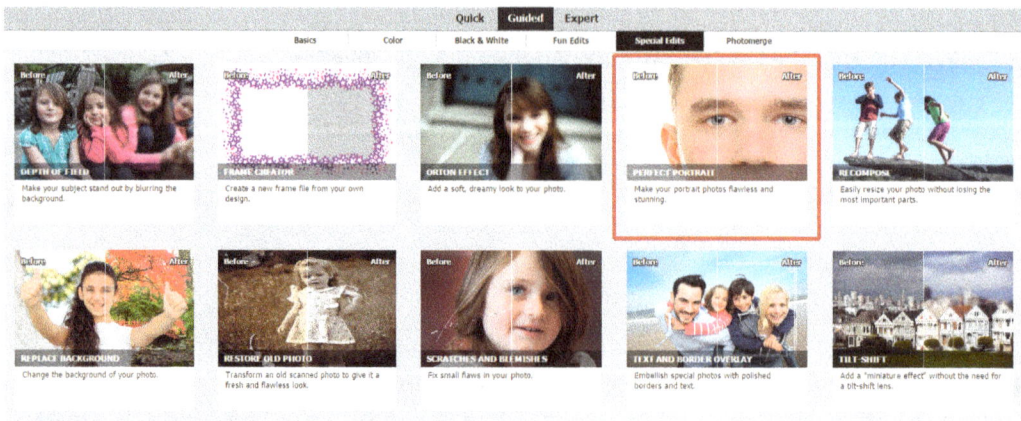

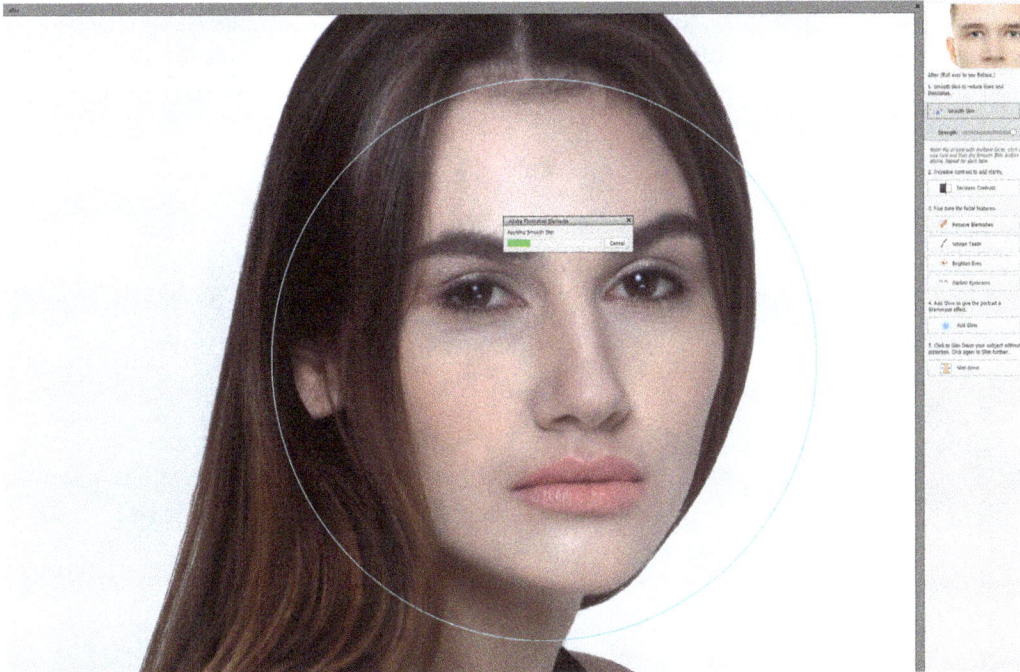

If you are stuck for time, or don't want the effort of learning the basics of retouching using the **Clone Stamp Brush** or the **Healing Brush** tools, use the **Perfect Portrait** feature or, maybe simpler still, use Elements' new **Enhance | Smooth Skin** feature. As you can clearly see in the preceding screenshot, **Perfect Portrait** also allows you to increase the contrast (which I did here), use the retouching tools, and add a beautiful glow, all in the space of a few minutes. It's a great feature that, like most of Elements semi-automated processes, works almost flawlessly, as seen in the following screenshot:

The new **Smooth Skin** feature, found under the **Enhance** menu, is simpler than **Perfect Portrait**. It isolates the face automatically (as you can see in the inset screen of the following screenshot), offering a degree-of-softening effect and a preview On/Off slider:

The result that you can see in the following screenshot is impressive, but note that it doesn't work unless the **artificial intelligence** (**AI**) can detect a face in the image:

Now, let's move on and see how the professional retouching tools—the **Spot Healing Brush** tool and the **Healing** and **Clone Stamp** brush tools—work.

Combining the Spot Healing Brush and the Clone Stamp tools

Removing the sensor spots would be my first job using the **Spot Healing Brush**. This should be an easy *click-and-move-on* process because the **Spot Healing Brush** simply copies pixels from the outer areas of the brush shape (usually a circle) and pastes them into the inner area, while matching those pixels' tones, color, and brightness. It's a magic tool and ideal for this step.

Make sure that the brush tip is about the same size as the blemish, or a little larger. If it's too large, it might copy in parts of the image you don't want to use for the repair. If the brush is too small, it might just leave a smudge. Don't forget also you can click-hold-move the cursor across the blemish to create a larger retouch area, as seen in the following screenshot. This works particularly well if the area to be fixed is an irregular shape. Note that the "healing" process only starts once the mouse button is released:

One great working tip is to use the square brackets ([]) to change the size of your brush or retouching tool. This is a much more efficient method than mousing down to the Options panel at the bottom of the screen all the time. Note that this keyboard shortcut works for all of Adobe's brush, retouching, and drawing tools. It will save you a heap of time, and the result can be seen in the following screenshot:

The preceding screenshot shows a closer view of the face. I held the mouse button and dragged the cursor along some straggly hair on the right-hand side of the face. Even though my freehand action was very wobbly, it worked quite well because the brush shape/size—the black dot upper right—covered the blemish area completely (once dragged).

In the lower example in the screenshot, I chose a far larger brush size, hoping to retouch the stray hair in one swipe of the brush. But as you can see, the model now has two chins. One important tip to remember is that the larger the brush, the further afield the software "looks" for pixels to bring into the brush shape. Running too close to the model's face in this example created pixel mayhem. Thank goodness for the **Undo** button!

Cloning is a different type of retouching process compared to the **Spot Healing Brush** tool. With the **Clone Stamp** tool, although it's a copy-and-paste process similar to the **Healing Brush**'s action, *it does not match the pixel's color, tone, or brightness*. Therefore, if you paste light pixels over dark pixels, it shows up as light on dark. So, how is this tool going to be helpful here? Follow these steps to find out:

1. Firstly, choose the **Clone Stamp** tool (by using the *S* key or selecting it from the toolbar). Choose a soft brush tip, setting its **opacity** to around 50–75%, then ensure that the **Alignment** checkbox in the tool's **Options** panel is set to **Off**.

2. What I did here in the next screenshot was to copy the highlights in the model's right eye and paste it over the (less bright) highlight in the left eye (arrowed). With a brush tip about the same size as the subject being copied, I chose *Ctrl/Opt*, then clicked into the right eye. This is referred to as the **Source area**. The program copies the pixels into the computer's virtual memory.

3. Release the mouse button, move the cursor from the **Source area** to over the Target area (arrowed, in the following example). Click once. In this case, the tool was set with a lowish opacity (75%), so it only transferred three quarters of the highlight from the right eye. A second click finished off the transfer, with the result seen in the screenshot overleaf:

'Target' area   'Source' area

As you see, the finished article, with equal brightness highlights in the eyes, looks 100% better. Don't forget the **Clone Stamp** can also be used to **add items to an image**. In the following bird shot, I cloned a single bird multiple times onto separate layers. Adding the cloned item to a different layer enables you to trim off excess pixels, resize the cloned image, and change its shape for the purpose, here, of fakery...:

The Burn, Dodge, and Sponge tools

The **Burn**, **Dodge**, and **Sponge** tools are probably the best unsung heroes of Elements. Why? Simple: they are easy to use and are very effective.

The **Burn** and **Dodge** tools are electronic representations of what I did for years in a black-and-white printing lab. "Burning-in" a photo was a technique for making part of a print darker than the rest of the image, using something such as a cardboard mask with a hole in it to make it happen. After the base exposure was done, I'd continue to expose the print—but only the bits of it that I needed to go darker—by holding the cardboard mask between the enlarger lamp and the photo paper. By gently moving the card mask so that the additional exposure only fell onto the area that I wanted to go darker, I could manipulate the global exposure so that it became a custom exposure. A dodging tool worked in reverse. This was a hand-cut bit of card taped to some wire and held between the enlarger lamp and photo paper to stop light getting to parts of the print that would have otherwise come out too dark.

When it worked well, the results were good, but it was hit and miss, and could not be repeated accurately. Then came Photoshop Elements, and my retouching and printing life changed forever.

The following image of an African elephant shows what you can achieve using these selective darkening/lightening brushes—add life to shady areas, while dramatically darkening other tones to add impact to the composition:

All three tools work just like a paint brush. The brush tip has a variable size for different problem areas, a variable hardness, and a massive range of different shapes. But the real strength of these tools is in the tonal range that you can set them to operate in: **highlights**, **midtones**, and **shadows** (note that the **Sponge** tool only has a **Saturate** and a **Desaturate** mode).

With these tools, I can paint additional darkness into the shadows, lighten the highlights, or increase the local color saturation of almost any part of almost any image. Here's what these tools can do:

- **Burn** tool: Use this brush to darken the shadows, midtones, or highlights of your image. It's best to start with the **Exposure** setting at 10% or 15%—any higher and your brushing becomes hard to conceal. You should also choose a largish brush size, and maybe a soft-edge brush tip to further conceal any brushing marks. The lower the **Exposure** (or speed of the effect), the more brush strokes are required, but the more subtle the effect. Burning in the shadows has the most dramatic effect; burning in a highlight, especially one that's nearly 100% white, often makes the area look muddy because there's no tone in that area to burn in, so scale it down a bit. I usually start by darkening the midtones first, then I move on to the shadows.

- **Dodge** tool: Use this tool to lighten details in the shadows, midtones, and highlights of your image. Trying to lighten details in the dark shadows often makes the tones appear grayish or ghostly—not a good look. This brush works best if it's used to lighten/brighten midtones and highlights. As with the **Burn** brush, you should keep the **Exposure** setting between 5% and 10% to avoid over-brightening the highlights and clipping tones (thereby losing detail permanently). Lightening highlights and darkening midtones/shadows really pumps up local contrast.

- **Sponge** tool: Use this feature to increase the **Saturation** (richness) of color that's already in the file or to **desaturate** the color until it eventually turns black and white. This is very useful when you want to knock back over-colorful parts of an image that are detracting from the subject matter.

In the following example, I am going to take one of my favorite images of an old bull elephant standing in front of Mount Kilimanjaro— a rare sight because Africa's highest peak is so often heavily obscured in cloud. The RAW image was underexposed in order to capture as much detail in the brilliant snowy peak, which left the tones in the lower section of the frame rather dull looking and in dire need of attention! Let's see what we can do to improve the image, as follows:

The first thing to do with this underexposed image is to use **Levels** (*Ctrl/Cmd + L*) to make it look brighter with a higher contrast. It's hard to assess any image if the color and brightness preclude an accurate inspection. By pulling the (Input Levels) sliders sliders in toward that central 'tone mountain', I made the highlights lighter and the shadows a bit darker, effectively boosting the contrast.

Tip

The **Sponge** brush tool is used for enhancing, or reducing just the color in the image. Colors under the brush tip saturate or desaturate (increase/decrease) depending on the type of brush tip (sharp-edged or fuzzy), its size and, importantly, the "flow" setting. Treat the last setting like a speed control. The higher the number (that is, from a scale between 0 and 100), the faster the effect—but the harder it is to control. Although technically a brush, one thing the **Sponge** brush tool will not do is add color where there was no color to begin with.

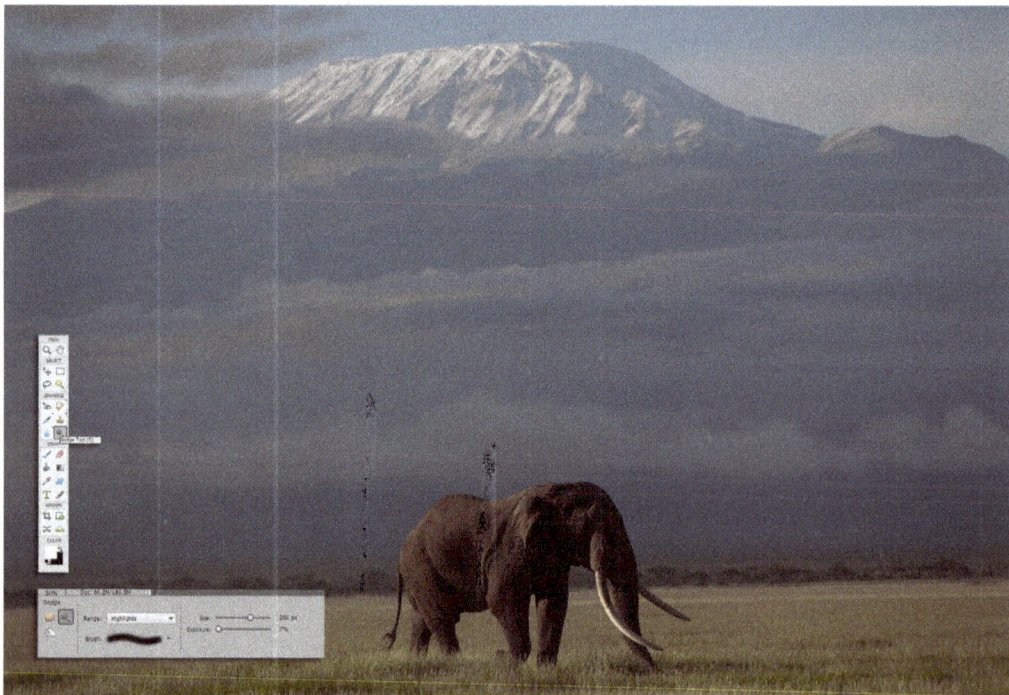

Then, I use the **Dodge** brush, set to **Highlights,** to lighten the snow on Mount Kilimanjaro in the distance. For this job, I set the **Exposure** to just 7% for the highlights—I know this sounds like almost nothing, but as the highlights are very nearly white anyway, you can't afford to rush the lightening process. Set the **Exposure** to a higher number and you'll see the white areas turning 100% white almost immediately, and, once done, there's no going back. 100% white means the tone is clipped—it's gone forever, producing a bleached-out look that can be unpleasant to the eye.

> **Tip**
>
> The **Burn** brush is possibly more useful than the **Dodge** brush tool. It works best when darkening existing tones, especially when set to **Midtones** or **Shadows**. However, it will not add tone to a brightly highlighted area. Burned-in highlights tend to go muddy when you over-burn these areas and are a sure sign that you have gone too far with your burning-in exercise.

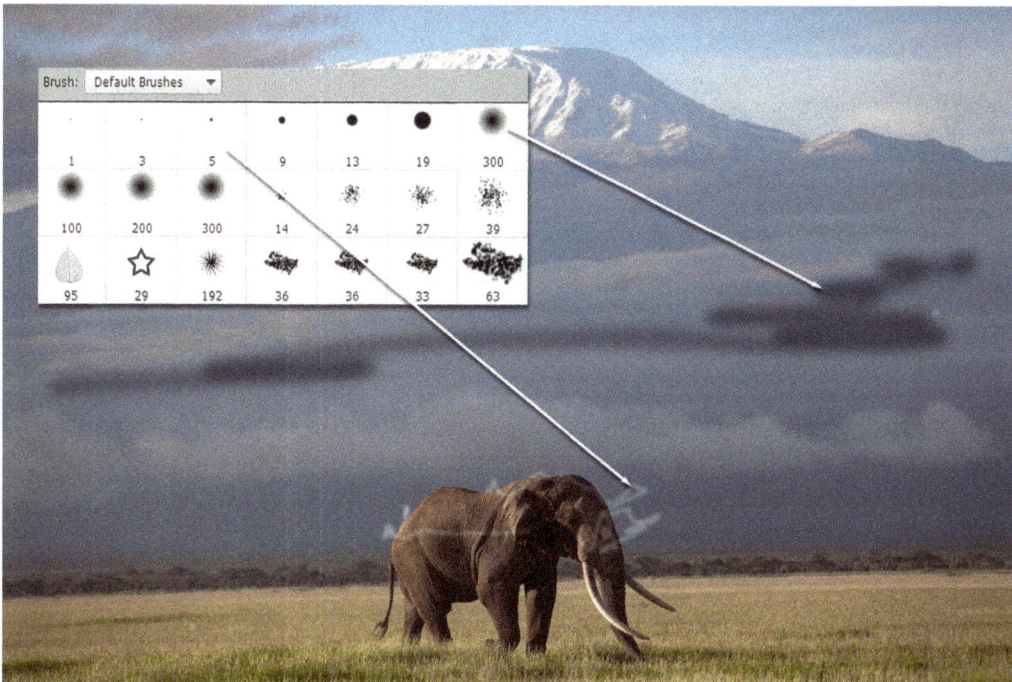

Be careful with the brushes that you use for the job—and the opacity settings.

Small, hard-edged brushes are not very useful in many instances as they leave a lot of tell-tale marks, as you can see in the preceding screenshot. Soft-edged brushes work better as they tend to blend the effect into the background more convincingly, especially when they are a larger size than you think you might need. In this illustration, I have deliberately used a brush that's too small, with an exposure setting that's too high (exposure describes the speed or intensity of the tool—in this example, how fast it darkens or lightens the pixels). No matter how dexterous you might be with a brush, if you use an exposure setting that's too high, the brush marks will show.

> **Tip**
> Although Adobe provides several hundred brush shapes and sizes by default, you can also find more online. I have used custom brushes downloaded from www.brusheezy.com very successfully. (More about this unique process in this chapter.)

Here's a close-up comparison of this old bull elephant, untouched on the left and dodged (carefully) on the right. I will never be able to lighten all the shadows on this subject because of the deep, late-afternoon shadows, but just lightening the already brighter parts of the pachyderm has made a noticeable difference.

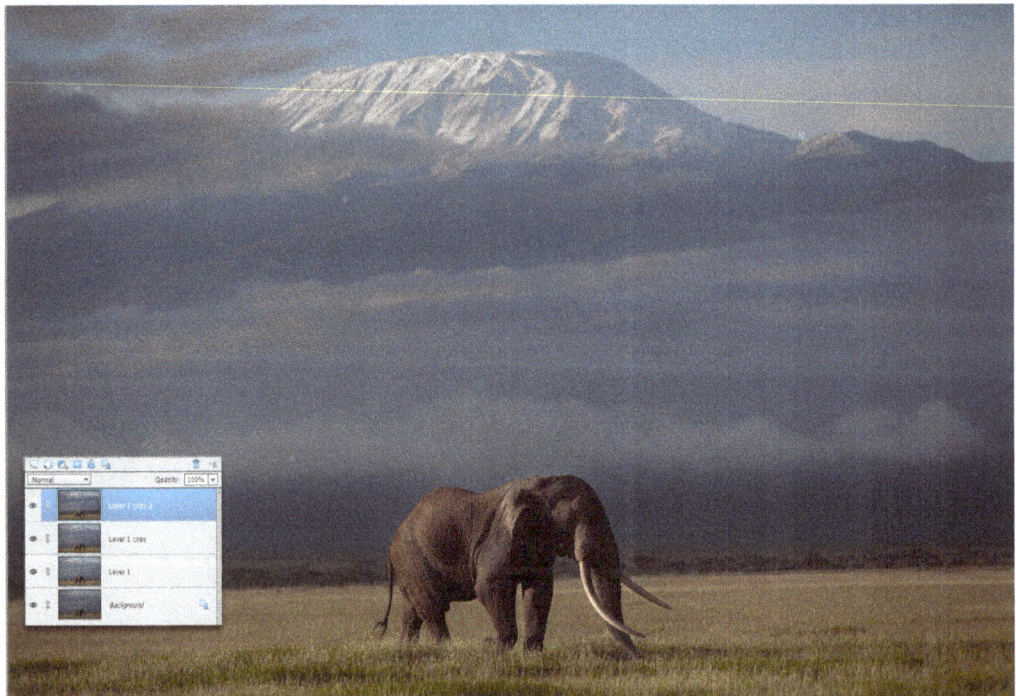

As I proceed with the dodging process, I make new layer duplicates, just so I can go back to previous versions if needed. It's not an essential part of the workflow, but I find it helps to have a series of backups—even if it is just to remind myself what the original looked like as a creative comparison.

With some slow and subtle changes to the dark areas under the clouds over the mountain, and some careful lightening of the whitish clouds directly above them, you can begin to see that the image tones are being made more dynamic and visually interesting.

One of the problems all photo-editing software presents to photographers—and a decision we have to make—is *knowing when to stop editing*. For this reason, when I get to a stage where I think I have finished, I duplicate that layer, in case I carry on with more editing.

Duplicating layers in this way allows me to save multiple versions in the one file, but it is also important to note that the more layers, the larger the resulting file.

The preceding screenshot shows the final version with significantly brightened clouds, warmer, more saturated colors in the foreground, and darker, more brooding clouds in the middle distance.

The selection tools

A **selection** is a feature that's used in Elements to apply an effect to only part of an image rather than, if no selection were made, to the entire picture. A typical example might be to select a pale sky to make it darker without affecting the rest of the image.

Photoshop Elements comes with a range of excellent selection tools, each designed to make the complicated and often tedious process of selecting objects a little easier.

Easy object removal

Interestingly, the program has two great new AI-driven selection features designed to make the selection process as painless as possible. These are **Object Removal** and **Subject Selection**. Let's have a look at these two new features first.

1. Open the image in question.

2. Choose the feature (**Guided Edit | Basics | Object Removal**).

3. Choose one of the selection tools to match the type or accuracy of selection needed—in this example, I used the **Selection Brush**, which lays a red mask over the painted area. You can modify the accuracy of this by choosing the **Add** or **Subtract** buttons. My selection was a bit over-generous, but once the Remove Object button is pressed, the magic happens. In the next example, the surfer in the background disappears in a few seconds. This is a really cool feature and opens massive potential for so many casual photographers (who'd not normally entertain the idea of a selection because of its implied complexity) because it's so quick, easy, and efficient.

In the final version shown in the following screenshot, you can see I not only removed the woman in the background but also the black object in the distance. Because the unwanted objects are quite separate from the main subject, this produces an almost flawless result:

Tip

What many who use this program might not appreciate is that each of the selection tools can be used in isolation or combined, simply by changing tools and continuing to click in the image. Holding the *Shift* key while clicking means that, as you click in the image, every click **adds** to the base selection. Holding the *Alt/Opt* keys while you click does the opposite, **subtracting** them from the base selection.

Although Guided Edit's **Object Removal** is a great feature, Adobe has developed another sophisticated AI-driven selection tool, simply named **Subject Selection**.

As its name suggests, its job is to select the subject in the image automatically. In this new feature, you don't even have to draw roughly around the subject, as Elements finds it for you. Really. And the good news is that in most of my test images, this worked seamlessly.

Selecting your subject

Here's another new feature to Elements 2020. It's called **Subject Selection** and is just the simplest and easiest process you could imagine for doing exactly what it claims—selecting a subject. Here's how it works:

1. Choose your image, then open it in the **Expert edit** mode, as follows:

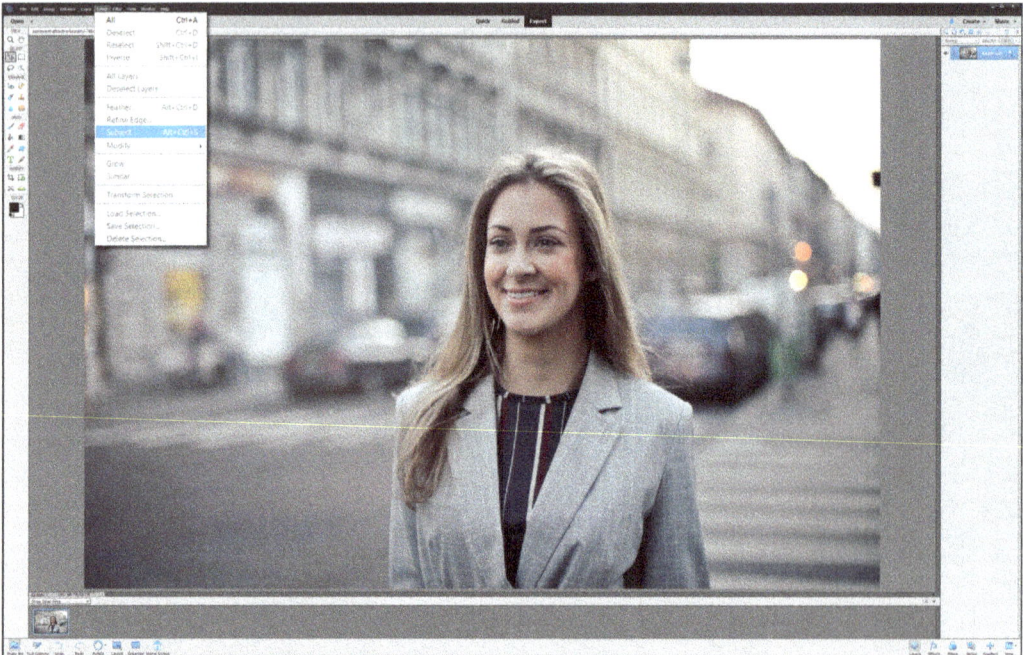

2. Go to **Select | Subject** (*Alt/Opt* + *Ctrl/Cmd* + *S* (see preceding screenshot) and sit back for five seconds to see the subject automatically selected—driven by Adobe Sensei (*Sensei* means teacher in Japanese), you'll get a preselected subject.

I tried with several picture examples where the subject stood out against the background, and this new feature did the job pretty well, with about 90-95% accuracy (around the subject). Not bad, considering I did nothing to the images other than open the files then try the selection process. Yes—it is a dumbed-down selection tool: there's no choosing the "right" tool, no tweaking or adjustments needed; it just does it.

The preceding screenshot provides an illustration of how well the selection process was executed. It's tricky—mostly because of the woman's hair. Hair (and fur) is notoriously hard to select, so some of the flyaway bits were missed—the solution to this would be to either ignore it or retouch the errant hair out of the picture (quite hard). In fact, depending on what you do with the image, you might never notice a few strands of hair missing from the selection. In this example I desaturated the background color using Hue/Saturation. The selection is not 100% perfect but, considering that it was an automatic operation, the result is more than acceptable.

You'll note that Elements' selection tools occupy their own space, called **Select**, on the **Tool Bar**. Adobe includes the very useful **Move** tool in this area, along with the **Elliptical** and **Rectilinear Marquee** selection tools. As their names might suggest, these are used principally for isolating square, rectangular, or circular objects.

Of far greater use are the freehand selection tools, which include the **Lasso**, the **Magnetic Lasso**, and the **Polygonal Lasso** tools. Because these are freehand tools they can be somewhat fiddly to use, simply because the problem of drawing with the mouse rears its ugly head once again. Those professionals who spend most of the day editing images for publication will use a **graphics tablet** and a **pen stylus**, which makes the freehand drawing of selections considerably easier and more accurate. Having said that, though, simple selections with the **Lasso** tool can be mastered quite easily, with a modicum of practice.

To finish off this stable of selection tools, we have the **Quick Selection** tool, the **Selection Brush** tool, the **Refine Selection Brush** tool, and the **Auto Selection** tool.

Of course, the real problem in working with the selection tools, and indeed many of Elements' other tools, is deciding which one to start with in order to get the job done. My suggestion is to have a good look at the object you are trying to select first because, in some examples, it's actually easier to select all the bits of the picture that you don't want selected. Once this is cleanly selected, you simply *invert* that selection, effectively swapping it from positive to negative, so that it flips from the surrounding area to the object itself (**Select | Inverse**).

An example of this might be a dark landscape with blue sky. If you want to brighten up the landscape without touching the blue sky, you would typically select the landscape and apply some tonal changes to that part of the image, but you might find that it's easier to select the blue sky using the **Magic Wand** tool, and then invert the selection so that it flips from the sky to the landscape.

From my years of experience, the most useful selection tools in this program are the **Lasso** tool and the **Magic Wand** tool, so let's have a look at how they operate.

The Lasso tool

As its name suggests, this tool, whose icon looks like a cowboy lasso, is used to draw around an object in order to select it. This can be quite a tricky operation if you don't have a steady hand and dislike drawing with a mouse. But practice makes perfect.

To *lasso* an object, select the tool, hold the mouse button down, and draw a line around the object that's to be selected, making sure that you join the end with the start point to complete the selection. If you get distracted halfway through drawing your selection and release the mouse button prematurely, you'll find that the start and (premature) finish points in the selection are automatically joined by a straight line. As I mentioned previously, by holding down the *Shift* key, you can **add to an existing selection** each time you click on an unselected part of the image, and jump from one selection tool to another just by clicking the relevant tool icons on the **Tool Bar**.

The following series of screenshots illustrate the simple procedure of selecting everyday objects using the **Lasso** tools:

Here's a busy city scene. First, I'm going to select the electrical box next to the wooden seat, on the right. The best selection tool for this? Probably the **Polygonal Lasso** tool, because this is ideal for selecting rectilinear objects. It works on a point-to-point drawing basis: click-move, click-move, click-move, just like connecting pins with a length of string. Selecting this box took about 15 seconds and five mouse clicks. The **Freehand Lasso** tool could also do this job, but as it's fully manual, it's hard to draw straight lines. The **Magnetic Lasso** tool would not work well because, in the background, the edges of the electrical box are so (tonally) busy, and it would not know what to select and what not to select.

This is my selection. I used the **Polygonal Lasso** tool to grab the pixels, then swapped to the **Selection Brush** as it has this great **mask display** feature (here, changed from the default red to yellow using the pop-out **Color Picker**, arrowed). The result can be seen in the preceding screenshot:

Once I completed the selection (and saved it), I used **Hue/Saturation** to change the electrical box to another color (using the **Hue** slider alone). That's how easy the **Polygonal Lasso** is to use. Not good for curves, but for anything with a straight line, it is excellent.

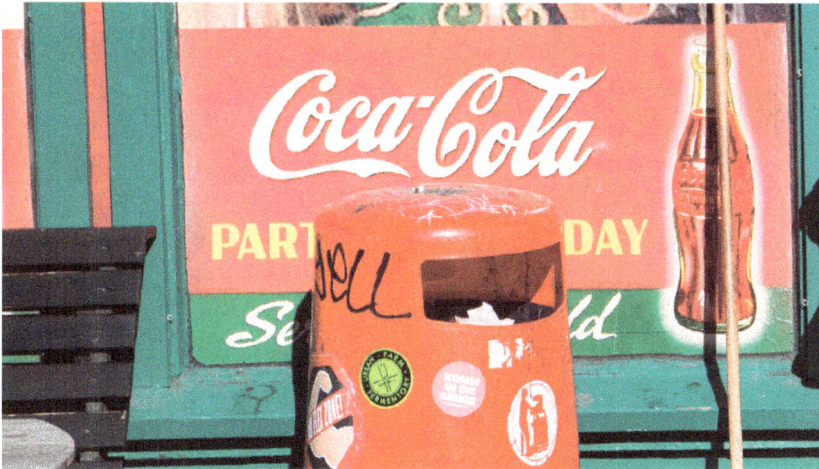

Here, I wanted to select the *Coke* logo. Using the **Magic Wand** made it easy, because it selects based on color only (see opposite page for more details). Once done, I copied and pasted that selection back into the same document (*Ctrl/Cmd + C, Ctrl/Cmd + V*) as a new layer, which could then be edited separately to the rest of the image.

I transformed the text to make it larger (*Ctrl/Cmd + T*). Note that this transformation process is fundamental to so many editing functions, such as copying and resizing images in one file, correcting perspective (covered later in this chapter), resizing text, and more. It's worth noting that there's a finite limit to the amount of resizing any image can accommodate before it loses quality. Any object that's pixel-based (that is, an image) can be transformed up to about 50% before it becomes noticeably soft. **Vector objects** (that is, text) can be transformed to any size, with no loss of quality.

Once the type had been resized and moved, I added red using the **Brush** tool.

> **Tip**
> The **Select | Inverse** command can be incredibly useful because, as luck would
> have it, often the object you are trying to select is harder to *grab* than the
> background it's sitting on. If this is the case, it's best to select the background
> first, then choose **Select | Inverse**, which flips the original selection from the
> background to the object.

Let's move on to discover the power of one of Elements' best all-round selection tools,
the **Magic Wand**.

The Magic Wand tool

The **Magic Wand** tool is one of the best selection tools on the planet because it selects
objects based on their color; plus, it's so easy to use. If I go back to my example of a blue
sky and a dark landscape, clicking on the blue sky will inevitably select everything that
is blue, but if the sky fades from dark blue to light blue, as most skies do, you might find
that the **Magic Wand** only selects a band of color, not the entire sky. This is because the
pixels that you click on represent a certain shade of blue. The tool will not automatically
select every pixel that's blue. Its **sensitivity** (to blue, in this example) is controlled by the
Tolerance slider. The default value for this is 3 2, so if I were to increase the tolerance
value it would grab a lot more of the sky.

Alternatively, you can hold the *Shift* key down to switch the tool to its **Add** mode, then
click on a darker or lighter part of the sky to add those pixels to the overall selection. It
sounds complicated, but once you're holding that *Shift* key and begin to click on other
parts of the sky, it works like magic, hence the name.

In the following screenshot, you'll see how relatively easy it is to add visual drama to an image simply by making a basic selection—in this case, of the sky—that can then be individually edited/enhanced to produce a significantly stronger-looking result, as shown in the following screenshot:

Look at the left-hand section of the preceding screenshot. How often do you see this: a potentially great image that looks a bit weak once displayed on a computer screen when we really wanted it to look more dramatic, as in the right-hand section?

The solution is to use the **Magic Wand** tool to select the sky (because it's mostly a similar color and brightness). Click on the sky once, and most of the sky in this scene will be selected.

By changing to the **Selection Brush**, then switching from **Selection** to its **Mask** mode, you will instantly see what has been selected (the clear areas) and what has not been selected (the red mask areas).

Interestingly, the two small red areas in the top left and top right of the preceding screenshot indicate that not all the sky has been selected—this is normal and easy to fix. In this example, the reason it is a slightly different tone from the rest of the sky (and therefore needs more attention when selecting) is that it suffers natural fall-off (i.e. slight edge darkening), which is typically produced when using a wide-angle lens. The fall-off can be very subtle and hard to detect with the naked eye, but because it might only be a tiny bit darker, the selection process can still pick it out as being different.

> **Tip**
>
> In Photoshop CC, all you do is press the Q key to jump into/out of this red, **Quick Mask** mode. Although it's a bit trickier to access in Elements, make a habit of jumping into, and out of, this **colored mask mode** while working on complex selections because it'll really help you visualize the accuracy of your selections. I use this feature all the time.

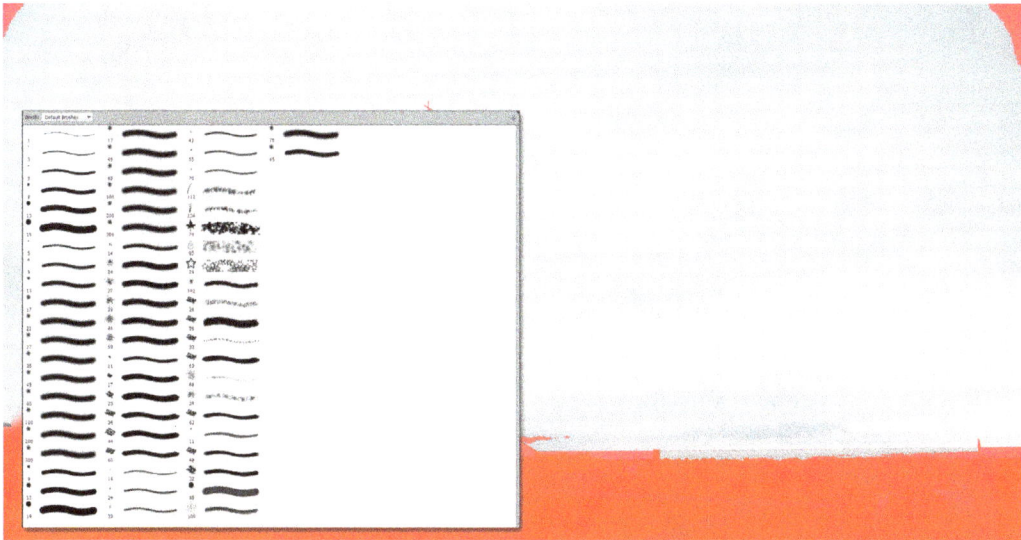

Choose a suitably sized brush (Elements has more than 250 brush shapes and thicknesses) and use the **Eraser** tool to remove the easy bits of the mask first (that is, the top-left and top-right sections of the screen).

Here's a *productivity tip*: To draw, retouch, paint, or erase in a straight line, click at the start of your line, hold the *Shift* key down, move the cursor to the end of the (imaginary) line, and click a second time. The **Eraser** tool draws a straight line between click A and click B. Keep holding the *Shift* key and click again. The straight erase line joins click B with click C, and so on. This works with all drawing, painting, retouching, and erasing tools.

If the features you are erasing around are linear, consider using a *square-shaped* brush tip. There's an entire sub-menu for square brushes in Elements' Preset Brush Picker in the tool options panel.

Use the keyboard shortcuts *Ctrl/Cmd* + + and *Ctrl/Cmd* + - to zoom in and out when erasing fine details (such as the sky under the church handrail). It's a lot faster than mousing over to the **Zoom** tool each time you want to enlarge something.

As you can see in the preceding screenshot, the point-to-point technique works well in tricky-to-select areas such as this. Note that the **Magic Wand** selection tool comes with a **Contiguous** checkbox—if checked, the wand will only select pixels of a similar color if they are touching each other. Uncheck the **Contiguous** box and it will select all the pixels that match that initial click. This can get you into a bit of (selection) trouble, so I suggest starting with **Contiguous** checked.

With all the red mask areas erased out of the sky (and some red mask areas added or extended across the ocean using the **Brush** tool), the next important step is to save the selection. Go to **Select | Save Selection** and then save the file in `.psd` format to retain the selection, just in case it's needed later.

Tip

Why does a **Joint Photographic Experts Group (JPEG)** file have to be saved as a `.psd` file when adding a selection? When we edit images, often some of the steps, features, and "extras" used in the edit process can also be saved into the same file—for example, selections, masks, paths (Photoshop CC only), layers, vector graphics, and text.

But JPEGs cannot contain anything but a single pixel-based image layer—which is where the Photoshop format file (`.psd`) comes in. With a `.psd` file, every extra feature used in a file (that is, a selection, type, or Adjustment Layers) can be saved into the same file. These can then be called up and edited further, when needed. If you save such a file in the JPEG format, all those extras will be lost.

Once the selection is saved (a habit that's well worth repeating in any exercise that requires a selection), add a **Feather** amount to the selection line. As with all selections, it's usually beneficial to soften the hard, 1-pixel-wide line with a **Feather** amount. In this case, I used a setting of 5 pixels. You won't see any change in this line until you either run a tone-changing tool over the selection or if you pop back into the **Selection Brush** and choose its **Mask** mode.

TIP

How do you know what **Feather** amount to use? This is a hard question to answer as there are so many variables: the resolution of the image (in **megabytes**), the selection size, the accuracy of the selection itself, and the purpose of the exercise. I generally work with 20-**megapixel** images and begin with a **Feather** of between 5-10 pixels. If I'm blending an object into a background, I might use a smaller pixel amount (especially if it's a tight selection), but if it's going into a similar-colored background, I'd increase the **Feather** to 20-50 pixels. Test different pixel widths before moving on to the next stage.

Another great tip is to use your selection in *reverse*. There are two ways to look at this: if you wanted to enhance the church and grass but not the sky, you'll find it very hard to select the lower part of the image because there are so many differently colored tones/ objects in this part of the file.

However, my tip would be to start with the sky, which is easier to select. Once that's selected, choose **Select | Inverse**, and the selection will magically flip into negative mode so that, suddenly, you have the grass and church selected and not the sky. It can be very handy in all those situations where selecting the subject is harder than selecting the background. To show you another way of using this **Inverse** command, in this example, I inverted the sky selection, then adjusted the contrast using Levels, then **Hue/Saturation** to bring up the color in the grass (and not the sky).

Saving a selection

One important feature that you'll find in this program is the ability to *save a selection* once it has been finished, as shown in the following screenshot. For me, this is very important because if you've spent a fair amount of time perfecting your selection, you really don't want to lose it should you have a problem with the software or the computer, which might require a restart:

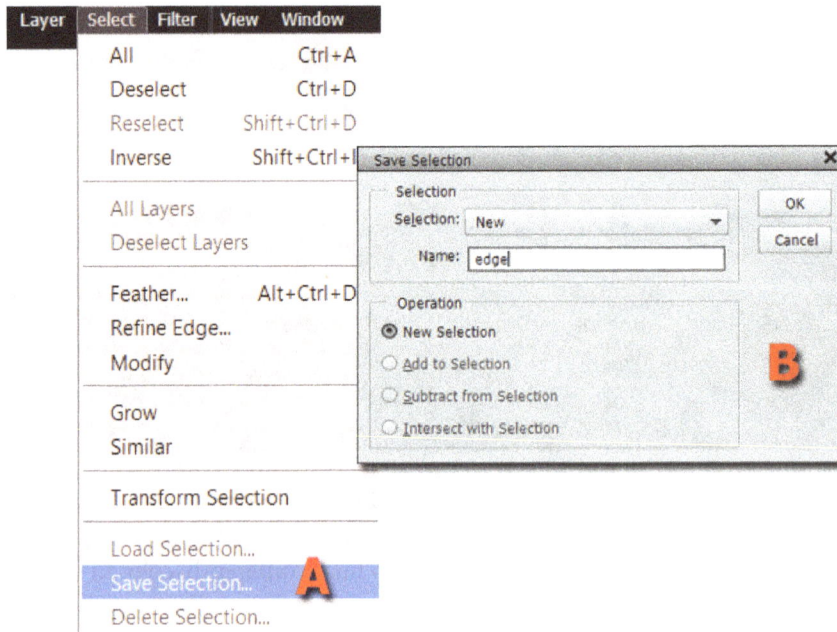

To this end, you'll notice that Elements has a dedicated selection menu at the top of the screen, and almost at the bottom of that pop-out menu, you'll find the **Save Selection** command (labeled with the red **A** in the preceding screenshot). Give the selection a memorable name in the **Save Selection** panel that opens (labeled with the red **B**) before clicking **OK** and moving on. If you plan on adding multiple selections to the same image file, it's probably worth naming your selections very specifically so they can be easily identified later, should you need to work on them again.

It's also important to note that, at this stage, your selection hasn't actually been preserved at all, despite using the **Save Selection** command. To save everything **permanently**, you must also save the entire file before moving on. When you do that, you'll notice that Elements forces you to save the entire file either in the **Photoshop** (`.psd`) or **Tagged Image File Format** (`.tif`). The other file formats discussed in this book, most notably JPEGs, cannot contain any additional information, such as selections, layers, paths, text, vector shapes, or masks.

Once the selection has been saved, you can close the image down and move on to a different task. If you need to work on that selection once more, open the image and, from the **Select** menu, choose **Load Selection**. If there's a single selection saved in that file, you'll see it in the **Load Selection** panel, which means you can click **OK** to open it back into the image. If you have multiple selections, choose the correct one from the **Select** drop-down menu in the **Selection** panel.

Remembering to save your selections will save you a heap of time and, more importantly, reduce your frustration levels by not having to recreate a selection from scratch.

Feathering selections

As you'll note from the start, the selection line around your subject is very sharp. It's a little like a scrapbooking exercise where the subject is cut out of the background using a craft knife. We frequently won't want such a sharp line because then, the selection we have made becomes obvious to the viewer. The solution is to use a feature called **feathering**. This effectively softens or blurs the selection edge by a certain amount, dictated by the **pixel radius**. This is probably one of the hardest numbers to judge when creating a selection because the fuzziness of your selection line is also influenced by many factors, including the file resolution.

Selecting an object from a 10-megapixel picture requires a much smaller feathering amount than if the image was 50-megapixel, as you can see in the following screenshot:

Experience helps you judge the feathering amount, although it's simple enough to experiment by starting with a 1-pixel radius. If that's not enough, undo the last action and try a different feathering amount. In the preceding screenshot, the left-hand image was set to 5 pixels while the fuzzy line in the right-hand image was set to 25 pixels. This is too much because, with such a soft edge, any enhancement added to the sky would bleed into the edge of the building, creating a halo effect.

The best way to preview selection-edge fuzziness is to swap whatever selection tool you are currently using for the **Selection Brush**. The tool has two modes: a **Selection** mode and a **Mask** mode. The **Selection** mode is the same, visually, as all other selection tools, but its **Mask** mode (which in Photoshop CC is called the **Quick Mask**) represents everything that's not been selected in the image as a red mask. This is one of the best ways to clearly display the extent of the current selection, but it also works as a technique for modifying it.

Because this red overlay is, in effect, a mask, you can add to it using the **Brush** tool, or you can remove from it using the **Eraser** tool, much in the same way that we can add to, or take from, a **Layer Mask** using a black or white brush (see the section on Layer Masking at the end of this chapter).

Once you're happy with the modifications that you have added using the **Mask** mode, click back into the **Selection** mode to view the traditional selection line of *marching ants* (as it's often described) before saving the selection and moving on. Look at the following screenshot:

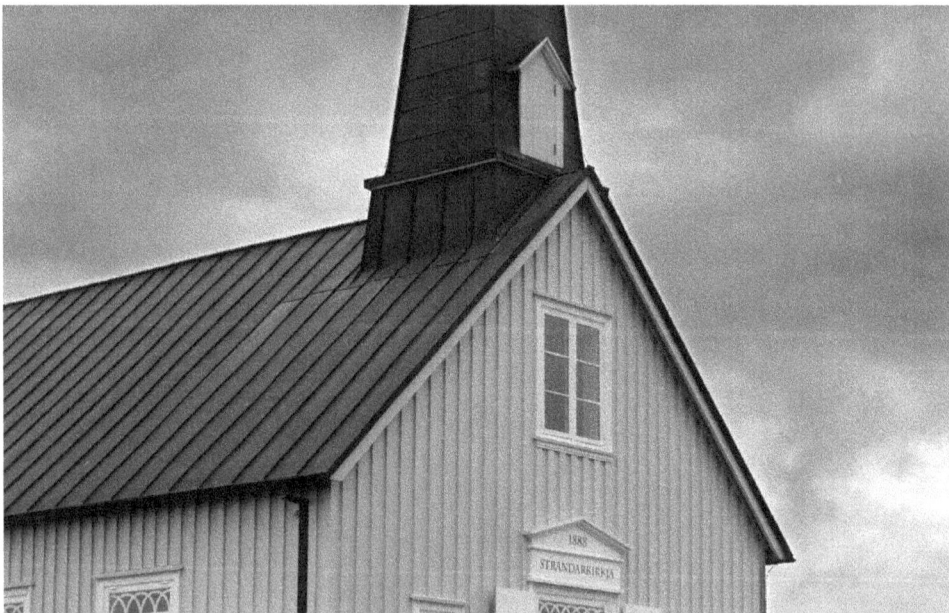

This is what it looks like if your feathering selection is used too much—once a tone change is applied to the image (in this case, darkening using the **Levels** tool), you'll see an ugly halo around the selected objects (in this example, it's the roof line). Undo a few steps to just before you applied the feather, apply a smaller value, and try again, or use the equally useful **Refine Selection** feature to reduce the feathering amount.

The Selection Brush tool

Photoshop Elements ships with a range of selection tools, all of which offer slightly different selection capabilities. Here's a very neat one called, simply, the Selection Brush!

The **Selection Brush**, which features the excellent **Selection** or **Mask Viewing** modes, operates just like a paint brush. Click and drag across your image and it will appear to draw two selection lines, one on each side of the brush. Swish the brush tip around a little bit and you'll see that it fills in those lines, making the selection larger and larger. For me, this tool's selection capabilities are reasonably user friendly, while its **Mask** mode is a feature I use all the time to preview what I have done, regardless of the selection tool that created it.

The Quick Selection tool

The **Quick Selection** tool certainly has a more instant appeal about it. Click and drag the cursor through the area that you want selected; it operates just like the **Magic Wand** tool, based on pixel color, while continually expanding its semi-automated selection process as you drag the cursor over different colored pixels.

Because of its design, you'll note that this selection tool is very good at *snapping* to the edges of same-colored objects. For example, selecting a red post box against a white wall is a very easy task—the sky against the black church roof is almost as easy to select.

Note that the **Magic Wand** tool might also be fairly effective with this kind of selection subject, but it would probably need lots of additional mouse-clicking to scoop up all the subtle tone variants, including shade, shadow, and other tonal inconsistencies that every picture throws at us. In this example, it's the shading in the clouds that's hard to assess—those tones are hard to see with the naked eye, but nevertheless will appear a challenge to select evenly using a tool such as **Magic Wand**.

The Refine Selection Brush tool

The **Refine Selection Brush** is not technically a selection tool; rather, it's a feature designed to refine an existing selection. In this context, it *sort of* replaces the process of adding to or taking from an existing selection by holding the *Shift* or the *Alt/Option* key while moving the cursor over the following screenshot:

The **Refine Selection Brush** throws up the red mask overlay, in exactly the same manner as the **Selection Brush**, but under its **View** menu, you can also set this tool to display the selection on a black or a white background. If you don't like the red overlay color, click on the color swatches button underneath the **Opacity** slider to change it to a color that suits your mood slightly better.

Where the **Refine Selection Brush** out-features the older-style *Shift* or *Alt/Opt* (to add to or take from an existing selection) is that its options not only include the ability to add to or take from the selection, but also the ability to push or move the existing lines in the selection. As with most of the other selection tools, you can, of course, change the size of the brush, as well as its softness, in order to give you greater control.

The Auto Selection tool

As with the **Refine Edge Brush**, the **Auto Selection** tool is relatively new to Photoshop Elements. It combines the action of the regular **Lasso** tools with the **Auto Selection** functionality of the **Quick Selection Brush**. What this means in practical terms is that if you want to make a freehand selection of a particular area using the **Lasso**, once you let go of the mouse, having completed the selection as close to the edges as you can, the line snaps to the nearest edge of contrast. In the **Tool Options** panel, you can also set this feature to **Auto Enhance** once the selection has finished drawing—sometimes, this is beneficial, sometimes not. You'll find the same process in the quirky **Whiten Teeth** tool in **Quick** edit mode.

If you search for examples of how this selection tool is used, you'll probably find it's only applied to a certain type of image. The reason for this is simply because every image that requires a selection is very different from every other image—no one selection tool is ideal for all selection tasks.

The Refine Edge function

Another useful feature is the **Refine Edge** function. Having made your initial selection, if you click the **Refine Edge** button in the **Options** panel, you'll see the selection view mode change to a white background. You can change this to a red mask background, a black background, or several other working *looks*, depending on how complex the picture is and how you like to view your selection work (as we'll soon see).

To use this panel effectively, move the sliders to see if it makes the selection around your subject more or less accurate, as shown in the following screenshot. Note that this is another easy way to view the effectiveness of feathering. Once this is done, click **OK**, and don't forget to save the selection:

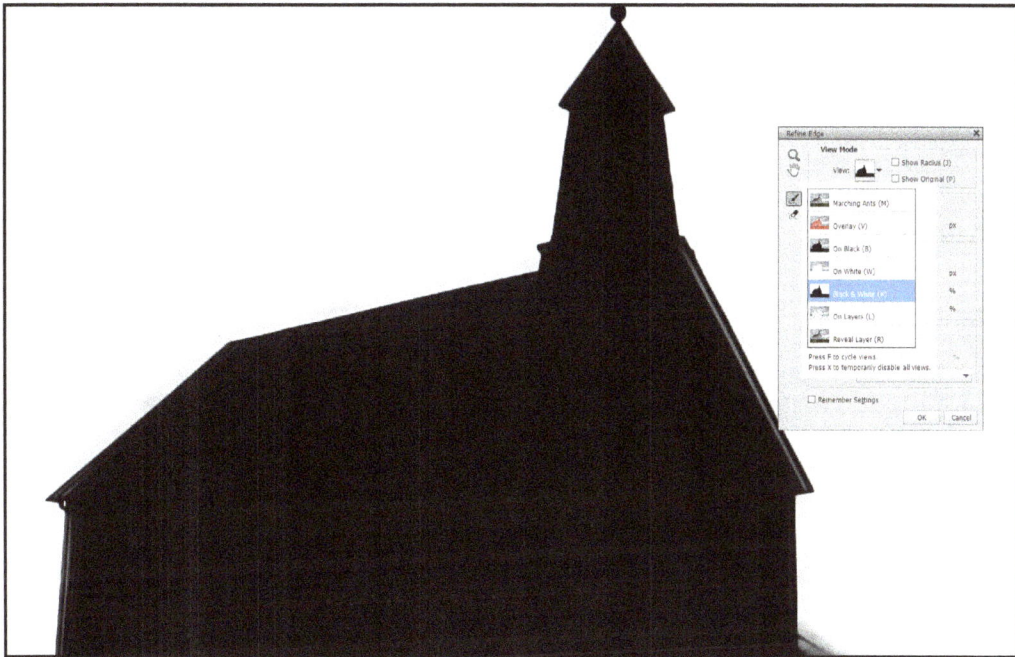

In the preceding screenshot, I have selected the **Black & White** display option, which gives the user instant feedback as to the accuracy of the selection made.

Removing large objects

Now that you have an idea of how selections actually work, let's take a look at how we can remove *large objects* from an image. Firstly, you might think: *OK—why not use the* **Healing Brush** *to remove an object?* Good question, but the answer is simple—the **Healing Brush** is both a copy-and-paste type retouching tool and a blending tool. The larger the object, the larger the brush that's needed to cover the object, and the larger the brush, the more pixels it needs to copy and paste over the large blemish. If this is then blended, especially at the edges, it can lead to a big mess. Let's look at the following screenshot:

Now you see it; now you don't. Removing large objects such as the girl in the forest should be a relatively easy task, but only if there are enough similar pixels to use the *cover-up* method. Before you start any large retouching job, it pays to study the relative **Source** area versus the size of the **Target** area.

It would be relatively easy to remove the girl on the right-hand side in the following image as most of the background contains very dark pixels, but it would be very hard to remove the three holy men to the right of the main subject in the following right-hand image simply because there are not enough free pixels for the cover up:

One sure-fire way to remove an object is to use a selection tool, such as the **Lasso** or the **Selection Brush**, to select a bunch of *good* pixels, feather the selection to soften the edges, then copy and paste the contents of that selection back into the image. Once it has been pasted back into the document, you'll need to move it over the *bad* patch and use the **Transform** function to resize and reshape the pasted pixels to fit over the errant part of the image.

Here's how it works:

1. In the following screenshot, I started by opening the girl in the forest image, then duplicated the layer (**Layer | Duplicate Layer**):

2. Now, loosely select the girl with the **Selection Brush** using a fairly thick brush tip—in fact, over-select the object by 15% or 20%. You can clearly see the selection line on the left and as a red mask on the right. As it is hand-drawn, it's not very accurate.

3. Now that your shape is selected, we have to move that *entire selection* over the part of the image that you are going to copy from (the **Source** area). Note that even though the selection is being moved, the selection line is still active.

4. With your selection shape dragged over the *good* pixels—the empty forest—turn the duplicated layer's visibility **Off** (by clicking the eye icon on that layer). We are going to use the still-active selection to copy some pixels from the **Background** layer, but before we do that, access the **Select** menu and add a **Feather** amount (how much depends on the overall resolution of the image—try 25 pixels). Then, from the same menu, choose **Select | Modify | Expand** and enter 25 pixels—this expands the selection further away from the original shape, as can be seen in the following screenshots:

In the preceding left-hand screenshot, you can see the rough selection around the girl's body in outline form and in red mask form, which is easier to judge. The right-hand screenshot shows the expanded selection line. You can do this freehand, or use the **Select | Modify | Expand** command.

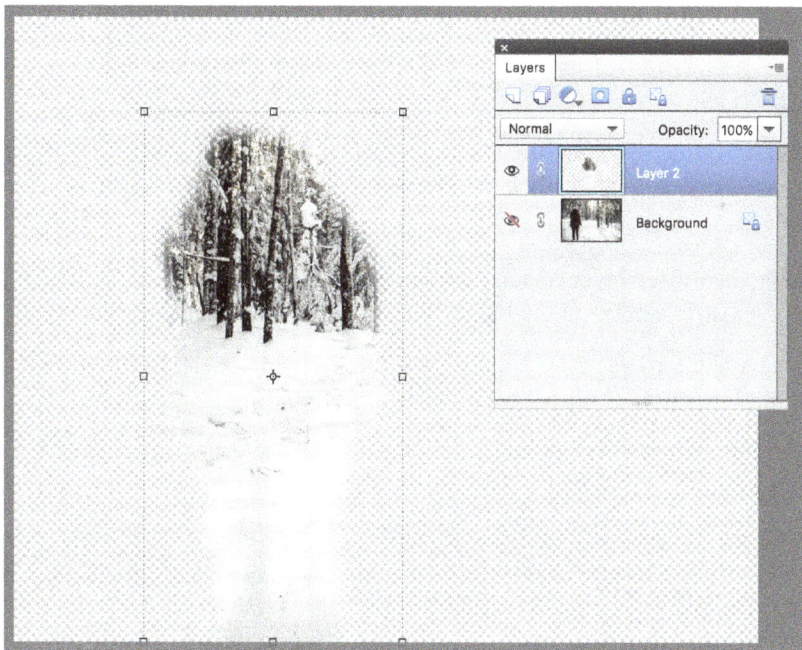

5. With an expanded and feathered selection active over the **Background** layer, copy and paste the content of the layer (by using *Ctrl/Cmd + C*, then *Ctrl/Cmd + V* to paste the copied content back into the document, or by using the **Edit | Copy**, **Edit | Paste** menu command). With the visibility of the base layer turned Off, you now see only what has been pasted back into the document - the fuzzy-edged forest selection, sitting on top of the original forest shot.

6. Finally, move the pasted selection over the object (in this case, to the left, over the girl), flatten the layer (**Layer | Flatten Image**), and you are almost done. When the layer is flattened into the background, retouch any tone inconsistencies out using the **Spot Healing** Brush, and you are done.

Finishing tips

As with all image editing, there are many things that can go wrong, causing your selection or edits to look rather amateur. Here are a few suggestions on how to improve your selection results:

- Try setting the pasted layer opacity to around 90% (using the field located at the top of the **Layers** panel) to help blend the pixels into the background.

- Always have the **Layers** panel open so you can see which layer is active (highlighted in blue).

- Use the layer visibility (eye) icon to turn the layer off and on to preview the layer beneath.

- Flick between the **Selection** and **Mask** modes while working with the **Selection Brush** to see how accurate your selection actually is (it's difficult to gauge just by looking at the marching ants selection line).

- If you are happy with the *patch* work, merge that pasted layer into the background (**Layer | Flatten Image**) and use the **Healing Brush** to blend any details in the frame that look *wrong*.

- If your selection does not quite cover the object being removed, try duplicating the pasted layer (in this case, it's snow), and shift it to the left or right to fully conceal your pixel wizardry.

Brush and Pencil tools

We have already discussed several uses of the **Brush** tool, notably in editing masks, but, it can also be used as a regular brush. To do this, you need to be adept at drawing with the mouse. If you aren't, you could buy a **graphics tablet**. These devices are perfect for artists because, instead of drawing with a mouse, you use a **pen stylus**, the same size and shape as a real pen, and draw onto the tablet. Tablets come in a range of sizes; larger ones provide more accuracy and features, but nevertheless, even a $50 model will serve you well. More on graphics tablets in Chapter 8.

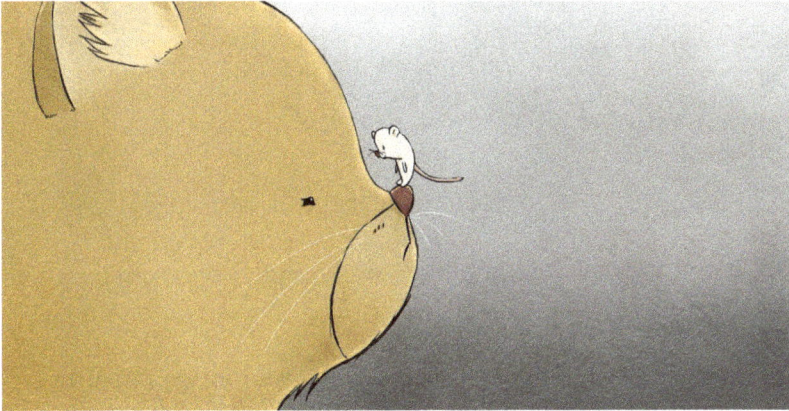

Elements has three types of brush tool: the **Brush** tool, the **Impressionist Brush** tool, and the **Color Change Brush** tool.

The **Brush** tool looks and works like (an electronic version of) a paint brush: choose a color from the **Color Picker**, pick out a brush tip from the 300+ on offer, choose the size and opacity, and off you go.

You can also choose to paint using a different tool **Blend** mode, depending on how you'd like the pixels to blend into each other.

With skill and the right brief, graphic artists can create impressive-looking artworks using Photoshop Elements and a graphics tablet.

Lastly the **Impressionist Brush** is fun as it sort of clones your image and turns it into large, fuzzy brush strokes while at the same time producing what passes for an impressionist look. You can broaden your impressionist look a little using the **Advanced** button, which takes you to a range of other brush strokes, tolerance settings, and more. I'm not sure what Edouard Manet or Claude Monet might have thought of this, but with the right image and textured paper to print on, the artistic effects can be quite persuasive.

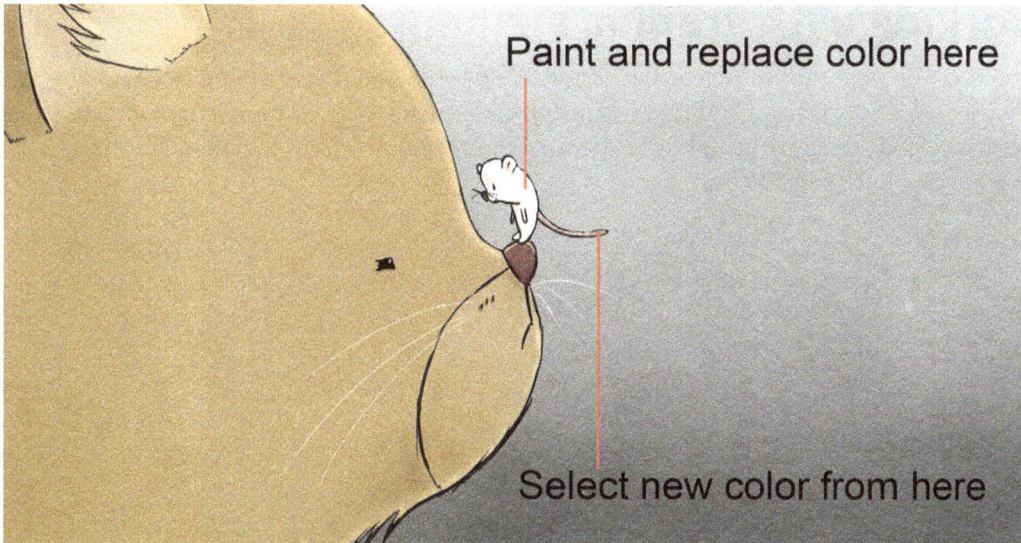

Paint and replace color here

Select new color from here

Lastly, we have the **Color Replace Brush**. As with many other tools, this one relies on applying the color change effect to similar-colored pixels. So, if I want to replace blue with red, providing that all the blue pixels are the same value, it will work well. But we all know that life in the digital-editing realm is not like this, so that's why we have the **Tolerance** slider to make Elements a bit more or less lenient when it is applying a color change. Increase the tolerance and it will apply the change to lighter and darker shades of blue. There are different brush styles to choose from, four different **Blend** modes (I find **Color** works best), and the inevitable **Contiguous** or **Discontiguous** checkboxes.

The **Pencil** tool, all alone on its own peg on the **Tool Bar**, is possibly the least used of all of Elements' many tools because, as I mentioned previously, unless you are a skilled graphic artist working with a graphics tablet, it's very hard to draw accurately with a mouse.

Working with graphic elements

Photoshop Elements is not Adobe Illustrator, by any stretch of the imagination, but it does contain a reasonably good range of **graphic elements** that can be added to images to enhance their design. The following screenshot includes the four gold photo corners, the textured photo plus the beer glass:

These graphics fall into the following groups:

- Graphics that can be added to existing semi-automated creative projects, such as the **Photo Book** and **Greeting Card**, found under the **Create** menu. These include a vast array of downloadable content, ranging from **backgrounds** and **picture frames** to **clip art** objects and preset **text styles**.

- Those that are designed to add benefit to single images—graphics such as **text boxes**, **copyright symbols**, **arrows**, **lines**, **speech bubbles**, **shapes**, and more.

Look at the following screenshot:

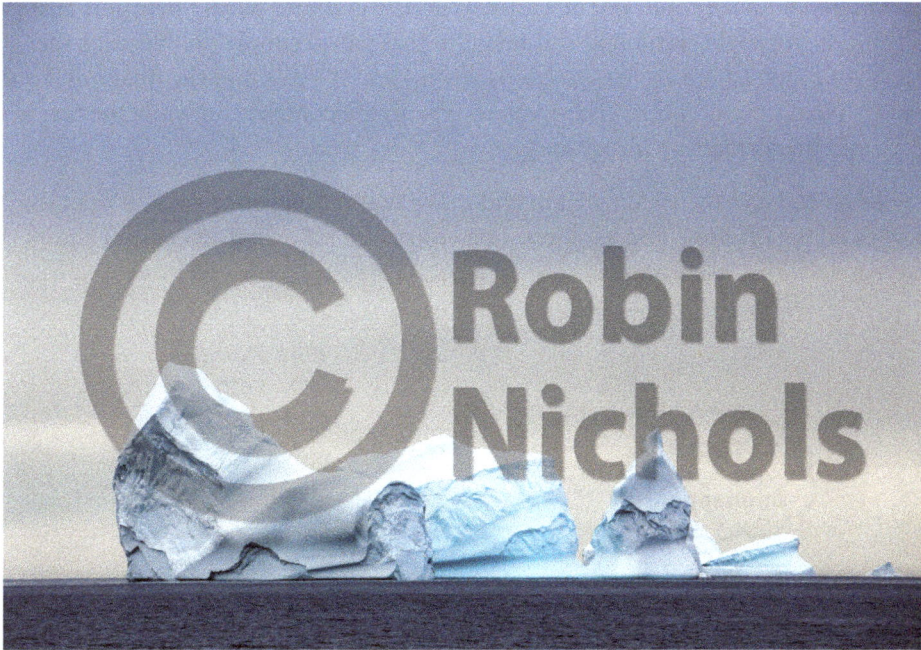

Graphics in this application are all **vectors**, made up from a mathematical formula rather than pixels. This means they are infinitely scalable, compared to a pixel-based image that can only be enlarged by around 50% before it begins to look soft.

The panel-based graphic elements on the right-hand side of the main screen (seen in the Swiss beer illustration on the previous page) be dragged off the **Graphics** panel. Most of these assets have to be downloaded from Adobe; you'll see the download timer appear briefly while this happens. It should only take a few seconds before they are added directly into the document.

The graphics can then be resized, flipped, and rotated using the corner handles (as you would when transforming a regular picture). You can even add tonal edits to a lot of these graphics, providing you *simplify them first* (that is, change the state from vector to pixel by right-clicking in the **Layers** panel and choosing **Simplify Layer** from the pop-out menu). They are very flexible.

You will find that most of these downloadable graphics are quite simplistic—these date back to the early days of Photoshop Elements, when it was very much the scrapbook hobbyist's plaything. Now, it's a far more sophisticated editing and design tool, so you might consider some of the effects to be a little dated and tired.

Text graphics

Adding text into an image could not be easier. With the graphics panel open, and Text selected from the top right-hand pop-out menu in that panel, simply double-click the desired text style icon (there are 40+ to choose from) and it loads into the image as 'Your Text Here'. All that's then required is for you to type in the content and while the text is selected, to add the formatting if required.

All you need to do is get the spelling right and make the text bigger or smaller to fit the page. Easy as falling off a log, and a lot less dangerous. The following screenshot shows what you can do with these features:

Regular Shape tool

Aside from the vector-filled **Custom Shape** tool, Elements has a few regular shapes that are useful in a number of different applications. These include the **Rectangle**, **Rounded Rectangle**, **Ellipse**, **Polygon**, **Star**, and **Line** tool, which can also be converted into an **arrow graphic**. Shapes can be helpful to photographers and designers - for example by adding a rectangular shape under text to make it more legible or by using the **Line** tool to direct the viewer to salient points in an illustrated graphic. It's not PowerPoint, and neither is it Illustrator, but these tools provide an excellent starting point for those wanting to take their photographic design into a more commercial arena. The following screenshot shows what you can do with these features:

Custom Shape tool

Custom shapes have been in Elements since version 1.0 and are a mix of handy items (such as the copyright symbol) and those that appear less practical. In short, there's something for everyone. To use them, go through the following steps:

1. First, choose a symbol from the pop-out menu (there are 548 to choose from—all are arranged under different sub-headings, such as animals, arrows, banners, crop shapes, and symbols).

2. To ensure that the custom shape does not distort while you drag the vector, hold down the *Shift* key while dragging.

Click anywhere in the image, hold down the mouse, and drag across the page. This *draws* the graphic symbol onto a new layer in the document. The further you drag the symbol, the larger it becomes, as shown in the following screenshot:

Cookie Cutter tool

Although not strictly a vector graphic, the **Cookie Cutter** tool is a cropping tool that uses vectors to create custom shapes instead of just removing bits of an image in a rectilinear fashion, as shown in the following screenshot:

I suspect that this tool harks back to the days when Elements 1.0 was just for moms and dads and their kids' school projects. That said, some of the cutting shapes are great fun and offer the user an opportunity for a different, neat, and quick look (I particularly like the **Crop Shapes**) to get away from the typical rectilinear photo edge by adding a very rough-cut, almost torn-edge look to any image.

It's a fun feature to play around with. As you can see in the following screenshot, the **Cookie Cutter** tool combines a range of preset shapes with one of your own images:

Photoshop Elements ships with a massive range of different **Cookie Cutter** shapes that you can choose from. In this case, a jigsaw shape is used to cut out part of an image of football players. In the following screenshot, you can see a small selection of Elements' many different **Cookie Cutter** shapes:

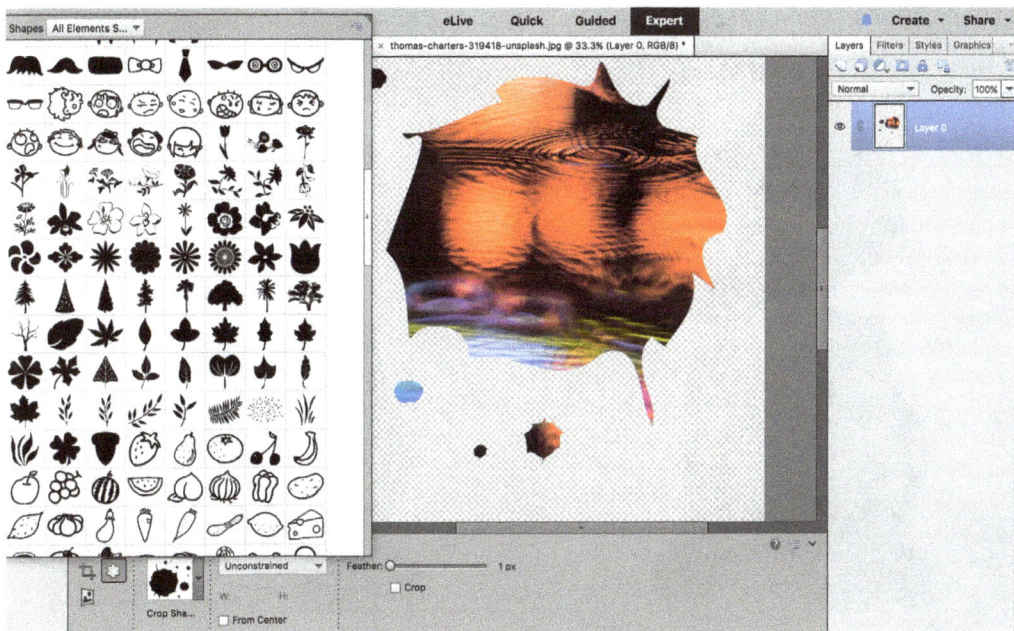

Paint Bucket tool

The **Paint Bucket** tool, as its name suggests, works like a real bucket of paint. Choose a color from the **Color Picker**, click in the image, and it will slop a bucket of that color across the image surface. OK—so your beautiful landscape is now all black (or whatever color was set in the **Color Picker**). By default, the **Paint Bucket** has several adjustments—the **Opacity** (which works as if you are watering the paint down), **Blend Mode** (which affects how the paint color reacts with the pixels it is poured over), **Contiguous** mode (which means it only affects similar-colored pixels if they are adjoining each other), and **Tolerance** (which dictates how sensitive it is to identifying similar-colored pixels over which it spreads). A default number of 255 means the paint slops over the entire image regardless of where you clicked. Set to a smaller value such as 15, and it only affects pixels that are very similar in tone to the ones initially clicked).

This large tolerance figure essentially means that it floods the entire canvas, but if it's set to 1, it only adds paint to the pixel you click on. So, if I'm looking at an image that has a solid block of color in it and I click on it, then that black color is instantly replaced with the new color, which stops at the boundary made by a different color. It's a good tool for recoloring all sorts of different parts of your images. How sensitive it is to the color that was originally clicked is controlled by the **Tolerance** slider. Look at the following screenshot:

A good use for this tool that few people realize is its ability to *add contrast* or a *color tint* to an image, especially if it's black and white, as shown in the preceding screenshot. Set the **Tolerance** to 255, **Opacity** to around 10%, **Blend Mode** to Overlay; choose black from the **Color Picker**; and then, click something that's already black in the image (the dog's body, in this example).

Each time the image is clicked, you add 10% more black to those shadows. If it doesn't work as expected, uncheck the **Contiguous** checkbox (in the **Tool Options** panel) and see if that improves the result. Using the **Overlay** Blend Mode ensures that the original tonal gradation of the picture shines through the black tone being added to the frame. Look at the following screenshot:

Another good use for this tool is to tint an image with color, or black and white (contrast). You can do this by going through the following steps:

1. Open the shot and choose a tint color (typically, photographers use this to warm up or cool down an image).

2. I chose yellow from the **Color Picker**, set the opacity to 10%, **Tolerance** to 255, and **Blend Mode** to Overlay, then clicked on the image. The **Overlay** Blend Mode gives the paint a specific *translucence* so that the tones in the image are not hindered by adding opaque paint, as they might be in real life.

3. With each click, the tint deepens by 10%. In the preceding screenshot, I have tinted a black-and-white image with deep yellow—once or twice, to give a pale sepia effect (as shown in the center example), and three or four times to warm it up considerably (right-hand example).

Adding text to images

Separate to the graphics panel text function just discussed, Photoshop Elements includes a sophisticated word-processing functionality, enabling text to be added to images and graphics. In fact, some of the more automated functions on offer are supplied complete with blank textboxes, ready for you to click and add your words of wisdom, so it's easy to do. Look at the following screenshot:

Using the **Myriad Pro Regular** font, I typed in `Stand up` (hit *Return*), `comedian:` (hit *Return*), and then typed `Vince Connolly` to get this triple-deck text layout. The text is left-justified, and the new type layer is placed automatically at the top of the layer stack.

The text tool is officially called the **Horizontal Type** tool. While the tool is active, you can choose a mode that types vertically (not always a good idea, because vertical text is hard to read).

To add text to a document, choose the **Horizontal Type** tool from the Tool Bar (or press the *T* key), click once directly on the image, and start typing. As soon as you click on the image, you'll note that a text layer appears in the **Layers** panel (keep that **Layers** panel visible so that you can keep an eye on which layer you are working on).

The first thing that you might notice is that the text you're typing appears either too small or too large. There's a simple explanation for this. Let's say that you are typing into a 20-megapixel image. The native camera file is set to a default of 72 **dots per inch (dpi)**, so it will print approximately 2 m x 1.5 m—that's huge. If you subsequently add 12-pt text to a document this size, you'll understand why it looks so small.

To remedy this situation, undo that last type layer, then open the **Image Size** feature (**Image | Resize | Image Resize**), make sure that the **Resample** checkbox is unchecked, and change the resolution from 72 to 300 dpi. Save the file, select the **Horizontal Type** tool once more, and when you add new text, you'll note that it appears much larger in the main window because, at 300 dpi, the new dimensions are considerably smaller (approximately 20 x 35 cm), so the 12-pt text looks larger.

If the image is destined for social media, you need to resize the overall dimensions of the picture first to a suitable web setting (such as 820 x 312 pixels for Facebook) before you start typing.

Once you have the document set to the correct resolution, it's time to *format* the text. To make changes to pre-existing text, it first must be *selected*. This is where many newcomers get into trouble. Selected text is highlighted in an opposite color—for example, black text is highlighted in white, and yellow text becomes highlighted in blue. This does look a little confusing.

If you just want to add a couple of words or even a short sentence to an image, the easiest, almost fail-safe method is not to use the **Type** tool at all, but rather open the image into **Expert** edit mode, go to the **Graphics** panel on the right-hand side of the screen, and from the sub-header drop-down menu, choose **Text**.

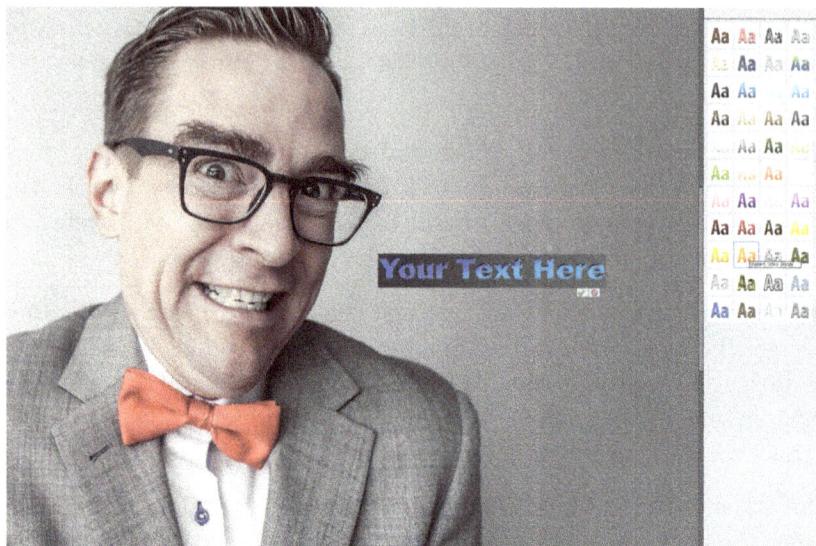

This panel contains a number of preset special effects; click one and it adds the words `Your Text Here` directly onto the page. All you then do is type over that text, and you are done. Look at the following screenshot:

I modified the font and text **Style**: `Stand up comedian` is **Myriad Pro Light**, while `Vince Connolly` is **Myriad Pro Bold**. Everything is the same font, but the style can add further **emphasis** to words by making them **semi-bold**, **bold**, and even **black**, which is even heavier than bold.

To emphasize text to a greater level, try using a **Drop Shadow**. With the type layer as the **active layer** (highlighted in blue), navigate to the **Styles** panel, find the **Drop Shadow** sub-menu, and click on a thumbnail. This instantly applies a drop shadow to that layer. Look at the following screenshot:

To give you an idea of your choices in terms of type styles, here's a small sample of what's possible using a regular font such as **Myriad Pro**, from the top of the preceding screenshot: black, bold, semi-bold, regular, light, light condensed, light extended, italic, and italic semi-condensed. Your choice.

Leading is a useful design feature that you'll find on the **Type** tool's **Options** panel; use it to add or remove space from between lines of text, or even from between single words. By default, this is set to **Auto,** which normally works OK, but if you particularly want two lines of text to be closer together, manually enter a figure and adjust accordingly.

Here's the leading reset to a smaller value than in the previous example. You can use leading to close the space between lines of text as a group (changing all three lines of text in one hit) or you can select a single line—say, the one at the bottom—then change the leading on just that to push that line further away from everything above it. Note that you must select *all* the text, including any spaces in that line, in order for the leading to work correctly.

A text box can be created by dragging the **Type** tool cursor over the image to draw a box. When you release the mouse, you can start typing. The text is held inside the parameters of that box. This is very useful if you have sourced your text from a word-processing document. Create a text box, copy the content from the word-processing document, then paste it into the Elements text box.

One of the golden rules in type design is to *avoid mixing your fonts* wherever possible; don't create a document that uses **Helvetica**, **Times New Roman**, and **Verdana** all on the same page. It looks messy and unprofessional. Using two different fonts is not bad, but use no more than that.

You can vary text emphasis with **styles**—these include bold light, extended, semi-extended, italic, semi-bold italic, and so on. Note that not all fonts have a wide range of these styles. I have used a font called Myriad Pro for many years simply because I bought additional fonts from Adobe for my design business, so now I have access to more than 35 (Myriad Pro) styles. Some fonts only have bold and italic, while others have more—and they are not necessarily all on your computer!

To select text that is currently being typed, use *Ctrl/Cmd + A* to select all. If the document has already been saved, then, with the **Type** tool selected, you need to first click inside the text once (to make it the active layer), then double-click the text to select a single word, or triple-click to select an entire sentence. If you're using a text box and want to select everything in that box, you will need to quadruple-click, very quickly, to select everything in that text layer.

Another way to select text is to click once into the text on screen to make that text layer the active layer, and then use *Ctrl/Cmd + A* to select everything on that particular text layer. I see students clicking and dragging the cursor around the text in the main window in the hope that this will select the text. It never works because you first have to wake up that text layer by clicking it to make it the active layer.

Using the Type options panel

Although this program certainly does not have the sophistication of a professional word-processing application, its tools—such as they are—can be quite creative. Aside from accessing all of your computer's different fonts, Elements offers different **styles** for those fonts (such as bold italic, light, extended, semi-bold, and so on), a **leading adjustment** (this controls the space between sentences), a **color swatch**, and a series of **faux styles** designed to apply a style to a font that doesn't normally have such options.

If the type is in the wrong place in your document, it's a simple operation to use the ubiquitous **Move** tool (*V*) to click and drag it to the new location; however, Elements offers another way to do this while you're typing. If you move the cursor slightly away from the text area while still in typing mode, it changes from the **Text Insertion** icon to the **Move** icon, and as soon as you see this, you can click, hold, and drag the entire text layer to another position in the main window. Then, you can double-click it to get back into the text layer and carry on typing. This is quite clever engineering on Adobe's part, but I have found that, in practice, if you're new to this program, it can cause more frustration when it does not work.

Text styles and special effects

The **Type** tool allows users to apply the usual font styles and colors to your text. But there's a lot more to using text than simply typing into an image.

With your text layer active (highlighted in blue), you can apply any of Elements' **Layer Styles** from the **Styles** panel that's located on the right-hand side of the main window. The most common style that's used with text is the **Drop Shadow**. Drop shadows are particularly effective for making text stand out from the page, especially if the background under the text is distracting.

Elements makes it easy to apply such effects. This is done by choosing **Drop Shadow** from the drop-down menu at the top of the **Styles** panel, choosing a particular drop shadow look, and clicking the icon to apply the style to that particular layer. If you don't like this effect, simply click another icon, and then that new look will replace the old one. It's a very easy system to work with. Using Styles in this way allows even relative novices to make their text productions appear professional in no time at all.

When the Style icon is clicked, it applies a preset recipe to that particular layer. If you don't like the recipe, it can be changed by accessing that particular layer's **Style Settings**. Open the **Layers** panel; you will note that a small **fx** logo has appeared next to the text layer's description. Double-click the **fx** icon to open up the **Style Settings** panel. In this window, you can see the exact recipe that creates the drop shadow as you see it. If you want to make the shadow darker or lighter, or appear further from or nearer to the surface of the document, fiddle with the sliders to modify that particular setting. You'll also find other special effects on this panel, including a **Glow**, a **Bevel**, and a **Stroke**, which is the Photoshop term for an outline.

You really don't absolutely need to use the **Type** tool to add words to your images or to a document. The text in this screen grab is from the text styles that you'll find in the **Graphics** panel. Click on a style that you like and it will drop `Your Text Here` into the main window. So, it is ridiculously easy to use, as well as quick. I personally don't like all the preset effects (drop shadows, glass looks, shaded color, bevels, and so on) that are added to these presets, but they are easy to use. Look at the following screenshot:

Useful styles that you'll find in this panel include **Bevels**, **Complex** (styles), **Image Effects**, and much more. When trying a **Layer** style, do bear in mind that some of them, such as photographic effects, will only work on pixel-based photos, and have almost no impact on text, and vice versa. If you try to apply a drop-shadow effect on a full-frame image, it won't work because the photograph occupies the entire screen; however, if you were to apply a drop-shadow effect on an image that has been reduced in frame size, it will display a drop shadow. The trick with text is to experiment with some of the styles to see which suits your project best. I will add that many of the styles that you see in Photoshop Elements have been with this software for a very long time (more than 10 years), so might appear somewhat dated.

Custom fonts

If you are looking for a special font to match a theme or character in one of your Elements projects, one thing you could consider is downloading a (free) *custom font* from a site such as www.dafont.com. Look at the following screenshot:

Find the font that you think suits your project (I entered the word *Japanese*) and click the **Download** button. Once downloaded to your Downloads folder (this should be fast because font files are very small) double-click the downloaded file. It will open a window displaying what the font looks like (as shown in the following screenshot). In the upper left-hand side of the font window, click the **Install** button. This will pop that new font into the shared font folder (this is the same process for both Mac and Windows):

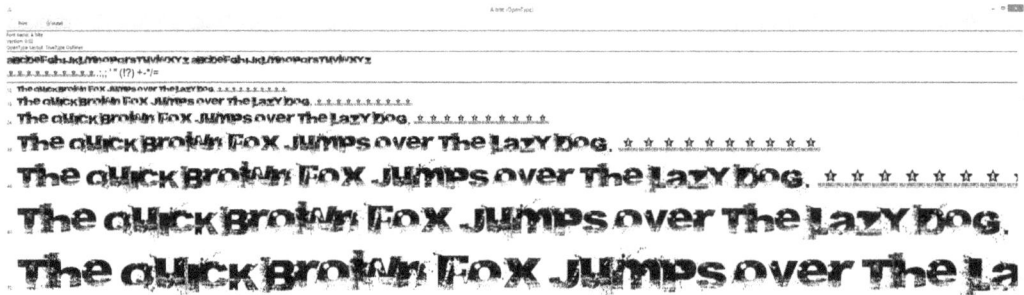

Now, it's best to restart Photoshop Elements. When you do this, you'll see the new font in the **Font** drop-down menu for the **Type** tool. In this example, I chose a font called **Papercuts**, which suited the **Autumn in Japan** theme of my book. (I first tried a very cool-looking font that was made up of chopsticks—very Oriental—but in practice, anything smaller than 18 points made it illegible, so I had to abandon that font and search for a more legible one).

> **A word of warning**
>
> Not all *free fonts* are fully functioning (from my experience). Around 80% of the fonts I download work fine, but some just don't function properly. I'm not 100% sure why this is the case, but I think it's usually easy enough to find an alternative font that looks similar that does work seamlessly...

Whenever I load a new custom font into my computer, I use the full-screen font display to print out a **paper record** that I keep on file—do this to remember what that non standard font looks like weeks or months later.

Keyboard shortcuts

As with most editing, you can lose sight of the image-making process and become too immersed in the more complex editing functions. Keyboard shortcuts are there to help spread the load, reduce **repetitive strain injury (RSI)**, and generally speed up your workflow. I use the first three in the following list all the time. It's also beneficial for you to memorize some of the tool access keys (letters) to make it easier to jump from process to process. Some of these are shown here:

- *Ctrl/Cmd + J*: Duplicate the (active) layer.

- *Ctrl/Cmd + D*: Use this to deselect or remove any active selection.

- *Ctrl/Cmd + T*: Use this to transform objects on the active layer.

- *Ctrl/Cmd + E*: Merge down.

- *Shift + Ctrl/Cmd + E*: Merge (all) visible (layers).

- *O*: **Burn**, **Dodge**, and **Sponge** tools.

- *A*: Selection brushes (**Quick Selection**, **Selection Brush**, **Magic Wand**, **Refine Selection**, and **Auto Selection**).

- *L*: **Lasso** tools (**Freehand Lasso**, **Polygonal Lasso**, and **Magnetic Lasso**).

- *S*: **Clone Stamp** tool (also the **Pattern Stamp** tool).

- *J*: **Spot Healing** and **Healing Brushes**.

- *B*: Brushes (**Brush tool**, **Impressionist Brush**, and **Color Replace Brush**).

- *E*: **Eraser** brushes (**Eraser**, **Background Eraser**, and **Magic Eraser** brushes).

- *K*: **Paint Bucket** tool.

- *G*: **Gradient** tool.

- *Alt/Opt + Ctrl/Cmd + S*: **Enhance | Select Subject**.

Out of the hundreds of possible keyboard shortcuts published for this program, I consider those on this page to the most important. They sum up the most practical features in this program and, once learned, will advance your understanding and editing proficiency tenfold.

Summary

In this chapter, we once more ramped up the depth of knowledge to present the best learning experience possible.

As you may well now be aware, it's possible to spend your entire working life immersed in the work of commercial photography and professional retouching. All the tools are here in Elements, but if you need to take the control you require to a higher level, this was the chapter for you, especially through the sections on professional-grade retouching, selections, burning, dodging, masking, text, and graphics.

We also highlighted a couple of simple ways to make selections—Adobe is continuously attempting to incorporate AI into its semi- and fully automated processes. In the case of its new **Subject Selection** feature, I think you'll agree it's a winner.

Having so many varied and powerful features at your disposal gives you a far wider range of creative options than just being able to add the odd preset effect to an image. If you can master this chapter, you'll be well on your way to becoming a retouching expert.

Coming up in the next chapter are plenty of in-depth sections for those who want more information about the power of illustration, graphics, drawing, and painting.

8
Advanced Drawing and Painting Techniques

This chapter will look at some of the more *esoteric* functions that you'll find in Elements. I use the word *esoteric* simply because these features are more graphic than *photographic*, more illustrative than *documentary*; however, as you'll see here, these features can be used to create standalone designs, or they can be incorporated into your day-to-day photography projects to produce outstanding results.

The main topics that will be discussed in this chapter are as follows:

- Illustration – drawing and painting techniques
- The View menu
- Using a graphics tablet
- Using brushes
- Brush behavior
- Drawing a sphere from scratch
- The Impressionist Brush
- The Color Replacement Tool

- Working with Brushes
- Importing and using Custom Brushes
- Custom lightening brush exercise
- Adobe vectors – using Adobe clip art
- Creating custom vector illustrations
- Working with effects filters

Illustration – drawing and painting techniques

For a Moms and Dads photo editing app, Adobe Photoshop Elements continues to amaze with what it can offer in terms of its processes, functions, and toolset. You'll find a staggering array of graphic elements that can be downloaded and installed directly from the Adobe servers, plus an impressive range of photo editing, design, and illustrative tools that go together to make it an all-in-one creative powerhouse.

Before I learned how to use **Adobe InDesign**, an industry-standard page layout application, I used Photoshop Elements to design, assemble, and produce my first 100-page magazine. It was quite hard work because Elements is basically designed for small tasks, snippets of text, and home projects, not commercial magazine production. Even so, the result, I might add, was excellent.

The following is a graphic illustration that was created using nothing but vector clip art picture frames and a background, downloaded from the **Graphics** panel (via the Adobe servers):

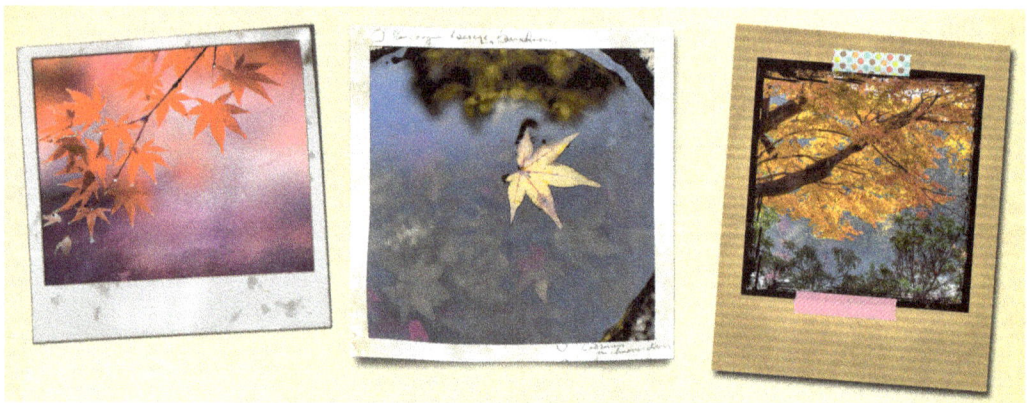

We'll look at its graphics capabilities in the following sections, but in the meantime, let's look at the illustrative capabilities of this program, starting with the essential design and layout helper: The **View** menu.

The View menu

Before you start any design project, it's important to have layout and lineup tools at your disposal – in the same way that before you start to type a letter, you need to have the margins, font and font styles set in place for a specific style or look.

The **View** menu repeats some of the keyboard shortcuts we've already mentioned elsewhere in this book, notably the **Zoom in** and **Zoom out** functions (*Ctrl/Cmd + +* and *Ctrl/Cmd + -*, respectively). These are two of the most important keyboard shortcuts because, as an image editor, you need to go in close to retouch, then zoom out to the see the global effect, then go in close again, then zoom out again, on a regular basis. Alternatively, you can use *Ctrl/Cmd + 0* (zero) to **fit the image** to the main screen – another handy shortcut.

Zooming to **Print Size** will show you how large it will print. If you have adjusted the file resolution so that it matches the output requirement (in the **Image Size** panel), this should provide accurate feedback on the display size.

In the following screenshot, I have opened the **Preferences** program (*Ctrl/Cmd + K*) at the **Guides** and **Grid** tab and have changed the **Grid** so that it displays in red, every 25%, with four subdivisions. This produces a clearer-looking grid with an easy to see (slightly thicker) vertical and horizontal center line:

> **Tip**
>
> Many might find the *"line of marching ants"* active selection line a bit distracting, especially when viewing the selection up close. Press *Ctrl/Cmd + H* to temporarily hide an active selection line. Just don't forget to press *Ctrl/Cmd + H* a second time to bring the selection line back, or use *Ctrl/Cmd + D* to deselect the selection before moving on.

Snap To is another handy feature, especially if you are using Elements for page layout or design and need to precisely align multiple elements (text boxes, images, or other graphics). Position a **Guide** somewhere in the page, then drag each element one by one into the vicinity of the guide – providing Snap To is turned on, it will "snap" or stick to the guide. I use this feature all the time because it works so well. If you are working on a project where positioning elements freehand is necessary, turn **Snap To** off so as to specifically stop those elements sticking to Grids or Guides.

Rulers are self-explanatory, but the **Guides** aren't. A **Guide** is a moveable line that can be positioned anywhere in the main screen, vertically or horizontally. You can have as many of these as are needed for the design job; just mouse-click and drag them off the ruler one at a time. To get rid of them, either drag them back off the screen into the ruler or choose **View | Clear Guides**. In the following screenshot, you can see the **Guides** (red) in action. **Guides** (*Ctrl/Cmd + ;*) are brilliant for lining up text and image layers for precise positioning. Guides and **Grids** do not print:

Using a graphics tablet

We have already discussed several uses for the **Brush** tool, notably in creating **layer masks**, in previous chapters, but of course, it can also be used as a real *brush*. To do this, you need to be adept at drawing with a mouse (which is akin to sketching with a bar of soap), or you might consider buying a **graphics tablet** or **graphics monitor**.

Tablet devices are perfect for artists because, instead of drawing with a mouse, you use a **pen stylus**, which is roughly the same size and shape as a *real* pen, and draw onto the tablet as if it were the screen itself. Interestingly, tablets are also available in the form of graphics monitors – digital screens onto which you draw – but these are significantly more expensive.

Tablets come in a range of sizes, though the larger the better since they provide more drawing accuracy and features, but nevertheless, even a $50 model will serve you well. One leading name in tablets is a company called Wacom, which produces a complete range of products from entry level to very expensive $700+ professional versions. If you just need a different and more accurate way to control your mouse actions, it's probably best to invest in a small or medium-sized tablet, which will set you back up to $300 or so:

Bluetooth-enabled models are slightly more expensive than non-Bluetooth models. If you can survive with a USB cable connection, you could save $40 or so. Larger models (8.5 x 5.5 inches and up) are easier to use because the active part of the tablet reflects the size of the screen more accurately. At the top end of town are tablets specially designed to work with real paper. Clip your favorite paper to the tablet and use the electronic stylus to either trace or draw through the paper to create an electronic file. Expect to pay over $600 for one of these bad boys.

If your work is 100% reliant on your penmanship (and your boss is OK with buying one for you), consider the top-of-the-range monitor tablet, which is essentially a 4K screen that you draw, design, and animate on. This is a beautiful product, but at $4,500+, it's out of the price range of most mere mortals:

Tips for getting the most from a graphics tablet

Unless you're incredibly gifted with manual dexterity, a graphics tablet is never a complete replacement for the mouse.

Buy the largest one you can afford – the larger the surface, the more realistic your drawing motion will be.

More expensive tablets have programmable buttons that aid productivity.

Make use of the **Tablet Menu** in Photoshop Element's **Brush Options** panel.

Despite being primarily a photo editing application, Photoshop Elements has an amazing range of graphic tools that are offered specifically to photographers and designers so that they can extend their creativity.

Here's a terrific graphic illustration that was created from a photo and over-painted with several different watercolor effects:

When using the **Brush** tool, note that Elements has a special **Tablet** menu (located in its **Options** Panel) that allows you to get more from the graphics tablet.

I have used tablets for many years and still find it hard to get exactly the right feel for drawing on a computer – but then again, I'm no artist and struggle to draw anything more basic than a loose sketch. That said, I have worked with designers who possess a masterful skill with the medium – they can churn out illustrations with these tablets that are truly beautiful.

Using brushes

Elements has several types of what I class as artist's brush tools. These are the **Pencil** tool, the **Brush** tool, the **Impressionist Brush** tool, and the **Color Change** tool.

The **Pencil** tool, all alone on its own peg on the **Tool** bar, is possibly the least used of all of Element's many tools because, as I mentioned previously, unless you are a skilled graphic artist experienced with a pen tablet, it's very hard to use:

Brush behavior

Though Elements is mostly a photo editing program, many of its tools rely on the use of a brush (and in my opinion, brush-based tools such as **Dodge**, **Burn**, and **Sponge** are some of the most creative in Elements).

But it doesn't end with these three excellent retouching brush tools. Elements contains a wide range of "real" (digital) brushes to paint, sketch, draw, and illustrate with, either by brushing on top of an existing image or starting from scratch with a blank canvas.

If that is not enough, Elements allows the user to change the characteristics of each brush – the shape, orientation, opacity, color, pressure, and appearance, all of which we will look at over the following pages.

On top of the expected hard and soft brush tips (the top two lines in the following screenshot), Elements provides a number of other brush characteristics, which include **Spacing** – if you are drawing and the line looks a bit lumpy, this is possibly because the **Spacing** slider is incorrectly set – which is the third line from the top. You can also angle the brush tip for an oblique look – this is more for users of a graphics tablet:

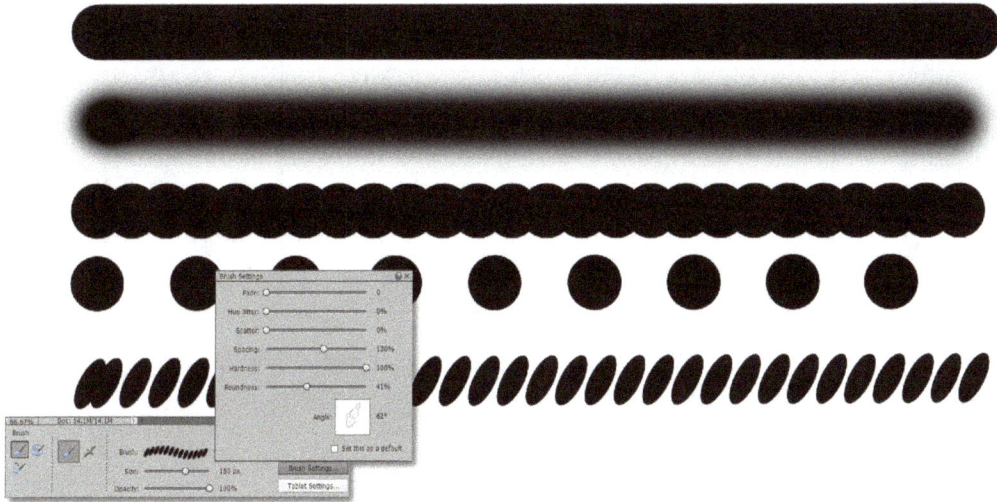

The following screenshot illustrates feature effects such as **Fade** (top), **Jitter**, and **Scatter** (which spreads the *paint* around, a little like the **Impressionist Brush**):

Now, let's learn how to draw the **perfect square or rectangle** using any of the brush-based tools in Elements. An example of this is shown in the following screenshot:

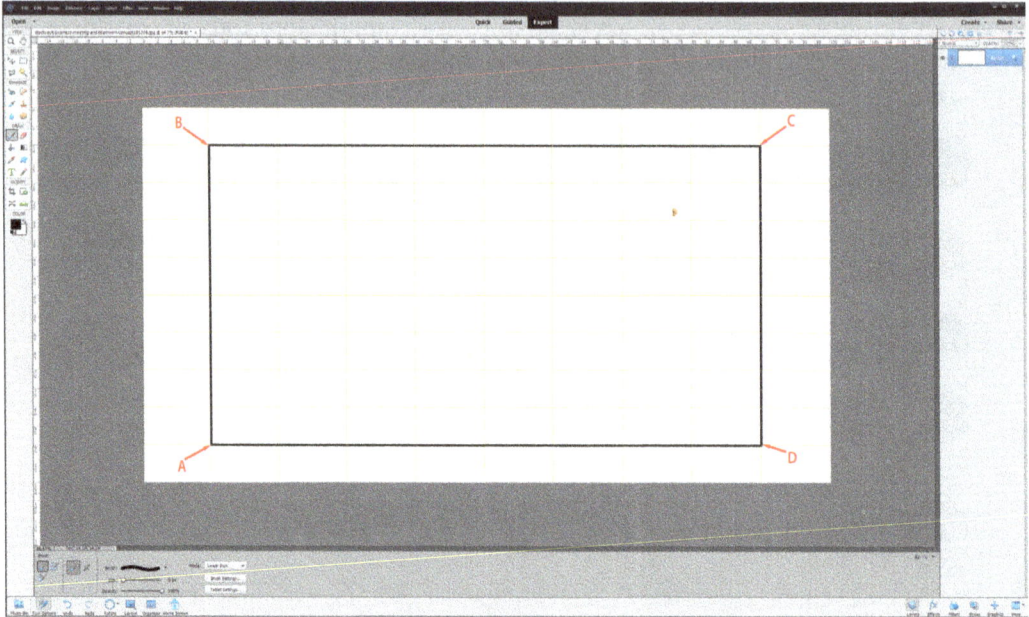

This point-to-point drawing technique works with all the **Eraser** and retouching type brushes, as well as the **Burn**, **Dodge**, and **Sponge** tools:

1. Turn on the **Grid** (*Ctrl/Cmd + '*).

2. Choose a drawing brush (such as the **Pencil** or **Brush** tool).

3. Mouse-click once on point **A**.

4. Hold *Shift* and mouse-click point **B**. The pencil line joins point **A** to **B** in a straight line.

5. Hold *Shift* and mouse-click point **C**. The pencil line joins point **B** to **C** in a straight line.

6. Hold *Shift* and mouse-click point **D**. The pencil line joins point **C** to **D** in a straight line.

7. Hold *Shift* and mouse-click point **A**. The pencil line joins point **D** back to point A.

Now, let's learn how to draw the **perfect circle** using the **Elliptical Shape** tool and the **Elliptical Marquee Selection** tools. An example of this is shown in the following screenshot:

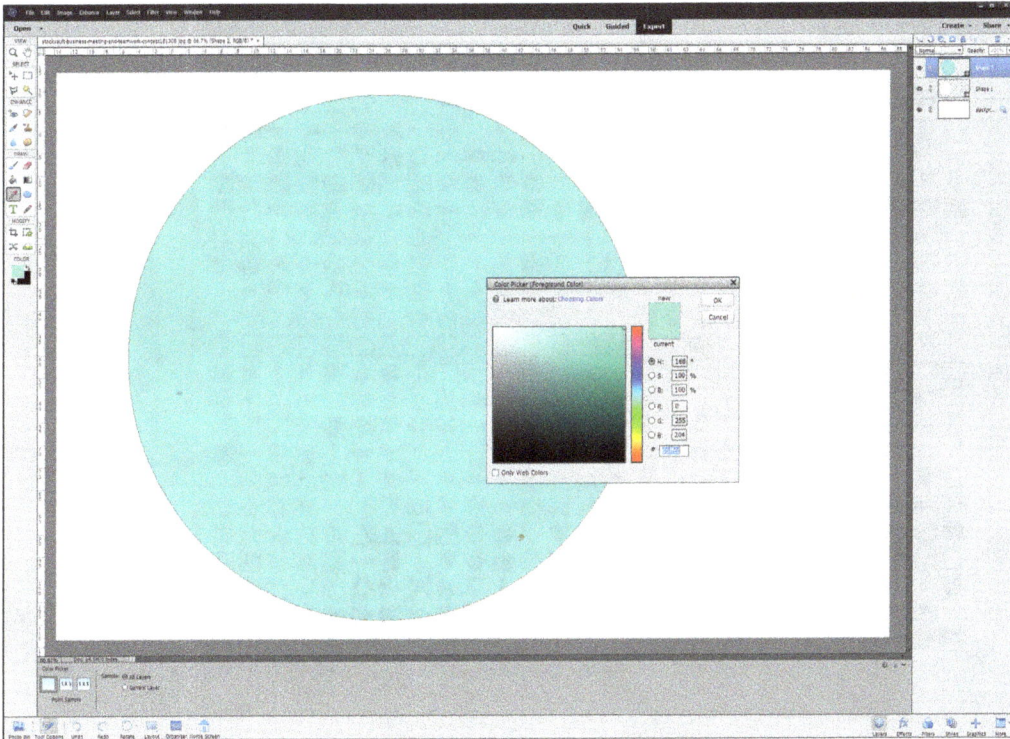

Let's get started:

1. Create a new blank document (**File | New | Blank File**).

2. Choose the **Elliptical** tool – normally, you'd click and drag in the new canvas to draw the shape, but it's hard to get it precisely symmetrical doing this freehand.

3. Hold the *Shift* key, then click and drag into the canvas. The *Shift* key locks the proportions, giving you a perfect circle. Note that if you want to add color to the graphic, you need to select the color first - in this case using the Color Picker, before moving on to draw the shape on the canvas.

Drawing a sphere from scratch

As a very simple exercise, the next few illustrations will show you how relatively easy it is to draw a three-dimensional sphere shape using Element's drawing tools:

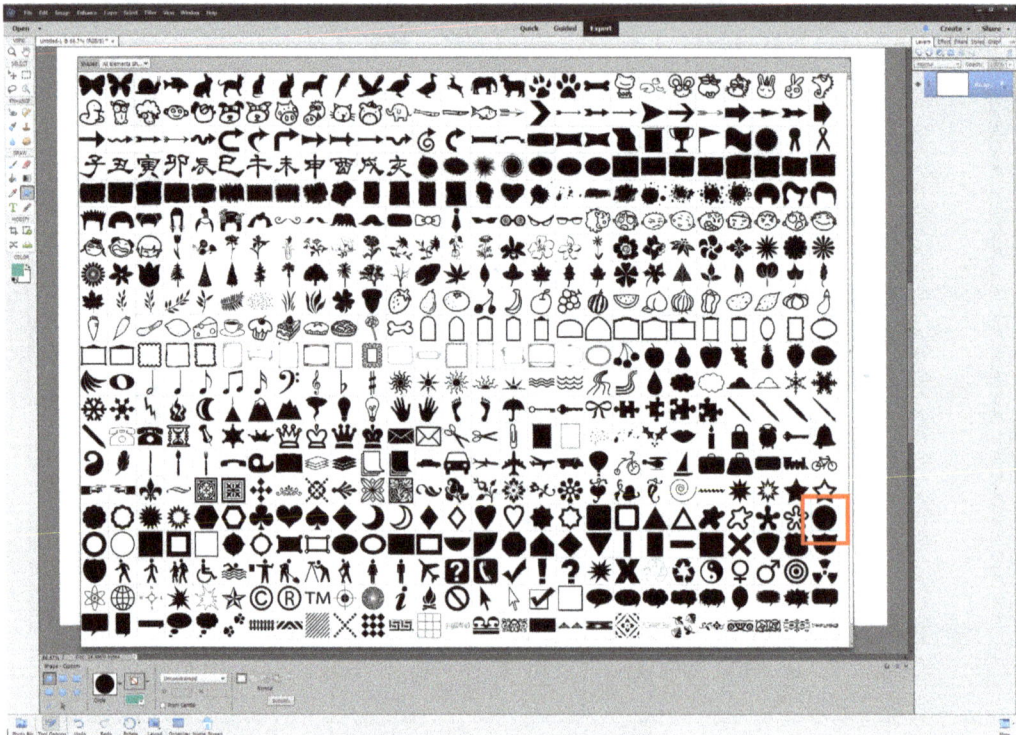

Let's get started:

1. Use the **Custom Shape** tool to draw a perfect vector circle, as highlighted in red in the preceding screenshot (tip: hold *Shift* when you do this to keep its proportions). Also, note that if you have not set your preferred color in the Tool bar's foreground Color Picker, it will default to black:

2. Add a shading effect. Using a large, soft-edged brush, I "painted" a darker shade of green into the lower part of the circle with increasingly deeper-colored brush strokes. I reselected from the color picker again and again, darkening the tint each time, to get the gradation just right. The brush must be large, soft-edged, and set to an opacity of 25% or so.

    It takes a while to slowly build up the shading effect that you can see in the following image, where the base is now almost black:

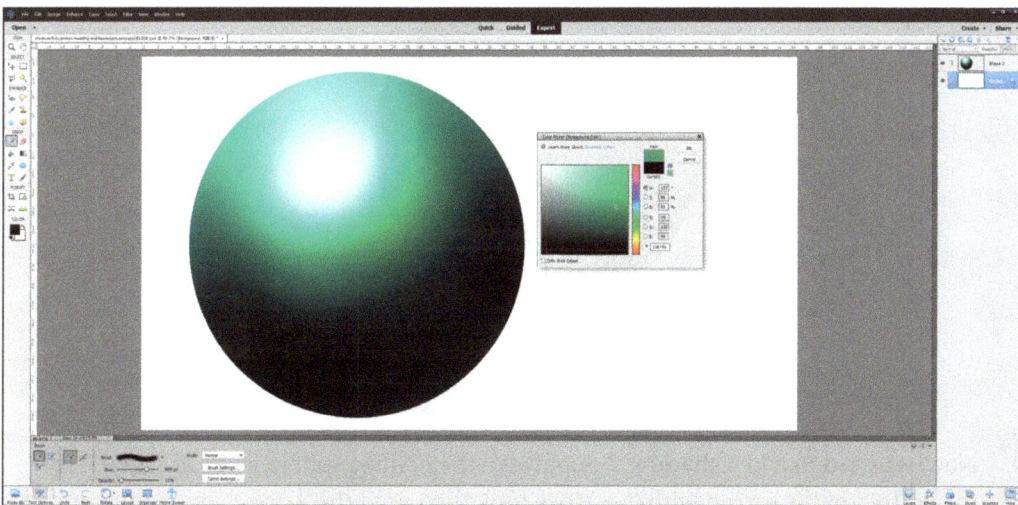

3. Once the color had darkened nicely around the base of the *sphere*, I chose white to "paint" in a light highlight at the top of the sphere. Once the tonal areas were more or less complete, I applied a **Gaussian Blur** (**Filter | Blur | Gaussian Blur**) to the entire area in the selection to smooth the tones:

4. Now, we need to add a **shadow**. I duplicated the *floating* sphere layer, dragged it to the bottom of the screen with the Move tool, then used the **Transform** feature and its **Scale** transform command to *squish* the shape, as you can see here:

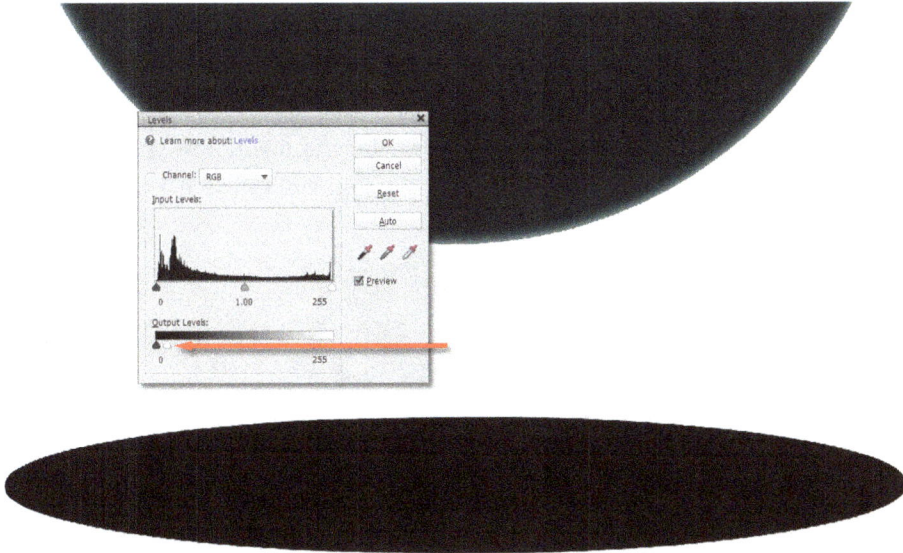

5. Then, I converted the squashed sphere to black using the rarely used **Output Levels** part of the regular **Levels** tool. Push the highlight slider all the way to the left (arrowed) to make it go black. This is now our shadow:

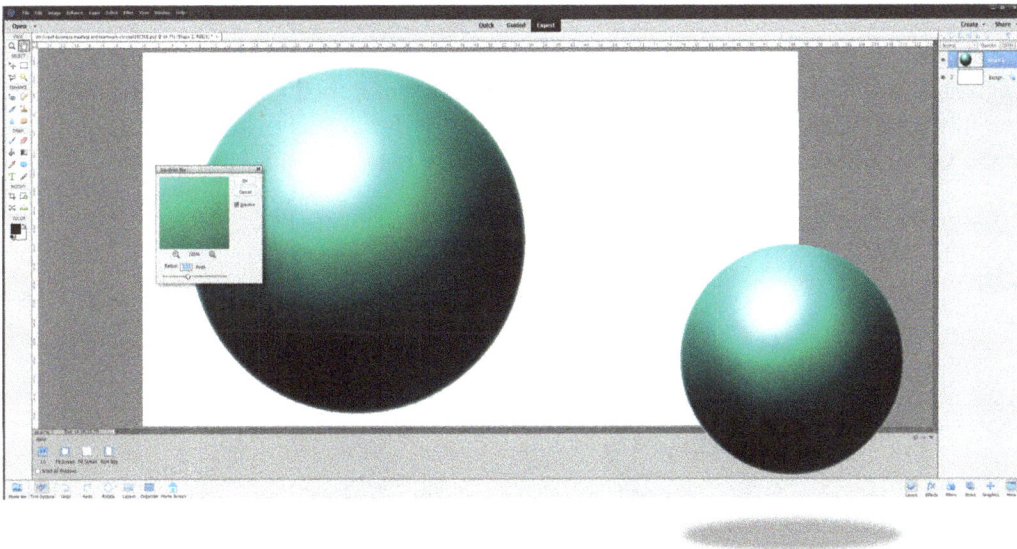

6. Finally, I blurred the black *shadow* layer using the **Gaussian Blur** filter and reduced that layer's opacity to give it a more realistic shadowy look. Now, it's finished.

The **Brush** tool looks and works like an electronic version of an artist's brush: choose a color from the **Color Picker** on the **Tool** bar, pick out a brush tip (300+ on offer), adjust its diameter (size) and its opacity (the speed of the brush), and off you go.

You can also elect to paint in different **Blend Modes**, depending on how you'd like the pixels to merge into each other. The default is **Normal**, but you can choose from one of the other 20+ Blend Modes for a special effect:

With skill and the right brief, graphic artists can create impressive-looking artworks using Photoshop Elements' illustration tools: the **Brush** and **Pencil** in collaboration with a graphics tablet. Here's another illustration. Essentially, this is only made up of 10 colors and is a **vector image**, saved in the GIF file format. Due to this, the file size is tiny:

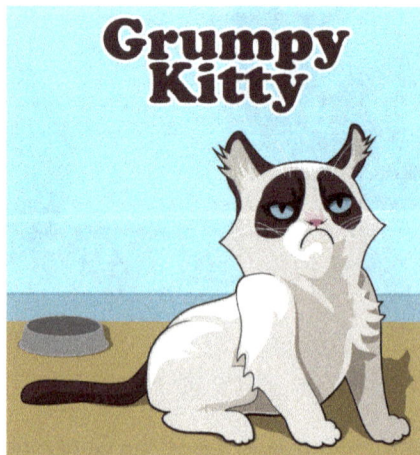

Impressionist Brush

The **Impressionist Brush** is fun as it *sort of* clones (copies) your image and paints it directly back into the canvas as large, fuzzy brush strokes, producing, I suppose, something that passes for an impressionist *look*. You can broaden your impressionist *look* a little using its **Advanced** button, which takes you to a range of other brush stroke options, **Tolerance** settings, and more. I'm not sure what *Edouard Manet* or *Claude Monet* might have thought of this process, but with the right image and textured paper to print on, the effects can be quite good.

This is the original picture:

I generally set the **Impressionist Brush Tip** to a large size when painting the background, but make the brush significantly smaller when working on the details – otherwise, the photo will just look out of focus or blurred. Another technique is to duplicate the layer first, apply the impressionist brush to the top layer, and then, with the **Eraser** tool (set to a low opacity of around 20%), carefully erase some of the top layer to reveal the *real* image beneath. Doing this produces a subtle blend of original image combined with the impressionist look. Sometimes this partial reveal process works better than just using the Impressionist Brush alone - but again, this does also depend on the nature of your original image:

Color Replacement tool

Lastly, we have the **Color Replacement** tool. Like many other tools, this one relies on applying the color change effect to similar-colored pixels. Take a look at this before and after illustration:

This isn't a bad result. I repainted the town hall in the background in a couple of minutes with the **Color Replacement** tool.

So, if I want to replace blue with red, providing all the blue pixels are the same value, it will work very well – but we all know that life in the digital editing realm is not like this, so that's why we have the **Tolerance** slider to make Elements be a bit more or less sensitive when it's applying a color change. Increase the tolerance and it will apply the change to lighter and darker shades of blue. You have different brush styles to choose from: four different **Blend Modes** (I find **Color** works best) and the inevitable **Contiguous** or **Discontiguous** check boxes.

Working with Brushes

Photoshop Elements comes with a number of artistic style tools, which includes a basic paintbrush. This tool has over 300 variants, which means you could spend a lot of time scratching your head deciding which style of brush you want to use.

The **Preset Manager**, which you'll find in the **Expert** edit mode, allows you to modify, monitor, import, delete, and rename **Brushes**, **Swatches**, **Gradients**, **Styles**, **Patterns**, and **Effects**.

Importing and using custom Brushes

If I were to download some custom brushes from the internet, I'd first open the **Preset Manager**, choose **Brushes** from the central drop-down menu, and then click the **Add** button, navigate to where the brush set has been downloaded to (such as into the computer's `Downloads` folder), and double-click to load them into Elements.

If I then click the **Done** button, this saves the brush (or brush set) into Elements for use later. I can, of course, rename that particular brush set, or even delete individual brushes that I don't like or use, in order to simplify my choice next time I'm looking for a brush type.

The following illustrations show the process of looking for, locating, loading, and then using custom brushes to enhance your images. Sometimes, this might just be the addition of something very small (such as a tiny cloud in an otherwise blue cloudless sky) or, at the other end of the scale, something far more dramatic, such as lightning bolts striking the Earth:

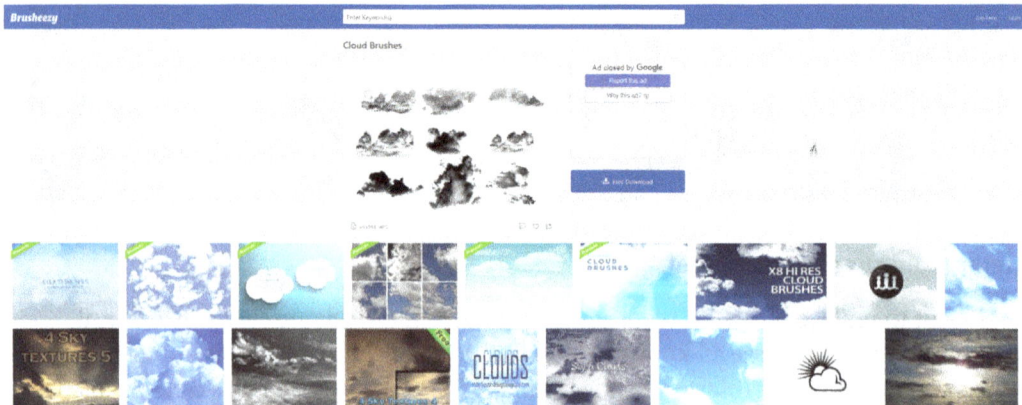

Let's learn how to import and work with Custom Brushes:

1. Here's what you'll find if you Google `Free Adobe brushes`. In this example, I searched for free **cloud brushes** and downloaded a set from a site I have found to be very reliable (`www.brusheezy.com`). Before you do this, please note that if you're not following the download instructions perfectly, you may find that, not only do you download a brush set, but that you may also download other software (from any website). Just be careful when you download and install anything because it might not be everything you were expecting, especially if that website is giving away stuff for free:

2. Here's the contents of my computer's `Downloads` folder – I download a lot of different brush sets! Here, you can see that some are in zipped folders waiting to be used, while the black and white icons named "brushes" are the unzipped brush sets waiting to be imported into Elements for use as a project:

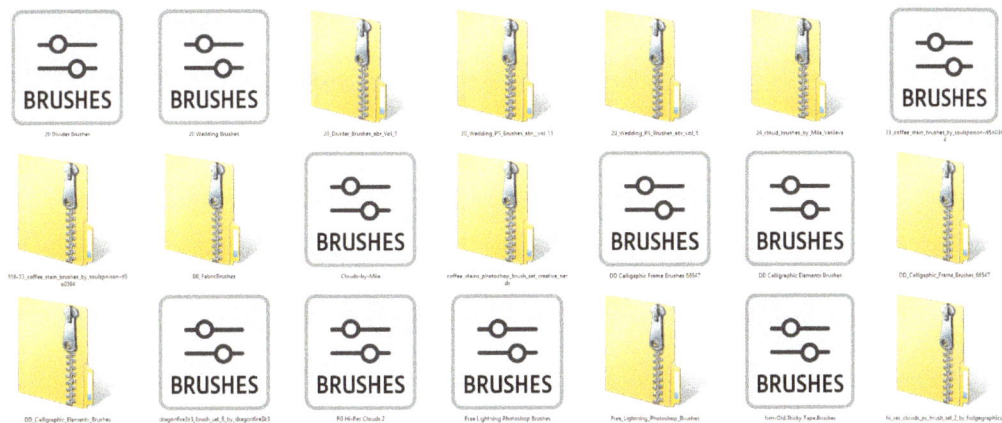

3. Right-click in the image to view the pop-out **Brush** panel. In the top right-hand corner, click the tiny button to view another pop-out contextual menu. This is where you can load newly-sourced brush files:

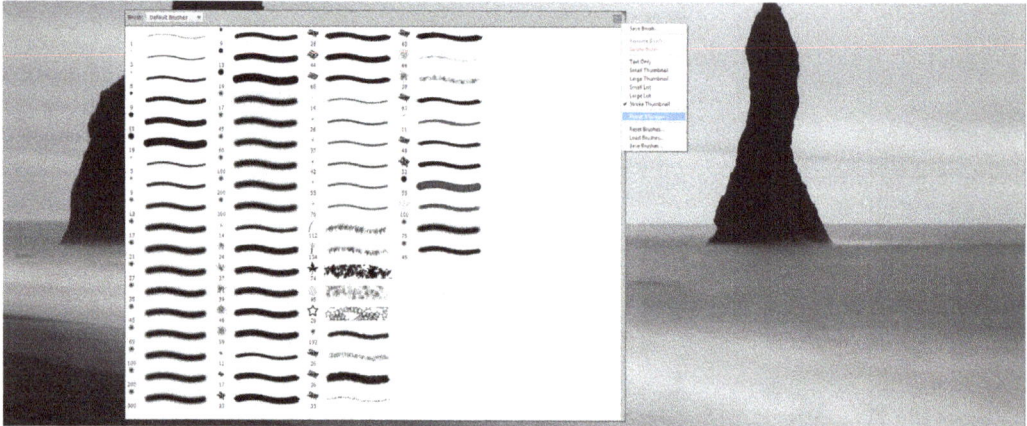

Once the new brush set has been loaded, you will see the new brushes in the **Preset Manager**, as shown in the following screenshot. Click **Done**:

4. In this example, the default cloud brushes I've installed are quite large (they were labelled as being more than 1,000 pixels across – the width of the brush is denoted in pixels underneath the brush thumbnail).

    They can, of course, be made smaller or larger as you can with any brush in Elements, either by changing the pixel width in the tool options panel or by tapping the left square bracket (to make it smaller) and the right square bracket to make it larger. By clicking once in the image, you add an image, not a brushstroke. If you click and drag, as you would when creating a normal brushstroke, the image of the cloud will be dragged across the canvas and would create a smeared line, which isn't what's wanted in this example. As you can see here, the single click has deposited a single black and white image of clouds over the surface of my seascape. The cloud is realistic but the positioning, over the sea, is definitely not!

5. If the image you're working on has a very clear separation between the sky and the landmass, you can simply choose a suitable color (white or black is a good place to start), adjust the size of the brush tip so that it fits in the sky area, and click once. As this brush is essentially created from a photo of clouds, clicking once drops in a graphic of those clouds. You might want to modify the opacity of the brush (that is, the density) and the color, depending on the effect you are trying to create (that is, stormy or sunny).

    In this example, the cloud brush is smaller than the previous illustration so that the cloud appears to fit neatly between the two rock stacks, exactly where you might expect to find a cloud – in the sky. In this example, I reduced the opacity of the brush slightly (to 85%) to make it appear as if it were blending with the tones in the original sky:

6.   Another way to make this *fake* cloud appear slightly more realistic is not to just stamp it in the middle of the sky, as in the previous example, but to try and **integrate it** behind the subject – in this example, behind the two dark rocks (this is the coast of southern Iceland).

Because the sky was essentially very pale in the original image, I can easily select it using the **Magic Wand** tool. Doing so means that if I now stamp my cloud brush into that sky area, the image will only appear in the sky, not on top of the dark rocks sticking up into the scene. This is because they are protected by the selection (this screen grab shows the extent of the selection in **Mask** mode).

Mask mode in Elements is the same as the Quick Mask mode in Adobe Photoshop CC and is a terrific way of checking the accuracy of the selection. However, it can also be edited as you see it here, using a brush to extend the mask or the eraser brush tool so that you can trim bits off it:

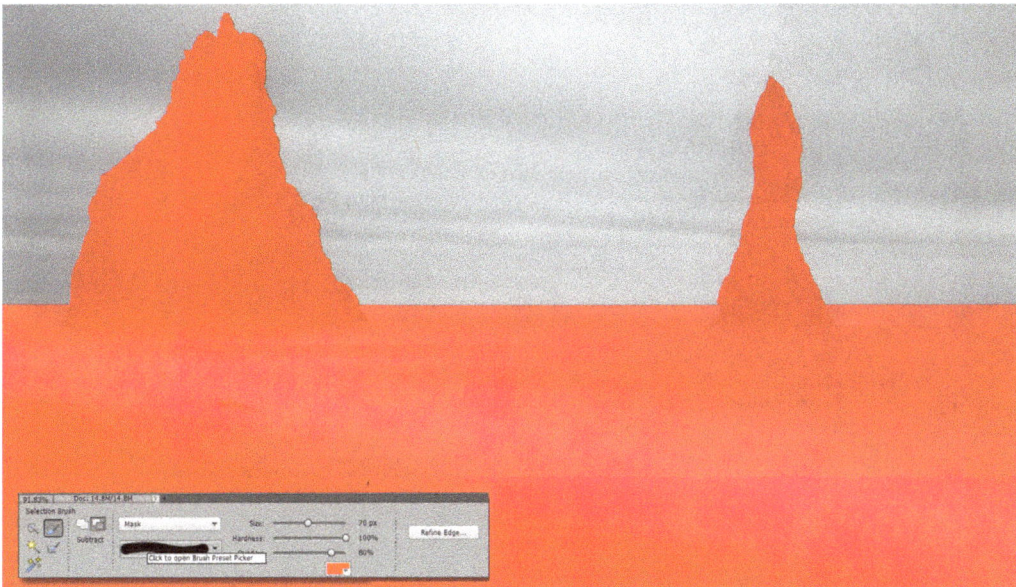

7. To fine-tune this process further, you may want to add a **Feather** amount to the resulting selection line – this should only be set to one or two pixels maximum, and it should be added **before** you start stamping. This small Feather amount will go a long way in helping blend the edge of the cloud brush with whatever object you're trying to place it behind. In this example, it's those two dark rock stacks off the beach. How can you judge the right pixel number for feathering? Generally, it's experience that teaches you how to get this right – too much and you'll see some fuzzy weirdness around the subject, too little and it doesn't work at all. The best advice is to test it first. If that does not work, undo the last action (*Ctrl/Cmd + Z*), add a different pixel value, and try again:

As you will appreciate while Googling for `Free Photoshop brushes`, there are hundreds of other types of free brush sets that you can download and incorporate in your artistic projects.

In fact, you might have seen a range of different brush effects in *Chapter 6, Advanced Editing Techniques*, in the traveler's journal illustration, which was recreated from over 40 different visual assets. This also included a number of special custom brush sets that I used from the web, including **coffee stains**, **watermarks**, and **sticky tape**, which are illustrated in the following image:

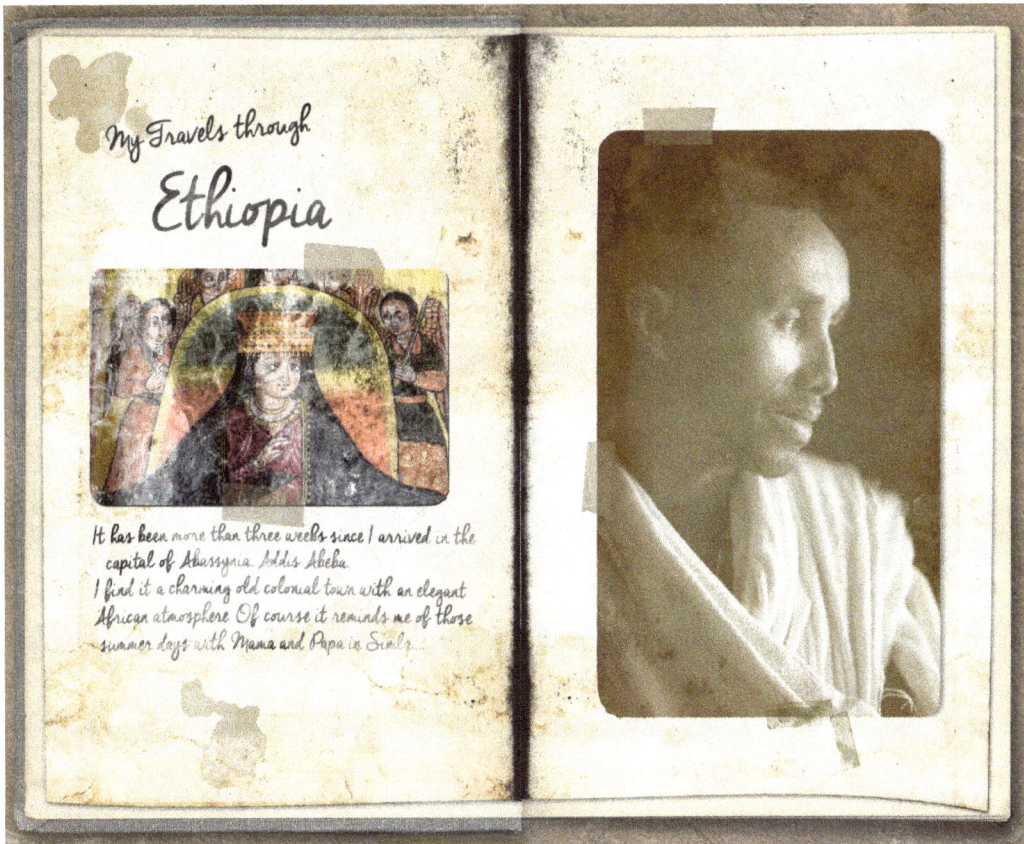

Custom lightning brushes

Cloud brushes are just a tiny part of the resources Elements users have access to on the web. You'll find an amazing range of free stuff online – just Google `Free Photoshop Brushes` and you'll get hundreds of responses. It's an opportunity to waste a lot of time because there's so much cool stuff to choose from.

From experience, some websites are excellent (such as the one pictured here), while others, although genuine, tend to include 'other' software in the *free* download. Be vigilant when you download and install!

Like the cloud brushes we profiled earlier in this chapter, there are **lightning brushes**, and a whole lot more to be had if you have the time to look for them. Most of the brushes I have tried worked really well, but as with anything downloaded off the internet, it pays to be a little careful in case you accidentally download more than you bargained for:

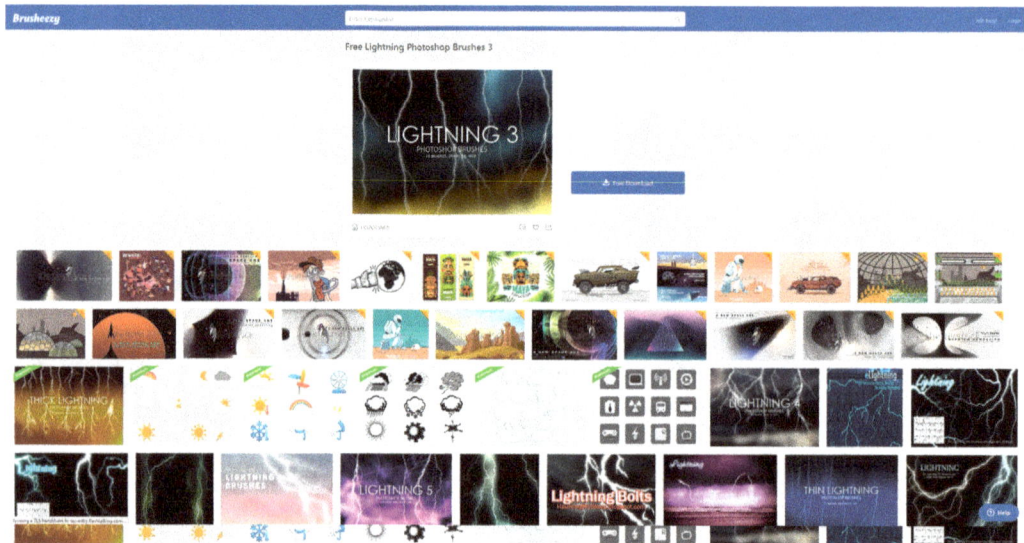

As with the previous step-by-step description of how to incorporate a cloud brush into your workflow, let's add some electric drama to a landscape using a lightening brush set!

Let's take a look at some custom lightning brushes:

1. I found a whole bunch of these **brushes** while searching for clouds. Again, these are from www.brusheezy.com, although there are many more sites offering similar brush files.

   Here's that brush set, already loaded into the **Preset Manager**, and now visible in the **Brush** panel that opens when you right-click anywhere in the image (or by clicking the **Brush Settings** menu in the **Brush** tool's **Options** panel). Note that the size of the brush is itemized as a pixel width under the small graphic of each lightning image:

2. Clearly just stamping one image of lightning into the main window isn't going to look genuine – lightning strikes never look like this because they emanate from the sky, generally from deep within a cloud system, so they will, more than likely, be part-obscured by more clouds - plus of course, this lightning bolt starts well below the top of the frame which looks somewhat fake:

3. To make this effect appear a little more real, I duplicated the landscape image layer first. Then, I made a new (blank) layer and clicked one lightning stamp into it. Because it is on its own layer, I dragged this lightning layer to the middle of the layer stack – the flash of lighting disappears immediately because it's now hidden by the (duplicated, and 100% opaque) top layer. Next, I reduced the top layer's opacity to around 80% so that I could see the lightning layer showing through it and carefully erased pixels from the top layer (with the **Eraser** tool set to 25%) to reveal the lightning on the layer beneath it. The good part of this exercise is that you don't have to be precise about erasing the exact same shape as the lightning bolt. Use a soft brush and erase a bit on either side. Also, note that I didn't erase all the pixels, so it looks like part of the lightning is actually still behind some of the darker clouds, which I think lends a greater sense of authenticity to the finished product. A meteorologist might look at this and find fault but to a casual observer, this effect, which took only a few minutes to complete, stands up well.

Adobe vectors

Photoshop Elements comes packed with vector **clip art** that you can use in your various projects. Actually, these assets are not in Elements when it's first downloaded, but every time you click an item in the **Graphics** panel, it will automatically download from Adobe. Since these are vector graphics, their size is tiny, so they take no time at all to download. Vectors are made from a mathematical formula and not pixels. Images are made up of individual pixels, which is why they take up a lot more space.

As an example, I am going to show you how make a **custom greeting card** using vector clip art. Let's get started:

1. To make your own custom greeting card, create a new document (**File** | **New** | **Blank Document**). Before you actually start the design process, I recommend that you search for envelopes that match your cards. It's very annoying if you go ahead and design a card and then find that no one makes envelopes to match the size of the card (yes, it's happened to me a couple of times). Find an envelope, measure its proportions, and create a new document that's twice its width or height, depending on whether you want the fold line at the top or on the left-hand edge of the card:

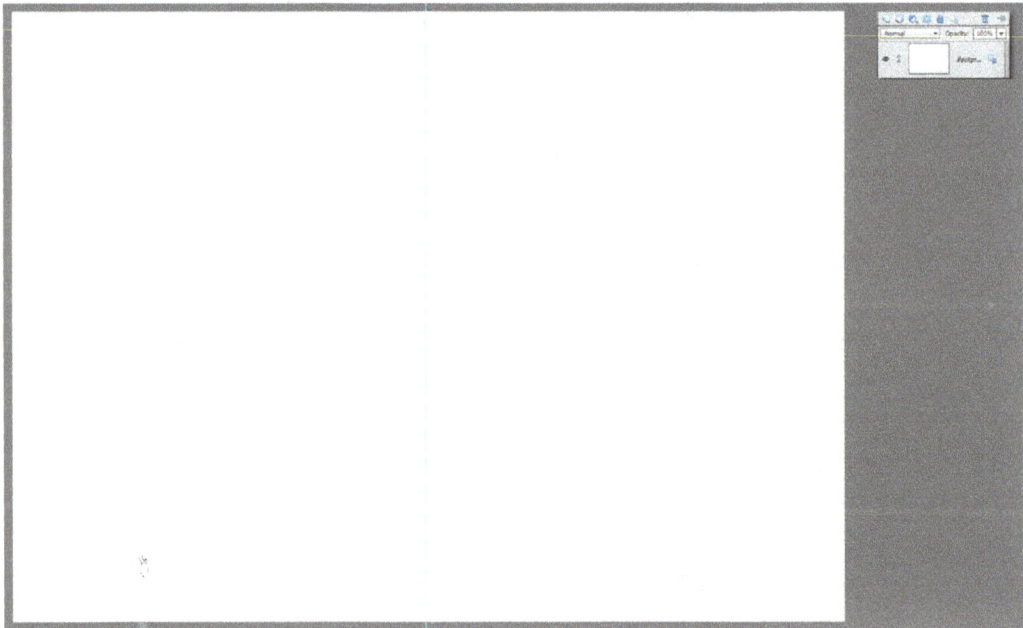

2. You can add some very nice preset text effects using the **Text** submenu in the **Graphics** panel. Double-clicking the text style from the listing on the right-hand side immediately adds it to the document open on the page as `Your Text Here`. Click this text to add your own greeting:

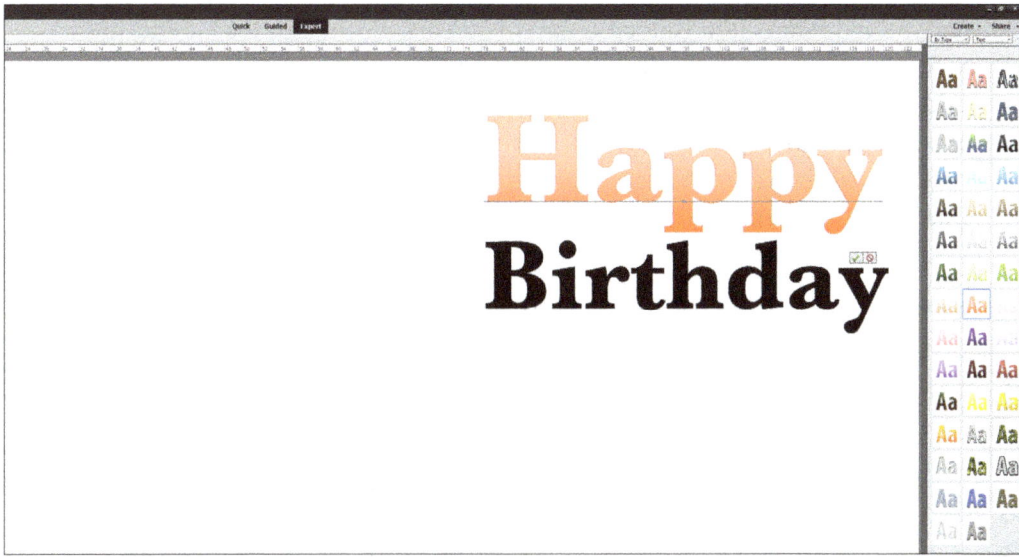

As an example, I chose **Backgrounds** from the drop-down menu, which is at the top-right in the **Graphics** panel, and clicked one of the thumbnails to automatically download and install it into my document:

3. My one problem with this otherwise good design feature is that it's hard to see what that design looks like before it is downloaded. But then, because it's only a small file, you can try one, and if it's no good, undo and try more.

4. If **Backgrounds** are not your thing, you can also drag entire designs, plus picture windows and frames into your custom card artwork. Again, this is a hit-and-miss process because some of the designs look quite different once they're in place. Simply undo and try another style before saving and printing it on your local inkjet or laser device. I sometimes spend a little more time making up a card design - then I save it in the Photoshop (.psd) format as my 'master' file. Once saved I can return to that same 'master' document again and again, changing just the main image to make it look fresh each time I need a new greetings card:

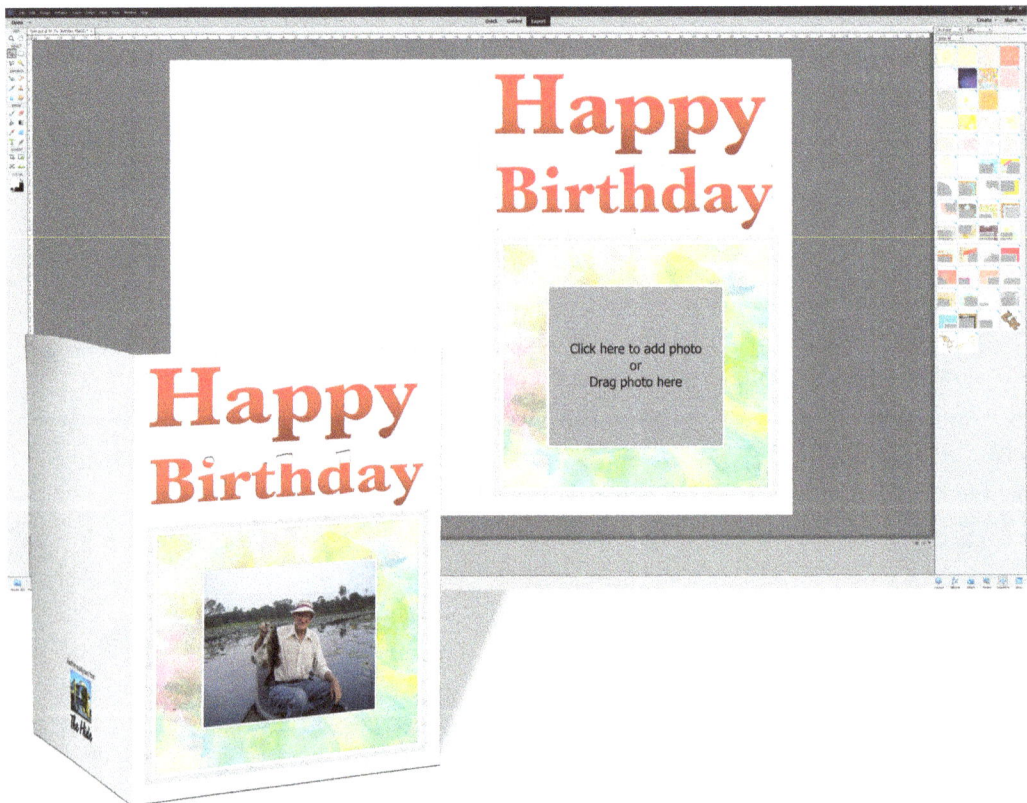

Creating custom vector illustrations

Surprisingly, Photoshop Elements has an amazing range of **vector tools** – shapes, text, and more. The beauty of these tools is that, since they are essentially made up of nothing more than a mathematical formula, they occupy very little space and can be resized to any size with no loss of quality.

In these illustrations, I am making a design for a book on Japanese food, experimenting with a custom font (**Paper Cuts**, downloaded for this project), as well as vector shapes as text boxes, plus a range of special effects, such as **Drop Shadows**. Let's get started:

1. In this example, I'm using scalable vectors to create a simple page design for a book on Japanese food. I have the main image open and have chosen a rounded edge panel as a starting point. Choose **Custom Shapes** from the **Tool bar**, select the **Rounded Rectangle Tool** (*U*), then click, hold, and drag into the image to add this vector shape to the document. It will go into its own layer automatically. Note that it doesn't matter if this is appearing at the right proportion or not because it can be resized at any time:

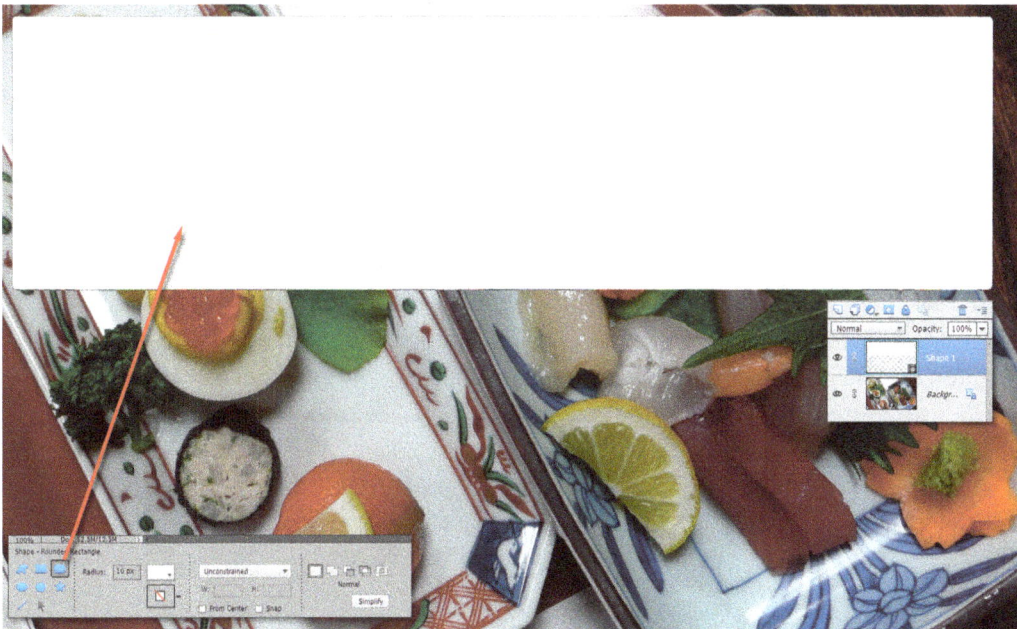

2. With this, I've added the first of my type layers. You can see that there are now three layers in this file: the background foodie shot, the vector shape layer, and the type layer on the top. At this stage, the font is just the default:

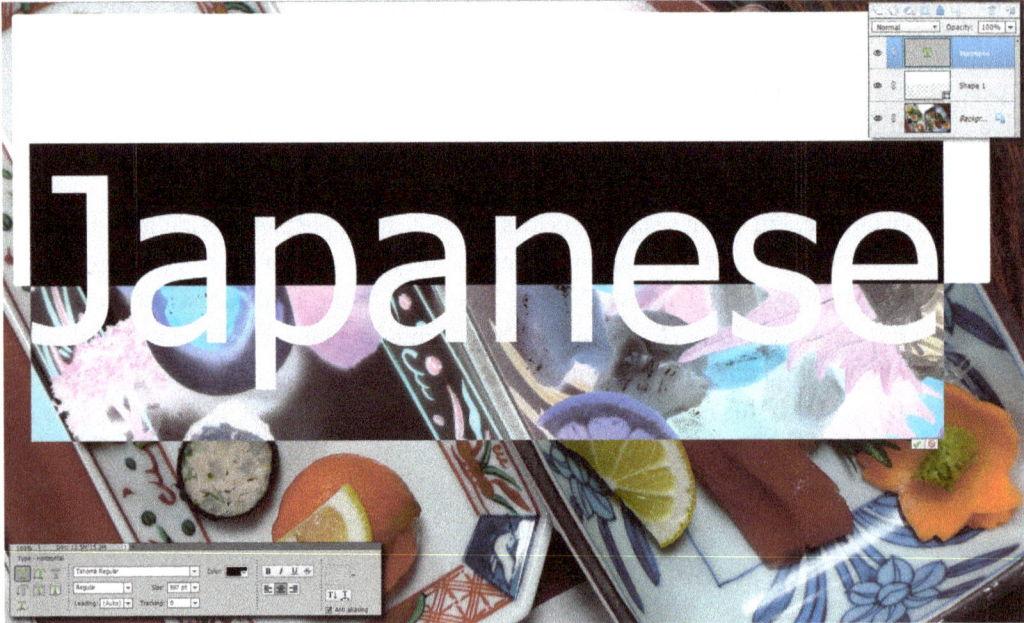

I changed the default font to a custom one called **Paper Cuts** (from a free site called www.dafont.com), which kind of suits the Japanese theme. Note that the **Rounded Rectangle** acts like a text box, into which text can be typed. This can be rather restrictive, especially if you're using a non-standard font, as I was here. In this instance, I created the new type layer away from the **Rectangular** panel, then dragged it on top, ensuring that it remained independent of the vector panel beneath it:

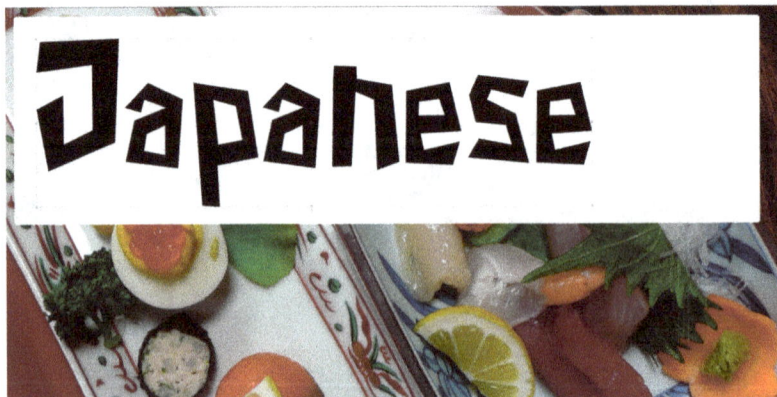

In this step, I duplicated the text and the vector layers. This is a handy shortcut that can be used in a lot of projects. By duplicating these layers, I don't have to go back to the **Tool bar**, select the **Custom Shape** tool, choose the **Rounded Rectangle** tool, and draw another shape (or create another text layer, for that matter). It's always far quicker to duplicate what you already have and then adapt the duplicate:

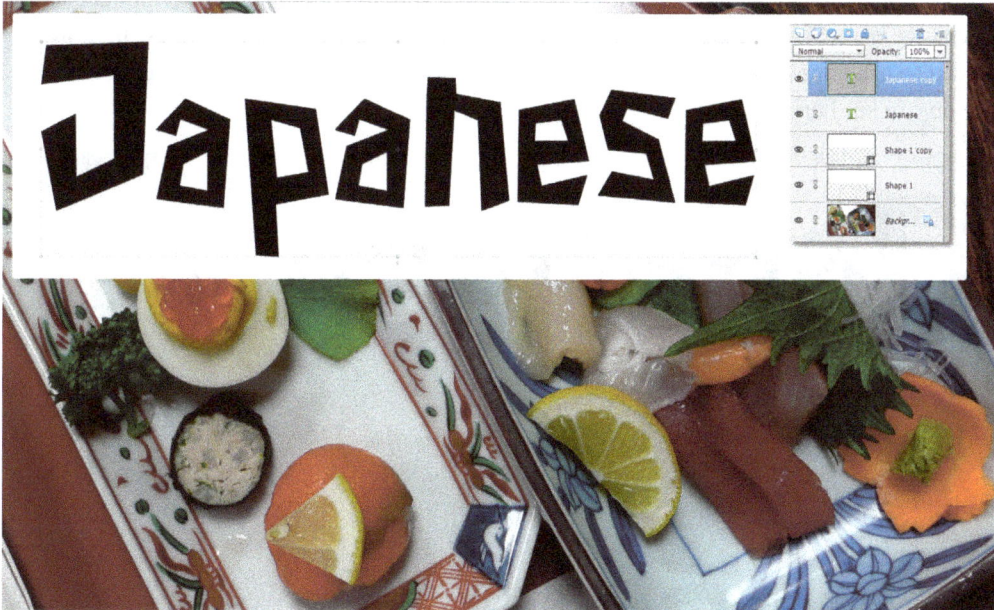

I've dragged both newly duplicated layers to the bottom of the page using the **Move** tool, and with the **Type** tool, edited the copied text layer so that it reads Kaiseki (an exquisitely presented traditional Japanese multi-course lunch or dinner). This process is much faster than trying to create a new type layer:

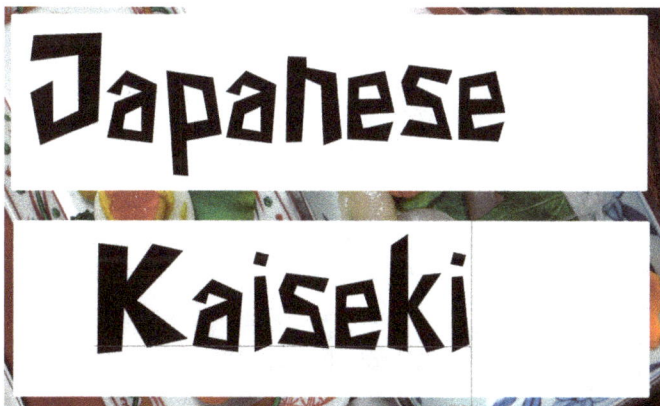

3. To add more irregularity to the shapes already created (I wanted it to look more retro), I transformed their shape. As these are vectors, you can resize them in any direction and to any magnification with no loss in terms of sharpness. *Ctrl/Cmd + T* puts the vector layer into transformation mode (confirmed by the appearance of corner handles around the shape). Grab any corner handle to stretch it larger, or push it in to make the shape smaller. Right-click inside the transform box to access the menu to change from **Scale** to **Distort**, **Skew**, or **Perspective**. I used **Distort** because it allows you to drag one corner only – which I did to reshape the rectangular proportions, as you can see here:

4. I duplicated the vector and text layer one more time to add the third component to the design:

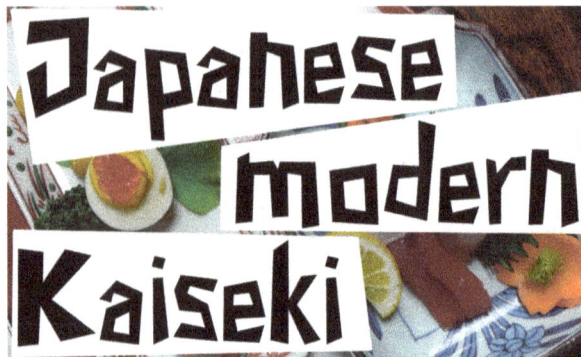

5. Double-clicking the vector layer thumbnail brings up the **Color Picker**, allowing you to add any color you like to that panel:

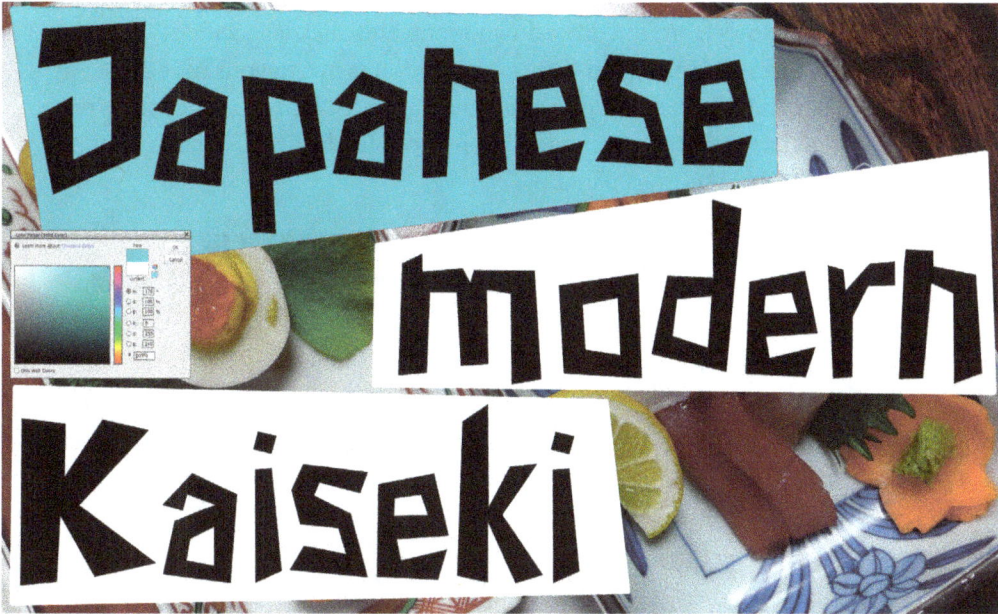

6. Adding color to the text is a slightly lengthier process. Select the text first, then choose a color from the **Options** panel. Alternatively, you can click in the **Color Picker** and add a color from there:

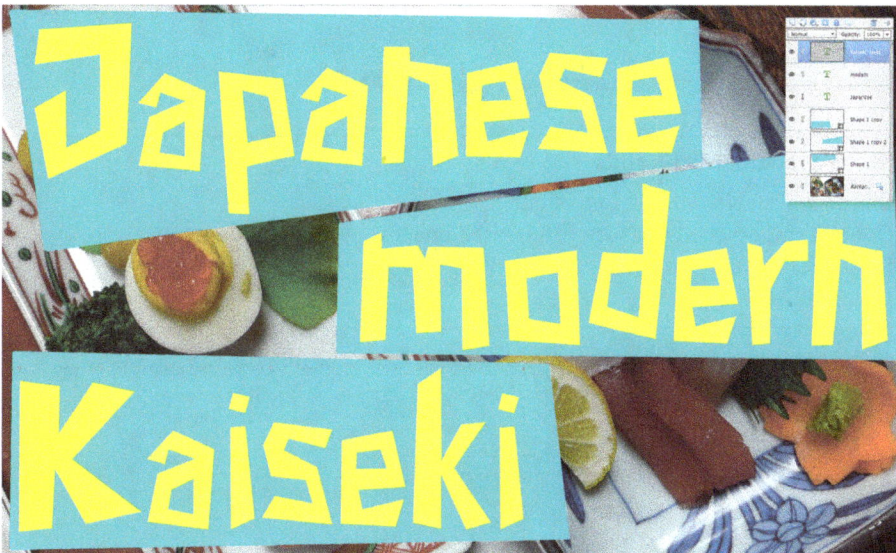

7. In the final stage, I added a small black drop shadow to the three text elements, just to lift them off the background color slightly. **Drop Shadows** are located in the **Styles** panel. Then select the appropriate text layer, go to the Styles panel, choose Drop Shadows from the drop-down menu and click a specific style (icon). The shadow is instantly applied to that text layer. If it is not to your liking, its characteristics can be edited and fine-tuned using the 'fx' button that appears on every layer that has a special effect added to it. Double-click that 'fx' logo on the layer to open the Style settings panel.

Vector graphics – key points

Infinitely scalable, with no loss of quality
Contain smoother edges (than pixel-based images)
Small files – fast downloads
Excellent for web use

Effects filters

Photoshop Elements comes with a huge range of **special effects filters**, which are located under the **Filter** menu at the top of the main screen. Many of these are **legacy items** that have been left over from previous iterations of this application – often very early versions. Because many of these are quite long in the tooth, it's quite difficult to find a practical use for them – personally, I think a lot of them could be removed to make space for newer features – but this is just an opinion. Try them out for yourself and see what you think.

One reason for not being impressed with some effects filters is because there are many excellent software plugins on the market that do the job of special effects far better than what Elements has to offer. That being said, you'll probably note that I have written about the **Gaussian Blur** filter in particular, and how useful it is, on a number of occasions. The **Filter Gallery** exists so that, rather than applying filters to an image one at a time (which is quite laborious), you can try a lot of the effects in a short time, one after the other, inside the **Gallery** itself.

One of my favorite filter effects, **Cutout**, reduces the number of colors in the image to give a colorful, silk-screen-printed, graphic effect. With this filter, you can choose how many color levels are used, with tools such as **Edge Fidelity** and **Edge Detail**:

The **Filter Gallery** is subdivided into six sections: **Artistic, Brushstrokes, Distort, Sketch, Stylize**, and **Texture**. In all, the **Filter Gallery** contains 56 different effects. Each effect has its own **Options** panel, allowing you to vary the intensity of the process to match the style that's required:

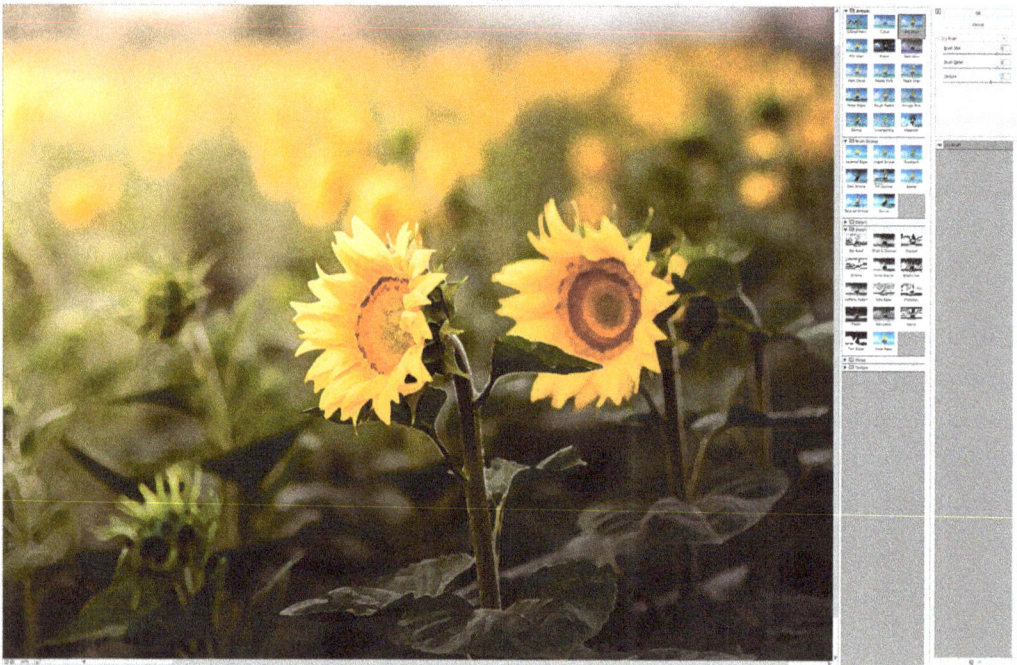

To help you untangle the mess of options in this utility, the **Filter** menu features a dozen subcategories: **Artistic, Blur, Brushstrokes, Distort, Noise, Pixellate, Render, Sketch, Stylize**, and **Other**. If you were to purchase and install a third-party plugin application, you'd see it appear at the bottom of the **Filter** list in the main window.

Keyboard shortcuts

Here's a list of some of the best (or most appropriate) keyboard shortcuts for this chapter:

- Create a new document: **File | New | Blank Document**.
- Zoom in: *Ctrl/Cmd* + "+".
- Zoom out: *Ctrl/Cmd* + "-".
- Fit image to page: *Ctrl/Cmd + 0* (zero).

- **Grid** (repeat the same to remove it): (*Ctrl/Cmd* + *'*).

- Show and hide the **Guides**: (*Ctrl/Cmd* + *;*).

- Use this to temporarily hide the selection line of marching ants. Repeat to show it: *Ctrl/Cmd* + *H*.

- Puts any object on a layer into **Transform** (resize) mode: *Ctrl/Cmd* + *T*.

- Hold the *Shift* key down while drawing with the Elliptical tools, Rectangular tools, or any of the Custom Shapes to lock the proportions.

Summary

So far in this book, we have discovered how this software application not only produces some outstanding results on regular image files, but that it can also be used very effectively as a graphic design and illustration tool.

We have discovered that working with vectors can be a completely different experience to pixel-based photos because, as we saw in this chapter, vectors can be infinitely scalable – while raster images cannot.

What's more, even if you have no desire to become the world's best designer, you can still use Photoshop Elements to produce simple artworks, add special filter effects to images, add text to your projects, and take your editing capabilities to the next level with custom brushes.

In the next chapter, we'll look at finalizing the edited image by starting with a recap on the best resolution settings for social media and the printed page, saving images specifically for the web, several methods for sharpening images, exporting the files, singly or en masse, and finally look at how to process image files in bulk using the very handy but much underused **Process Multiple Files** feature.

9
Exporting the Finished Work

Having successfully navigated the often-complex world of advanced editing and illustration using Photoshop Elements, this chapter is all about setting up those images to achieve the best results when exporting your work to online resources or to print.

To start, we will revisit the concept of **resolution** just so you understand the differences between pixels and dots per inch, compression, and web display speed because all of these factors can have a massive impact on how your work appears on **Facebook**, **Flickr**, or in a luxuriant **digital photo book**.

In this chapter, we will cover the following topics:

- Resolution revisited
- **Local Printing**
- **Save for Web**
- Sharpening techniques
- **Haze Removal**
- **Export as New Files**
- Batch processing using **Process Multiple Files**

Resolution revisited

Although we discussed resolution in some depth in *Chapter 3, The Basics of Image Editing*, it's worth going over some of its salient points again before committing ourselves wholly to the subject of output.

Here's a brief reminder of how resolution works.

Resolution is vital for many reasons, especially when preparing **images for output**. Even if the image is only destined for **Facebook**, it pays to produce a well-edited image containing enough pixels to display it at its best for specific output display sizes, however limited they might be by the host (such as Facebook) or the technology (such as laser printing). Some uses are covered in the following subsections.

Online – web and blogging

Online display is typically set to 72 **dots per inch** (**dpi**), which is a standard resolution for viewing images online. Since this is a fixed resolution, the more pixels there are in the file, the larger, physically, it will be displayed. However, most websites (and blogs) have a finite size for displaying images, which is impacted by the design intent, the speed of the internet connection, and storage space, but, ultimately, by the company offering the service. I use **Google Blogger**, which is free. It offers several image display sizes, topping out at only 640 pixels wide for the largest image view.

So, if the resolution (number of pixels) in your file exceeds the number that's needed to display an image at a fixed size and resolution, it's essentially pixels wasted, and might slow the display on screen significantly (and potentially switch your audience off). If you use a commercial site, such as **Google Blogger**, the file size is automatically restricted in the upload process. But if it is your own domain, you can technically upload any sized file. Note also that uploading full-resolution images might tempt less-upstanding members of the public to steal your work by downloading the high-quality file and using it in some way for their own profit.

Later in this chapter, we will discuss using the **Save for Web** utility, a feature that's designed specifically to optimize file sizes as well as download and display speed.

So, if your images are destined for the web (you might have your own domain and website), the ultimate size (resolution) of your images is essentially in your hands—you decide their dimensions and how much optimization has to be added to each file to produce the fastest download speeds.

Facebook

According to Facebook guidelines, *high-resolution* images can be as large as 2,048 pixels (wide). This particular dimension will produce the best visual result—even if Facebook's **automatic compression algorithms**, which are added to every upload, are heavier (more damaging) than most people might be comfortable with. Unfortunately, there's nothing you can do about the compression level. If the images don't appear as good as you hoped, try re-editing them and upload them again—this only takes a few minutes. Facebook is the world's largest repository of images so, with something like 300 million images uploaded **every day**, I'm surprised that its compression algorithms aren't even more aggressive.

One typical method of reducing the resolution of an image that is destined for posting on a personal website or social media would be to use the **Image Size** tool (**Image | Resize | Image Size**). This is fine for one or two images but tedious if you are uploading more than a handful. You can, of course, upload a full resolution image directly to Facebook but, again, if there are a few to upload, this is going to use up a lot of bandwidth and take a lot of time. If you want the fastest uploads, resize everything to fit the exact display proportions first. I usually size images a bit larger than the recommended size (for example, 2,500 pixels wide):

As a reminder, this is what happens if the JPEG compression added to a file is too much—it produces softness, lack of color, and low sharpness, as in the following figure, compared to the original in the preceding screenshot:

Instagram

As another ever-growing repository of images and video data, **Instagram** recently increased its standard image resolution requirement to 1,080 pixels per square inch. It's not much, considering the original resolution of most cameras is 24 million pixels or more, but this has been an attempt to keep up with the ever-higher screen resolutions coming onto the market. When I first started writing about imaging technology, a 17-inch screen was a big deal. Now, if it's not 22, 24, or even 30 inches wide, it's considered old technology. 4K screens are fast becoming standard, with higher-resolution 5K screens just around the corner.

Flickr

As one of the world's largest image resources, **Flickr** is ever-changing in terms of its online resolution requirements. Currently, you may still upload high-resolution files to this site, but you can elect to set the online display resolution of those files to a maximum of 2,048 x 1,463 pixels or smaller, should you wish. Again, the real danger of uploading full-resolution files while having them in the public domain is that it might attract unsavory characters wanting to download and use your work for free (see the *Copyright symbol* section in this chapter). Some folk are happy to do this, but if you are hoping to make a commercial business from your photography, only upload low resolution, copyright-stamped versions, and store the best, high-resolution work on external drives or use a cloud-based service such as **Dropbox**.

To get your images out of Elements and uploaded to a **Flickr account**, it might be best to have the image open (and preferably edited) on the desktop. Then, find the **Flickr** tab from the **Share** drop-down menu in **Editor** (note that you can also upload directly to Flickr from Organizer):

If you have never done this before, you'll have to first authorize the transaction between Flickr and Elements. Just agree to all of the conditions and you'll get a thank-you from Adobe once it's completed. The process takes a few seconds. Click **Complete Authorization** in the Flickr panel, and you are good to start uploading directly into your Flickr Photostream:

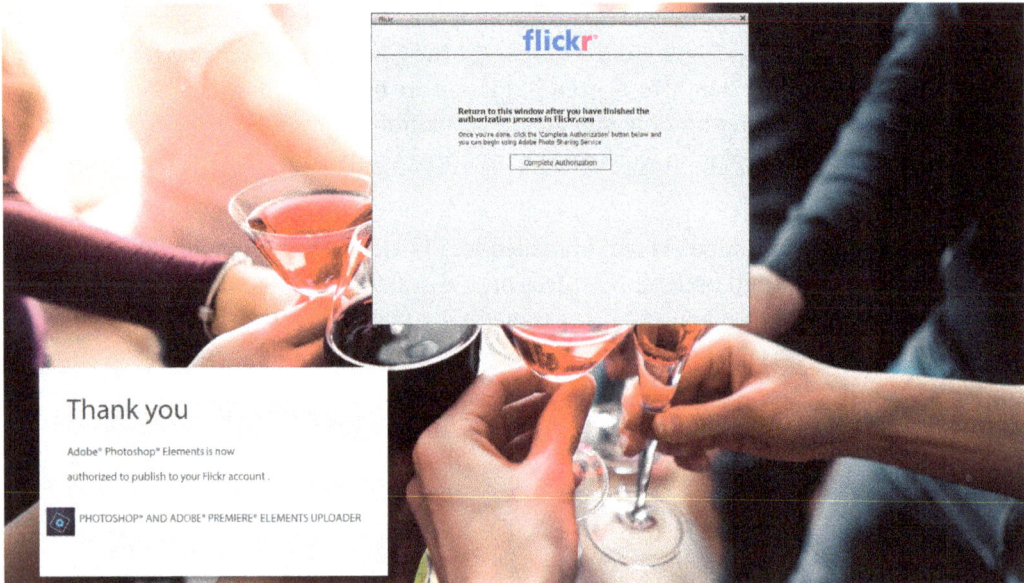

The upload process is easy from here on. Select one or more images and select an album to display them on Flickr, or create a new one for them to go into. Then, add a description, if needed, and hit **Upload**:

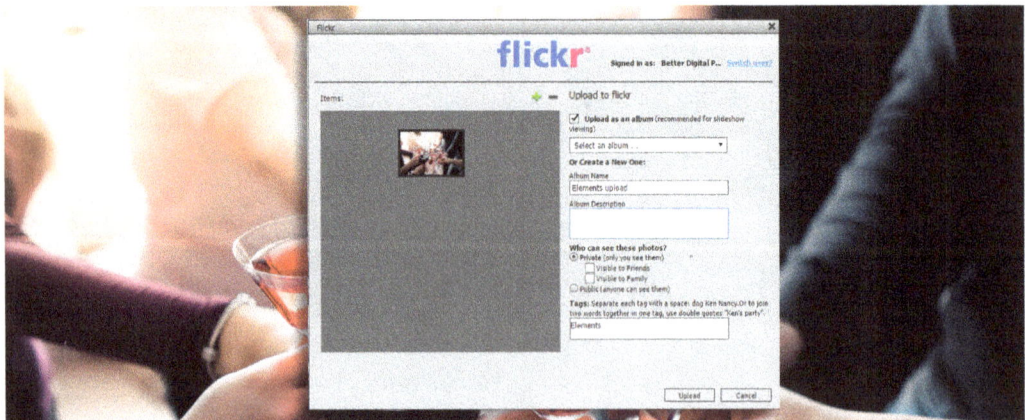

Print resolution

All print work (such as photo inkjet, laser, newspapers, magazines, photo books, and four-color lithographic printing) has to be set to a resolution of 300 dpi as a best practice, so the files that are used are going to be far larger than those for web display. It's called the *standard print resolution* because it produces a seamless, continuous tone image with no visible pixelation or color banding.

That being said, thanks to some fantastic **resampling software**, inkjet printers and most commercial four-color CMYK print devices can produce awesome results using lower-than-recommended resolution files. If you're not sure, check with your local business before you start outputting for print:

All terrestrial-based book-making software only functions with JPEG or PNG files. If they are RAW, TIFF, or PSD files, output and convert them, using the **Export as New Files** feature, to a folder on the desktop. Then they can be imported into the book software:

Here's an example of how you can use PNG files to **preserve transparency**—in this case, images with a ripped edge effect on the left and with a non-rectilinear three-dimensional lift-off-the-page effect on the right-hand side of the lower image.

Local printing

Elements is well equipped for print output if you have access to a laser printer or an inkjet device (note that photo-quality inkjet printers will always produce better photographic quality than laser printers). If you have spent time resizing your images to fit your favorite paper sizes, then it's an easy process to choose **Print (File | Print)** and send the data to the printer. As a bonus, Elements allows you to queue multiple files for printing. If you forgot to load an image into this queue, it's easy enough to add (and subtract) images at a later date.

This is the Elements **Print** panel. I think it is overly complex and poorly designed:

To get an idea of both its capabilities as well as its complexity, the following screenshots illustrate the various steps needed for a regular home print, plus all of the many options it includes. Let's go over these now:

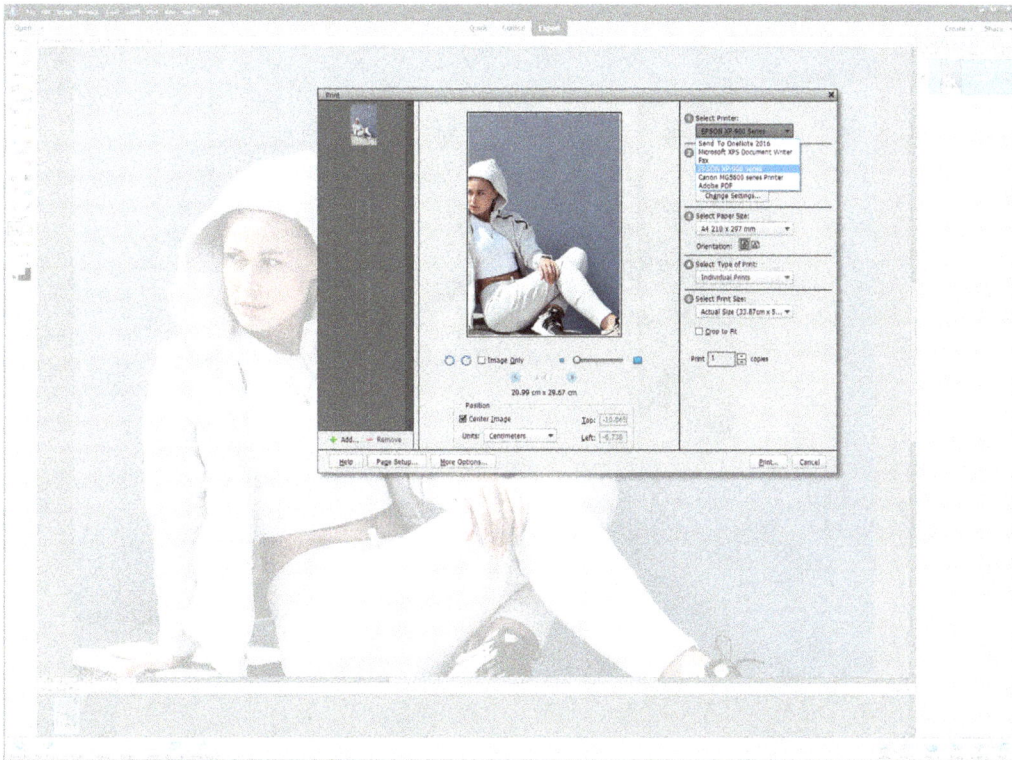

Select Printer: If you only have one device connected, that's the default; otherwise, hit the drop-down menu and select the appropriate print device (note that if you have recently replaced a printer, the software driver for the old one will still show up in this list unless you take the time to delete it). Otherwise this is, a good feature because, increasingly, businesses use multiple printers - laser printers for basic office work, dye-sublimation printers for fast photo quality reproduction, and a range of inkjet printers for presentations, portfolios and more.

Printer Settings: If it's not already displayed, click the **Change Settings** button here and choose the paper type to use for the current job. It's important to get this right because each paper surface has slightly different characteristics (look at the difference between gloss and matte paper) and if it's set incorrectly, it might affect the brightness and even the color of the resulting print:

Select Paper Size: This is a no-brainer, but I'm always mildly surprised at how easy it is to just press the print button in a hurry, only to find it was set to 5 x 7 inches and not **A4**, so I have to start over. Also, don't forget to check the paper orientation (**Landscape** or **Portrait**) in order to match the image being printed:

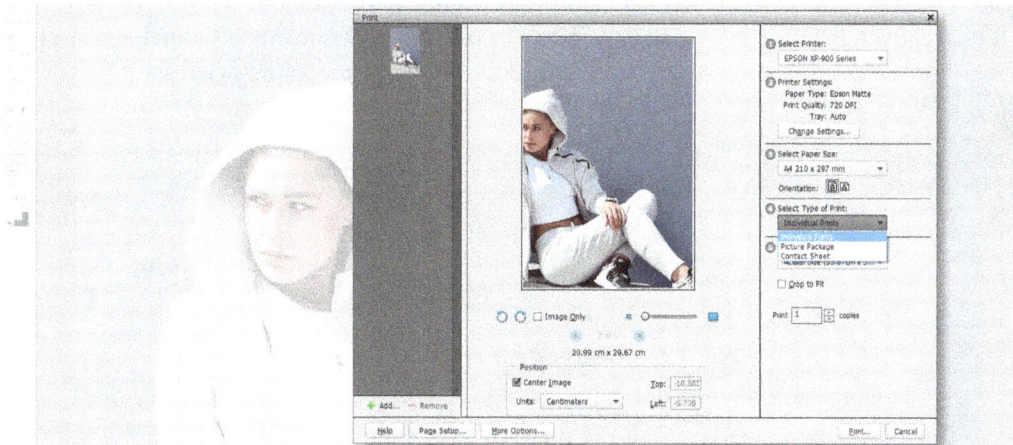

Select Type of Print: Most photographers will expect to fill the page with one image (choose **Individual Prints**) but Elements offers two other options, as you can see in the following screenshot:

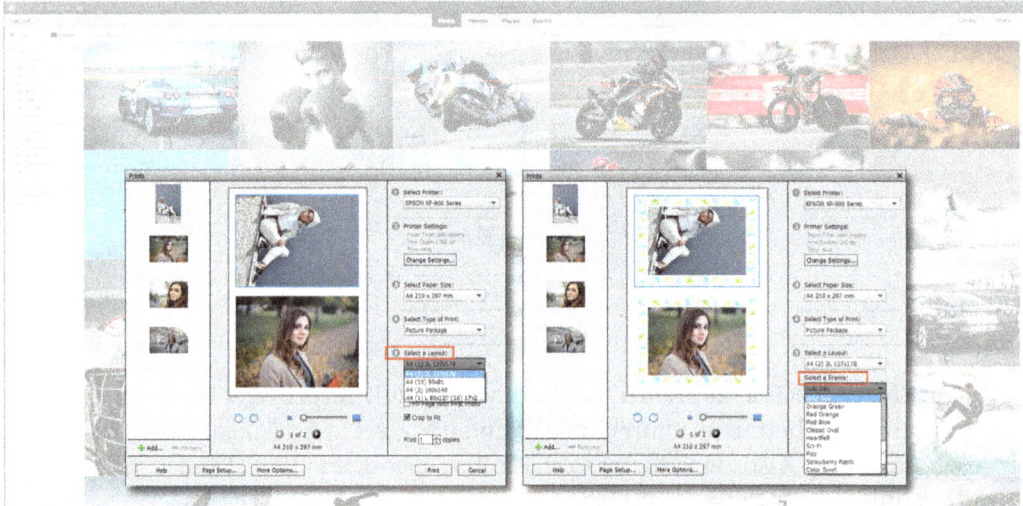

Picture Package: This function arranges multiple photos onto a single page according to the layout chosen from **Select a Layout**. There are only four layouts for **A4** paper—two-up (127x178mm), ten-up (55 x 91mm), two-up (100 x 148mm), and 16 assorted sizes (a true *package*). Other paper sizes have a different number of options available:

Contact Prints: This used to be one of my favorite features because it mimics the photo darkroom contact print format. It adds as many images as you want to each page (actually, you can only add nine columns, which makes the images about the size of a small postage stamp). You can also include the date, caption, and filename of each image in the sheet if required.

In all of these printing modes (**Individual**, **Package**, and **Contact Sheets**), if you add more images than can fit on one page, Elements adds another page so that everything fits—a very nice touch:

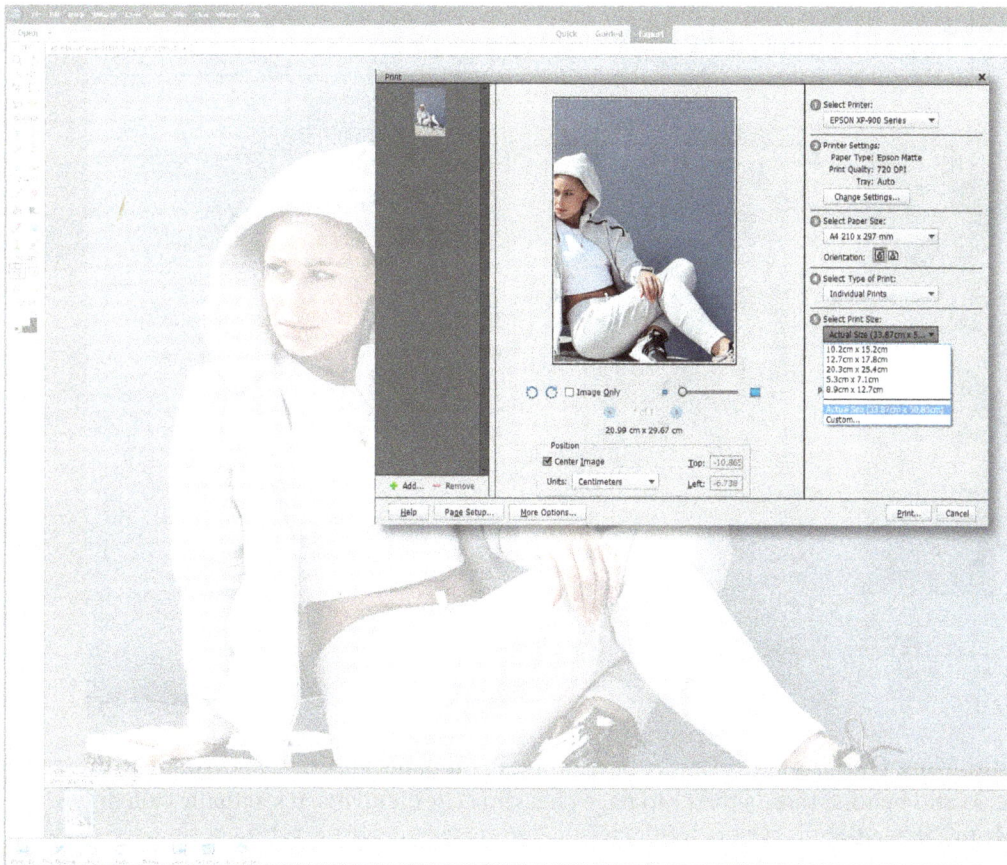

Select Print Size: This final section allows you to set the print size smaller than the paper chosen—effectively giving it a white border, which is a nice touch if you are adding your work into a folio or presentation case, for example:

Fit to Page?

You might note that if your file size is larger than the paper size chosen, there's no **Fit to Page** checkbox obviously visible in this busy **Print** panel.

I think this is a massive oversight on the part of Adobe. In fact, you might agree with me when I say the entire print panel is ridiculously complex, especially if all you want is one quick print. (I think most print software utilities are poorly designed and unnecessarily complex—many are different for Windows or Mac and, like this one for Elements, most feature several confusing panels. I think it's high time the industry has a rethink about how it designs these handy software widgets, but as the move to the web and social media gains momentum, I suspect this might never happen.

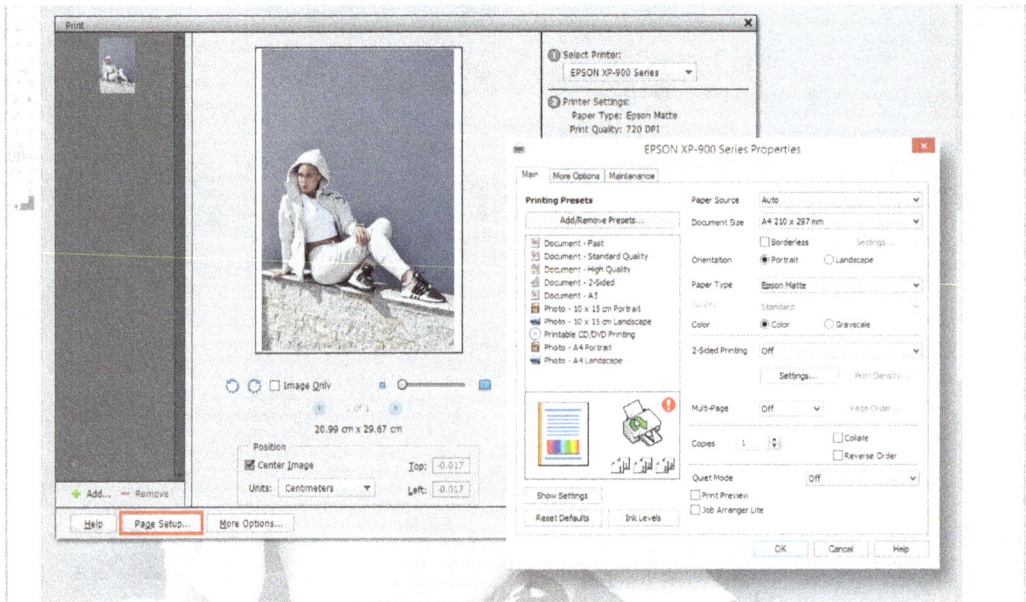

Hit the **More Options** button at the base of the **Print** panel and, under **Custom Print Size**, lo and behold, there's the fit to page checkbox (in Elements, it's actually called **Scale to Fit Media**).

Page Setup

This button takes you to the printer software where you can also set the paper size, paper type, and other printer-specific features, such as two-sided printing, borderless printing, checking ink levels, and turning the printer's color management software to **Off** (it's always better to let Photoshop Elements handle the color management):

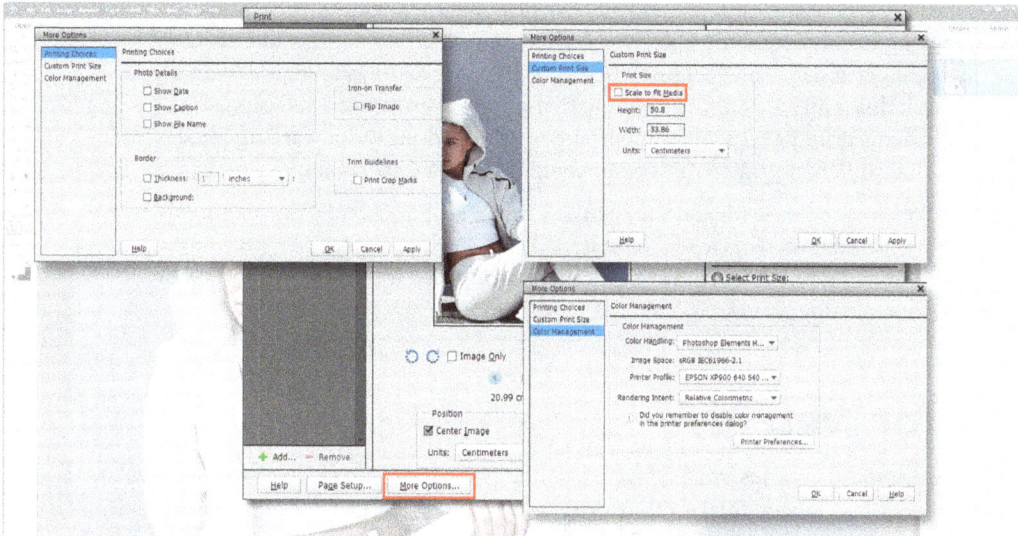

More Options: This button reveals three more panels for adding photo details and a border, checking **Scale to Fit Media** (custom sizes), and using **Color Management** (set this so that Photoshop Elements manages colors). It's where you'll find the **Scale to Fit Media** checkbox.

Now, you are good to click the **Print** button!

> **A word of warning**
>
> As you might be aware, the software that comes with your printer might look totally different on a Mac than it does on Windows, and it's almost guaranteed that different printer models and brands each have their own uniquely designed operating software. All of them essentially do the same thing, but the design and layout of the features you'll find might be radically different. It can be very confusing, especially if you have just upgraded your local printer by buying a different brand. Once you have set Elements up to print, the process might get easier as it will 'remember' your previous settings on that device. I think this is an area of image editing that is long overdue for a redesign. The Elements print panel needs simplifying, while third-party software supplied by various different printer companies could do with a total revamp.
>
> If you are preparing images for print, it's worth noting that any sharpening that's added to the image will be softened in the print process, so it's a good idea to add more sharpening to files that are destined for print to counter that slight softening process.

Save for Web

Photoshop Elements comes with a feature called **Save for Web** (**File | Save for Web**), a slightly simplified legacy feature that was passed down from Adobe Photoshop. You would use this feature to specifically fine-tune image output so that they perform optimally on web-based media, such as blogs and websites. Note that although this is an excellent process for perfecting web-bound images, uploading to some social media sites might produce a slightly different quality because those sites (such as Facebook and Instagram) might apply additional manipulation, particularly with regard to **file compression**, but also in relation to maximum permissible file sizes.

Before you start using this feature, it's probably best to reduce your files to a reasonably manageable size before fine-tuning with **Save for Web**. For most web applications, if the file's longest edge is 1,000 or 1,200 pixels, this is a perfectly sufficient resolution. It's not too big but, then again, it's not too small either:

To use **Save for Web**, the image must be opened in the **Expert** edit mode. Then, follow the **File | Save for Web** command:

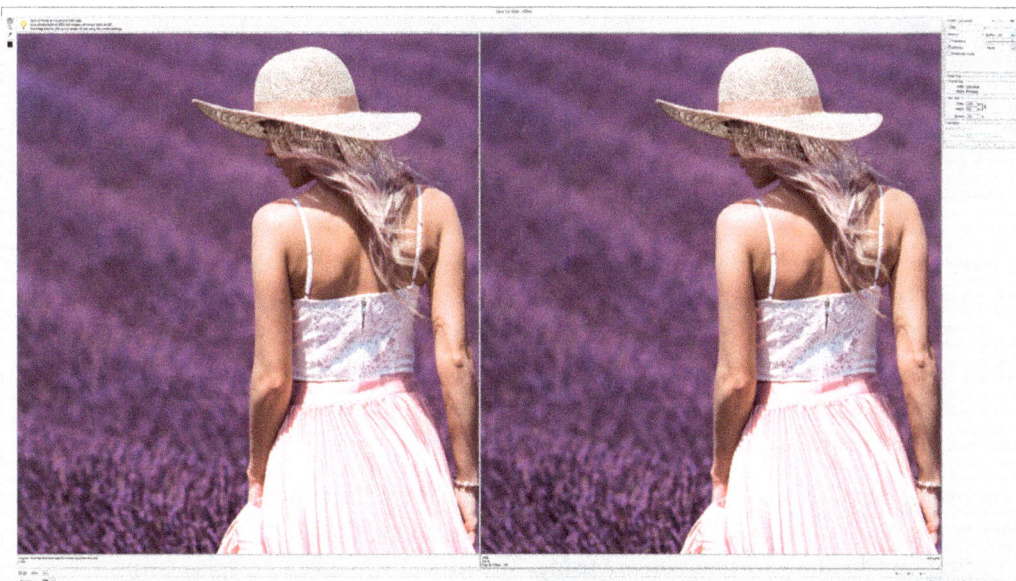

Here's the twin-screen configuration with the untouched version on the left and the processed version on the right.

Display speeds are listed at the base of the image while the file format, compression, dithering, and color size are adjusted through either the drop-down preset menu, on the top right-hand side of the screen, or by setting the edit parameters manually using the sliders and menu choices. Note that you can also use this utility to reduce its file size, if you haven't already done so. I'd use this file reduction panel if I were only processing a couple of images; otherwise, I'd use the **Process Multiple Files** function to bulk-reduce image resolution because it's so fast (you will see how this works later in this chapter).

You should have the JPEG quality set to the best result—which, in this case, is the least compression, but because it's not compressed quite so much, the file will be larger and will take a lot longer to load:

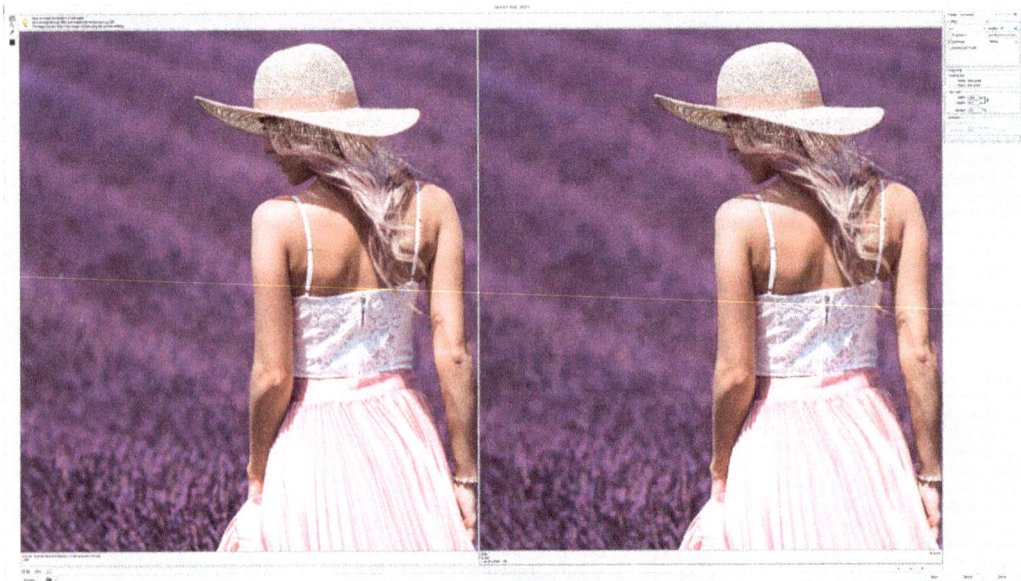

The **Save for Web** panel has a number of presets to get you started if the process of editing for the web is a new concept. Elements provides presets for saving **GIF**, **PNG**, and, of course, **JPEG** files, all of which can be set to different compressions and/or dither amounts (dithering is a clever computer technique where adjacent pixels are blended to create colors that might not be normally visible in the often-limited color range offered by GIF files—the more dithering, the larger the file size).

By choosing one of these presets, you'll see how much impact an additional compression, dither amount, optimization, or scan will have on the saving process. These options vary depending on which file format you are using. The time it will take to display using a range of internet speed samples can be adjusted from an excruciatingly slow 28 kilobytes per second to figures of around two megabits per second, depending on the resources available or the client's requirements.

The following is another good example of the varied quality output this feature can serve up. In this case, I have set the file format to **GIF** because the image is simple and contains few colors and no gradation. By choosing only **64** colors and adding a dither amount, the original (JPEG) file size is 1.5 MB, while the GIF version is only 48 KB. In practice, what dithering does is merge the pixels in such a way as to hide the blockiness some GIFs suffer from when their color palette has been pared down to the bare minimum. I suspect that many of these features are not as important now as they were five years ago before cable internet became an accepted default for many consumers. Of course, if you live in a country with poor internet speeds and access, you'll find these tools helpful. Note that in reality, you would never normally use the GIF file format for photographic images.

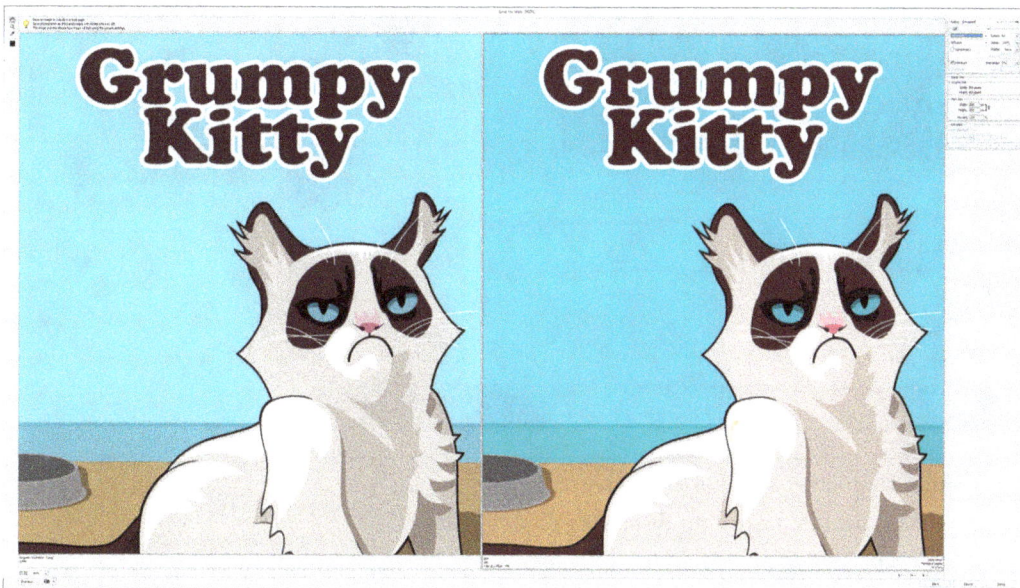

The idea behind working with this tool is to tinker with the settings that are available so that you get the fastest possible download speed without (too much) loss of image quality. It also gives you a great opportunity to swap between those (three different) file formats that produce, according to your settings, significantly different results. These can be accepted or rejected depending on the type of image, the placement in the web page, and the application of the web page (such as a personal portfolio, professional services, commercial shop front, or social media page).

The beauty of preparing images for use on the web is that, even if you've never done this before, it only takes a few minutes to upload the new material and, if it doesn't look good, it's quick enough to undo, fix, and replace.

Save for Web also has this sensible feature called **Preview**, which shows you what the image looks like in an internet browser:

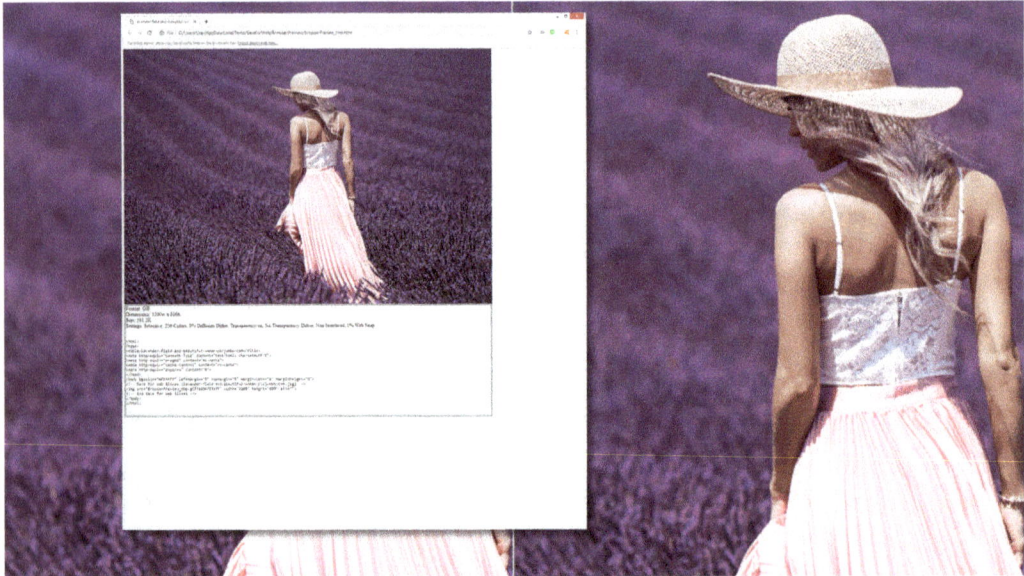

Important note: Web file formats

JPEG is the best format for displaying photographs.

PNG24 is also a good format for photographs. The PNG24 format comes into its own when you are saving transparency—for example, an image with a ripped edge effect or a logo that's not 100% square or rectangular. PNG files can be larger than JPEGs.

GIF is the format to use for displaying line art and illustrations that feature large areas of solid color and sharp detail and text. Animated images are also in the GIF file format.

PNG8 is an alternative to GIF in that you can set the number of colors it uses and therefore restrict the file size accurately.

For the best results, it's best to test your processed images on different browsers and computers:

Here's the same file I have been using as an example, but in this version, it has a ragged edge made from **transparent pixels**. If this is saved as a JPEG, those transparent edges would be filled in with white (by default), so it has to be in the PNG format to preserve transparency, which is producing those rough edges.

Sharpening

The process of sharpening has always confused photographers, especially those new to the profession, simply because one of its names is unsharp masking, which doesn't seem to make any sense. Let me explain this a little more.

The way software sharpens an image is by increasing the contrast along the edges of objects inside the image. If this is a portrait, the software will try and increase the contrast around the edges of the eyes, the nose, the lips, and the hairline—those kinds of dominant features. There's no point in applying the same amount of sharpening to the smoothest skin tones because, if you enhance the skin pores, the result will not be flattering.

To this end, the Unsharp Masking tool creates a black and white mask in the background, which limits the sharpening effect to those (contrast) edges, and not to the open areas of skin.

Elements has several sharpening tools, including the **Sharpen Filters**, **Unsharp Mask**, **Adjust Sharpness**, and the **Shake Reduction** features, most of which are located under the **Enhance** menu.

Unsharp Mask

We looked at the sharpening process in *Chapter 3, The Basics of Image Editing*, but I think it's worth going over some of the more important points again to ensure that your output quality is 100%. The regular **Unsharp Mask** filter from the **Enhance** menu has three sliders and a small preview window:

- The **Amount** slider is the amount of enhancement that's added to the edges of the contrast.

- The **Radius** slider controls how much attention is spent on either side of the contrast edge.

- The **Threshold** slider has the effect of blending or softening the contrast edge.

If the **Amount** and **Radius** sliders are increased too much, the sharpening effect looks very gritty and unpleasant to the eye. Adding a **Threshold** amount will help to soften the overall result.

Unfortunately, the downside of using this particular filter is that it's not possible to physically control the actual mask part of Unsharp Masking. We can do this in the **Camera RAW** window - also covered in Chapter 3:

The **Unsharp Mask** filter, as shown in the previous screenshot, is accessed via the **Enhance** drop-down menu and is quick and easy to use, but it doesn't give you the same level of control you get with the **Detail** panel in **Camera RAW**.

If you open your picture in the **Camera RAW** editing window, Elements offers a far superior way of controlling the sharpening process. If you are editing a RAW file, this sharpening process is part of the normal procedure, but if you're working on a JPEG, TIFF, or PSD file, you must open it in the **Camera RAW** window using **File | Open in Camera RAW**.

Once the image is open in **Camera RAW**, go to the **Detail** tab, and note that the sharpening panel has the same **Amount** and **Radius** sliders as the **Unsharp Mask** filter from the **Enhance** menu. Note that it also has **Detail** and **Masking** sliders. Here's how to get the best results from this feature:

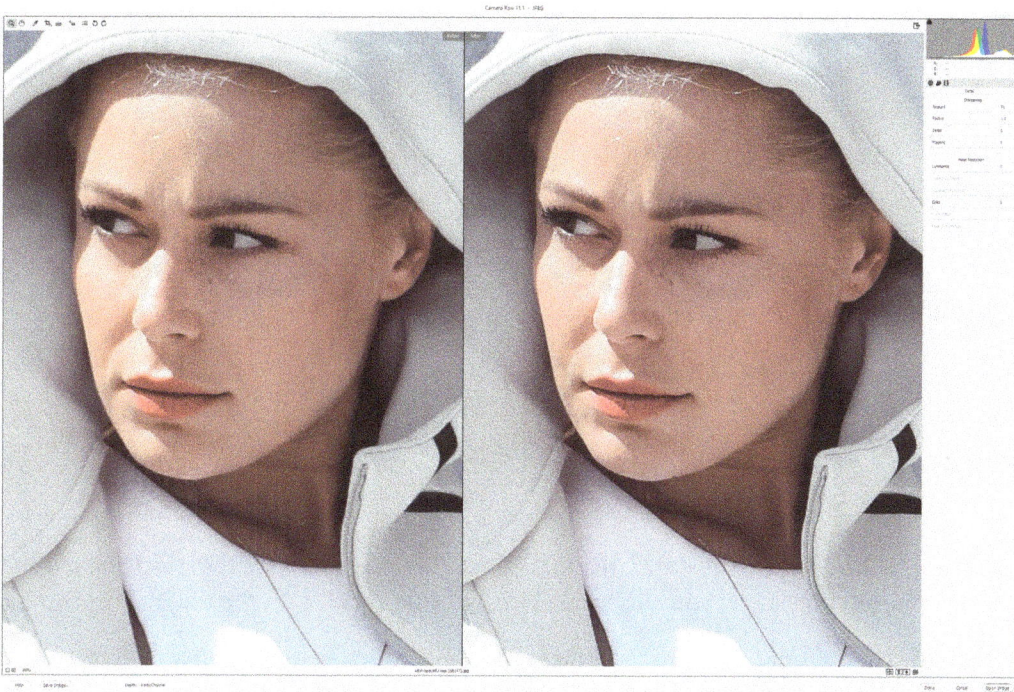

To open any file that's not a RAW file in the **Camera RAW** window, use **File | Open in Camera RAW**. This works for JPEG, TIFF, and PSD files. Set the **Amount** (of sharpening) and **Radius** as you would have done using the regular unsharp mask filter.

By holding the *Alt/Opt* key and then shifting the masking slider at the same time, you'll see the black and white mask appear in the main screen. For a portrait, you probably want to move the slider to the right, to a point where the smooth skin areas are all black—this indicates that no sharpening will be applied to that area. As you can see in the following screenshot, I have shifted the **Masking** slider to the right-hand side. This effectively restricts the spread of the sharpening effect to only the white regions, which means you only sharpen the parts of the image that benefit most. In a portrait, there's little or no reason to sharpen the open areas of skin because it can produce quite unflattering results:

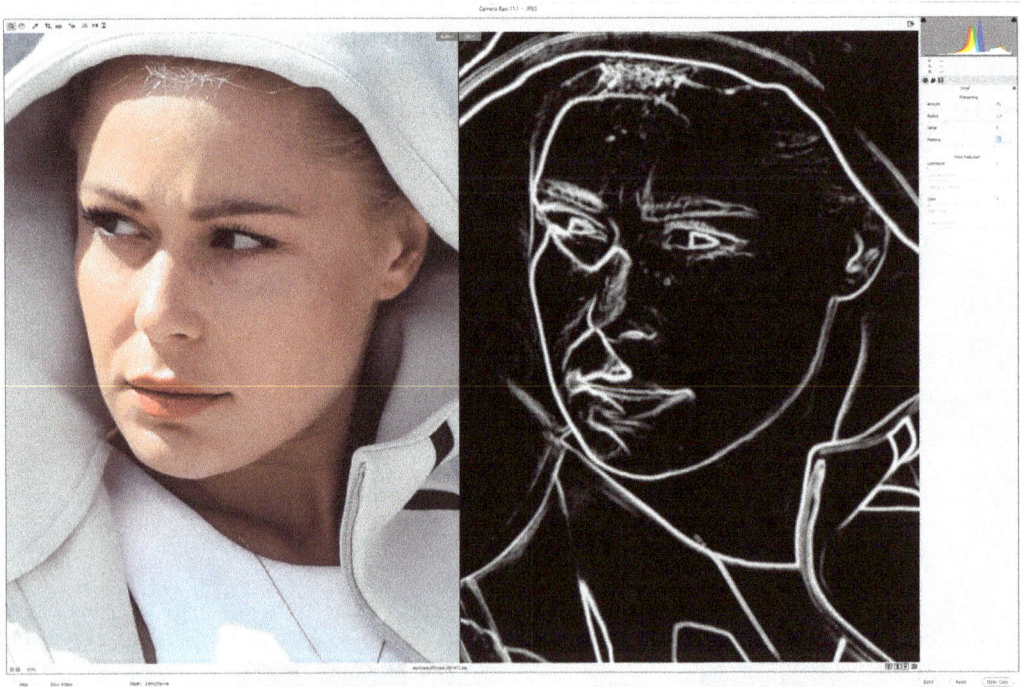

As soon as the *Alt/Opt* key is released, the mask is hidden, and you'll see the effect applied to the real image, especially if you enlarge that image beyond 100%, in the original version.

Another tip is to hold *Alt/Opt* while shifting the **Details** slider so that it displays the added emphasis it applies to the edges. Use this to fine-tune the mask effects further.

One problem you'll encounter when sharpening images is, if the file has been exposed using a high ISO number (such as 1,600 ISO+), chances are any sharpening will also increase the visual presence of **digital noise**, which is never a good look. Underneath the **Sharpening** panel, you'll find the **Noise Reduction** settings—use these to help reduce the unflattering effects too much noise produces.

Digital photos generally suffer from two kinds of noise: luminance and color.

Luminance noise is essentially graininess that appears in high ISO images. Note that many cameras have built-in **noise reduction filters**, which are designed to reduce the negative effect of shooting at high ISO ratings. Some of these filters are quite effective, but, to be honest, I usually prefer to reduce the amount of noise using Photoshop Elements because it's easier to see what you are doing on a large computer screen. Once a camera has passed its noise reduction filter over the file, that's it—you can't reverse the process.

The second type of noise is color noise, and this produces an ugly, multi-colored pixelation, mostly in the dark, shady areas of the final file. We typically shoot at very high ISO numbers when the lighting is poor, and because noise is created by under-exposure, this is why we can see a lot of visual problems in photographs taken indoors, at night time, early morning, and anywhere you experience poor lighting:

It's very easy to add too much noise reduction. To remove ugly noise artifacts, the software has to effectively blur the image slightly, which makes it look weird. In the preceding example, I have added way too much filtration so that the skin tones not only appear smooth, but the subject has also lost all of her freckles.

When you look at the **Noise Reduction** panel underneath the **Sharpening** panel, you'll note that only the **Luminance** and the **Color** sliders are active. As soon as you shift that **Luminance** slider to the right, the **Luminance Detail** and **Luminance Contrast** sliders become active. Shift the main slider first to reduce the grittiness created by the noise, then fine-tune the results using these other two sliders. In reality, their effectiveness is very subtle, but persevere and they might reintroduce more detail into the image without increasing the noise.

If your image suffers from color noise, something my Canon files are particularly prone to exaggerate, then try shifting the **Color** slider to the right. This effectively turns the color speckling into black and white noise, something which most photographers can live with compared to ugly color-noise pollution:

By manipulating the detail sliders associated with both the **Sharpening** and **Noise Reduction** panels, it's possible to dial back some of the softness and add some additional detail—all without increasing the noise artifacts.

Of course, images are not all the same and will require a different amount of sharpening and treatment. I find that using the mask feature goes a long way in illustrating, in a very black and white way, how the sharpening process works and, more importantly, precisely where it is directed.

The Adjust Sharpness tool

If you just want a quick sharpening fix, the tool to head to is called **Adjust Sharpness**.

The **Adjust Sharpness** tool, which can be found under the **Enhance** menu, is a little simpler to apply than the Unsharp Mask tool in Camera RAW. Use the **Amount** slider to increase or decrease the amount of contrast added to the edges, the **Radius** slider to control how wide that edge contrast is, and the **Remove** menu, which features **Lens blur**, **Gaussian blur**, and **Motion blur**, to try and mitigate the often-harsh effects of the sharpening process.

The tool also gives you the scope to modify the sharpening effect of the shadows and highlights via the drop-down menu at the bottom of the panel, but in reality, I find this has an almost negligible effect. The best way to get the most from this feature is to try it and see for yourself:

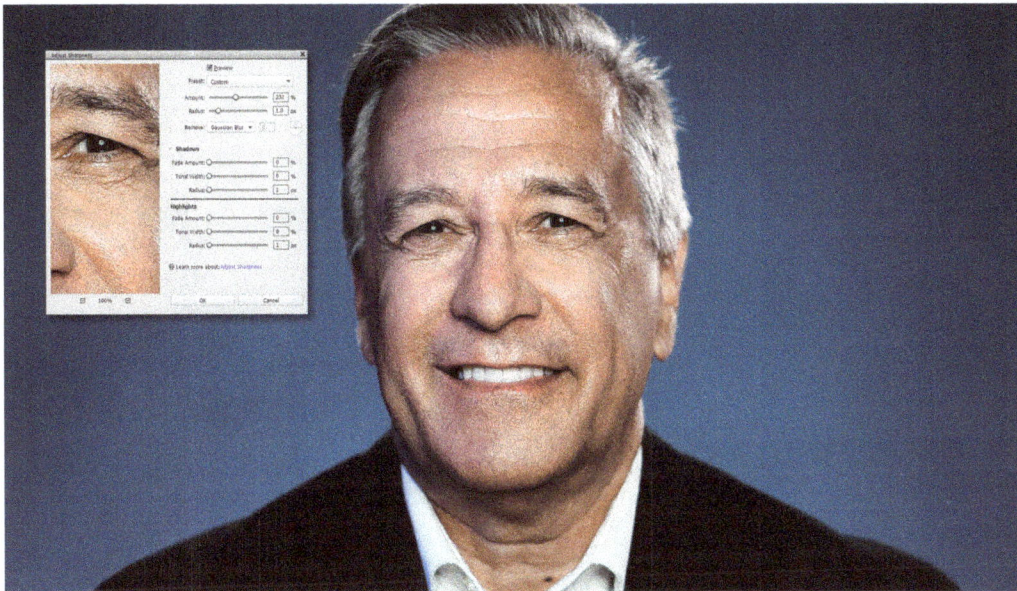

I never fully understood why Adobe always left the sliders in features such as **Adjust Sharpness** with a scale that ran off the map. By dragging **Radius** to the right, you create a very ugly halo, as in the following screenshot. Avoid over-compensating like this at all costs:

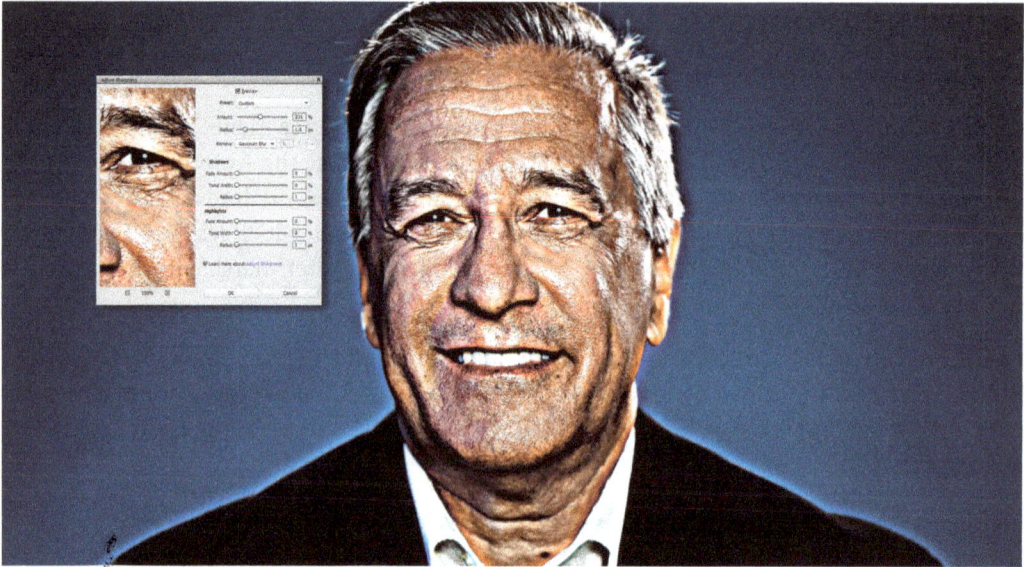

The previous example was quite sharp to start with. This one of an Ethiopian priest is just a little blurred so you see no improvement in its apparent clarity. I'd be better off using the **Shake Reduction** tool to try and improve this picture:

I generally recommend an amount of between 100 to 200%, with a radius of around one pixel. The higher the **Radius** setting goes, the more the image looks like a special effect, which is something you really don't want to see. Let's move on to look at another example of how effective Shake Reduction can be.

The Shake Reduction tool

As the name suggests, **Shake Reduction** is included in the sharpening itinerary and specifically targets those pictures that are not 100% pin-sharp. I've always been a bit suspicious of a tool like this because, let's face it, if the image is really blurred, surely there's very little we can do to make it really sharp?. This tool allows you to select a portion of the image onto which shake reduction, a very processor-intensive process, can be imposed:

In the preceding example, it actually works very well (see the bottom half), but it won't work quite so well with all blurry images. Its efficiency depends on the degree of shake, and the area the problem covers in the file. But don't take my word for it—try it yourself and see whether it works on your images.

The High Pass sharpening technique

Another neat way of applying sharpness to an image is to combine a fairly obscure filter called **High Pass** with a layer blend mode. The **High Pass** filter applies a mid-gray mask over the image, which highlights any differences in contrast—much like the masking feature we saw in the **Unsharp Mask** tool. The gray areas are exempt from sharpening while the edges that you can see in the gray filter get sharper. If you really want your images to *pop*, try this using the **Hard Light** blend mode:

To achieve this technique, first duplicate the layer (**Layer | Duplicate**) and choose the **High Pass** filter from the **Filter | Other** menu at the top of the screen:

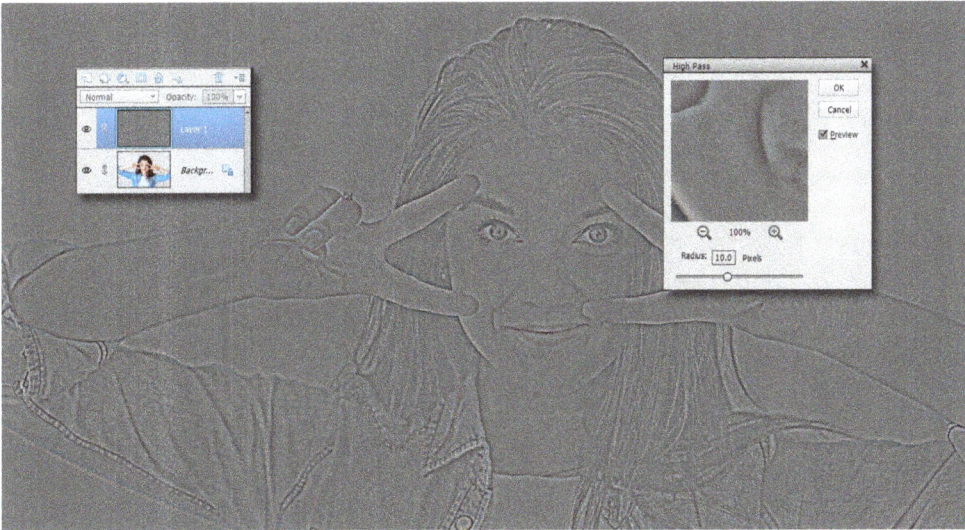

This is what the **High Pass** filter looks like at a value of 10 pixels. Weird. In essence, the *popping* effect we are about to see is added to the parts of the image that are not mid-gray—essentially, the highlighted edges of the subject only:

Change the duplicated layer's blend mode from the default, **Normal**, to **Overlay** or **Soft Light** or even **Hard Light**. The former produces quite an abrupt change and **Soft Light** often produces the best, most natural result, while **Hard Light** is very dramatic:

In this sample, I added the **Overlay** blend mode in the left-hand pane and left the right-hand as the original to compare the *look* that was created. This is a simple and highly effective way to add a lot of *punch* to your work.

> **Tip**
>
> When using this technique, I prefer to start at a High Pass filter value of 10 pixels, although this can be varied depending on the image resolution, the *look* required, and the Blend Mode that's chosen.

General sharpen filters

Elements has several other places where it's possible to add sharpness to an image. This includes the **Basic** mode, the **Guided** mode, and the **Enhance** menu in the **Expert** mode. All three work well but can be a little heavy-handed, and, of course, somewhat lacking in control, which is one good reason to use the better-featured Unsharp Mask or Adjust Sharpen tools:

I rarely use any of the auto filters scattered throughout this program because they don't offer much in the way of control. Even the **Sharpen** feature in the Guided edit mode, as in the preceding screenshot, is really quite aggressive and hard to temper without the luxury of a mask.

The Haze Removal tool

Another great feature to be found in Photoshop Elements is the **Haze Removal** tool. It's really a tool that's designed to boost the mid-tone contrast in your images, and it works incredibly well on hazy, misty, steamy pictures where the clarity is suffering. You'll note, in the examples shown here, that once processed using haze removal, the finished images look sharper. This is because sharpening is all about the contrast differences along subject edges, so it might not only fix the climatic conditions, but also make it appear sharper.

However, you might not know that it's also great to use on some black and white images, low-contrast images, and sometimes it's just good to add to a picture to add a bit of *punch*.

Elements features two of these filters: one is the **Auto Haze Removal** tool, which does a good job, but if it's control you need, it's best to go for the regular **Haze Removal** tool in the **Enhance** menu and use its sliders to perfect the effect on each image, one at a time:

The following is more of a snowy image than a hazy image. The sky is indistinct due to slight overexposure and the low cloud. Select **Enhance | Haze Removal** from the **Enhance** menu:

This is the easiest filter to play with. Use the sliders at the base of the filter panel to make adjustments. For some reason, this doesn't update your slider changes in the main window until the **OK** button is pressed, then it's too late. If you don't like the result, undo then redo it again:

The finished product looks 100% better than the slightly overexposed, light, and indistinct features of the original:

Here's another use of the haze removal tool, where we are enhancing a slightly low-contrast (but not hazy) image. Because this feature adds **mid-tone contrast**, it's perfect for adding a bit of *punch* to the image. Of course, this doesn't work for all images, but when it does work, it's impressive:

This feature keeps on giving. In this example, I have an old print that has been scanned and retouched, but its tones are still flat. It's an ideal image to test the Haze Removal tool on:

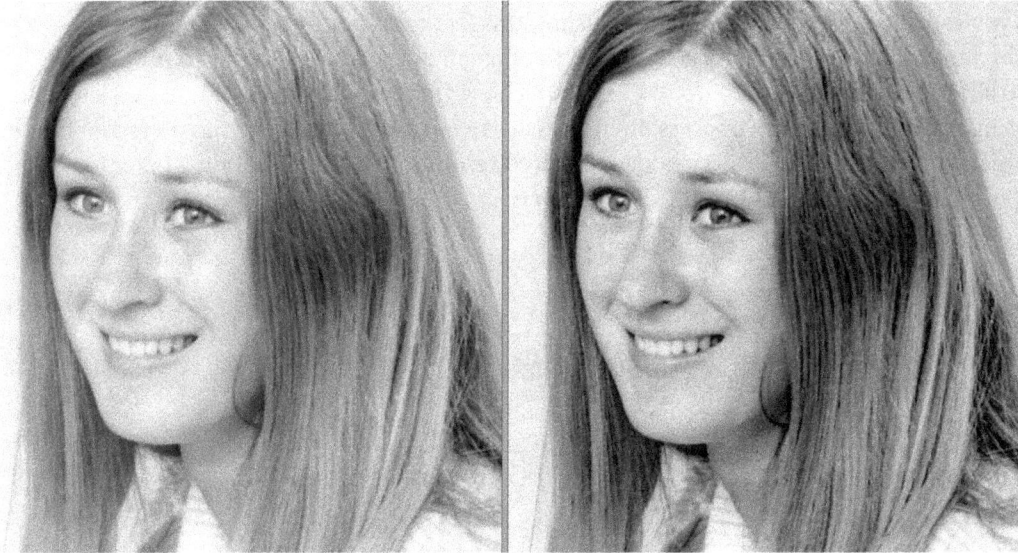

As is clearly visible in this before-and-after illustration, haze removal is also a good bet when it comes to adding a bit more contrast *punch* into your scanned images. It doesn't work with all images, but it's certainly effective in this example.

Export as New Files

Resizing images one at a time in order to upload them to Facebook, Instagram, or another social media site is one technique that works well for a few images at a time. But if you have a lot of material you'd like to resize and need it done fast, the Organizer's **Export as New Files** tool might be your best option.

It has many advantages. You can export a lot of images to a specified location, add a common name to all exports, change the file format, and even choose a specific image dimension. It takes around two minutes to export 200 images, so it's fast.

As you can see from the following screenshot, this feature is handy because it works right out of the Organizer (there's no need to open all of the images in the editor first). It also allows you to add more into the **Export as New Images** window if you missed a few during the initial selection process, then all that's needed is to change to the preferred file format (such as PNG or TIFF), choose a desired resolution, set the location where the exported images get saved to, and click **Export**:

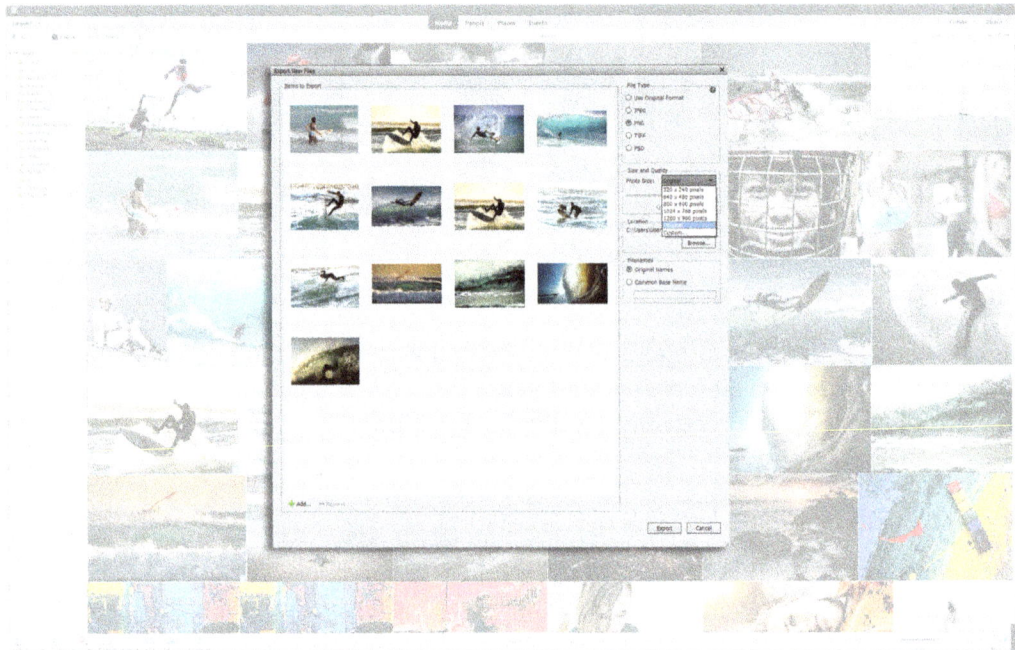

It's a very neat little utility but one concern is that you can't save it at the best resolution to upload to Facebook (2,048 pixels). **Export as New Files** goes as high as **1280 x 960 pixels**. As a workaround, it's possible to use the **Custom** feature at the bottom of the drop-down **Size and Quality** menu. Enter 2048 and 1150 pixels. Note that this is never going to work 100% of the time because, although 2,048 is the correct measurement for the longest edge, the short edge will vary with every different camera file (because cameras have different-shaped sensors). If it's clearly distorting your exports, then turn to the **Process Multiple Files** utility (which we'll look at next) and reduce the images that way.

Process Multiple Files

I don't think **Actions** in Photoshop Elements is a very strong feature because every action recorded originates from Photoshop CC (you cannot record actions in Elements). Because they originate from a different application, some automated features might not work in Photoshop Elements because its toolset is different - and that leads to frustration.

Process Multiple Files, on the other hand, works brilliantly for many automated editing operations. For example, you can use it to change the file format, reduce the file size, and add unique names to files. And, as its name might suggest, you can use it to process a couple of files or a few hundred in one go. Providing it's set up correctly from the outset, you'll find that it's a handy tool that performs extremely quickly:

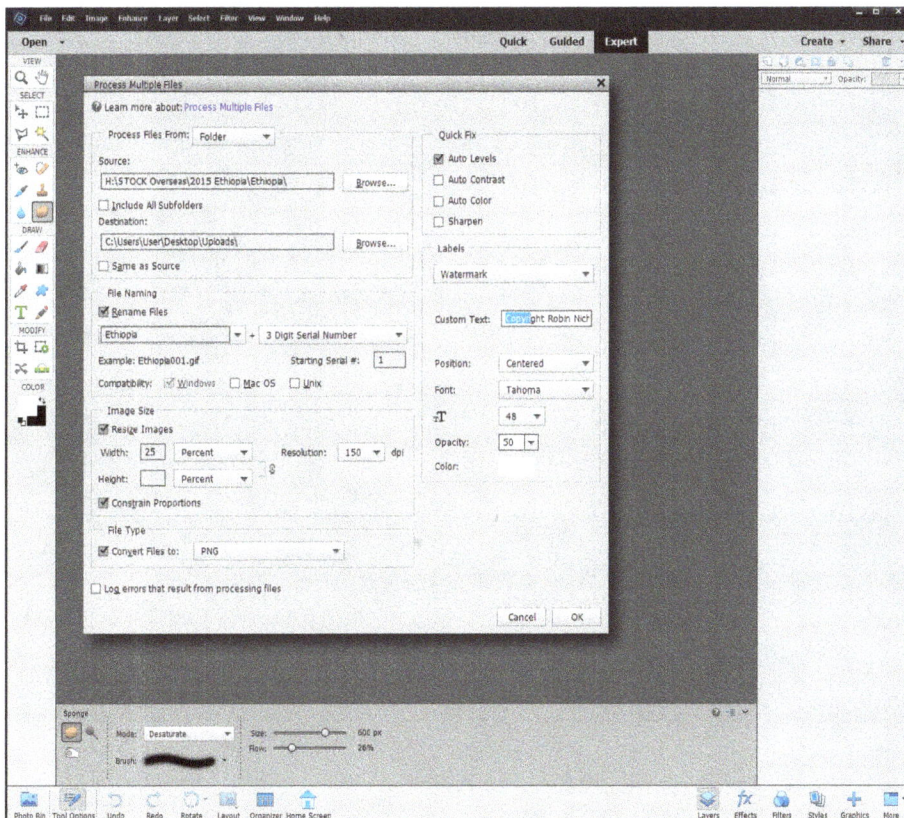

How does it work? I use this tool to reduce the size of processed RAW files from my 20-megapixel Canon camera in order to upload them to my blog. Rather than using the one-at-a-time **Image Resize** dialog box, I place all of the images to be uploaded into the same folder, and then simply run **Process Multiple Files**, resetting the image size to a maximum of 1,000 pixels along the longest edge (this figure might vary depending on your quality requirements).

The **Process Multiple Files** feature will work on files that are already open, or you can take them from a specific folder of images. In my workflow, I typically edit my pictures, save them to a specific folder (in a place where I can find them quickly), and then create a new, empty folder on the desktop, which is used to store the processed files (I put them on the desktop so that they can be seen and accessed easily):

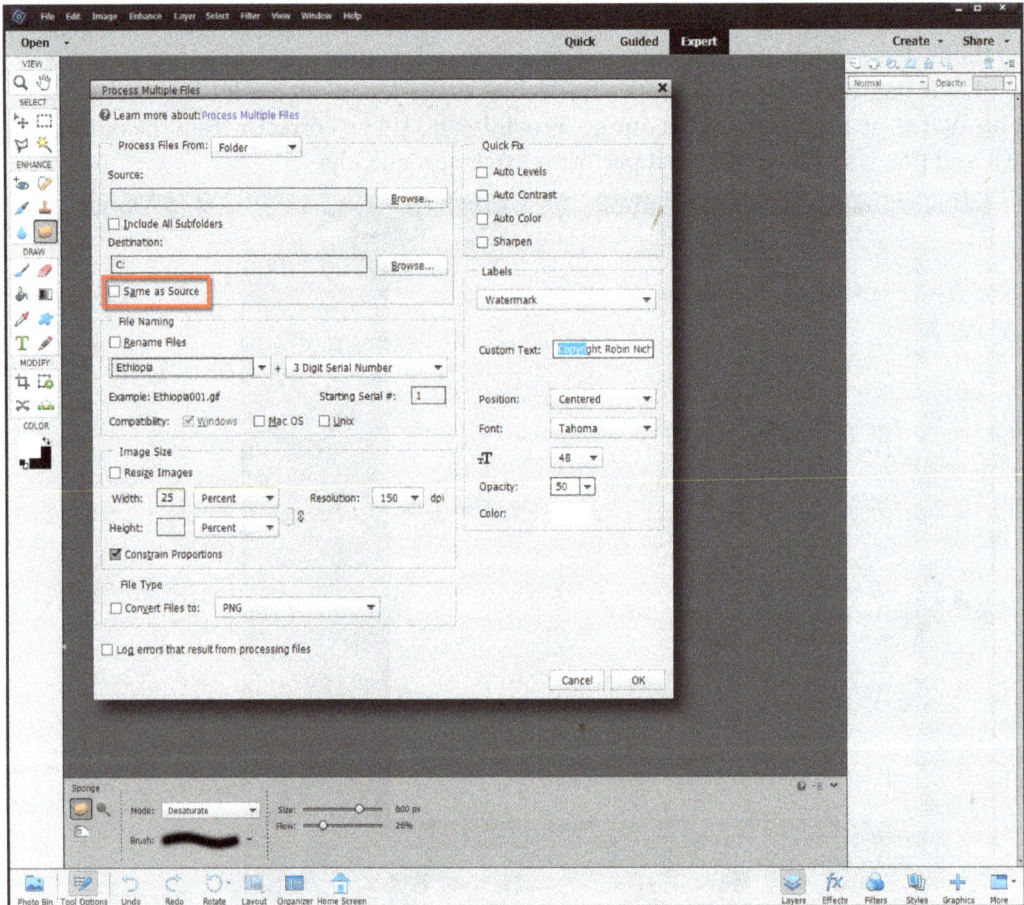

Elements offers the option of adding the (processed) pictures back into the same folder. I'm a little nervous about recommending this in case the program overwrites your original pictures and you are left with nothing but low-resolution web versions of the originals that can't be reinstated. Best practice suggests that you leave the **Same as Source** checkbox unchecked (red outline) and always create a new folder as the destination into which Elements can save your processed files:

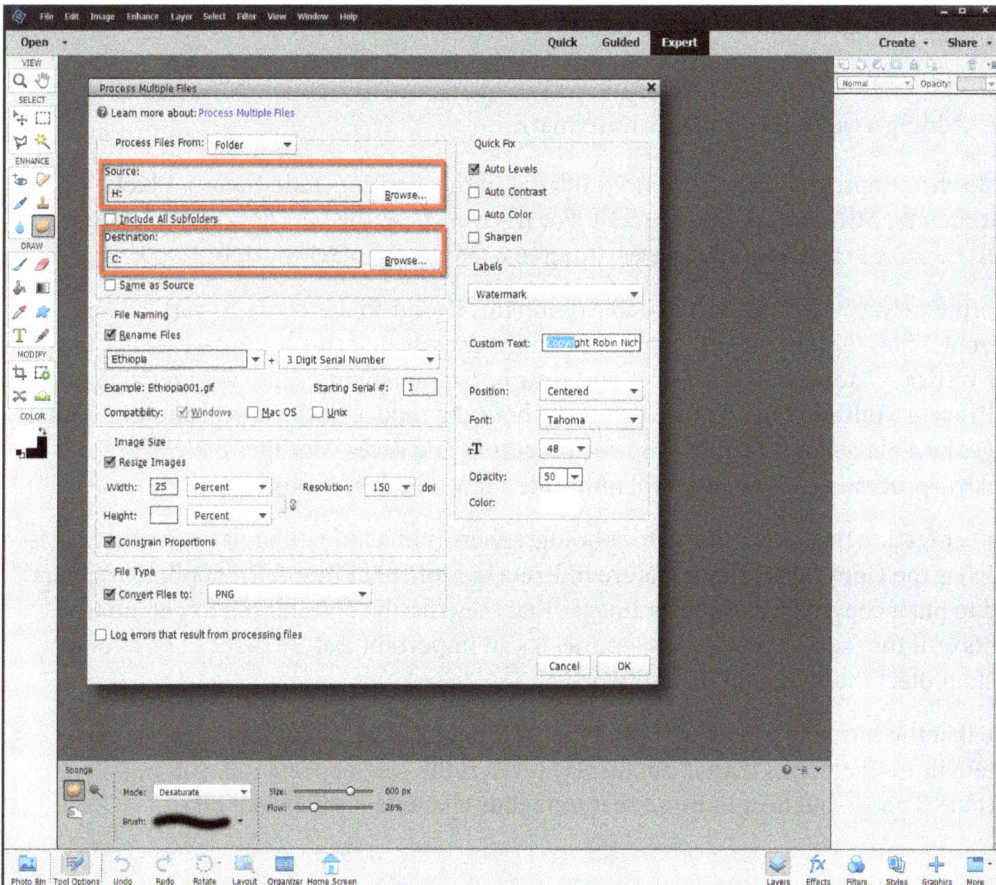

Two fields that are very important to fill before you start processing files are **Source** and **Destination**.

The features that are offered by **Process Multiple Files** include the following:

- Renaming files
- Resizing files
- Converting files into a different format
- Adding a range of quick-fix edits
- Adding a caption or a simple watermark

For down- or upsizing files, the options offered in this panel include **Inches**, **Pixels**, **Centimeters**, **Millimeters**, and **Percent**. For my workflow, the best option is to choose **Pixels** because I can then reduce everything to a maximum pixel width of 1,000.

Unfortunately, you will run into trouble doing this if your folder contains vertical and horizontal files (because they'll come out at different sizes). If this is the case, either put your vertical pictures into one folder and your horizontal pictures into another and run the **Process Multiple Files** feature twice, or choose to reduce both vertical and horizontal images by a percentage. Elements opens, processes, and saves your files incredibly quickly—processing 100 images will only take a few minutes at most.

Another feature that's very useful for photographers (but a little difficult to control how it works) is the **Copyright Stamp** feature in **Process Multiple Files**. A lot of photographers need to put a copyright stamp over images that they may be distributing to potential clients or if they're displaying them online. It's an important feature that can go a long way to protect the copyright of your work.

Note that the tiny field into which you type your personalized copyright message can contain more characters than it can display (even if the field appears full, you can continue typing—but bear in mind that too many characters will be cut off).

The program automatically adds 50% opacity to the text—you can set it to a slightly lower opacity if required so that your copyright warning doesn't obscure the impact of the image. It's a handy and easy-to-control method for adding a basic copyright message on hundreds of pictures in a matter of minutes:

This is what happens when the files being processed are different resolutions. The copyright stamp has been set for the original high-res files, but there were some smaller resolution files in there too—these are not big enough to accommodate the overlay. Verticals also suffer from the same issue—in this case, it might be best to run **Process Multiple Files** twice, once on horizontal files and once on vertical files:

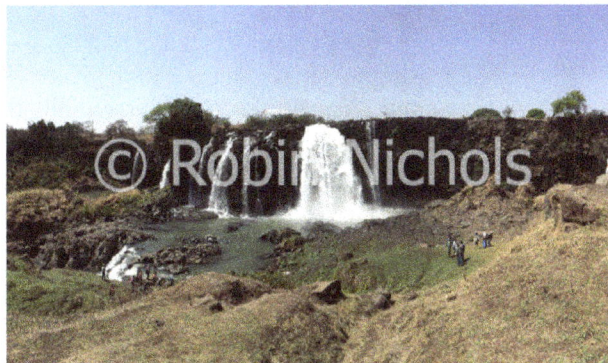

This is what your result should look like: a big copyright statement through the middle of the frame, making it hard for even a skilled image retoucher to steal your work.

In this example, I used Microsoft Word to supply the copyright symbol (you'll find this symbol in most word-processing apps). I typed it into a Word document, then selected and copied it into the clipboard before pasting it into the **Custom Text** field of **Process Multiple Files**, which is arrowed on the left in the following screenshot. On Windows, you can make a copyright symbol by using the *Alt + 0169* keyboard shortcut (on the number pad only). On a Mac, use the *Option + G* command to add a copyright symbol:

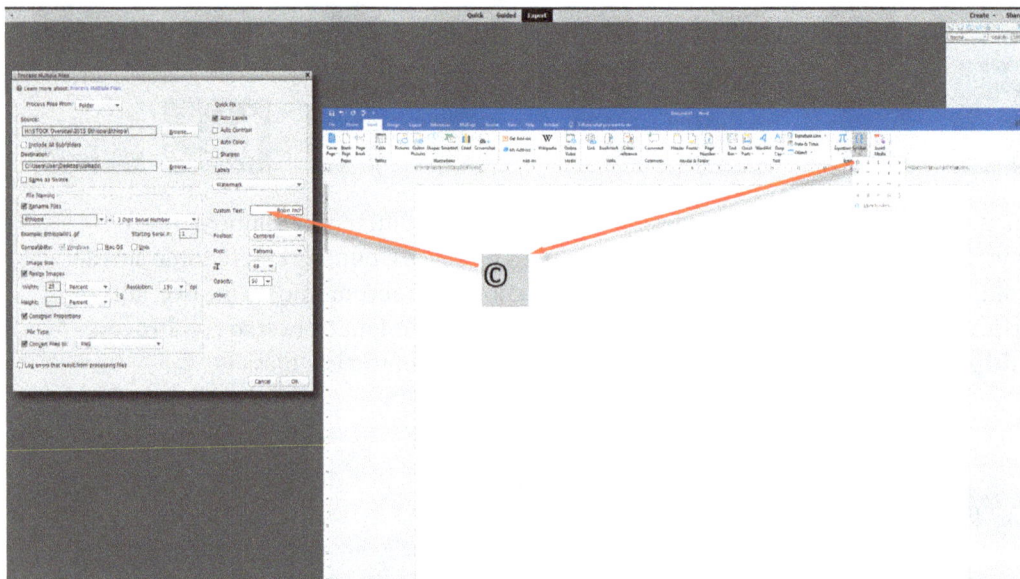

Alternatively, you can apply a **caption**, which is essentially the filename, its description (if present), and the date modified—details, I think, that are not always very useful to have displayed in the image. Try it and see for yourself.

If you're in a hurry and haven't had time to edit your pictures, you can also use the **Quick Fix** checkboxes in this panel to apply **Auto Levels**, **Auto Contrast**, **Auto Color**, and a Sharpen action on the images being processed.

Personally, I find that although the Process Multiple Files panel appears to be a little big and scary at first, its functionality is brilliant because, once you have done this a couple of times, you'll be into bulk processing in no time at all.

Some key things to remember when adding a copyright symbol are as follows:

- Test the process on one image first to make sure that the text will fill the frame and is legible but doesn't dominate the image. You want to make it tricky for anyone to copy and retouch the copyright stamp out of the file, but not too bold as to obscure the image.

- Center the text. I see a lot of copyright symbols placed in out-of-the-way places in the frame because the photographers are loath to obscure their beautiful works of art. The problem is, if it's at the edge of the frame it can be removed using the **Healing Brush** in a few seconds, or cropped out entirely. Don't make it easy for unscrupulous people to steal your work!

- It works best if all of the images are the same orientation and resolution.

- Copy and paste a copyright symbol from MS Word (**Insert | Symbol**) into the **Process Multiple Files** caption field.

Keyboard shortcuts

Here are a few handy keyboard shortcuts that fit nicely with the topics we discussed in this chapter:

- **Export as New Files**: *Ctrl/Cmd + E*

- Change resolution and image size: **Image | Resize | Image Size**

- Copy, resize, name, and format change images in bulk: **File | Export as New Files (Organizer)**

- Copy, resize, name, add tone changes, file format changes, add a copyright stamp, and export in bulk: **File | Process Multiple Files**

- Send the current image to a local printer: **File | Print**

- Optimize the image for best online web display: **File | Save for Web**

- Open non-RAW files in the Camera RAW editor: **File | Open in Camera RAW**

- Used in conjunction with a layer blend mode to make image sharpness *pop*: **Filter | Other | High Pass**

- Add mid-tone contrast to remove haze and mist and to make tones pop: **Enhance | Haze Removal**

Summary

Exporting your work is the final process of the Elements workflow. In this chapter, we have summarized resolution by looking at the different settings that are required for a range of social media and print spaces. We also looked at the features Elements offers for preparing images for export, including **Save for Web**, **Sharpening**, and **Haze Removal**, and exporting to various places on the computer and cloud. Don't forget to try the excellent **Process Multiple Files** feature—this is one of those often-missed little gems that can be used to really speed up output.

Our next chapter discusses what to do if image-making goes wrong. In that chapter, we'll be discussing how to reinstate a lost or damaged catalog, how to search for missing files, and how to work with the excellent **Find** menu—a powerhouse of search options. There's also a section about how to add new pixels to a file (resampling), how to fix grossly over exposed or underexposed images, how to make blurry images appear sharper, and how to copy and paste body parts from one image into another using the amazing Photomerge **Face Swap** utility.

At the end of that chapter, I will run through a couple more composition helpers, most notably the **Content-aware Move** tool and the **Recompose** tool.

10
Best Practices

Nothing ever goes entirely to plan when shooting pictures, which is why we use Photoshop Elements to help fine-tune things such as **composition**, **color**, and **image clarity**. But even then, things can still go wrong with the software.

Adobe does a great job of updating the security and stability of Photoshop Elements, but since almost everything in this industry is updated or replaced every few months, it's not surprising that problems can arise from time to time.

In this section, you will find the solutions to some of the most common imaging problems, including the following:

- Finding lost/disconnected files
- Using the **Find** menu
- Missing keywords
- Adjusting metadata dates for different time zones
- Reinstating the catalog
- Resampling – adding or subtracting pixels
- Gross under- and over exposure (dealing with excess digital noise)
- Techniques for fixing blurred images
- People and face-swapping (using **Photomerge**)
- The **Content-Aware Move tool**
- Poor composition (**Recompose tool**)
- Using the **Help** menu

Finding lost or disconnected files

Elements keeps all your original files, plus all your edited material, displayed in the Organizer – but only if you ask it to by checking the **Include in the Elements Organizer** box in the **File | Save As** window. That's the theory, but as we all know, in real life, things rarely go 100% to plan. Pictures can be corrupted, get lost, or just go missing. The following are a few strategies to initiate if you can't find images you thought were already part of Elements' Organizer:

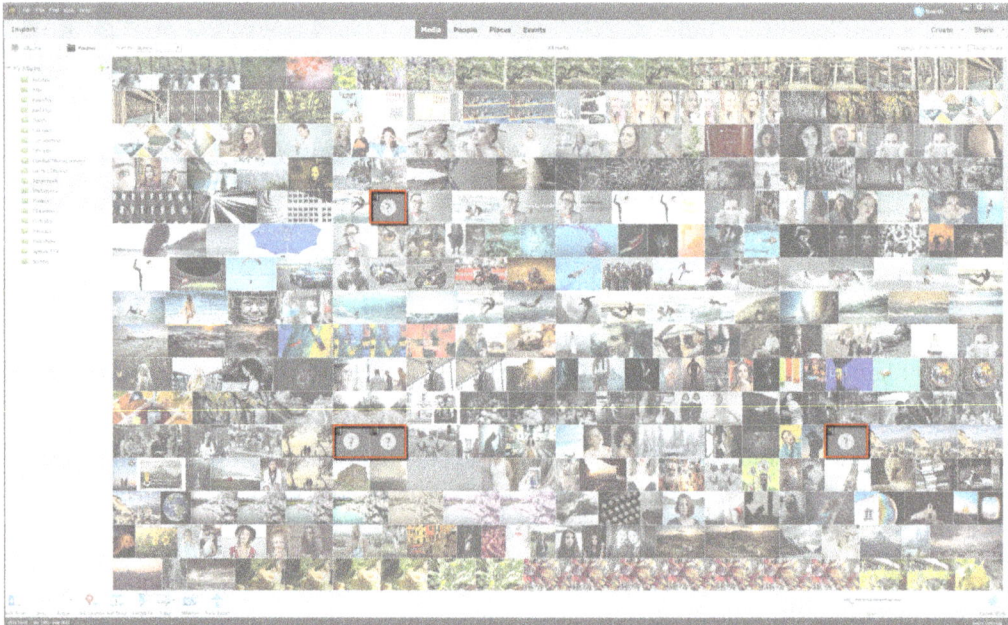

Check the Organizer: If your image was originally imported into the **Organizer**, but has disappeared for whatever reason, you will still be able to see its **thumbnail icon** in the main **Organizer** window – even if it's just a question mark. Despite the fact that the original image might be *missing*, Elements remembers what the file's name was and immediately searches for it.

On any typical day, you might see a missing file or two in the **Media** area of **Organizer**. In my experience, Elements is very good at finding these errant files, providing it has the time (that is, you don't cancel the search prematurely) and that it is still in existence (that is, the image has not been deleted or renamed).

Double-click the thumbnail for the missing file and you'll see the following **Elements Organizer** screen: **Searching for missing file**. It might take a few minutes, or more, but providing that the missing file has not been deleted, it will be located:

Double-click the thumbnail to let the **Organizer** know you want to enlarge the file to full size. If it's lost the **connection** to the original, full-resolution file, you'll immediately see a **Search** panel appear.

In my experience, if you leave it long enough, Elements will find that missing file – providing the original is still on your drive. Elements' ability to locate lost files makes it one of the best picture editing programs:

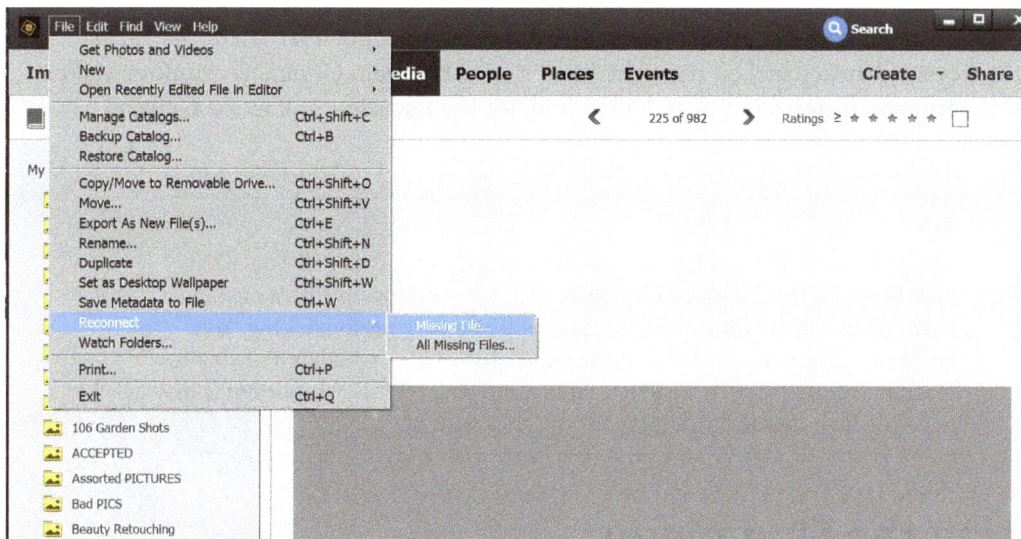

If, for whatever reason, Elements cannot find and reconnect a missing file but you know where it has been moved to, try choosing **File | Reconnect | All Missing Files…**, or simply move the file to where it should be and try again, as shown in the preceding screenshot:

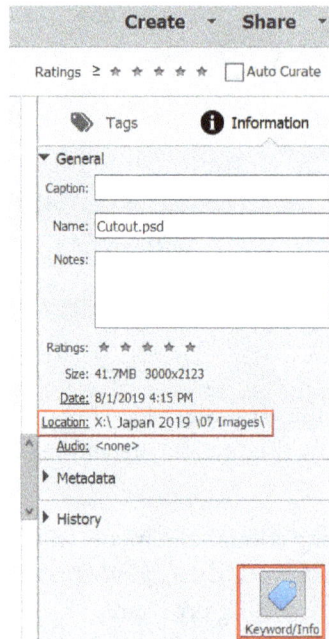

To find where an image **should be** (or where it was before it got *lost*), check out the path in the **Keyword/Info** panel on the right-hand side of the main Organizer window. Make sure the **Information** tab is checked, then look for the **Location** link in the **General** comments area.

> **Tip**
>
> The lesson to be learned here is to avoid renaming or moving files once they have been imported into the Organizer. Begin by coming up with a plan in terms of how to file your work; this plan will be a very personal thing. You know best how to label your shots or folders full of files, whether it's by dates, real names, events, work, holidays, family, and so on. What's important is that once you have decided on a method, you stick with it!

Using the Find menu

The **Find** menu is perhaps the most useful tool in the arsenal of search functions found in Elements. With this drop-down menu, you can search through the following categories:

- **Metadata** (including camera and shooting details)
- **Media Type** (such as photos, video, audio, projects, items with audio captions, and so on)

- **History** (including **Imported on**, **Emailed to**, **Printed on**, **Exported on**, **Shared Online**, **Used in Projects**, and so on)

- **Caption**

- **Filename**, including the following:

- **Version Set**

- **Stack**

- **Untagged items**

- **Visual Search** (including visually similar photos and videos, objects appearing in the photo, or duplicate photos)

- **Saved Searches**

You can even search for an image using terms such as **Items with Unknown Date or Time**, **Untagged Items**, or even **Items not in any Album**:

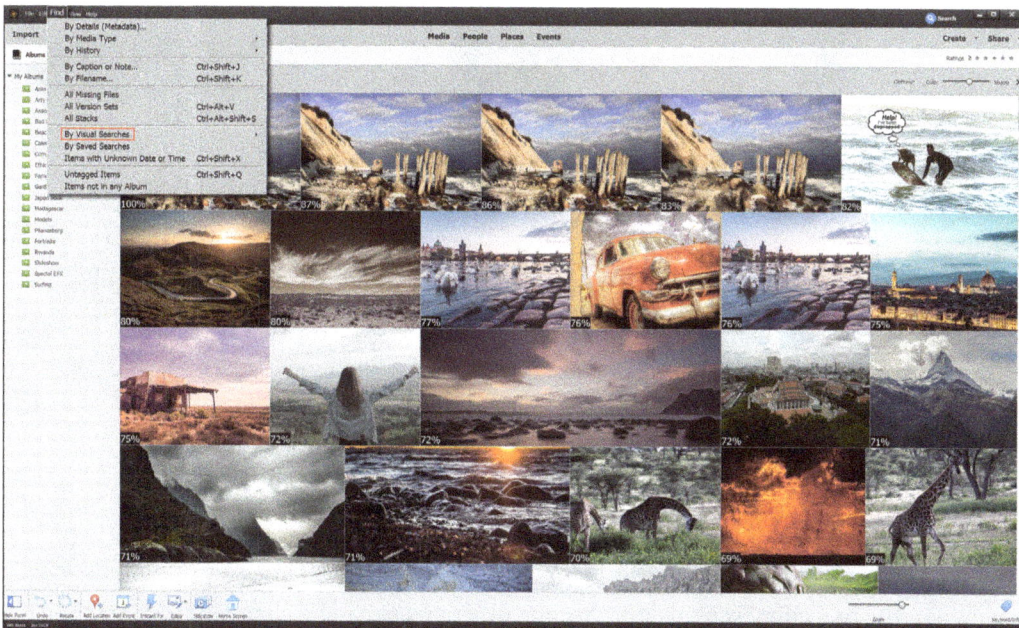

In the preceding screenshot, I searched for images that were visually similar to the one I originally picked. The result was immediate, finding and ranking the other three files that were near-identical in a few seconds. Although the image of a man and his dog on a surfboard has an 82% visual match to the original landscape, that is not considered a close match. When considering the distance between Elements' successful choices (the three most similar landscapes and *the rest*), an 82% match is actually far down the list.

The Find menu has a very comprehensive list. Personally, I find the *visually similar* search quite useful. It doesn't get it right all the time, as you can see in the preceding example, but when it does get it right, it can save you a heap of time.

Adjusting dates for different time zones

One thing that's going to mess up an image search is if the date is set incorrectly on your camera. If you fail to set the correct date, the results of the Elements search will be inaccurate, as it will be searching for a different date.

If the date on your camera is set correctly, you must also be aware of time travel! What I mean by this is traveling across a different **time zone**, which will also throw your searches into a state of confusion. Simply traveling north or south is not the issue, but moving from east to west can confuse any search parameter:

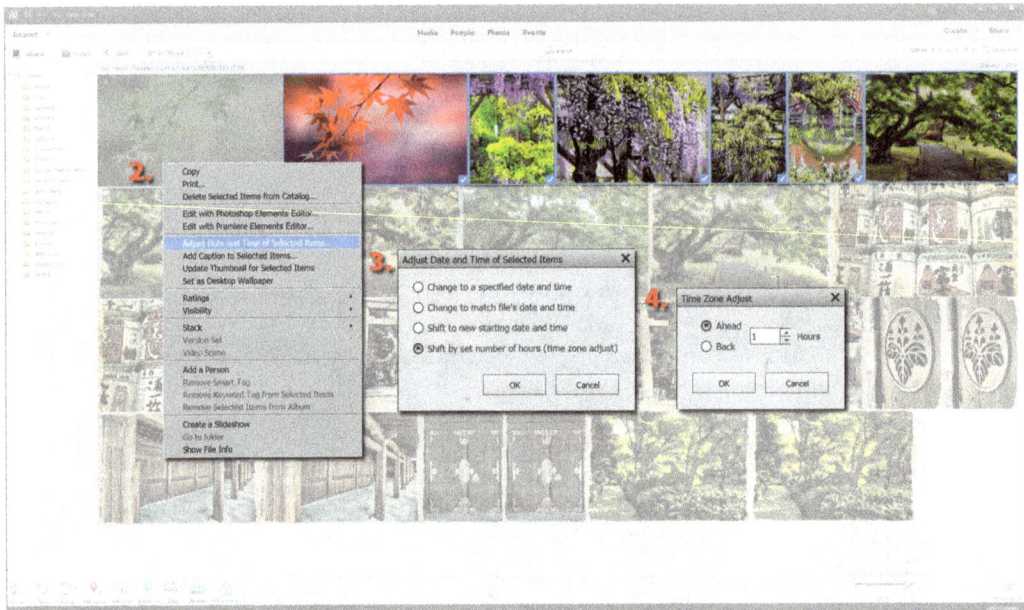

As shown in the preceding screenshot, the date of an image can be changed in Photoshop Elements by editing the metadata.

Here's how it works:

1. Select the images with dates you want to change in the Organizer.

2. Right-click the images, and from the pop-out menu, choose **Adjust Date and Time of Selected Items…**.

3. In the **Adjust Date and Time of Selected Items** dialog that opens, select the fourth option: **Shift by set number of hours (time zone adjust)**.

4. In the **Time Zone Adjust** panel, set the time difference based on the **Ahead** or **Back** options. Easy. Now, you should be able to find those glorious sunset shots you took from that Hawaiian beach rather than pictures of relatives waving you off at the airport the day before you arrived!

Reinstating your catalog

The catalog (or catalogs) is saved to a computer's hard drive by default, although it can be saved to any drive, even a removable one.

Catalogs should be **backed up** on a regular basis (use the **Organizer | File | Backup Catalog** command to do this), preferably to a removable drive or even to the cloud. Never back up to the same drive that you use to run Elements from because that wouldn't really be a true backup. Always back your catalogs up to a different drive:

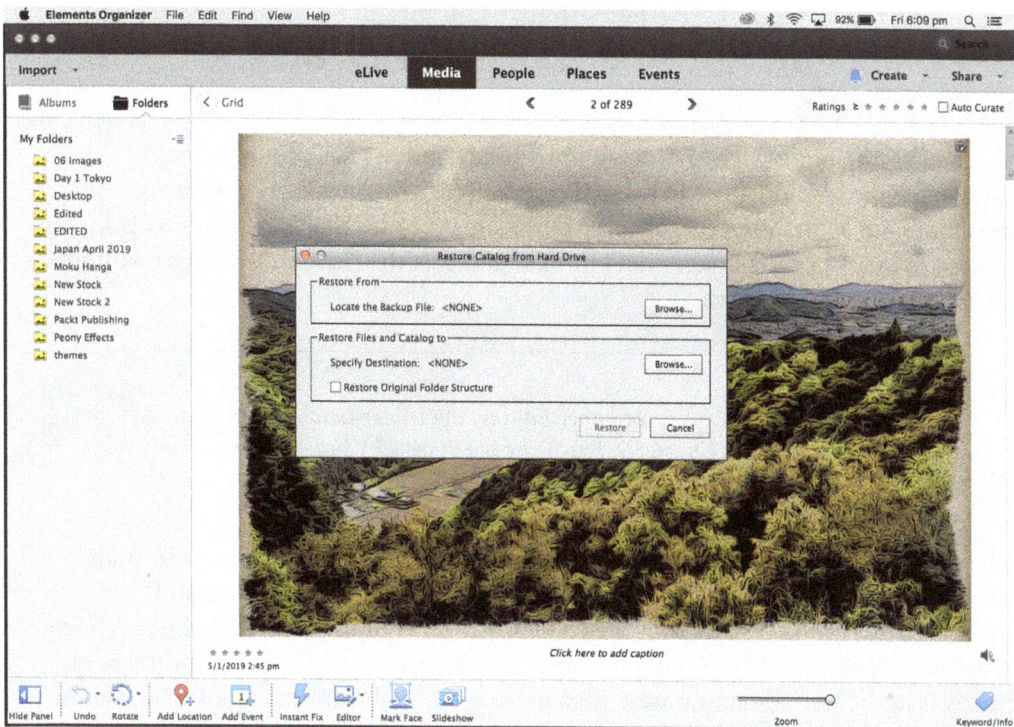

I know the prospect of backing up is boring, but trust me, you only have to lose everything once – whether to a mechanical or electronic failure, or even a virus – to fully appreciate how important the simple process of backing up can be.

So, how do we reinstate a catalog if we suffer data loss? The first thing is to make sure that the computer is 100% virus- and problem-free. There is no point in risking the loss of your data a second time if the computer is not fixed.

Plug in the drive containing the backed-up copy, start the **Organizer**, and select **File | Restore Catalog**. This will present you with two fields to fill out. First, you must find where the backup is located, navigate to the location where you want it reinstated, and click **Restore**.

> **Important note**
> If you just want the catalog restored to where it was initially installed by default, select the **Restore Original Folder Structure** checkbox.

Resolution problems – resampling or adding more pixels

Occasionally, you might have to deal with pictures that don't have a high enough resolution for the task you have in mind. For example, let's say you are preparing a family photo album but soon discover that some of the older photos that were scanned from the originals are too small; the images can't be enlarged past the size of a matchbox without them appearing soft and fuzzy.

> **Important note**
> Refer to *Chapter 3, The Basics of Image Editing*, the *Understanding picture resolution* section; and *Chapter 9, Exporting the Finished Work*, the *Resolution revisited* section, for more information.

Much of the free software available for producing digital book products have in-built warning symbols that appear as soon as you over-enlarge an image on a page. These warnings are there mostly to protect the company from complaints that the images being used are low-resolution. You could, of course, still complain, but the proof for the book company is in the low-resolution **warnings** that appear in the original book file, as shown in the following screenshot:

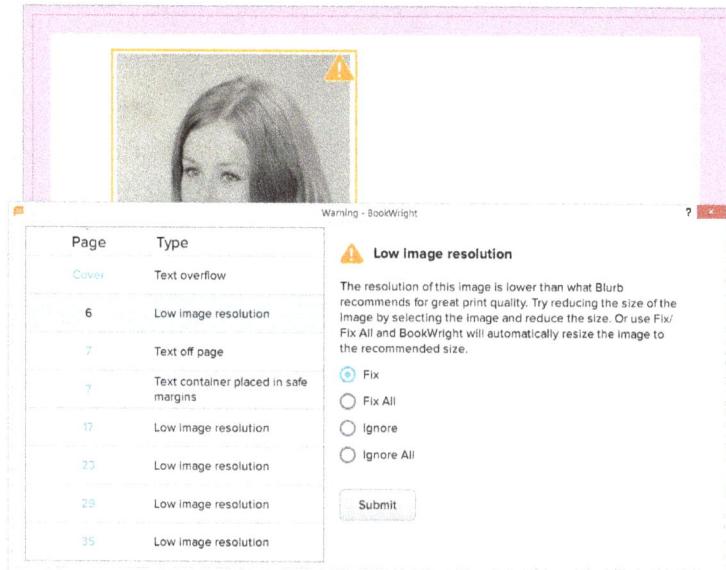

Page	Type
Cover	Text overflow
6	Low image resolution
7	Text off page
7	Text container placed in safe margins
17	Low image resolution
23	Low image resolution
29	Low image resolution
35	Low image resolution

Warning - BookWright

⚠ **Low image resolution**

The resolution of this image is lower than what Blurb recommends for great print quality. Try reducing the size of the image by selecting the image and reduce the size. Or use Fix/Fix All and BookWright will automatically resize the image to the recommended size.

◉ Fix
○ Fix All
○ Ignore
○ Ignore All

[Submit]

The low-resolution warning symbol in the preceding screenshot is from Blurb's excellent **BookWright** software, a free application that's designed for making coffee table books, but this type of resolution warning should pop up in most free bookmaking software:

As shown in the preceding screenshot, in Blurb, clicking the yellow warning icon automatically resizes the file so it displays at the correct size for the number of pixels in the file. The resolution for print is 300 dpi. In this example, my old scanned family snap is on par with the size of a postage stamp – not the size I had envisaged for my book. It needs to have additional pixels before it can be printed larger, which should also stop that annoying warning sign in the book's software from popping up:

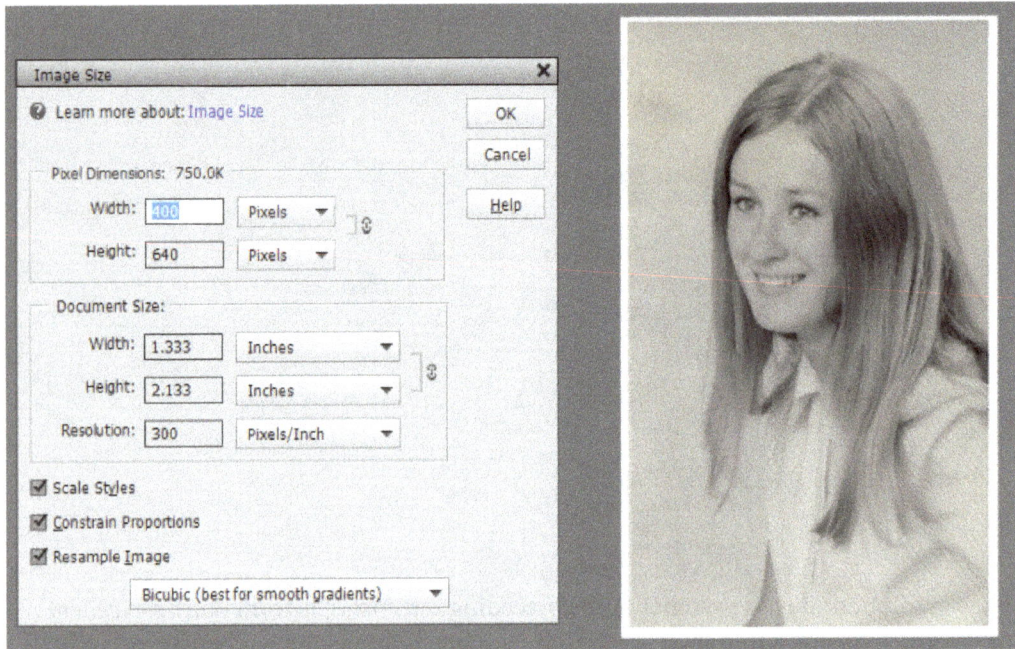

Luckily, Photoshop Elements has an amazing feature called **resampling**, which allows you to add or subtract pixels to and from image files that need resizing. Before you jump with joy, however, note that the quality of a resampled file is directly determined by the quality of the original file, so if it starts off really small, you can only increase its size by a few percentage points before affecting the quality. If the original image is of good quality (over 10 MB+, for example), you can probably double or even treble its size and still produce a clear, sharp-looking result.

> **Important note**
>
> Note that it's important to check the **Constrain Proportions** box so that any increase or decrease in image size is proportional. If this is not checked then the image will be distorted.

If you have any special effects applied to the image (such as a drop shadow), checking the **Scale Styles** box ensures that the effect is also scaled to match the increase in image size. If the drop shadow distance (that is, the height) is set to 20 pixels, but the image is resampled to twice the size without **Scale Styles** being checked, for example, the drop shadow effect remains at a height of 20 – which might look out of proportion to the rest of the image:

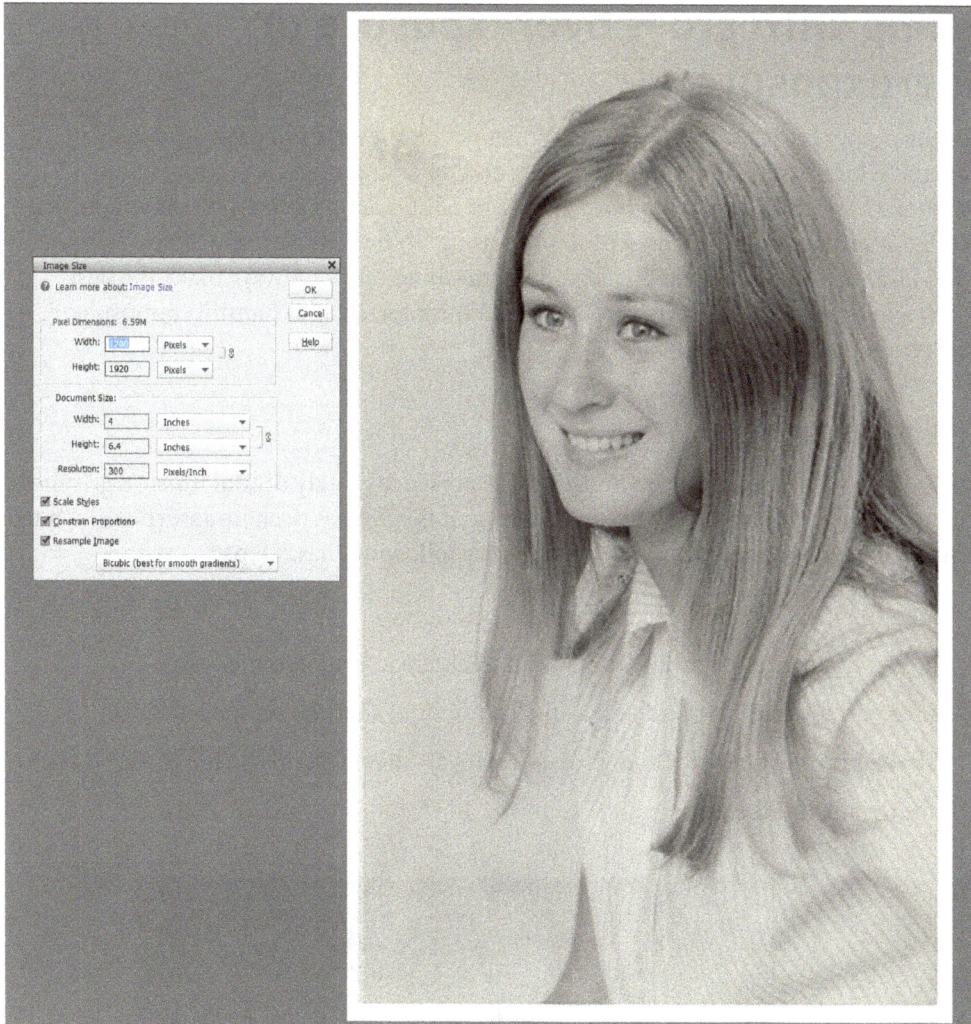

It's important to remember that although you can enter almost any enlargement figure that takes your fancy, results are not always guaranteed. In this example, I checked the **Resample Image** checkbox at the bottom of the **Image Size** dialog panel (**Image | Resize | Image Size**), then added what I thought was a more appropriate pixel width for the book. Note that this updates the **file size**, which gives you a good idea of whether the image will be big enough for the page in question. In this example, the image changed from 400 pixels to 1,200 pixels wide, which was enough to boost the overall file size from 0.75 Mb to 6.5 Mb. Because a large percentage of new pixels were added to a low-resolution original, the resulting file doesn't look entirely sharp, but it's a better result than having to reduce the file to the size of a postage stamp. Note that you can also **sharpen the file** to compensate for any softness introduced by the resampling process.

Dealing with gross overexposure or underexposure

One of the main reasons for shooting RAW files is that they are not processed in the camera, which essentially means that they end up containing a lot more picture information than you'd find in a typical JPEG file. JPEGs are processed in-camera, which is a bit like running them through a mini processing lab before the result appears on the camera's LCD screen. It's a great concept, but a machine cannot always make the best decisions when there are so many variables to account for, such as lighting, atmosphere, and the photographer's intent.

Underexposure

The main issue with underexposed images is the presence of ugly **digital noise**, a grittiness that appears mostly in high ISO files, and more so if the file has been underexposed. To fix the visual problems created by underexposure, try following these steps:

1. Open the RAW file in the **Camera RAW** window.

2. Use the **Exposure**, **Highlight**, and **Whites** sliders to brighten the scene.

3. Move to the **Detail** tab, and add a small amount of sharpening if needed.

4. Use the **Luminance** and **Color Noise** (removal) sliders to rid the file of excess noise.

5. Save the file in Elements:

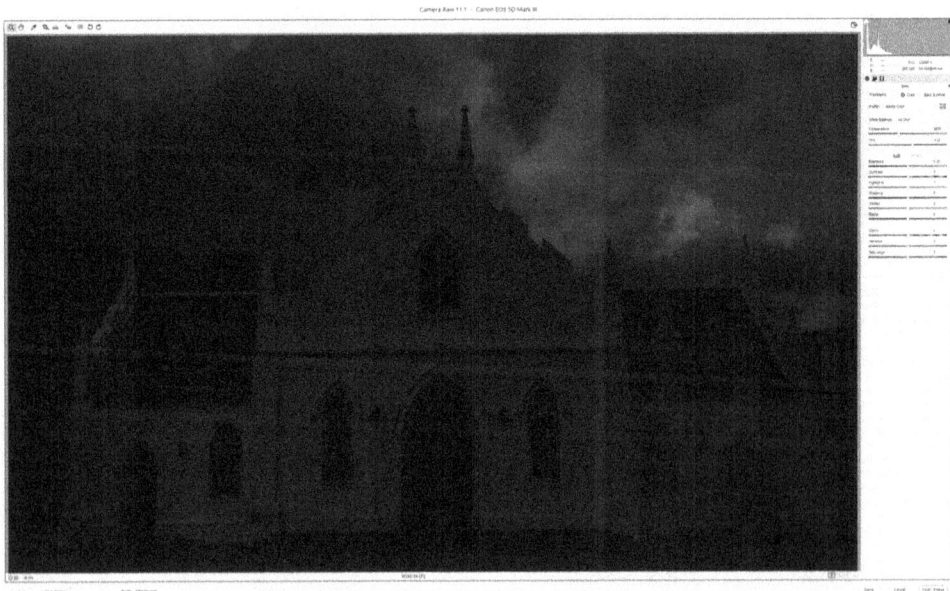

As shown in the preceding screenshot, underexposure can usually be fixed in the Camera RAW utility:

If you take a look at the preceding image, you may consider it *fixed*. The previously poor levels of brightness has been improved to the point that, unless you look closely, the image appears to be well-balanced. Again, as with most things to do with digital editing, how much time and effort you spend on 'fixing' an image is dependent on its ultimate usage. At what size will it be displayed, is it for social media or print, inkjet or commercial lithographic presses? Knowing exactly how the image is to be used goes a long way in helping you gauge how much time to spend in the digital darkroom!

Now, as you can see from the preceding screenshot, there is too much noise. If you take the time to examine the image closely, you'll see that it's rife with ugly examples of **color noise**, a defect that becomes more prevalent when heavily underexposed images are significantly lightened. Some cameras suffer more from color noise than others – for example, Nikon DSLRs remove color noise in-camera, while Canon DSLRs are less effective. Luckily, color noise can be filtered out in Elements:

By applying not only Brightness and Sharpening, but also **Luminance** and **Color Noise** removal in the **Camera RAW** window, it's possible to restore most of the quality in the preceding file, as if it were properly exposed in the first place:

As you can see in the preceding example, the final edited image looks as bright and as noise-free as the scene itself when it was captured.

Overexposure

Overexposed files have a different set of (visual) problems to underexposed images. Where the detail is mostly recoverable in an underexposed image, overexposure loses data – a process called **clipping**. This is especially prevalent in JPEG files possibly because of all the in-camera processing and compression levied on the file, but it can also happen with a grossly overexposed RAW file, too.

If you have a file that has been overexposed, follow these steps:

1. Open the RAW file.

2. Check if the highlights have been clipped by clicking the **Highlight Warning** button at the top right-hand side of the histogram (highlighted in red). If you see red in the brighter parts of the image file, it means those pixels are over-bright - and probably clipped.

   In this case, if you hover over those areas with your cursor, you'll note that the **RGB readout** (detailed under the histogram) reads R: 255, G: 255, B: 255, which is the maximum brightness (note that, in the preceding screenshot, all of the tone sliders are set to zero):

3. To bring detail back into those areas, try reducing the **Exposure** (via its slider) to a point where you start to see the gamut warning color shrinking or disappearing, as shown in the preceding screenshot. If you have to darken the entire image to achieve this, that's OK, the result may be 'murkier' than expected.

4. If the image does turn a bit murky, try shifting the **Highlight** or the **Whites** sliders. In the preceding screenshot, both values have been altered so that the red warning color is no longer present. We can now see detail in the image's brighter areas:

5. In the preceding example, **Vibrance** and **Clarity** were added to the image to finish off the tonal rescue. Because most of the file was overexposed originally, there's less need to add any kind of noise removal filter. Once your image has been successfully altered, save the resulting masterpiece.

Fixing blurred images

The sad truth is, if your image file is really **blurred**, there's not much that software can actually do to bring it back to a point of sharpness. However, if it's just a little blurred, you can try increasing the contrast or using one of the specialist tools available in Elements to make it at least appear at least a bit sharper.

The following are some tools that might improve the overall look of a blurry image:

- **Levels** (refer to the *Adjusting contrast using Level* section in *Chapter 3, The Basics of Image Editing*).

- **Contrast** (refer to the *Camera RAW* section in *Chapter 3, The Basics of Image Editing*).

- **Clarity** (refer to the *Camera RAW* section in *Chapter 3, The Basics of Image Editing*).

- **Unsharp Mask** (refer to the *Unsharp Mask* section in *Chapter 9, Exporting the Finished Work*).

- **Shake Reduction** (refer to the *Shake Reduction* section in *Chapter 9, Exporting the Finished Work*).

- **Haze Removal** (refer to the *Haze Removal* section in *Chapter 9, Exporting the Finished Work*).

Although most of these sharpening-type tools have already been mentioned throughout this book – some in great detail – it's worth revisiting one of the most effective tools in solving this problem: **Shake Reduction**.

As you can see from the following screenshot, I tried to photograph a mounted horseman, galloping past at 65 km/h while aiming an arrow at a target. I had never seen this before and did not have much time to think about the settings, so I considered 1/500s @f8, ISO 3200, to be sufficient for the job. As you can see, it was not fast enough to totally freeze the archer's movement, thus providing me with an excellent opportunity to test the **Shake Reduction** tool (Enhance | Shake Reduction):

As you can see from the preceding screenshot, reducing the camera shake in this example worked surprisingly well. Bear in mind, however, that **Shake Reduction** is not a feature that works perfectly all of the time, as there are many *degrees* of shake possible, such as camera shake, lens shake, subject movement, and photographer shake. In the example of this horseback archer, the camera's original shutter speed wasn't enough to freeze the motion of the rider, but by applying the **Shake Reduction** utility at full strength, the clarity of the image significantly improved, as follows:

People and face-swapping

Ever taken a snap of friends only to discover, after they have all gone, that one of them is looking in the wrong direction or has their eyes closed?

This is a common error that many of us will have experienced at one time or another. Before Elements came along, the only way to remedy this was to get your friends back together to recapture the image, or to spend time selecting, copying, and pasting figures from one picture to another. Correcting such an error was a time-consuming and complex process, so most people didn't bother doing anything further.

Fortunately, Elements has a fantastic feature called **Face Replace** that can help. The Face Replace tool is built around the same computer code that's used in the **Panorama** stitching and **Scene Cleaner** features (as discussed in *Chapter 5, Easy Creative Projects*), and it essentially enables you to remove a face from one image and transfer it to another, all without the need for making selections or complex masks. This is all put together into a very easy-to-follow and effective process located in the **Guided** edit window – right next to **Photomerge Panorama**.

The only proviso with this feature is that you have **more than one image of the group** available. (If you're using the more specific Photomerge **Face Swap** function, you'll need a second or third face to copy and paste.) I generally advise anyone shooting snaps of their friends or family to set the camera's drive mode to *high speed* and to take at least two or three images as, in my experience, someone is bound to have their eyes closed or be looking away when the shutter is pressed. If you still end up with every picture having something wrong with it, **Face Replace** can help.

Here's how this amazing feature works:

1. First, open the images in Elements. You can select up to 10.

2. Select the **Guided** edit mode, as shown in the following screenshot:

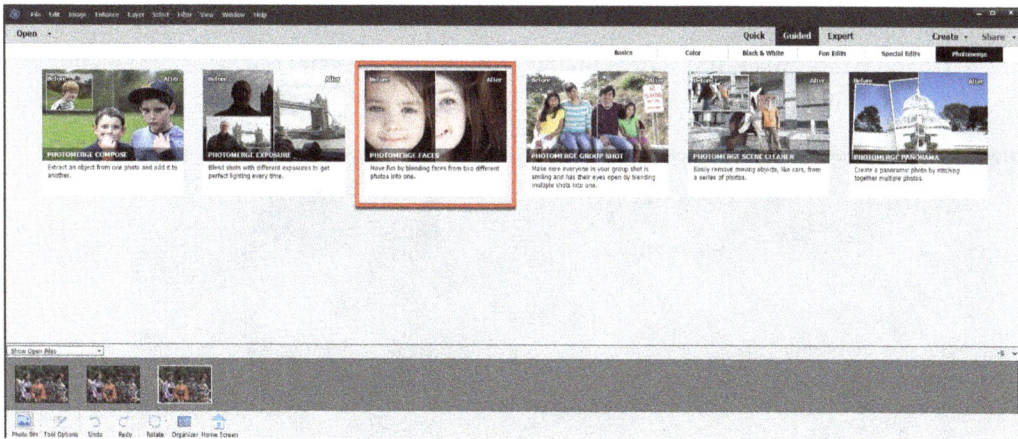

3. From the **Photomerge** tab, choose **Face Replace**.

4. Elements will ask you if you want to open all of the currently open images in Face Replace. Click **Open All**:

5. Two windows appear. The right-hand window contains the *master* or base image – in other words, the best shot. Identify the best photograph and drag it from the **Photo Bin** into the right-hand window, as shown in the following screenshot. Double-clicking any one of the thumbnails in the photo bin will load it into the left-hand pane. This is the source image, from which we can select a better facial expression, angle, or overall look:

6. In the preceding screenshot, there are two different photographs of the same Japanese women in Kyoto. In the right hand frame, the right hand woman is looking to the right hand side, away from my camera.

7. To fix this, use the image of the (same) woman in the left hand window - where she's looking at the camera and use the **Pencil** tool to roughly draw around the face you'd like copied to the right-hand image. You don't need to be accurate – simply sketch a mark in the area you want to copy, and Elements will transfer the surrounding area to the image in the right-hand window. If only part of a face is transferred, simply draw around the *donor face* a bit more and wait for the update. It's an amazing process to watch, but this tool will only work if you remember to take additional shots when in the field.

Elements uses a cleverly-designed color-coding system, which allows you to identify where each face comes from. This feature is not important when you're working with a small number of images, but if you're working with a maximum of 10, you'll find the color coding very helpful.

8. As you can see in the preceding screenshot, the woman in the flowery kimono was looking at the ground in the right-hand frame, but with a quick pencil stroke and the use of the green image as a donor, the problem was fixed seamlessly.

9.   In the following screenshot, I swapped the face of the woman in the orange kimono using the blue sample. Once done, press the **Next** button and save the resulting masterpiece:

Perfecting the process

To fine-tune this process, there are a number of tricks you can apply, as follows:

Use the effective **Alignment Tool** if multiple images don't line up precisely. This is an excellent feature and makes the subsequent face replacement process much more accurate.

Use the program's **Eraser** tool if you overdraw around an object and too much copies across.

Note that you can also check the **Show Regions** checkbox to highlight, in color, what has been copied into the right-hand pane and from which image.

Content-Aware Move tool

A tool that might help fine-tune your composition is the **Content-Aware Move tool**. Essentially, this is a big **Healing Brush**, but instead of clicking repeatedly over an image hoping that it can copy, paste, and blend pixels over a problem area, this tool works on a much larger scale. With this tool, draw around the object you want to move, drag the entire object to a new position, and release it – Elements will do the rest.

Here, *the rest* means assessing the pixels around the target site and then blending them into the canvas. However, like many of the magic auto-fix tools in this application, some examples work much better than others.

The **Cloning** process, can at times be a little too aggressive, copying objects into the area to be covered that are inappropriate. That's the nature of the beast. Elements provides some control over the power of the **Healing** action (via a slider), plus **Add** or **Subtract** modes for the initial selection process.

After it has performed, however, I have to fine-tune the results with the **Clone Stamp** or the **Healing Brush** to tidy up some of Elements' visual mistakes. That said, the **Content-Aware Move tool** is not a bad feature with which to recompose certain types of images, especially if it's applied to a photo where there's room for the moving and blending process to actually maneuver:

The preceding image demonstrates this feature because the object I want to move has plenty of reasonably uniform space around it (the ocean), which will probably work well in terms of blending over the area once occupied by the boat:

Start by drawing a simple line around the object you want to move. It doesn't have to be accurate, but be careful not to include any of the object you are trying to shift (in this case, the fishing boat). Because the healing brush works by assessing the brightness and texture in the pixels around the target and source locations, it's important to work with a **simple image** rather than one that's busy. Drag the object to its new location, and once you're happy with its position, click the green checkmark:

You can see the result in the preceding screenshot. Although there are some slightly weird textures in the ocean where the boat once was, the result is acceptable (especially from an automated action):

As you can see in this final shot, the area where the boat was looks a bit muddy – this is the **Content-Aware Fill** process. If this is the case, use one of Elements' retouching brushes to tidy up the automatic tool's shortcomings.

Recompose tool

Another composition helper is the **Recompose tool**. Personally, I think its results can be very hit and miss, almost as if Adobe has bitten off more than it can chew on.

We all have snaps in our libraries where we might wish the composition to be slightly different – people a bit closer to each other, landscapes a bit wider, or formats changed to a square shape, for example. The **Recompose** tool sets out to provide the solutions to these problems. Follow these steps to learn how to use it:

1.   First, open the image in question.

2. Note that you have two types of brush available: green and red. The green paintbrush is for preserving the shape of objects, while the red paintbrush indicates that the selected pixels can be deleted:

3. I like the empty openness of this scene, but want to try to stretch it further to give the image more of a panorama *look*:

4. I need to add more to the right-hand side of the file using the **Canvas Size** feature. I wasn't 100% sure how much extra real estate I was going to need, so I added extra because it's easy to crop off later:

5. As you can see, by using a big brush, you can paint over the objects in an image you want to keep, and over those you want to remove. If you make a mistake use each brush's **Eraser** tool:

6. Once the regions are set, as shown in the preceding screenshot, carefully grab one of the handles; in this case, it was the center handle on the right-hand edge that was dragged in order to stretch the image to a wide panorama format:

As you can see in the preceding screenshot, the result is subtle. Although the final result was not as wide as I had originally hoped, if the image had been dragged any further to the right, the scene would have been distorted.

Using the Help menu

Although I hope that much of the information you need to understand Elements is in this book, there might be some questions it can't quite answer. If you need any more information on this powerful editing program, try Google, or, failing that, the Elements **Help** menu.

Under the **Help** menu, you'll find a number of areas of interest, including the following:

- Photoshop Elements Help
- Getting Started
- Key Concepts
- Support
- Video Tutorials
- Forum

The following screenshots give you a brief idea of the backup Adobe provides for its ever-growing following:

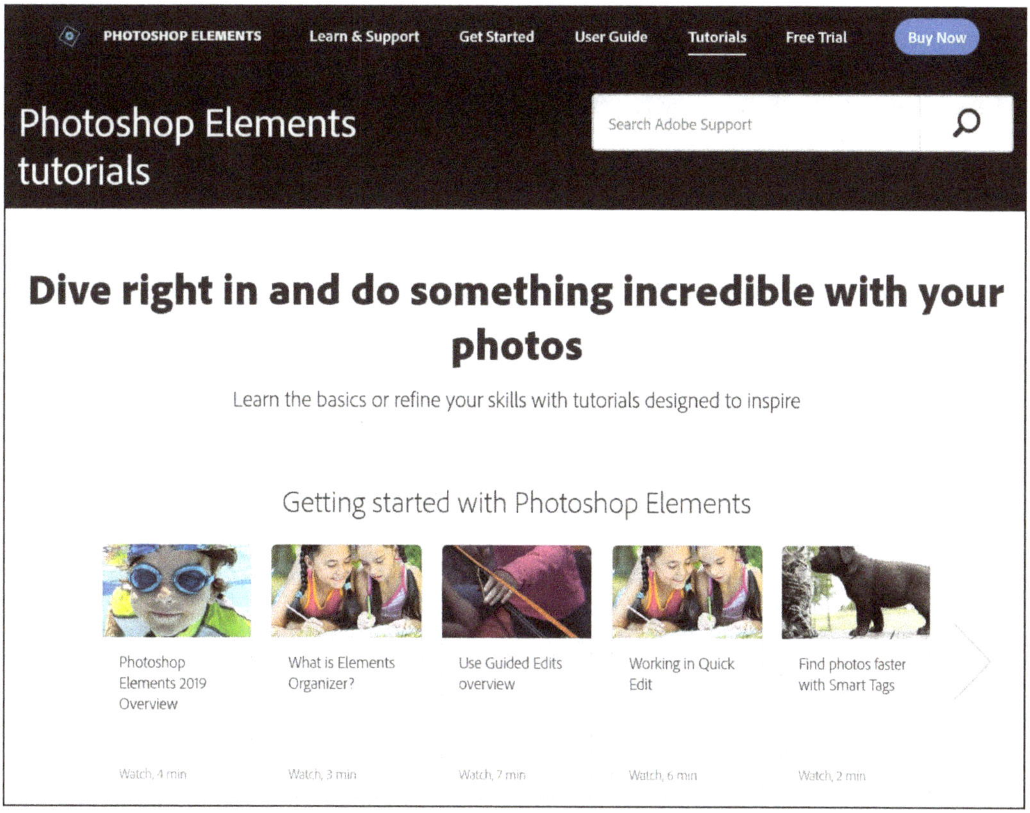

As you can see, Elements directs its users to an amazing array of instructional videos. They might not specifically address your exact requirement, but they do provide a great starting point for anyone who needs help with their editing:

Summary

I trust that this penultimate chapter has helped you iron out any residual questions you might have about the features found in Adobe Photoshop Elements. This chapter has covered most of the basic and commonly encountered problems in the program. Speaking from experience, you'll find that any problems you come across derive from either your computer operating software or mistakes that were made while shooting, rather than a failure of Elements. Now in its sixteenth version, and continually improving and upgrading, Elements provides a very stable platform on which to work.

In the next chapter, we will summarize Elements' common features: all of its tools, panels, filters, menus, and project opportunity features.

The upcoming chapter will also act as an important **reference point** for you to visit if you ever need a little more information on certain tools and functions you may be unfamiliar with.

11
Feature Appendix

This appendix features a summary of what I truly hope is every **important tool**, **panel**, and **feature** to be found in this amazing photo editing program, plus an overview of what you'll find among its many **menus**.

Not everything you find in this application is perfect, so I have also endeavored to add my personal thoughts on the usefulness of some of the tools and features to help prevent novices from wasting time by choosing less effective tools for the job. Though this chapter is by no means comprehensive (that would require another book), this section is designed to shed additional light on the workings of this multifarious editing application.

Treat it like a quick reference section – if you are trying to achieve a specific effect, flick through these pages to find the right tool or process for the job at hand...

By way of a quick reference, here's a list of the topics covered in this chapter:

- Home Screen
- Organizer – Import (button)
- Organizer – the five view spaces
- Expert Edit mode – the Tool bar (including the View, Select, Enhance, Drawing, Modify, and Color tools)
- Quick Edit mode - Adjustments (including Smart Fix, Exposure, Lighting, Color, Balance, and Sharpen)
- Guided Edit mode (including the following sections: Basics, Color, Black and White, Fun Edits, Special Edits, and Photomerge)

- Quick and Expert Edit mode drop-down menus (including the File, Edit, Image, Enhance, Layer, Select, Filter, View, Windows, and Help menus)

- Panels overview (including the Layers, Effects, Filters, Styles, Graphics, Actions, and Color Swatches)

- More tabs (covering Histogram, Favorites, Navigator, and the Info panels)

- Create Menu (for the Organizer and Editor), which includes the following: Slideshow, Photo Collage, Photo Prints, Photo Book, Greeting Card, Photo Calendar, Instant Movie, Video Story, Video Collage, and DVD with Menu.

- Share Menu (includes Email, Twitter, Flickr, Vimeo, YouTube, Burn Video DVD, and PDF Slideshow)

Home Screen

Start by double-clicking on the Elements icon on your Windows or Mac and you'll get the following options.

This window is essentially what used to be called the eLive screen—it's what you first see when Elements opens. It provides creative inspiration by offering brief examples of slideshows, Pattern Brush, Painterly, B&W Selection, Depth of Focus effects, collages, special text effects, and more using your images rather than random stock shots. You can also use it to search for further inspiration online or simply to start the **Organizer**, **Editor**, or **Video Editor**.

Organizer – Import (button)

The big button in the top-left corner of the **Organizer** window is pretty much where it all starts. Use this to import images into the Photoshop Elements database (called the **Catalog**). Choose from **Import from Files and Folders**, **Camera or Card Reader**, **Scanner**, or **Bulk**. (You can also import files using the **File | Get Photos and Videos** drop-down menu.)

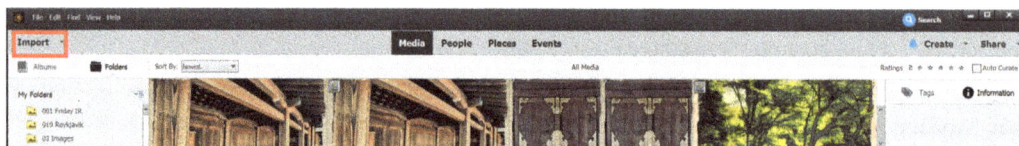

Organizer – the five view spaces

Media: This is the window in which you see all of your photos, sound tracks, music and video files, and graphics stored in the catalog. Use it to further sort images by dragging them into **Albums**.

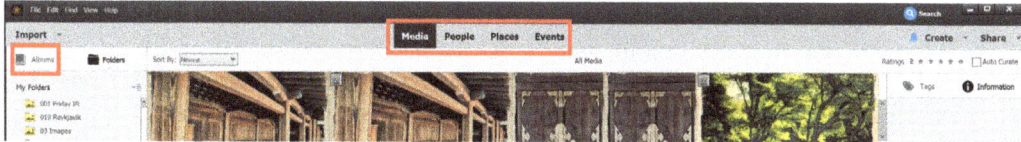

People: If you decide to analyze your image database, Elements can file your images based on the people it identifies in each image. This is a very clever feature that seems to work well.

Places: This is an internet-reliant viewing mode that's geared toward photographers whose cameras are GPS enabled. Images appear on a Google map according to the coordinates taken from the file's metadata. This is a nice feature for anyone embarking on a road trip or perhaps researching travel. Curiously, this feature has been made unavailable to all previous versions of Elements.

Events: Use this feature to group your images based on the date. This is very handy if you need quick access to files that were shot at specific times. If they are holiday snaps taken in a different time zone, remember to change the date in each file to make searching more accurate.

Albums: Albums can be created inside the general media area to hold specific groups of images. They are a very effective way to further organize your images—rather than having everything display together in the one **Media** window.

Folders: The folder view displays the computer's folder hierarchy. Only those folders that feature already-imported images appear in this display.

Auto Curate (checkbox): Turn this on to see what Elements regards as the top 50-500 *best* images (you select from how many). Good luck with that!

Keyword/Info: This is an essential panel in Organizer as it displays the basic metadata for that file, along with the history (that is, the edits). The **Tag** part of the same tab displays any keywords or tags that have been attached using Elements or other applications.

Expert Edit mode – the Tool bar

Tools on the **Tool** bar are divided into six groups, each pertinent for specific picture editing tasks: **View**, **Select**, **Enhance**, **Draw**, **Modify**, and **Color**.

> **Important note**
>
> While hovering the cursor over the Tool bar, a letter in brackets will appear for each tool icon - this is the single letter keyboard shortcut for that tool, or group of tools. If that letter/shortcut refers to multiple tools in a group (for example, the Custom Shape tool (U) has seven different tools with the same shortcut), you can cycle through them by pressing the single letter shortcut while holding down the Shift key.

View tools

Zoom tool (*Z*):

Use this tool to click and enlarge your image in the main screen. Note that you can also do this by using the keyboard shortcut: *Ctrl/Cmd* + "+" or "-".

Hand tool (*H*):

Use this tool to move the image around the main screen. It only works when it's enlarged to a size that is bigger than the main screen. If you are working with any other tool at the time and need to shift your image in the main window left/right or up/down, hold the *Spacebar* and the **Hand** will appear, allowing you to shift the image and release the Spacebar so that the tool you were originally using reappears.

Select tools

Move tool (*V*):

This is one of the most useful tools in Photoshop Elements. Use it to click, hold, and reposition images, objects, or text in multilayered files.

Rectilinear Marquee tool (*M*):

As the name suggests, you'd use this for making quick rectangular or square selections. Once drawn, only the pixels inside that selection can be altered. Those outside the selection are protected. To cancel a selection, choose **Select | Deselect** or *Ctrl/Cmd + D*. To draw a perfect square, hold the *Shift* key while clicking and dragging in the image. To move the selection already made, click immediately inside the cropping marquee and click and drag it to reposition the *live* selection. In this case, using the Move tool will not only move the selection, but all of the pixels inside the selection too.

Elliptical Selection tool (*M*):

As the name suggests, use this to create an elliptical or a circular selection around your subject. To create a perfect circular shape, hold the *Shift* key while clicking and dragging in the image to create your selection.

Lasso tool (*L*):

The Lasso tool is exactly that: click and then drag the cursor to draw a line around your subject. Because it's a freehand operation, accuracy is quite hard to maintain. If your editing style requires you to work with selections frequently, l would highly recommend purchasing a graphics tablet. These devices basically replace the clumsy mouse with a pen-shaped electronic stylus, making it far easier to execute fine and very accurate brush strokes.

Polygonal Lasso tool (*L*):

This selection tool is particularly good for selecting geometric shapes because it operates on a **point-to-point** basis. Click the mouse once, reposition the cursor and click a second time, reposition the cursor and click a third time, and so on. Each time you mouse-click, it pins the straight selection line to the canvas. Drawing a square selection takes just five clicks.

Magnetic Lasso tool (*L*):

This is also a freehand type of drawing tool, except for the fact that, as its name suggests, the selection line's *qualities* are to stick to the edges of objects with measurable contrast. So, if you're selecting a black object on a white background, it will work seamlessly with little or no real draftsmanship. As long as you follow the outline of the object roughly, it will make the line for you. The *magnetic* qualities of the tool can be increased/decreased, depending on how defined the contrast edge in the subject is.

Magic Wand tool (*A*):

This is an all-time favorite for most editors because its selection capabilities are based on the color of the pixels that you click. Vary its effectiveness by increasing or decreasing the **Tolerance** levels so that it selects a wider, or narrower, range of the color that was initially clicked. Like all of the selection tools, if you hold the *Shift* key while clicking in an image, each subsequent click *adds* to the overall selection. If you over-select something (because the **Tolerance** is set too high), you can also subtract from the overall selection by holding the *Alt/Opt* key while clicking. You can also set the tool to contiguous (which limits the color selection to those pixels of a specific color that adjoin the sample), or discontiguous, in which case all pixels of that color, regardless of where in the image they are, get selected.

Enhance tools

Red Eye Removal tool (*Y*):

By clicking and dragging a small selection marquee (square shape) over the offending red eye, Elements *looks* for red pixels and turns them gray. Essentially, it removes the ugly red-eye effect by making the pupils appear gray. Although your subject might have green or blue eyes, gray eyes are far more preferable to red eyes. Note that this tool also has a check button for removing pet eye.

Spot Healing Brush tool (*J*):

This is probably the most useful of all retouching tools because it's so easy to use, and it's very effective. Choose a brush size, move the cursor over the blemish, and click once. Photoshop Elements copies the pixels from around the outside of the brush shape and pastes them inside, virtually erasing (covering up) the blemish in the original image. It works like magic in most retouching situations, providing the blemish is not too near other strident details, such as hair, in which case it might copy unwanted items into the target area. Making the brush smaller usually solves this problem.

Healing Brush tool (*J*):

This retouching tool works in a similar format to the **Spot Healing** brush, except that you must first select a *source* area by holding the *Alt/Opt* key and clicking in a *good* area of the image. This *tells* Photoshop Elements where you want to copy pixels from. You then shift the cursor over the area to be repaired and click a second time to paste the copied pixels over the damaged pixels. This is especially useful if the retouching area containing *good* pixels is a long way from the area requiring repair. For larger repairs, you can easily click, hold, and move the brush over a larger or misshapen area, before releasing the mouse to fix it. Remember that the larger the brush size, the further afield Elements looks for a good source area, which increases the possibility of copying inappropriate details, as well as good stuff.

Smart Brush tool (*F*):

This is one of Elements' clever *all-in-one* tools where the brush operates as a selection tool, detecting the edges of the object you paint over, while automatically adding to that selection one of the visual effects available (these are chosen off of the quite extensive menu—lighting, nature, portrait, tints, black and white, special effects, and many more). Success here relies on your object having a defined edge that the selection tool can identify. If it goes over the bounds of the image, you can simply paint in reverse mode or fine-tune the effect using the **Refine Edge** feature found in the tool's options panel.

Detail Smart Brush tool (*F*):

This is the big brother to the **Smart Brush** in that it relies on your painting and drawing skills as opposed to letting Elements just automatically select edges. Because of this, I find this tool hard to use. Again, a graphics tablet would make this tool much easier to use.

Clone Stamp tool (*S*):

I like the healing brushes because they blend the color and tone from the source into the target area. With this tool, what you select is exactly what is copied into the target area (although you can adjust the opacity of the sample). So, if you need to repair some lighter-colored pixels, it's important to find some equally light-colored *good* pixels to use as your source area, otherwise the transfer of pixels in the copy and paste operation will be visible. Use this tool, with the **Opacity** set to a very low number, to copy and paste good pixels over the bad pixels in very transparent layers. It takes considerably longer doing this, but it's also easier to cover your (retouching) tracks, and can give you a more professional-looking result.

Pattern Stamp tool (*S*):

This is similar to the **Clone Stamp**, but instead of copying and pasting pixels from the same or even a different image, this tool applies textures. I think it has limited application in photography, but I can see it being an asset for designers and web builders.

Blur tool (*R*):

As its name suggests, use this brush-based tool to add softness to critical areas of your images. This tool is very useful for blurring small areas, but works too slowly if you try and apply it to a large area with a big brush on a high-resolution image file. For big jobs, I'd use a selection and one of the blur filters.

Sharpen Brush (*R*):

This works in the opposite manner to the **Blur** brush in that you can literally paint in some sharpness to small areas of a picture. It's incredibly useful for fine-tuning portraits, for example, but it's easy to go too fast with this, which produces a jarring, pixelated look in the image. Use with care.

Smudge tool (*R*):

This effects brush allows you to push pixels around as if they were made of wet paint. It works well, but if the image file is of low resolution, manipulating the pixels makes the image appear defocused and blurry—the higher the resolution in the original file, the better the results.

Dodge tool (*O*):

This (along with the **Burn** and **Sponge** tools) is one of the *unsung heroes* of the image editing world because it allows you to make significant changes to parts of the image without the need for complex selections or masks. It's an adjustable brush-based tool that allows you to *paint* lightness into three distinct tonal ranges: the **highlights**, **midtones**, and **shadows**. How fast this effect materializes is controlled using the tool's **Exposure** slider.

Burn tool (*O*):

This adjustable brush works in the opposite direction to the **Dodge** tool. The **Burn** tool allows you to *paint in* darkness to three distinct tonal ranges: **highlights, midtones,** and **shadows**. How fast this happens is controlled, like the Dodge tool, by using the **Exposure** slider. These tools benefit by choosing a low-exposure setting. The slower the process goes, the less noticeable it is in the finished product.

Sponge tool (*O*):

This brush-based tool operates by increasing or decreasing the saturation (color intensity) over which the brush passes. You can increase the color, or decrease it, to the point where it turns black and white. Note that it will only have an effect if the original contains visible color information—it won't work, for example, if you try and increase the saturation of a sky that looks white because it has been overexposed.

Drawing tools

Brush tool (*B*):

Not surprisingly, this [paint] **Brush** tool works just like an artist's brush. Choose color from the Color Picker at the bottom of the toolbar and start painting. For the best results, use a graphics tablet.

Impressionist Brush tool (*B*):

As its name might suggest, this clever tool copies the pixels over which you brush and represents them, in one smooth action, in a blurred, impressionistic style, hence the name. You can choose from a range of impressionist brush stroke styles.

Colour Replacement tool (*B*):

This brush-based tool allows you to choose one specific color in the image, and by choosing a second color from the Color Picker, you can simply replace the color that was initially picked from the picture with the new color that's been chosen from the Tool bar. This is quite an effective tool.

Eraser tool (*E*):

As its name suggests, this tool is used to erase pixels from any image. It is especially useful for jobs such as cutting objects out of a background or blending images together from different layers.

Background Eraser tool (*E*):

This is another type of selection tool that works on the edge contrast in the image—you set the parameters with the brush **Size** and **Tolerance**. Set it up, and then click and drag just away from the object you want the background removed from and it removes the background pixels while hopefully leaving the subject. I write *hopefully* because I find this tool hard to control. You be the judge. You can work in Contiguous or Discontiguous modes. Much of its success relies on the type of image you are trying it out on.

Magic Eraser tool (*E*):

I suspect that this tool is based on the same pixel-grabbing design as the **Magic Wand** selection tool, except that, instead of selecting pixels, it removes pixels based on their color. You can adjust its efficiency using the **Tolerance** slider. I find this a lot easier to control over the **Background Eraser** tool.

Paint Bucket tool (*K*):

This feature has been in Photoshop Elements forever, and is used, as its name suggests, to slop *paint* (color) over the image. Like most of Photoshop Elements' tools, how far the paint spreads across the canvas (the image) can be controlled using the **Tolerance** slider, the **Contiguous** check box, and the tool's **Blend Mode**. And by changing its **Opacity** value, you effectively water the paint down. I use this tool quite a lot to *throw* a color wash over an image if I want to give it an old, faded, or different emotional feel. You can also use it in conjunction with an **Adjustment Layer**, or a mask, to darken, lighten, or color selected parts of an image file. It is a very handy, yet underutilized, feature.

Gradient tool (*G*):

This is used both as a photographic tool and for graphic design applications. Click and drag the gradient line through the image in any direction to apply it to the picture—in combination with the tool's **Blend Mode** and the **Opacity** slider. Photographers use this feature in the same way as they might a **graduated neutral density filter** that slides over the front of the lens, specifically for landscapes and for artists, to re-color images. It can be especially effective with black and white files. In my opinion, this is another underutilized Elements tool.

Eye Dropper (*I*):

This is a very useful, but nevertheless underrated, feature in Photoshop Elements. Use the eye dropper to sample the brightness levels in any part of your image, specifically to check the density of the shadows or highlights. This tool is especially useful if your screen is not calibrated because it can indicate possible tonal loss in very bright or dark regions of the file, irrespective of what you might actually see on screen.

Custom Shape tool (*U*):

This tool shares space with the **Rectangle** tool, the **Rounded Rectangle** tool, the **Elliptical** tool, the **Polygonal** tool, the **Star** tool, and the **Line** tool. All of these are **vector shapes** and can be applied to photographs, or used solo, as part of a design or illustration. Since they are vectors, they can be enlarged or reduced with no loss of quality. Use shapes as text boxes, design elements, or the Custom Shape Tool itself to apply features such as a copyright stamp to pictures. There are 560 (yes, I counted them all) different *shapes* to choose from under the submenus: **Animals, Arrows, Banners and Awards, Characters, Crop Shapes, Dress up, Faces, Flowers, Foliage and Trees, Food, Frames, Fruit, Music, Nature, Objects, Ornaments, Shapes, Signs, Symbols, Talk Bubbles**, and **Tiles**. Phew!

Horizontal Type tool (*T*):

Use this tool by clicking in the main window and typing in order to add text. Its features mirror those of a typical word processing application. Text is placed on its own special vector text layer, which can be edited independently of the image into which it has been placed. This is a very useful feature.

Pencil tool (*T*):

You use this in exactly the same way as you would a regular artist's HB pencil. It works best in conjunction with a **graphics tablet**, which will give you significantly more drawing accuracy than if you use a regular mouse.

Modify tools

Crop tool (*C*):

Click, hold, and drag inside an image to draw a **crop marquee**. Click **OK**, and all of the pixels outside of this marquee will be removed from the file. Use this to recompose a shot at the editing stage. The **Crop** tool can also be used to rotate an image, as well as crop it. It can also be used to add a **border** to an image first by dragging the Crop tool to the extremities of the image and then, in a second action, pulling the edges of the **Crop Marquee** off the image and onto the surrounding canvas area. When you click **OK**, that section between the edge of the image and the canvas becomes a color border. Choose a color from the **Color Picker** before you create the border.

Recompose tool (*W*):

A relatively new addition to Photoshop Elements, the **Recompose** tool uses the power of **Photomerge** (originally used to stitch panoramas together) to bring separate subjects closer together or further away—in the same frame. It's somewhat tricky to use, and, like many of the fully automated tools in Elements, it doesn't always produce good results simply because every picture is completely different to the previous one. It's worth a try, though.

Content-Aware Move tool (*Q*):

This is a select, copy, and paste tool. Draw a generous line around the subject (the **Source**) that's to be moved and drag the entire selection to a new location (the **Target**). Using Elements' content-aware AI, it analyzes the **Target** area and blends the copied pixels into the new background. In my experience, this doesn't work as convincingly as a manual copy, paste, and blend adjustment, but if the situation is right (if there are enough pixels in the source area), it does the job beautifully.

Straighten tool:

This tool is used to level all of those photographs that have uneven horizons. Click, hold the mouse, and drag the ensuing *line* across the real horizon in the shot, and when you release the mouse button, the image rotates to make the line you drew 100% on the level. Amazingly, this also works for vertical lines.

Color

Color Picker (*P*):

This feature, located at the base of the **Tool** bar, allows you to change the color of the Foreground and Background palettes. Pressing *D* on the keyboard resets the Color Picker to its default black foreground/white background state. Pressing the *X* key swaps black with white, foreground, and background. Use this feature to select a color whenever using any of Photoshop Elements brush tools, pencils, drawing tools, **Paint Bucket**, and anything else that requires coloring in. Note that, instead of clicking the small color square at the base of the **Tool** bar and then choosing a color from the **Color Picker** panel, you can move the cursor off the **Panel** and over the image to choose a tint from the image itself.

Quick Edit: Tool bar

This tool bar shares many common features that are also found in Expert Mode, including **Zoom**, **Hand**, **Quick Selection**, **Redeye**, **Straighten**, **Type**, **Spot Healing**, **Crop**, and **Move**. One that is unique to this tool rack is the curious **Whiten Teeth** tool.

Whiten Teeth (*F*):

This tool produces a *select and brighten* effect. If you click and drag across teeth, or anything else that might need a bit of brightening, it selects the area (based on edge contrast) while adding a brightness boost. This isn't a good substitute for regular visits to your dentist, however.

Adjustments

On the right-hand side of the **Quick** edit space, you'll find this handy tone fixing utility. It features the **Smart Fix**, **Exposure**, **Lighting**, **Color**, **Balance**, and **Sharpen** tools, all of which can be adjusted using a slider or by clicking on one of the nine tiny thumbnails under each sub-header. It's easy.

Tool Options panel(s):

Every tool in this application has its own **unique settings** that can be used to modify that specific tool's efficiency. If you find that the tool you are working with doesn't work as effectively as you had hoped it would, simply open the options panel at the bottom of the screen and adjust the settings to make it work more effectively.

Guided edit space

Guided offers 53 step-by-step editing processes—from a basic color fix, to far more sophisticated processes, such as **panorama stitching**, **tilt-shift**, and **watercolor** effects. It's a neat feature that works very well, plus it's a good place to look for image editing **inspiration**. This excellent edit space is subdivided into the following subsections:

Basics

Brightness and Contrast – fundamental editing for most digital photos.

Correct Skin Tone – fixes color casts and inconsistencies.

Crop Photo – trims bits off the image to improve composition.

Levels – an easy to use and powerful contrast and brightness adjustment feature – an essential tool.

Lighten and Darken – a simple feature, not as effective as Levels.

Object Removal – a very impressive new feature that automatically removes objects from a scene using Adobe AI and the Healing Brush tool. All you have to do is draw roughly around the offending item and it disappears as if by magic.

Resize your Photo – a quick way to resize any image.

Rotate and Straighten – a self-explanatory function.

Sharpen – a process to add clarity, especially if the image is to be printed.

Vignette Effect – adds a darker edge around the image, which, in turn, emphasizes the subject in the center of the frame.

Color

Enhance Color – uses the powerful Hue/Saturation feature to boost color. Essential.

Lomo Camera Effect – creates a cool soft focus, plus heavy vignette effect. A nice tool.

Remove a Color Cast – good for correcting weird colors.

Saturated Film Effect – a simple, one-click color booster. Easy to use, and effective.

Black and White

Black and White – simply converts a color shot to black and white.

B&W Color Pop – same as above, but it retains a single color, which you choose, as a special effect.

B&W Selection – same as above, but in this version, you select an area of color to retain (could be single or multiple colors).

High Key – a great, graphic result.

Line Drawing – as above, producing a very distinctive graphic effect.

Low Key – the opposite to high key; this is good for those dark, extra moody shots.

Fun Edits

Double Exposure – blend one picture into another for a neat, sixties look.

Effects Collage – a very simple but effective way to split an image into 'parts', like a dyptich (two panel) or triptych (three panels), each with a slightly different visual look applied to them. Easy to use and effective.

Meme Maker – an easy way to create a neat graphic for Instagram or Facebook.

Multi-Photo Text – the same as the Photo Text effect, except this one uses a different image for each letter of the effect.

Old Fashioned Photo – combines a graphic photo effect, with a sepia toning look as well as some texture overlays.

Out of Bounds – a three-dimensional effect that looks cool, but I find that it only works with selected subjects.

Painterly – adds rough brushstroke effects to any image. Especially good if you print the image onto watercolor or textured papers.

Partial Sketch – converts the image into a graphic, monochromatic line drawing, with some of the original color showing through the layer. Very illustrative.

Pattern Brush – a new feature that automatically selects the subject in the frame and adds a pattern to the background and then behind the subject. Effective.

Photo Text – fills text with any image for a bold, graphic look. Works best with bold or extra bold fonts.

Picture Stack – produces a nice 'stack o' prints' look to a collection of images.

Pop Art – Andy Warhol-type posterization effects.

Puzzle Effect – splits an image into a jigsaw look using a simple graphic overlay.

Reflection – this effect is designed to look as if the lower part of the frame is water or glass, into which the top part of the image is reflected. Does not work on all images...

Shape Overlay Effect – have fun using the Cookie Cutter tool. Use this to add a bit of scrapbooking design to your projects.

Speed Effect – adds a sense of movement using a Motion Blur filter.

Speed Pan – adds a blur to the left and right, simulating the look of a panned shot.

Zoom Burst Effect – makes it look like you zoomed into the subject with the lens at the time the shutter was pressed.

Special Edits

Depth of Field – selects part of a photo and makes it blurry to create the look of selective, wide-aperture focus effects.

Frame Creator – adds a graphic frame to any picture.

Orton Effect – adds a heavy soft focus effect to your image. Maybe looks a bit dated, but nice anyway.

Perfect Portrait – great for flattering any portrait sitter. Easy to apply and very useful.

Recompose – uses the Photomerge engine to push and recompose parts of an image using components from other snaps.

Replace Background – a semi-automated select and replace feature. If you don't have the right background, Elements provides a few samples.

Restore Old Photo – a bit of a powerhouse feature involving 11 different processes to make an old snap look like it was shot yesterday.

Scratches and Blemishes – uses the retouching Healing and Spot Healing Brush tools to refine and retouch any image to make it look professionally edited. An excellent feature.

Text and Border Overlay – adds a graphic border over your photo.

Tilt-Shift – produces over-the-top softness in parts of the image, which, in turn, gives that wonderful close-up look that makes a full size subject appear as if it's really a miniature figure.

Water Color Effect – a lovely overlay filter effect used for adding a bit of extra creativity to any shot. Good to use if you go on to print the created art on watercolor inkjet paper, or similar.

Photomerge

Photomerge Compose – use this tool to select and transfer a person or object from one picture to another. It's a simple process where you (roughly) draw a line around the subject and the software automatically copies, pastes, and blends the object from one picture to another.

Photomerge Exposure – Elements' nearest equivalent to a high dynamic range effect (HDR). Combine multiple exposures of the same shot to produce an image that contains a wider tonal value than is possible with a single snap.

Photomerge Faces – use in the same way as the Compose feature. Select one face from a picture and paste it on top of another face in a different shot. Good for group shots where not everyone is smiling in every scene, for example. The trick, however, is that you must remember to take multiple versions of your groups so that you can find suitable 'replacements'.

Photomerge Group Shot – same as above, but designed for groups of people.

Photomerge Scene Cleaner – shoot multiple frames at a busy scene (preferably without moving the camera) and then remove some of the people by copying and pasting selected empty spaces over the busier parts of the scene. Sounds complex, but it is easy to do and works remarkably well.

Photomerge Panorama – works brilliantly by lining multiple snaps of a scene up to produce a seamless panorama. Sections of the panorama must be shot with a good 20% overlap, with the same exposure and focus point to get the best results (Photomerge only works if you remember to shoot multiple frames in the field!).

Quick and Expert Edit – drop-down menus (top of the screen)

File menu

Use this important menu to do the following:

- Create new, **blank documents**.
- **Open** existing files.
- Force-open **non-RAW** files in the **Camera RAW** utility (*Alt/Opt + Ctrl/Cmd + O*).
- Find **recently edited files**.
- **Duplicate** an (open) image.
- Close a single picture, or groups of pictures, with one action (*Ctrl/Cmd + W*).
- **Save** your progress (important: *Ctrl/Cmd + S*).
- Save your progress and rename/relocate the file (**File | Save As** or *Ctrl/Cmd + Shift + S*).
- Save a file specifically optimized for display on the web (*Alt/Opt + Shift + Ctrl/Cmd + S*).
- Access file information (**File Info** = metadata).

- Place images inside other images.
- Organize already opened files.
- Process multiple files in bulk (this is a great productivity feature).
- Have access to various print functions.

Edit menu

This is quite an important menu because it gives you multiple undo/redo commands. In fact, Photoshop Elements allows you to go backward as much as required. Also, try using the *Ctrl*/*Cmd* + *Z* (undo) and *Ctrl*/*Cmd* + *Y* (redo) commands.

Use this menu to copy and paste data into an image or to do any of the following:

- Revert to its original state (that is, undo ALL changes; *Shift* + *Ctrl*/*Cmd* + *A*)
- Copy (*Ctrl*/*Cmd* + *C*).
- Copy merged layers (*Shift* + *Ctrl*/*Cmd* + *C*).
- Cut (*Ctrl*/*Cmd* + *X*).
- Paste (*Ctrl*/*Cmd* + *V*) selected data.
- Paste clipboard content into a selection (*Shift* + *Ctrl*/*Cmd* + *V*).
- Delete the content of a selection.
- Fill a selection.
- Apply a stroke (line) to a selection.
- **Define** brushes or patterns in the library.
- Clear the contents of the **History, Clipboard** content, or both (good to use if your computer has limited RAM or a full hard drive).
- Adjust the (global) **Color settings** (*Shift* + *Ctrl*/*Cmd* + *K*).
- Edit your brush presets in the **Preset Manager** (advanced).
- Access the program's **Preferences** (concerning grids, guides, plugins, allocation of RAM, and more).

Image menu

In this menu, you'll find all of the functions that apply directly to the image. This includes the following:

- **Rotating** (the image, the image layer, flipping the image vertically and/or horizontally).

- **Transforming**: *Ctrl/Cmd + T* changes the size, proportion, or perspective of any object on a layer—this is a valuable function that you'll use a lot.

- **Cropping** accesses the **Crop** tool (*C*).

- **Recomposing** accesses the Recompose tool (*W*).

- **Resizing**: Use **Image Size** to change the number of pixels in a file (*Alt/Opt + Ctrl/Cmd + I*), and use **Canvas Size** (*Alt/Opt + Ctrl/Cmd + C*) to add pixels to the image canvas (the border around the image).

- **Mode**: Use this function to set/change the image mode (that is, Grayscale, RGB, Indexed color, and Bitmap).

- A feature to **Convert Color Profile** (advanced).

Enhance menu

In this powerhouse menu, you'll find all of the features and tools you need to improve the tones and clarity in your creations:

- **Auto Smart Fix** (*Alt/Opt + Ctrl/Cmd + M*)

- **Auto Smart Tone** (*Alt/Opt + Ctrl/Cmd + T*)

- **Auto Levels** (*Shift + Ctrl/Cmd + L*)

- **Auto Contrast** (*Alt/Opt + Shift + Ctrl/Cmd + L*)

- **Auto Haze Removal** (*Alt/Opt +Ctrl/Cmd + A*)

- **Auto Color Correction** (*Shift + Ctrl/Cmd + B*)

- **Auto Shake Reduction**

- **Auto Sharpen**

- **Auto Red Eye Fix** (*Ctrl/Cmd + R*)

- **Adjust Color**: Includes **Remove Color Cast, Hue/Saturation** (very useful – *Ctrl/Cmd + U*), **Remove Color** (*Shift + Ctrl/Cmd + U*), **Replace Color, Adjust Color Curves, Adjust Color** for **Skin Tone,** and **Defringe Layer**

- **Adjust Lighting**: Includes **Shadow Highlight, Brightness**, and **Contrast**, and the very useful **Levels** (*Ctrl/Cmd + L*)

- **Adjust Smart Fix** (*Shift + Ctrl/Cmd + M*)

- **Convert to Black and White** (*Alt/Opt + Ctrl/Cmd + B*)

- **Colorize Photo** (*uses Adobe AI to select and colorize parts of a black and white or color image. Excellent new feature with an auto and a manual override feature*)

- **Haze Removal** (*Alt/Opt + Ctrl/Cmd + Z*)

- **Adjust Sharpness**

- **Smooth Skin** (*uses Adobe AI to isolate the facial features before adding a soft smoothness. This is mostly hands-free, producing a satisfying result in portraits.*)

- **Open Closed Eyes** (*both this and the next feature rely on automated facial recognition (Adobe AI). Fun to use and both produce effective results.*)

- **Adjust Facial Features**

- **Shake Reduction** (*a feature used to add contrast and the appearance of sharpness back into a shaky file. Works OK.*)

- **Unsharp Mask**

Layer menu

Not surprisingly, everything pertaining to the use and the modification of **Layers** is found under this menu:

- Create a **New Layer** (*Shift + Ctrl/Cmd + N*) or a new layer via a Copy (*Ctrl/Cmd + J*).

- **Duplicate** an existing (selected) layer.

- **Delete** a (selected) layer.

- Rename a layer.

- Apply a **Layer Style** (for instance, drop shadow, bevel, stroke, and glow).

- Add a new Fill Layer (with a solid color or gradient).

- Add an **Adjustment Layer**.

- Create a **Layer Mask** (advanced).

- Create a **Clipping Mask** (*Alt/Opt + Ctrl/Cmd + G*—advanced).

- Make a **Layer Group** (advanced).

- **Hide** layers (*Ctrl/Cmd* + ,).
- **Merge** (layers) down (*Ctrl/Cmd* + E).
- **Merge Visible** (*Shift* + *Ctrl/Cmd* + E).
- **Flatten** all layers in a file.

Select menu

As its name suggests, this menu is everything to do with **Selections**. Use its features to do the following:

- Select an entire object (*Ctrl/Cmd* + A).
- **Deselect** the current selection (that is, turn it off – *Ctrl/Cmd* + D).
- **Re-select** that selection (*Shift* + *Ctrl/Cmd* + D).
- **Invert** the current selection (that is, **Select | Inverse** or *Shift* + *Ctrl/Cmd* + I).
- **Select** all of the layers in the document.
- **Deselect** all of the layers in the document.
- **Feather** a selection (an important feature that's used to soften the hard edge of a new selection).
- **Refine Edge** calls up Elements' handy selection edge modification utility.
- **Subject** (*Alt/Opt* + *Ctrl/Cmd* + S). An impressive new feature that uses AI to find and select the subject of the image. If the subject is clear, it works well.
- **Modify** opens up a range of selection modification features, including Border, Smooth, Expand, and Contract. Vital for perfecting the accuracy of a selection.
- **Grow** is a selection modifier (makes the selection larger by a set pixel amount).
- **Similar** is a selection modifier.
- **Transform Selection** is a handy tool for adjusting the size and shape of an existing selection.
- **Load Selection** allows you to import or load an already-saved selection.
- **Save Selection** allows you to preserve your selection work (in TIFF or PSD file formats only).
- **Delete** is a selection modifier.

Filter menu

There are too many filter tools to mention here.

Under the **Filter** menu, you'll find a huge range of filter **special effects**, some of which are designed to lend an artistic look to your work. I use filters for jobs such as blurring pixels (depth-of-field effects) and some for distorting, sketching, stylizing, adding texture, and even for adding more digital noise. All filter effects can be used globally or simply applied to a smaller part of the image once they're confined inside a **selection**.

View menu

The tools that are found inside the **View** menu are used principally to line up, arrange, enlarge, or reduce the image size that you're currently viewing. Note that none of these overlay *helpers*, such as **Grid**, **Ruler**, or **Guides**, which show once the images are printed or uploaded to the internet. They are merely there in order to assist your page layout and design:

- **Zoom In** (*Ctrl/Cmd + =*)
- **Zoom Out** (*Ctrl/Cmd + -*)
- **Fit on Screen** (*Ctrl/Cmd + 0*)
- **Actual Pixels** (*Ctrl/Cmd + 1*)
- **Print Size**
- **Selection** (*Ctrl/Cmd + H*—very handy when you're working with selections, but don't forget to turn it back on – *Ctrl/Cmd + H* again)
- **Rulers** (*Shift + Ctrl/Cmd + R*)
- **Grid** (*Ctrl/Cmd + '*)
- **Guides** (*Ctrl/Cmd + ;*)
- **Snap To** (makes the grid and guides *magnetic*, making it easier to align multiple objects quickly and accurately)
- **Lock Guides** (*Alt/Opt + Ctrl/Cmd + ;*)
- **Clear Guides** (removes all guides)
- **New Guide**

Window menu

In this drop-down menu, you'll find references to all of the panels inside Photoshop Elements. This includes the following:

- **Actions**: A rather limited feature in Elements in my opinion.

- **Adjustments**: Very useful in Quick Edit.

- **Colour Swatches**: Useful for setting, saving, and reusing text and painting colors.

- **Effects**: Excellent bunch of preset effects—inspirational (*F2*).

- **Favourites**: Drag often-used features here so that they can be found again quickly.

- **Filters**: Too many to mention here—hundreds of filters and creative possibilities (*F3*)

- **Graphics** (*F7*).

- **Histogram**.

- **History**.

- **Info**: Used to measure the brightness of pixels, irrespective of screen calibration (*F8*).

- **Layers**: Important for all multi-image and text-based image projects.

- **Navigator**: When working on a highly zoomed-in image, use Navigator to keep an eye on exactly where it is in the image that you are looking/working.

- **Styles** (*F6*).

- **Panel Bin:** All open images are visible in this pop-up bin area.

- **Reset Panels** (use this if your desktop is awash with panels and you need a fresh start).

If the name of the panel has a check mark next to it, it's open somewhere on the desktop. If there is no check mark, it's closed.

Help menu

The **Help menu** provides a shortcut to the online Adobe help manuals, as well as subjects such as the following:

- Tips for getting started

- Key concepts

- Support

- Video tutorials online

- The Adobe forum
- Updates
- A direct link to your account settings

Panels overview

Layers panel:

This is possibly the most important panel in this program, especially if you're working with multi-image files or images with text (because different image elements can be placed on separate layers). In some of the more complex operations offered by Photoshop Elements, this panel is hidden unless you specifically search out its advanced mode. (It's hidden because, since that process might involve a very complex list of functions, having everything visible might be a recipe for disaster. Deleting, moving, or renaming any one of those layers might prevent the (prerecorded) action from being completed).

Effects panel:

As its name might suggest, this panel is all about choosing a special effect to apply either to a pixel-based **image** or to a vector-based **text layer**. From the drop-down menu inside this panel, you can choose to view everything (**Show all**) or choose one of the sub-headers, which includes **Faded Photo, Glow, Monotone Colour, Painting, Panels, Seasons, Textures,** and **Vintage**.

Filters panel:

Like the Effects panel, this panel offers a wide range of special effects that can be applied in a range of ways to your image files. Like the Effects Panel, these filter effects, of which there are more than 300, are subdivided by a drop-down menu inside the main panel. Subheadings include **Artistic, Blur, Brushstrokes, Distort, Noise, Pixelated, Render, Sketch, Styles,** and **Other**. Another way to access these filters is to use the excellent **Filter Gallery**, which is located under the filter drop-down menu at the top of the screen.

Styles panel:

Like the previous two panels, **Styles** incorporates a number of special effects, most of which are legacy items from the early days of Photoshop Elements. This is the panel where you'll find **Drop Shadows, Bevels, Image Effects,** and **Photographic Effects**. Other subheadings include **Complex, Glass Buttons, Inner Glows, Inner Shadows, Outer Glows, Patterns, Strokes, Visibility, Wow Chrome, Wow Neon,** and **Wow Plastic**. Some of these can be applied directly to images, while others work especially well on text layers. They can also be used to create graphic effects if you're designing web pages or creating vector art.

Graphics panel:

This panel perhaps has more than all of the other panels put together (with more than 1,500 downloadable assets). To give you an idea, you can use the **By Type** drop-down menu at the top of the panel to display the numerous options a little more clearly. **By Type** includes **Activity**, **Color**, **Event**, **Mood**, **Object**, **Seasons**, **Style**, and **by Word**.

The right-hand drop-down menu features headers that read **Backgrounds**, **Friends**, **Graphics**, **Shapes**, and **Text**. Note that these need to be **downloaded first** before you can incorporate them into a project. They are vector clip art files, so they are very small and are ready for use almost immediately.

Actions panel:

An **Action** is a pre-recorded set of instructions for a specific editing process, such as a resolution change, brightness adjustment, or file format change.

Actions are created (recorded) using Adobe **Photoshop CC** and can be replayed on a single image or in bulk. Since many of these **Actions** are recorded using functions that are not present in Photoshop Elements, you'll find that, if you download and import new **Actions** (from the internet), it's more than likely they'll not function correctly. Adobe has included the same pre-recorded **Actions** as a *starter pack* in Elements for years—which would suggest to me that they are no longer worth pursuing—because most of the Photoshop CC-recorded actions will not work in Elements. That being said, Elements does have an outstanding feature for bulk processing called **Process Multiple Files**, which we will look at in *Chapter 9, Exporting the Finished Work*.

Color swatches:

Adobe supplies Elements with a range of **color swatches**, which can be treated like a student paint box. Each swatch has a range of different colors. You can choose from **Photo Filter Colors**, **Web Hues**, **Web-Safe Colors**, **Web Spectrum**, **Windows**, or the **Mac OS**. Alternatively, you can create and save your own **custom swatches** for specific jobs.

More tabs

Histogram panel:

The **Histogram**, that curious *mountain range* depicting where in the image the tones sit in relation to absolute black and absolute white, is a very handy tool. At a glance, you can tell whether the image is overexposed or underexposed.

History panel:

This panel contains a list of all of the steps and mouse clicks that are made while editing a single image. Everything is recorded in a linear fashion, so it's entirely possible to go back in time to a previous edit state in order to rework a specific part of the edit process. It doesn't allow you to combine different states—once a state has been deleted, everything later than that is also lost.

Favorites panel:

Use this Panel to store frequently used clip art, filters, effects, and text simply by dragging the effect thumbnail into this panel. This is a huge time-saver because all of your favorite and most often-used features can be stored here for fast access.

Navigator panel:

This small panel displays a large thumbnail of the image that's displayed in the main screen. If this is enlarged beyond the bounds of the screen, it clearly displays the proportion of the enlarged image that's currently visible as a bright red rectangle. Click in this shape to shift your view of the enlarged image. This is useful when you're editing highly enlarged images because it allows you to navigate around the image far faster than if using the regular scroll bars.

Info panel:

Use this panel to measure the brightness or darkness of any part of the image that's displayed on the main screen. It doesn't matter what tool you happen to be using at the time—mouse over the area of concern and the **Info Panel** will give you an RGB (brightness) readout. If you have just edited the picture and then read the **Info** panel, it cleverly displays both the before and after RGB readout values together. This is a very useful tool, especially for all of those photographers whose monitor is not 100% calibrated.

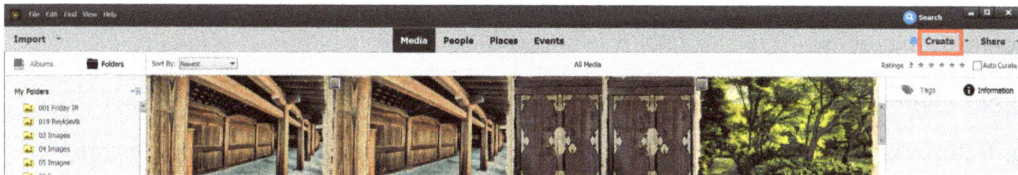

Create Menu (Organizer and Editor)

Slideshow:

This is one of the easiest ways to create a slideshow (.MP4 movie format) and probably the fastest. Because it's so quick, you get very little input and a few style choices and that's it. Previous versions of Elements enjoyed quite a sophisticated and feature-rich slide-making utility. This new version has been dumbed-down—it's fast and easy, but if you want greater control, you'll have to turn to a third-party application such as Pro Show Gold.

Photo Collage:

This is an amazing feature that takes a bunch of images and assembles them into a nicely designed collage. To achieve this the traditional way, that is, using layers and masks, would take a long time. This feature takes a few seconds. Brilliant.

Photo Prints:

This is a feature that links your Elements output to a local printer. Options include Local printer (single prints), Picture Package (a set of differently sized pictures all up on one sheet of paper), or Contact Sheet (multiple images arranged in a grid across the page—good for reference).

Photo Book:

This feature allows you to add multiple images into a preset page layout—you choose the number of pages and the design, which is then downloaded from the Adobe servers. Populating the pages is as simple as drag and drop.

Greeting Card:

A rather dated-looking set of preset card designs mark this feature as one that hasn't been upgraded for many years. That being said, it is easy to use and produces reasonably good results. With a little experience, anyone could produce a far better, more personal design by doing it manually.

Photo Calendar:

This feature runs in a similar fashion to the Greetings Card utility—choose a style and design, download it from the Adobe servers, and drag and drop your images from the Photo Bin into the monthly pages. To finish, print this on a local printer and get it bound at the local office services outlet. Many other companies, most notably, digital photo-making businesses, produce far superior products.

Instant Movie:

This is only applicable if you also own Adobe Premiere Elements (video). I thought this was one more of those *big claims with mediocre results* type products. How wrong I was. If you shoot video but don't know how to edit your clips, or don't have the time, this feature is truly amazing. Add the clips and let it make an instant video. It works well.

Video Story:

A slightly more serious and complicated video editing feature (compared with the Instant Video feature), this was designed, as its name suggests, to tell a story, thereby incorporating text and graphics with your video clips. Again, this is a brilliant, entry-level video widget.

Video Collage:

This is another beautifully designed utility that allows you to make a split-screen, multi-clip video with virtually no prior experience of editing clips. A great design that works well.

DVD with Menu, **CD Jacket**, **DVD Jacket**, and **CD/DVD Label**:

These four projects are somewhat dated—they have been present in Elements for several versions—and I suspect they are no longer used that often.

The fad of creating your own DVD labels has long since faded into the downloadable distance. Like many of Elements' project-based features, these processes were very easy to use with a drag and drop design, but with limited designs. I used to make all of my DVD labels and CD jackets—it was great fun but quite labor-intensive.

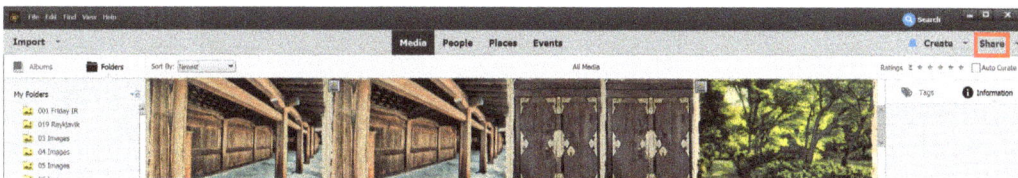

Share Menu (Organizer and Editor)

Email:

Link your email account with this utility to attach images easily and efficiently.

Twitter:

Sign up, and then upload your images directly to the Twitterscape.

Flickr:

Sign up, and then load images directly into your Flickr Photostream.

Vimeo and **YouTube**:

Both of these features are only relevant for video—linking your Vimeo and YouTube accounts to provide a direct link between the two features makes posting so much simpler.

Burn Video DVD:

This is like the previous point; this is a simple method for getting your data onto DVD media (requires Premiere Elements to function).

PDF Slideshow:

Here, you can add multiple images in the PDF slideshow window. Then, the software binds it all together into a universally readable PDF file that can then be distributed via email, a blog, website, disk, or USB media.

Other Books You May Enjoy

If you enjoyed this book, you may be interested in these other books by Packt:

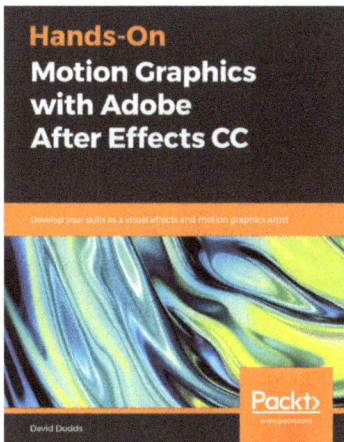

Hands-On Motion Graphics with Adobe After Effects CC
David Dodds
ISBN: 978-1-78934-515-5

- Create a lower third project for a TV show with complex layers
- Work with shape layer animation to create an animated lyrics video
- Explore different tools to animate characters
- Apply text animation to create a dynamic film-opening title
- Use professional visual effects to create a VFX project
- Model, light, and composite your 3D project in After Effects

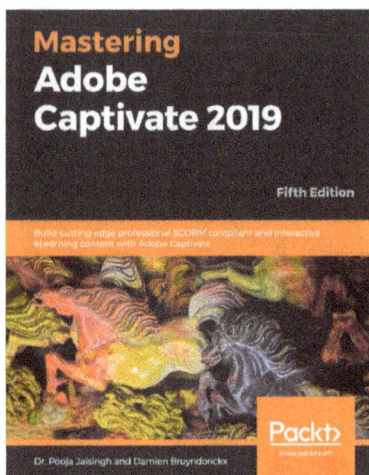

Mastering Adobe Captivate 2019 - Fifth Edition

Dr. Pooja Jaisingh, Damien Bruyndonckx

ISBN: 978-1-78980-305-1

- Learn how to use the objects in Adobe Captivate to build professional eLearning content

- Enhance your projects by adding interactivity, animations, drag and drop interactions, and more

- Add multimedia elements, such as audio and video, to create engaging, state-of-the-art learning experiences

- Use themes to craft a unique visual experience that reinforces the learning process

- Use question slides to create SCORM-compliant quizzes that integrate seamlessly with your favourite LMS

- Make your content fit any device thanks to the responsive features of Adobe Captivate

- Create stunning immersive 360° experiences with the all new Virtual Reality projects of Adobe Captivate 2019

- Integrate Captivate with other applications (such as PowerPoint and Photoshop) to establish a professional eLearning production workflow

- Publish your project in a wide variety of formats including HTML5 and Flash

Leave a review - let other readers know what you think

Please share your thoughts on this book with others by leaving a review on the site that you bought it from. If you purchased the book from Amazon, please leave us an honest review on this book's Amazon page. This is vital so that other potential readers can see and use your unbiased opinion to make purchasing decisions, we can understand what our customers think about our products, and our authors can see your feedback on the title that they have worked with Packt to create. It will only take a few minutes of your time, but is valuable to other potential customers, our authors, and Packt. Thank you!

Index

A

active layer 225, 257
adjustment layer
  about 241-243
  considerations 245
  masking 243-245
Adjust Sharpness tool
  using 429, 430
Adobe InDesign 360
Adobe Photoshop Elements 2020
  Home screen 4, 5
  new features 2, 3
Adobe RGB (1998) 28
Adobe vectors
  about 390-392
  custom vector illustrations,
    creating 393-398
advanced panorama techniques 199, 200
AI-driven creativity 187-192
Alignment tool 472
Apple Mac 136
artificial intelligence (AI) 294
artistic effects
  adding 181-183

autocorrection tools
  using 104, 105
  with Expert edit mode 105, 106
Auto Selection tool 328

B

Background Eraser tool 277
background layer 242
Basic tab 77
beauty shot
  Clone Stamp tool, using 288
  customizing 288
  retouching, example 290-294
black and white conversion
    techniques 120
black shadow layer 373
blending modes 234-239
Blend Mode 175
blogging 404
blurred images
  fixing 466-468
BookWright software 457
brush behavior 366-369
brusheezy
  URL 379

brushes
   download link 303
   importing 378-384
   using 366-384
   working with 378
brush modes
   Block 277
   Brush 277
   Pencil 277
Brush Options panel 364
brush tool
   types 335
Burn brush tool 302
burning in technique 299
Burn tool
   about 299
   using 299-305

C

calibration 136
Camera RAW toolbar features
   about 86
   Crop 87
   Hand 86
   Preferences 87
   Red Eye 87
   Rotate Image (L) 87
   Rotate Image (R) 87
   Straighten 87
   White Balance 87
   Zoom 86
catalog
   about 7, 8
   managing 61, 62
   reinstating 455, 456
Catalog Manager 8, 61
Central Processing Unit (CPU) 34

clipping process 464
Clone Stamp tool
   disadvantages 289
   using 288, 289
cloning 297
cloud brushes 379
coffee stains 385
color
   adjusting, with Hue/Saturation 113-118
Colorize Photo 187
color management
   options 65, 66
Color noise 84
Color Replacement tool 377
color spaces 28
Content Aware mode 157
Content-Aware Move tool 473-475
contrast
   about 107
   adjusting, with Levels 107-113
Cookie Cutter tool 342, 343
copy-and-paste tool 288
copyright stamps 230
copyright symbol
   adding 447
Create menu 16, 17
Create Menu (Organizer and Editor)
   CD/DVD Label 509
   CD Jacket 509
   DVD Jacket 509
   DVD with Menu 509
   Greeting Card 508
   Instant Movie 509
   Photo Book 508
   Photo Calendar 508
   Photo Collage 508
   Photo Prints 508
   Slideshow 508

Video Collage 509
Video Story 509
Create Texture mode 157
creative edit workflow
    about 134
cropping feature 92
Crop tool
    about 93
    working 93, 94, 95
custom Facebook page
    creating 216-218
custom fonts 355, 356
custom greeting card
    creating 213-215
    creating, with vector clip art 390-393
custom photo calendars
    creating 209-212
Custom Shape tool
    about 341
    Cookie Cutter tool 342
    Paint Bucket tool 344
custom vector illustrations
    creating 393-398

D

dates
    adjusting, for different time zones 454
Detail tab
    about 81
    noise reduction 84, 85
    sharpening tools 82-84
digital illustration 161
digital negative file 30
digital noise 84
distort 264
dithering process 90, 229

Dodge tool
    about 299, 366
    using 300-305
dots per inch (dpi) 89, 347
drawing techniques 360
Drawing tools, Expert edit mode
    Background Eraser tool (E) 491
    Brush tool (B) 490
    Color Replacement tool (B) 490
    Custom Shape tool (U) 492
    Eraser tool (E) 491
    Eye Dropper (I) 492
    Horizontal Type tool (T) 492
    Impressionist Brush tool (B) 490
    Magic Eraser tool (E) 491
    Paint Bucket tool (K) 491
    Pencil tool (T) 492
drop shadows 231

E

editing workflow 71
edit modes
    about 9
    Expert edit mode 13-15
    Guided edit mode 11, 12
    Quick edit mode 9, 10
effects filters 399, 400
Elements Organizer
    media, importing into 39-42
    photos, importing into 39-42
eLive screen 4, 484
Elliptical Marquee Selection tool 369
Elliptical Shape tool 369
Enhance tools, Expert edit mode
    Blur tool (R) 489
    Burn tool (O) 490

Clone Stamp tool (S) 489
Detail Smart Brush tool (F) 489
Dodge tool (O) 490
Healing Brush tool (J) 488
Pattern Stamp tool (S) 489
Red Eye Removal tool (Y) 488
Sharpen Brush (R) 489
Smart Brush tool (F) 488
Smudge tool (R) 489
Sponge tool (O) 490
Spot Healing Brush tool (J) 488
Eraser Brush tool 277
Eraser tool 472
Events category 54-56
Expert edit mode 13-15
Expert edit mode, Organizer
  about 486
  Color 493
  Drawing tools 490
  Enhance tools 488
  Modify tools 492
  Select tools 486
  View tools 486
Export as New Files tool
  Process Multiple Files feature 441
  using 439, 440
exposure 221
eye icon 167
Eye tool 11

F

Facebook
  about 405, 406
  automatic compression algorithms 405
Face Replace feature 468-472
Face Swap function 469-471

facial expressions
  modifying 126, 127
file formats
  characteristics 30-32
  JPEG 29
  RAW 29, 30
file formats, for saving edited RAW files
  JPEG 87
  PNG 87
  PSD 87
  TIFF 87
files
  saving 101, 102
files, editing
  best practices 71
Find menu
  using 452, 454
Flatten Image command 240
Flickr 407, 408
flyers 252-258
fonts
  reference link 173
font style 231

G

gamut warning 79
Gaussian Blur filter 246
global tone-changing tools 272
Google Blogger 404
Gradient tool 280
graphic elements
  Regular Shape tool, using 341
  text, adding 340
  working with 338, 339
graphics monitor 363
Graphics panel 360

graphics tablet
  about 169, 363, 492
  using 310-365
Grid View mode 43
gross overexposure 460
Guided edit mode 11, 12, 184

H

Hand tool 11
Haze Removal tool
  about 435
  using 435-439
Healing Brush tool 11
Help menu
  using 478, 479
high-impact black and white images
  creating 118, 119
High Pass sharpening technique
  using 432-434
Histogram feature 78
Home Page 178, 180
horizons
  straightening 95, 96
Horizontal Type tool 170
Hue/Saturation
  used, for adjusting color 113-118
Hue,Saturation, Brightness (HSB) 24

I

illustration 360
image
  editing, workflow 134
image makeover
  examples 135-175
impressionist brush 375

Instagram 406
Instant Fix feature 100

J

jigsaw panorama
  creating 200
Joint Photographic Experts
      Group (JPEG) 319-321
JPEG file format
  about 29, 30
  options 103

K

keyboard shortcuts 218, 219, 284, 285, 400
keyword tags 49-52

L

large objects
  removing 330-334
  selection results, improving 334
Lasso tools
  about 310-314
  Freehand Lasso tool 311
  Magnetic Lasso tool 311
  Polygonal Lasso tool 311
layer masks 363
layer opacity 240
Layer panel
  about 232, 240
  features 232, 233
layers
  about 223-231
  merging 240
leading design feature 350

legacy items 399
Levels
   used, for adjusting contrast 107-113
light blue 274
lightning brushes 386-389
lines per inch (lpi) 89
Lithograph effect 182
lost or disconnected files
   finding 450-452
Luminance noise 84

M

Magic Eraser tool 277
Magic Wand tool 310-320, 383
mask 241
masking feature 82
Mask mode 383
media
   backing up 38, 58-61
   importing, into Elements
      Organizer 39-42
   reviewing 43, 44
Merge Down 240
Merge Visible 240
metadata
   using 47, 48
Modify tools, Expert edit mode
   Content Aware Move tool (Q) 493
   Crop tool (C) 492
   Recompose tool (W) 493
   Straighten tool 493
Move tool 11
multi-image poster
   creating 252-259
Myriad Pro
   using 349

N

noise reduction 75, 76

O

Object Removal 13
opacity 240
Opacity slider 277
Open Closed Eyes tool 128, 129
optical distortion 259
Organizer
   about 6, 7, 17
   adjustments 494
   basics 494
   Black and White tools 495
   Color tools 495
   Expert edit mode 486
   Fun Edits tools 496
   guided edit space 494
   instant photo fixing 100
   keyboard shortcuts 67
   Photomerge tools 497, 498
   Quick Edit 494
   Special Edits tools 497
   Tool Options panel(s) 494
   using 484
   view spaces 485
overexposure 464-466

P

padlock icon 225
Paint Bucket tool
   using 344, 345
painting techniques 360
Panel Bin
   working with 19, 20

panels
  Actions 22, 506
  Adjustments 21
  Color Swatches 23, 506
  Effects 21, 505
  Favorites 23, 507
  Filter 21, 505
  Frames 21
  Graphics 21, 506
  Histogram 23, 506
  History 23, 507
  Info 24, 507
  Layers 21, 505
  Navigator 24, 507
  Styles 21, 505
  Textures 21
  working with 19
panorama
  setup requisites 195-198
panorama stitching
  tips 198
Paper Cuts 394
paper record 356
Pattern Brush 12
Pattern Stamp tool 12
Pencil tool 204
pen stylus 310, 335, 363
People mode 56-58
perspective
  correcting, with transformations 259-263
perspective correction lens 260
perspective, transformation modes
  about 263
  free rotate layer 263
  skew 263
photo-editing computer
  setting up 33-37

photo, for editing
  opening, ways 72
Photomerge 493
Photomerge Scene Cleaner
  using 201-205
photos
  importing, into Elements
    Organizer 39-42
  organizing 45
  star-rating 46
Photoshop files 30
Photoshop LE 1
Photoshop PDF files 31
picture resolution 89-92
pictures
  combining 252-258
pixels
  adding, to images 456
pixels per inch (ppi) 89
Places feature 53
plugins
  installing 64
  working with 63, 64
Portable Network Graphics (PNG) files
  about 31
  options 103
  point sizes 231
posters 252-259
Premiere Elements
  working with 17, 18
preset 136-139
print resolution
  about 409
  local printing 410-416
  page setup 417, 418
Process Multiple Files feature
  working 441-447

profile browser 80
ProPhoto RGB 28
pseudo layer masks 245-251

Q

Quick and Expert Edit
  Edit menu 499
  Enhance menu 500, 501
  File menu 498, 499
  Filter menu 503
  Help menu 504
  Image menu 500
  Layer menu 501, 502
  Select menu 502
  View menu 503
  Window menu 504
Quick edit mode 9, 10
Quick Edit, Organizer
  Whiten Teeth (F) 494
Quick Selection tool 11, 326

R

Random Access Memory (RAM) 34
RAW files
  about 30
  editing 73
  overview 74-76
RAW processing tools 77
Recompose tool 475-478
Refine Edge function 329
Refine Selection Brush tool 327
Regular Shape tool 341
repetitive strain injury (RSI) 357
resampling 97, 98, 458
resampling software 409

resolution
  about 404
  working 404
resolution problems
  solving, by adding pixels 456-459
  solving, by resampling 456-459
retouching tools 134
RGB application 146

S

saturation 272
Save for Web feature 404-423
Save Image command 88
Scale transform 372
Scene Cleaner 201
screen calibration 66
selection
  about 306
  feathering 323, 324
  saving 322, 323
Selection Brush tool 325
selection tools
  about 306
  Auto Selection tool 328
  Lasso tool 310
  Magic Wand tool 314
  Object Removal feature 306, 307
  Quick Selection tool 326
  Refine Edge function 329
  Refine Selection Brush tool 327
  Selection Brush tool 325
  used, for selecting subject 308-310
  using 289
Select tools, Expert edit mode
  Elliptical Selection tool (M) 487
  Lasso tool (L) 487

Magic Wand tool (A) 487
Magnetic Lasso tool (L) 487
Move tool (V) 486
Polygonal Lasso tool (L) 487
Rectilinear Marquee tool (M) 486
sensor spots 143
sensor swabs 292
shadow 372
Shake Reduction tool
    using 431
Share menu 16, 17
Share Menu (Organizer and Editor)
    Burn Video DVD 510
    Email 510
    Flickr 510
    PDF Slideshow 510
    Twitter 510
    Vimeo 510
    YouTube 510
sharpen filters
    using 434, 435
sharpening process
    about 75, 76, 423
    Adjust Sharpness tool, using 429, 430
    High Pass sharpening technique,
        using 432-434
    Shake Reduction tool, using 431
    sharpen filters, using 434, 435
    Unsharp Mask tool, using 424-428
Simplify Layer process 256
skewed perspective, correcting
    about 264-270
    erasing tools, using 277-279
    Gradient tool, using 280-284
    layer masking 272-276
    working tips 271
skin smoothing 122

skin tone color
    perfecting 120, 121
slideshow
    creating 205-208
Smart Object 256
Smart Tags 5, 18
Snap To feature 362
soft-edged brush 149
solid state drives (SSDs) 37
SoulMission font 230
special effects filters 399
sphere
    drawing, from scratch 370-374
Sponge brush tool 301
Sponge tool
    about 299-302
    using 300-305
Spot Healing Brush
    about 123
    combining, with Clone
        Stamp tools 295-298
    using 150
    working 124, 125
sRGB color space 28
sticky tape 385
Straighten tool 11, 95, 96
styles 351
Subject Selection feature 25

T

Tablet Menu 364
Tagged Image File Format (TIFF) 322
text, adding to images
    about 346-352
    Brush tools, using 335, 336
    custom fonts 355

Pencil tool, using 337
    text styles and special effects 353, 354
    Type options panel, using 352
text boxes 230
TIFF file format
    about 31
    options 103
tilt-shift lens 260
Tolerance slider 277
tonal zones 144
Transform feature 372
Type tool 11

U

underexposure 460-463
Unsharp Mask tool
    used, for sharpening images 424-428

V

vanishing point 271
vector image 374
Version Sets
    saving 101, 102
video
    working with 17, 18
View menu 360-362

view spaces, Organizer
    Albums 485
    Events 485
    Media 485
    People 485
    Places 485
View tools, Expert edit mode
    Hand tool (H) 486
    Zoom tool (Z) 486

W

watermarks 385
web file formats
    GIF 422
    JPEG 422
    PNG8 422
    PNG24 422
Whiten Teeth tool 11
white rectangle 243
white thumbnail 273
widescreen panoramas
    creating 193, 194

Z

Zoom tool 11

9 781800 204201